AUSTRALIAN PAINTING

. . . by making art the perfect expression
of one time and one place it becomes art
for all times and of all places.

TOM ROBERTS, July 1890

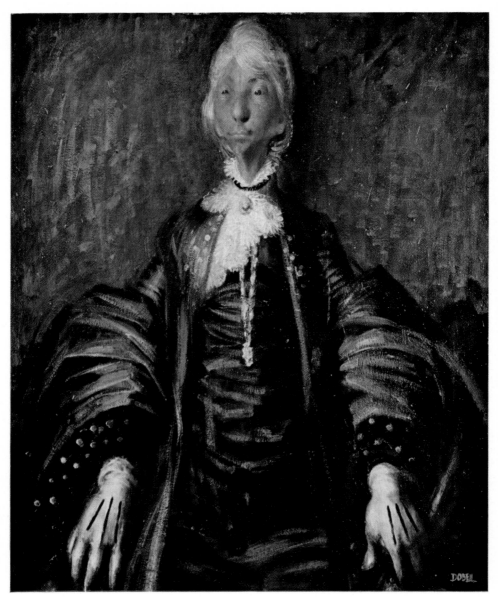

Frontispiece WILLIAM DOBELL *Dame Mary Gilmore, O.B.E.*, hardboard, 36 x 29, 1955-7, Sydney

AUSTRALIAN PAINTING

1788 - 1960

Bernard Smith

MELBOURNE
OXFORD UNIVERSITY PRESS
LONDON   WELLINGTON   NEW YORK
1962

Oxford University Press, Amen House, London, E.C.4

GLASGOW NEW YORK TORONTO MELBOURNE WELLINGTON
BOMBAY CALCUTTA MADRAS KARACHI LAHORE DACCA
CAPE TOWN SALISBURY NAIROBI IBADAN ACCRA
KUALA LUMPUR HONG KONG

The publication of this book has been assisted by grants from the Commonwealth Art Advisory Board and the Australian Humanities Research Council.

Registered in Australia for transmission by post as a book
PRINTED IN AUSTRALIA BY BROWN, PRIOR, ANDERSON PTY. LTD.

To KATE my wife

CONTENTS

INTRODUCTION

WHEN compared with that of other nations the story of Australian art is a comparatively short one, but it is, nevertheless, full of fascination and interest. For the Australian nation, though young, has been fashioned by people from the older nations of Europe (at first, mainly from Britain) and Australian art has naturally drawn quite constantly upon European traditions throughout its short history. Indeed, in one sense, it may be said that Australian art is a European art flourishing in the South-East Asian world. But that is not the whole truth. From the beginning of settlement in 1788 the physical environment of the country and, later, the social character and composition of the new nation have influenced the course which art has taken in Australia. In consequence Australian art has gradually acquired qualities as distinctive as the social attitudes and speech of Australians. To observe how these peculiarities have asserted themselves is one of the fascinations of the study of Australian art.

But it is by no means the only satisfaction. Australian artists have constantly returned to refresh themselves from the deep fountains of European culture and civilization. And it is equally fascinating to study the ways in which traditional links have been preserved, especially when the points of view of local artists and critics of art have tended to become insular, ultranationalistic, or narrow in their range of sympathies.

And there is yet another fascination. The study of Australian art is the study of an art in its beginnings. A national tradition always matures slowly and in the arts very slowly indeed. So in this book we study a seed-time, the harvest being still beyond knowledge. How rich that harvest will be it would not be wise to conjecture. One thing is certain, however: Australian art will not emerge fully formed until it has produced masterpieces which fashion from the Australian experience of life something of lasting value for the whole field of human experience. And masterpieces are not produced without an awareness of tradition. For the Australian artist there are two traditions of special importance, the European tradition itself and the local Australian tradition which is itself a variant of the European tradition. Strangely enough, it is the local tradition which is less well understood by Australian artists today. To clarify the Australian tradition and to make it more widely understood is one of the main aims of this book.

ACKNOWLEDGEMENTS

ALTHOUGH it covers a somewhat similar field this book is in no way a second edition of my earlier *Place, Taste and Tradition* (1945), from which only two or three paragraphs have been incorporated. Apart from a few critical comments which have already appeared in *Meanjin*, x (1951), in *Nation*, 18 June 1960 (whose respective editors I thank for permission to reprint) and in the John Murtagh Macrossan Lectures for 1961, the material herein has not been published previously.

It is not possible here to thank everyone individually who has helped me in preparing this book during the past six years but I wish to record my thanks to them all. A book of this nature could not possibly be published in Australia in its present form without financial and personal assistance from many quarters. Both the publishers and I wish to express our thanks to the Australian Humanities Research Council and the Commonwealth Art Advisory Board for the co-operation and assistance they have provided. We are also indebted to the Bank of New South Wales and Mr G. A. W. Robertson, the editor of the *Etruscan*; Dr Norman Behan of Brisbane; the Clarendon Press, Oxford, and the Art Gallery Society of Victoria for their assistance in providing blocks.

It is my duty to thank the Trustees of the Art Galleries of New South Wales, Queensland and Western Australia; of the National Galleries of Victoria and South Australia; of the Tasmanian Museum and Art Gallery, Hobart; of the Queen Victoria Museum, Launceston; of the Castlemaine Art Gallery; Mr Brian Johnstone of Brisbane; and the Council of the Museum of Modern Art of Australia for permission to reproduce work in their collections. I wish also to thank the directors of these institutions for their co-operation and assistance.

I wish to express my deep appreciation to those artists and relatives of artists who have answered my questions and provided me with reliable information. To several people I owe a special debt of gratitude: to Mr Daniel Thomas, of the Art Gallery of New South Wales, for his prompt and never-failing attention to innumerable inquiries over two or more years and his many helpful suggestions, including his invaluable assistance in reading and correcting the proofs; to Mr Brian Finemore, the Assistant Curator of the Australian Collection at the National Gallery of Victoria, for his patient and helpful replies to my many queries; to Mr Robert Campbell, the Director of the National Gallery of South Australia, for his friendly co-operation and personal interest in the book; and to Professor A. D. Trendall, the Master of University House in the Australian National University, for reading the manuscript and making helpful comments. I also want to thank the librarians of the Mitchell and Dixson Libraries, the National Library of Australia and the Art Gallery of New South Wales for their constant good service. I must express also my gratitude to all those people who have kindly allowed me to reproduce works of art in their possession.

This book was completed before it was possible to take advantage of some valuable research work completed by Honours graduates of the School of Fine Arts in the University of Melbourne, during 1961, but I wish to acknowledge here the value of work by Miss Virginia Spate on Tom Roberts and his times, and Mr Eric Thacker for his work on *art nouveau* in Australia. I also wish to thank Professor Burke and my colleagues in the Fine Arts Department of the University of Melbourne for their encouragement and patience, and the University itself for providing financial assistance for research in the subject.

I am deeply indebted to Dr Ursula Hoff, the Keeper of the Prints at the National Gallery of Victoria, who has given me invaluable help in reading and correcting the proofs. The errors that have survived the scrutiny of my friends are indeed my own. Finally I wish to thank my publishers and their printer for the great care they have taken in the production of the book.

SANDRINGHAM, VICTORIA   B.S.
DECEMBER 1961

ABBREVIATIONS

AA	*Art in Australia*, 1916-42: The Sydney art quarterly
AE	*The Australian Encyclopaedia*, 10 vols, Sydney, 1958
Brit. Mus. (Nat. Hist.)	British Museum (Natural History), London
Burl. Mag.	*The Burlington Magazine*, London
CAO	*A Catalogue of Australian Oil Paintings in the National Art Gallery of New South Wales*, Sydney, 1953
C.A.S.	The Contemporary Art Society of Australia
DAB	Percival Serle, *Dictionary of Australian Biography*, 2 vols, Sydney, 1949
DNB	*Dictionary of National Biography*, 22 vols, London, 1960
EVSP	Bernard Smith, *European Vision and the South Pacific*, Oxford, 1960
Journ. RAHS	Journal of the Royal Australian Historical Society, Sydney
N.L.A.	National Library of Australia, Canberra
PTT	Bernard Smith, *Place, Taste and Tradition*, Sydney, 1945

The State Galleries are indicated by the name of the capital cities in which they are located, thus:

ADELAIDE	The National Gallery of South Australia
BRISBANE	The Queensland Art Gallery
HOBART	The Tasmanian Museum and Art Gallery
MELBOURNE	The National Gallery of Victoria
PERTH	The Western Australian Art Gallery
SYDNEY	The Art Gallery of New South Wales

CHAPTER ONE

THE FIRST ARTISTS
1788 - 1824

'. . . *the whole appearance of nature must be striking in the extreme to the adventurer, and at first this will seem to him to be a country of enchantments.*'

THOMAS WATLING, *Letters from an Exile at Botany Bay to his Aunt in Dumfries* (1794)

WHEN Lieutenant James Cook discovered the eastern coast of Australia in 1770 in the *Endeavour*, the ship's company included Joseph Banks, a young gentleman of considerable wealth and social standing, who possessed keen scientific interests and was especially devoted to the study of botany. Young men of his class usually made a tour of the European continent, often lasting two or three years, in order to complete their education and improve their taste. The tour was known as the grand tour and its high point was the ancient towns of Italy. But Banks liked to do unusual things. The Royal Society had helped to sponsor the *Endeavour's* voyage and through its recommendation Banks, who was a member of the Society, was allowed by the Admiralty to travel with Cook to the South Seas. When his friends asked him why he did not make the far safer trip to Italy he replied: 'Every blockhead does that; my Grand Tour shall be one round the whole Globe.'[1]

In order to obtain permanent graphic records, grand tourists often included artists among the suite of servants who attended them. Banks included two young artists, Alexander Buchan and Sydney Parkinson (*c.* 1745-71), in his party, Buchan was to make drawings of native peoples and natural scenery; Parkinson, drawings of plants and animals. The voyage, unfortunately, ended in tragedy for both artists. Buchan, who was an epileptic and a very bad sailor, died soon after the *Endeavour* reached Tahiti in 1769. Parkinson, who made many drawings of plants, animals, natural scenery and native peoples in the Society Islands, New Zealand and Australia, and also compiled a splendid journal of the voyage,[2] proved himself a most able and observant artist-traveller. But he too died (from malaria) shortly after leaving Batavia where so many had fallen ill.

Some of the drawings made by Buchan and Parkinson were used to make engravings to illustrate John Hawkesworth's *Voyages* (1773),[3] which contained the first official account of Cook's discoveries. Several of Parkin-

B

1 *An Animal of New Holland*, engraving after George Stubbs, 7¾ x 9⅝, Hawkesworth's *Voyages*, vol. iii, 1773

son's drawings were also engraved for his *Journal of a Voyage to the South Seas*, which was published by his brother, Stanfield Parkinson, in 1773, but was not made available to the public until 1784.[4] By means of such engravings the British public was introduced to the Australian scene. The engraving of a kangaroo (1) in Hawkesworth's *Voyages* after a painting (from a specimen) by George Stubbs helped to establish the country's reputation as a wonderland of natural curiosities. Another engraving, entitled *Two of the Natives of New Holland Advancing to Combat* (2), was intended to depict the Australian aborigine, but was accurate only in the rendering of the tattooing and the bone ornaments. Everything else: the shield, sword, dart, the pose of the figure and method of dressing the hair, owes far more to the engraver's knowledge of classical sculpture than to his knowledge of the Australian aborigine.

This is not surprising. The two natives who defied Cook at his landing with such primitive weapons were rightly regarded as men of courage. Artists of the time made a practice of using poses and gestures selected from well-known pieces of classical sculpture in order to represent heroism and nobility in the figures they drew. In this engraving the native holding the shield is posed rather like *The Borghese Warrior*, a well-known piece of Hellenistic sculpture by the Ephesian sculptor Agasias. Furthermore, many educated people of the time firmly believed that all primitive people were naturally noble and heroic because their lives were lived close to nature free from the complexities and temptations of civilization. They considered them, in other words, to be noble savages.[5] And quite

2 *Two of the Natives of New Holland advancing to Combat*, engraving by T. Chambers after Sydney Parkinson, 8⅝ x 7½, from *Voyage to the South Seas*, 1784

the best way to represent a noble savage was to cast him in the mould of a Greek hero or a Greek god. So it came about that the first engraved illustrations of Australian aborigines depict them as noble savages.

The Voyage of Governor Arthur Phillip to Botany Bay, which was published in 1789, sixteen years after the printing of Parkinson's *Journal*, continued to illustrate Australian aborigines in this fashion, though one contemporary reviewer of the book, William Wales, criticized the tendency to depict native peoples after the manner of classical sculpture and to

3 *A Family of New South Wales*, engraving by William Blake after Governor King, 7½ x 6⅜, from John Hunter's *Historical Journal*, 1793

make their huts look like booths in English fairs.[6] The convention, however, lingered into the 1790's; and the finest of all the engravings which render the aborigine as a noble savage was also one of the last. This was William Blake's *A Family of New South Wales* (3), which was engraved from a drawing by Lieutenant P. G. King and published in John Hunter's *Historical Journal of the Transactions at Port Jackson and Norfolk Island* (1793).

Cook's voyages were undertaken to promote the cause of science and geographical discovery, and to advance Britain's position as a maritime power. Governor Arthur Phillip's task was more mundane. He had to establish a penal settlement upon an unknown coast. The Admiralty did not supply him with artists as they had Cook on his second and third voyages. But drawing played a significant part in a naval officer's training. He was expected to be able to draw maps, charts and profiles of coasts, and to keep a journal, when visiting unknown or outlandish countries, which would contain an accurate record of all interesting and curious observations. Furthermore, many naval men shared the current enthusiasm for collecting and describing new plants and animals; others, with some skill in drawing,

4 THE PORT JACKSON PAINTER, *Black Swan*, water-colour, 9 x 7½, *c.* 1790, 'Watling' Drawings, Brit. Mus. (Nat. Hist.)

were well aware that specimens and drawings of 'non-descript' products of natural history sent back home to scientists and collectors with influence in official circles often led to preferment or advancement.

In this connexion no one had more influence than Sir Joseph Banks who, as a young man, had collected plants in New Holland in 1770 and had become, by 1788, the President of the Royal Society, the most important and influential body of scientists in the world.[7] Banks had done more than anyone else to interest the British Government in the establishment of the penal settlement at Botany Bay. But he also had a deep personal interest in the place, for he hoped to obtain from there many rare specimens for his magnificent natural history collection. And few things delighted him more than a fine illustration of an exotic plant carefully drawn and coloured from nature.

Governor Phillip was well aware of Banks's interests and sent him many specimens and drawings of plants and animals found in the neighbourhood of Port Jackson.[8] But Phillip was no draughtsman, so he employed someone to make drawings for him. It is not possible to say for certain who this person was. Yet since most of the drawings made were illustrations of the plants, animals and native people of the Port Jackson neighbourhood, it will be convenient to call him the Port Jackson Painter.[9]

The Port Jackson Painter's known work consists of over 250 water-colour drawings, most of which are now in the British Museum (Natural History)

at South Kensington. The drawings include maps and coastal
profiles, and illustrations of birds,
snakes, insects, fish and other animals collected in the neighbourhood of Port Jackson and Norfolk
Island. There is also a number of
drawings of aborigines, and of
incidents which took place at the
settlement during Phillip's governorship (1788-92). A painting
of a black swan (4) provides a
good example of the Port Jackson
Painter's natural history drawings.
An elegant silhouette is used to
convey the essential qualities of
the bird with a minimum of fuss
and detail. The subject was a
matter of unusual interest for
Europeans. The Roman poet
Juvenal declared black swans to
be as rare as good wives,[10] and

5 THE PORT JACKSON PAINTER,
Balloderree, water-colour, 9¾ x 8, *c.*
1790, 'Watling' Drawings, Bris. Mus.
(Nat. Hist.)

writers had recalled his words down the centuries. Their discovery by the
Dutch navigator, Willem de Vlamingh, in Western Australia in 1697,
aroused great interest. The black swan, like the kangaroo and the platypus,
came to be cited as evidence that in Australia (a country itself at the
antipodes of Europe) the laws of nature were somewhat upside down.

The Port Jackson Painter did not depict aborigines as noble savages in
the way English engravers (who had never seen them) did. Consider, for
example, the portrait of Balloderree (5), a young native well known about
the settlement, who upon one occasion visited the Governor bedecked in
war paint to inform him that he proposed to revenge himself upon some
white men because a party of convicts had destroyed his canoe. The Port
Jackson Painter has portrayed him with a naïve realism which is tinged
with kindly sentiment and a hint of amused superiority. He did not, it
would seem, dislike the aborigines, nor did he represent them idealistically
in the manner of Greek heroes. His drawing sought rather to record their
customs and habits, as in the fine drawing called *Method of Climbing
Trees* (6) which depicts their methods of obtaining food. 'The Hunted
Rushcutter' (7) which records, doubtless, an actual incident, reveals the
lively sense of humour so often present in his work. But it was the country's
curiosities, its plants, animals and people, which held the centre of the

6 THE PORT JACKSON PAINTER, *Method of Climbing Trees*, water-colour, 11 x 6¼, *c.* 1790, 'Watling' Drawings, Brit. Mus. (Nat. Hist.)

artist's interest. The local landscape as a whole yielded no such fascination, being drawn in a rudimentary fashion. And this is true in general of the work of the other naval draughtsmen who accompanied Phillip to Sydney Cove: George Raper, John Hunter, William Bradley and Arthur Bowes.[11] A professional painter would certainly have attempted to render the character of the local landscape.

Governor Phillip had not been provided with professional artists because his was not a voyage of discovery and scientific investigation. The practice of providing professional artists for scientific expeditions was, however, continued by the Admiralty when preparing for Matthew Flinders's exploration of the Australian coastline in the *Investigator* (1801-3). William Westall (1781-1850) was appointed as a landscape and topographical artist, and Ferdinand Bauer (1760-1826) as a natural history draughtsman.

Westall had been trained as an artist, first under his brother Richard Westall, and later at the Royal Academy Schools. Benjamin West, the President of the Academy, recommended him for the position when William Daniell, who later became famous for the scenes he painted in India, declined to accept the position.

As was usual, among artists attached to surveying voyages, Westall made many off-shore drawings of coastal and harbour views. These, when engraved in the atlases to the published accounts of such voyages, were an aid to later navigators. Westall's coastal profiles and harbour views are among the finest ever made by a professional artist attached to a voyage of discovery and survey. He also made drawings of natives encountered upon the voyage. In most of them something of the neo-classical conventions in which he had been taught to draw still lingers. Westall, that is, could not help seeing aborigines to some extent as noble savages. He also painted a number of particularly fine water-colour landscapes, such as his *King George's Sound from the Isthmus Below Peak Head*[12] which is treated with

7 THE PORT JACKSON PAINTER, 'The Hunted Rushcutter',
water-colour, 6⅜ x 11¾, c. 1790, Banks MS. 34, Brit. Mus.
(Nat. Hist.)

great breadth and fluency. As the expedition proceeded, however, Westall became increasingly concerned with the peculiarities of Australian vegetation. This led to individual studies of trees and shrubs, and a more careful and precise treatment of foreground vegetation in his landscape. It is likely that such interests were developed by Ferdinand Bauer.

Some of the oil paintings which Westall executed for the Admiralty after his return to England reveal him grappling with the problem of depicting the light, atmosphere and vegetation of the tropics; a novel problem in landscape painting at that time, but one which, under the stimulus of the great German geographer, Alexander von Humboldt,[13] was soon to occupy the attention of many travelling artists. In Westall's *View of Cape Townshend,* he is clearly seeking to render the visual effect of a tropical morning shortly before sunrise; in his *View in Sir E. Pelew's Group* (8), the blinding sunlight of a tropic noon; and in his *View of Malay Road from Pobasso's Island,* the dramatic effects of a tropical storm.

The *Investigator* circumnavigated Australia and was finally abandoned at Sydney in 1803 because of its unseaworthy condition, the ship's company transferring to the *Porpoise* and *Cato* which were, however, wrecked in northern Queensland waters. After the party was rescued, Westall made his way to China and thence to India, drawing scenes wherever he travelled. He arrived home in England in 1805, but the island of Madeira had attracted him on the journey out and thence he returned in the same year, later making a trip to Jamaica. By 1807 he was back in England again and held an exhibition of paintings from drawings made on his extensive travels.

8 WILLIAM WESTALL, *View in Sir E. Pelew's Group, Gulph of Carpentaria*, canvas, 23 x 33½, c. 1802, The Admiralty, London

But his exotic subjects did not appeal to the buying public, and in the years following he turned to sketching in Worcestershire, the Wye Valley and the Lake District.

Westall held a very poor opinion of the Australian landscape as a subject for painting. But his work and travels are of considerable value for an understanding of the beginnings of Australian art. Improvements in the art of navigation, Britain's growing mastery of the high seas and the desire for a life of adventure all helped to attract many young artists to engage upon long voyages whenever the opportunity presented itself. Sometimes, as in Westall's case, they gained a paid position as a topographical or landscape artist to a scientific expedition; at other times they had to content themselves with gaining a passage as best they could. They were assisted by the fact that during the first half of the nineteenth century many fine travel books, magnificently coloured by means of aquatint engraving, were published both in London and Paris. Illustrations for such books were provided by artists prepared to journey to the ends of the earth in order to paint lands and peoples no European artist had painted before.[14]

The Austrian artist, Ferdinand Bauer, Westall's companion on the *Investigator*, was one of the greatest of all botanical draughtsmen. Few, if any, natural history painters have equalled the beauty, accuracy and sensitivity which Ferdinand and his brother, Francis, achieved in their drawings of plants and flowers. Indeed, Ferdinand Bauer's work evoked the praise of the poet Goethe, who said that it revealed that the service both of art and science, though difficult, was still possible. Bauer was born in Vienna and was the son of a painter to Prince Liechtenstein. The Abbot of Feldsberg, recognizing his ability at the age of fifteen, engaged him to paint flower studies which later passed into the Prince's collection. In 1786 Bauer journeyed to Greece with John Sibthorp, the Sherardian Professor at Oxford, and returned with him to England where the two men collaborated in the production of the now famous *Flora Graeca* (1806-40). Francis followed him to England and, through Sir Joseph Banks's patronage, became draughtsman to the Royal Botanic Gardens at Kew. And it was through Banks's recommendation that Ferdinand Bauer became Flinders's natural history draughtsman, with a salary of £300 per annum including rations for himself and his servant.

When Bauer arrived in Sydney on the *Investigator* in February 1802, he was so impressed with the great wealth of botanical material awaiting classification that he decided to remain in Australia longer than he had first intended. From Sydney he made many successful botanical excursions including a visit to Norfolk Island in August 1804. He arrived back in England in 1805 with Robert Brown, the great English botanist who was another member of Flinders's expedition, and began to prepare the plates for his *Illustrationes Florae Novae Hollandiae* (1813). But the time was not favourable for flower books and, after the issue of fifteen plates, the project was abandoned (9). Disappointed, Ferdinand left England and bought a small house in Vienna where he completed his drawings of Australian plants, animals and flowers before he died there in 1826. A large number of his drawings of Australian plants are now in the collection of the British Museum (Natural History), South Kensington, many more in the Natural History Museum, Vienna, and others at Göttingen University.[15]

9 *Grevillea Banksii*, engraving after Ferdinand Bauer, from his *Illustrationes Florae Novae Hollandiae*, 12½ x 10, London, 1813

Bauer's achievement was possible because men like Sir Joseph Banks combined a keen interest in science with a delight in fine drawing. Few men of his time had wider or more varied interests than Banks, but the central passion of his life was his botanical collection. Running through years of correspondence with the early governors of New South Wales there is one dominant theme, his tireless interest in the 'non-descript' productions of New Holland. He used his influence with the British Government to provide special facilities for the safe transport of specimens of Australian flora to England. Botanists and horticulturalists were keen to obtain floral rarities from New Holland, and the colony benefited because Banks was equally interested in transmitting useful plants from England to Australia. Indeed the need to transplant Australian specimens to England and to acclimatize English plants in Australia led to the early establishment of botanical gardens in the colony. Amateur collectors like John White, the surgeon of the First Fleet, and Philip Gidley King, the Governor of New South Wales (1800-6), were aware of the great interest in Australian natural history and did all they could to maintain a constant supply of specimens and illustrations from the colony.

But amateurs were not able to cope with the increasing demands of botanists, nurserymen and the directors of botanical gardens. For this reason professional collectors were sent to the country. Among the first to arrive was George Suttor (1774-1859) and George Caley (1770-1829), both sent out by Banks in 1800. Suttor brought a collection of grape vines, apples, pears and hops with him. He proved to be an excellent colonist and forty-three years after his arrival was able to publish *The Culture of the Grape-Vine and Orange in Australia and New Zealand* (1843). Caley also established a botanical garden for the transmission of plants to and from the colony and made several botanical excursions to the south and west of the settlement at Sydney.

Australian plants were received with great interest and enthusiasm in England. The Linnean Society, a scientific society specially devoted to the study of botany, had been founded in 1788, a few months after the foundation of the settlement at Port Jackson. This society from its beginnings took a special interest in Australian flora. James Edward Smith, the President and a close friend of Banks, published his *Specimen of the Botany of New Holland* (1793-4) less than six years after the foundation of the settlement. The book reveals how the propagation of Australian flowers was becoming quite a fashionable pursuit in England. We learn that the Dowager Lady de Clifford was the only lady in Europe who had a waratah growing in her garden, though up to the time of publication it had not flowered. Lord Viscount Lewisham's *pimelia*, however, had flowered, in February 1794. *Mimosa* had been raised plentifully from seeds brought from Port Jackson, and, wrote Smith, 'is not uncommon now in our greenhouses'. The enthusiasm for Australian plants continued for many years. In 1828 Robert Sweet, another Fellow of the Linnean Society, published *Flora Australasica: or a Selection of Handsome, or Curious Plants, Natives of New Holland, and the South Sea Islands; containing coloured figures and Descriptions of some of the choicest species most proper for the conservatory or greenhouse, and many which will endure the cold of our climate, in the open air, with very little protection; with magnified dissections of their most essential parts, their names, descriptions, a full account of the best method of cultivation and propagation. The greater part are handsome evergreen shrubs, and many produce sweet-scented flowers; as they are generally of free growth, and easily managed, they may be considered as the most desirable plants for cultivation.* The title of the book alone is sufficient to indicate that the interest in Australian plants arose partly from scientific curiosity, partly from a fashionable desire among gardeners to possess exotic rarities from the antipodes.

In any case, the interest in the 'non-descript productions of New Holland' stimulated the production of hundreds of drawings of Australian plants and animals during the early years of settlement. Most of these drawings found their way to England. Some were used to illustrate voyage and travel books relating to Australia, others books and journals associated with the study of natural history. The naval and natural history draughtsmen who first worked in Australia were more interested in depicting its natural curiosities, such as its plants, birds, fish and insects, than in depicting the landscape as a whole. Reactions to the landscape itself varied. Some, noting the lack of undergrowth and the open forest character of the vegetation, compared it with an English nobleman's park. Early engravings representing Australian scenery often resemble an English park, though tropical plants, such as palm and the grass tree (*Xanthorrhoea*), are usually added for local colour. Others, oppressed by the bushland stretching away on all sides, spoke of its monotonous effect.[16] In such country the eye could not look far into the distance; it was trapped, as it were, in a foreground of primeval bushland which offered little variety from its dull evenly-toned olive-grey. Furthermore, early settlers had reason to fear the natives and the danger of getting lost in forests which lacked edible fruits, and in which water was often difficult to find. However fascinating and curious the plants and animals, the landscape as a whole was felt to be drab, fearsome and melancholy. This attitude to Australian nature may be studied in more detail in the work of Thomas Watling, the first landscape painter to work in Australia.

Thomas Watling (*b.* 1762) was a young coach-painter of Dumfries, Scotland, who was transported at the age of twenty-six for forging guinea

10   THOMAS WATLING, A *Direct North General View of*
Sydney Cove . . . in 1794, canvas, 36 x 51, Dixson Galleries

notes of the Bank of Scotland. He appears from his work to have been
professionally trained and he either taught or was prepared to teach
drawing, for among the documents exhibited at his trial there was a drawing
sheet, which read: 'Ladies and Gentlemen taught Drawing at Watling's
Academy. Admission per month One Guinea.' Watling, though to all
accounts a somewhat shifty young man, received a good Scottish education
and imbibed a great deal of the picturesque taste and romantic sentiment
current during his day. He arrived in Sydney in October 1792 and remained
in the colony until at least 1796, when he received a conditional pardon.
During the period of his conviction he spent a good deal of his time making
drawings of birds, native people and views of the settlement for officials
like John White, the Surgeon-General, and David Collins, the Judge-
Advocate. A number of his drawings have been preserved in the British
Museum (Natural History) at South Kensington, and some of his letters
home were published in *Letters from an Exile at Botany Bay, to his Aunt
in Dumfries* (c. 1794). This book enables us to appreciate his reactions to
the Australian scene.
   Watling had been trained in the picturesque mode of landscape painting,
a mode which made much use of old and gnarled trees, winding mountain
paths, peasant cottages, jagged and rocky cliffs. Consequently the local
scene depressed him. 'The landscape painter', he wrote to his aunt, 'may in

11 THOMAS WATLING, *Taken from the West Side of the Cove*, pen and wash, 15 x 20, *c.* 1794, 'Watling' Drawings, Brit. Mus. (Nat. Hist.)

vain seek here for that kind of beauty which arises from happy-opposed off-scapes. Bold rising hills, or azure distances would be a kind of phaenomena. The principal traits of the country are extensive woods, spread over a little varied plain.'[17] This was an accurate enough description of the Sydney neighbourhood in its virgin state. But Watling knew well enough that picturesque paintings were not simply transcripts of nature but that they were painted by selecting and combining motifs drawn from a number of sketches. So he proceeded to outline to his aunt a programme for painting the local scenery.

I confess that were I to select and combine, I might avoid that sameness, and find engaging employment. Trees wreathing their old fantastic roots on high; dissimilar in tint and foliage; cumbent, upright, fallen or shattered by lightning, may be found at every step; whilst sympathetic glooms of twilight glimmering groves, and wildest nature lulled in soft repose, might much inspire the soul.[18]

How Watling selected and combined to avoid the 'sameness' of the landscape and render it picturesque may be seen by comparing his oil painting *A Direct North General View of Sydney Cove . . . in 1794* (10) with the wash drawing (11) from which the larger work appears to have been painted. Picturesque painters preferred serpentine curves to even

12   W. S. BLAKE, *A View of the Town of Sydney*, aquatint, 9⅝ x 16½, 1802

curves, dark foregrounds to light foregrounds, and a generalized treatment
to sharp details. A comparison of Watling's painting with his drawing
reveals the following: the horizon line of the drawing curves in one long
shallow arc; in the painting the line has been softened, broken by verticals
and altered to a shallow serpentine curve; the foreground of the painting
is much darker than the foreground of the drawing and is also more
generalized in its treatment; large trees have been introduced into the
foreground of the painting as side-screens to the view; a group of natives
gathered around a fire, and a naval and military man conversing on the
high road add a touch of local colour. All these alterations helped to trans-
form a topographical drawing into a picturesque painting. The painting
was intended to be what Watling himself called a 'picturesque description',
and was probably sent back to England by an official to indicate the growth
of the settlement at Sydney after seven years.

Some of Watling's views and drawings of natives were used to illustrate
Collins's *Account of the English Colony in New South Wales* (1798-1802).
Watling was himself anxious to publish an illustrated book on the colony,
for in a projected advertisement which he sent in one of his letters to his
aunt in which, incidentally, he calls himself 'Principal Limner of New South
Wales', he proposed: 'the Execution of a Picturesque Description of that
Colony; in an highly-finished Set of Drawings, done faithfully upon the
Spots, from Nature, in Mezzo, Aqua-tinta, or Water Colours'.[19] But the
project came to nothing. Watling received a conditional pardon in 1796 and
nothing is known of his work after that date. He may, however, have gone

13 *Part of the Harbour of Port Jackson*, aquatint by Robert Havell
after James Taylor

to Calcutta where a Thomas Watling was practising as a miniature painter
between 1801 and 1803.[20] But by 1804 he was definitely back in Dumfries,
for in that year he is alleged to have forged five-pound notes of the Bank
of Scotland. He was tried in January 1806, but the witnesses emitted their
depositions viva voce, contrary to Scottish law, and Watling obtained a
verdict of 'not proven'. In 1806 Watling was forty-four years of age, but
what happened to him after that date remains unknown.[21]

Watling had sought to combine the topographical view and the picturesque landscape in his 'picturesque descriptions'. Though the need for
topographical views of the colony continued, by 1800 there was in England
an influential body of opinion opposed to the fashionable affectations of
the picturesque mode of landscape painting. For instance, Edward Dayes
(1763-1804), a well-known water-colour painter and mezzotint engraver
published a scathing criticism of picturesque painting in his *Essay on
Painting* (1805). 'We must give up our understanding', he wrote, 'if we
call that landscape fine which represents dirty, rugged grounds, scrubby
bushes, poor scraggy ill-formed trees, shapeless lumps of antiquity, and
muddy pools peopled with gypsies and vagabonds, dirty beggars clothed
with rags . . . or nasty swine on filthy dunghills'.[22] In 1804 Dayes had himself

engraved a *View of Sydney Cove*[23] which is more topographical in approach than Watling's picturesque view of *Sydney in 1794*, though it may have been engraved from an original Watling. Another representative topographical view of this time is W. S. Blake's engraving of Sydney in 1802 (12); its documentary precision and spick-and-span appearance would have appealed to Dayes. The layout and situation of the town are indicated clearly; such details as houses, roads, cultivated land and wharves are indicated with appealing simplicity and welded into a well-balanced composition. A similar manner of working is to be found in the topographical drawings of the convict, John Eyre (14), and the surveyor and explorer, George William Evans.

John Eyre (*c*. 1771-1812), the son of a woolcomber of Coventry, was transported to New South Wales for seven years for breaking and entering. He arrived in Sydney in June 1801. As a convict he was paid from the Police Fund to paint numbers on Sydney's houses at 6*d*. per house. Several of his topographical views (14) were published in D. D. Mann's *Present Picture of New South Wales* (1811) and A. West's *Views in New South Wales* (1812-14).[24] George William Evans (1778-1852) was born at Warwick and articled to an engineer and architect. He arrived in Australia in October 1802 and was appointed acting Surveyor-General of Lands in August 1803. Evans drew several topographical views of Sydney, and also of Hobart after he had taken up the post of Assistant-Surveyor of Lands at Port Dalrymple in 1812.[25] Others followed Eyre and Evans; and many topographical views of Australian colonial towns were drawn and engraved during the next forty years. For this was the great age of picturesque topography. In both London and Paris superb travel books lavishly illustrated with coloured aquatint engravings were being published. One of the greatest of the British publishing houses of the time was Robert Havell and Sons, which published, among other things, the great bird books of John Audubon, the famous American ornithological artist. Havell also published three views of Sydney (1823) drawn by the military surveyor, Major James Taylor, a section of which is illustrated (13).

Taylor arrived in the colony in 1817 as a member of the 48th (Northamptonshire) Regiment and left for Madras in 1824. Unlike Eyre, whose paintings are rather devoid of life, Taylor animated his precisely-drawn panorama with a wealth of local activity. We see a man ploughing a field; a group of men idly gossiping while two doze in the afternoon sun, leaving a third to chop wood—the first illustration on record of what has always been known in Australia as the Government stroke![26] We see travellers on the road; a field full of sheep and cattle; ships at anchor in the harbour; many yachts and native craft. In the middle ground we may note the natural parklands which early travellers so frequently commented upon as

14 JOHN EYRE, *View of Sydney from the West Side of the Cove*, water-colour, 13½ x 25½, 1806, Dixson Galleries

15 *Interior Mount Gambier*, hand-coloured lithograph, 9¾ x 14, by J. W. Giles after George French Angas from *South Australia Illustrated*, 1846

being similar to English parks. By way of contrast, the horizon line is crowded with trees, a feature which gave the landscape that shut-in quality which Watling and many travellers complained about. Into the scene Taylor has carefully inserted two native camps, and has fringed his foreground with native flowers, such as the waratah, the grass tree and the wild iris. In another part of the panorama, Taylor draws English plants growing in the garden of the military hospital. The panorama is clearly not intended to be simply a transcript of nature but seeks to satisfy three allied yet distinct interests: an interest in the progress of the settlement, in the contrast between savage and civilized life, and in natural history.

Panoramas were a specialized development of topographical landscape. One painting was attached to another until the running set provided a graphic description of a large area as seen from one vantage point. The first mechanical panorama was invented by Robert Barker (1739-1806), an Irish painter resident in Edinburgh, who conceived the idea of painting a completely circular view of the city and placing it on a revolving drum. It met with great success and Barker took it to London in 1789 and exhibited it at the Haymarket.[27] It was so successful that a permanent panorama was set up which continued for many years. Panoramas became popular both in England and America during the first half of the nineteenth century, and several panoramic views were painted in the Australian colonies at that time with the ultimate intention of providing material for this highly popular form of entertainment. Robert Burford (1791-1861), for instance, painted panoramas of Sydney and Hobart from drawings made by Augustus Earle in 1825 and 1827. They were shown in London in 1829 and 1830. Several others were painted before 1850: but in the second half of the century the panorama steadily declined in popularity. A highly popular form of art, it reduced pictorial topography to its most hybrid and least satisfactory form.

The topographical view recorded urban progress. It looked in towards the centre of the town, not out into the primeval wilderness flanking the frontiers of settlement. By 1813, however, the Blue Mountains to the west of Sydney were crossed. In Tasmania, where Hobart had been established in 1804, movement into the interior of the island, slow at first, made rapid progress under Governor Arthur following his appointment in 1824. The opening up of the interior confronted artists with new types of landscape. And the first man to paint them, indeed, we might say the first man to paint Australian landscape with a vision unsullied by current artistic conventions, either picturesque or topographic, was John William Lewin (1770-1819).

Lewin was a natural history draughtsman and field naturalist who came of a family of ornithologists. He arrived in Sydney in January 1800 with a recommendation from the Duke of Portland, who was then the Home Secretary, and he also had an undertaking to collect Australian insects for Dru Drury, a well-known London naturalist who was a friend of Banks and possessed the finest entomological collection in Britain. During 1803-4 Lewin drew, engraved and coloured plates for his *Prodromus Entomology: Natural History of Lepidopterous Insects of New South Wales*, which was published in London in 1805. His second book, *Birds of New Holland*, was published in London in 1808. During these years Lewin also painted many views of Sydney.

16   JOHN WILLIAM LEWIN, *Cox's River*, water-colour, 8¾ x 7, 1815, Mitchell Library

Governor Macquarie took a special interest in Lewin and helped him in several ways. In 1815 he accompanied the Governor when he made his famous progress over the Blue Mountains to Bathurst. On this progress, Lewin made a number of water-colour paintings of scenery through which the company passed. These paintings constitute the first successful attempt to paint the local scenery with an eye unfettered by current artistic conventions. Lewin's work as a naturalist had enabled him to acquire an honest eye for visual facts. A naturalist, he succeeded in painting a naturalist's landscape; his water-colours are, to the best of his ability, transcripts of nature. In his *Cox's River* (16), for instance, the foreground is light in tone, and contains nothing more than a collection of rocks, grasses and trees, honestly seen and drawn. There are no side-screens of picturesque foliage, no noble savages. Lewin has grasped the nature of the eucalyptus, its light translucent foliage through which the horizon may be seen, and the nature of the slender and feathery grasses of the interior. He succeeded, too, in portraying an authentic bush atmosphere. In *Springwood* (17), for example, we see Macquarie's party preparing to camp among tall

c

17   JOHN WILLIAM LEWIN, *Spring-wood*, water-colour, 8¾ x 10¾, 1815,
Mitchell Library

gum saplings as the rakish light of the evening filters through the foliage to cover everything with a rosy tone. The horses have been unharnessed from the wagons and men are standing about or sitting in groups yarning under the trees. In *Sidmouth Valley* (Mitchell),[28] a family is seen camped in the bush, their chattels spread out around their wagon and tents. A woman prepares an evening meal while a man sits on a chest and watches. In Lewin's Blue Mountains paintings the landscape is no longer seen, as it was by the Port Jackson Painter, as an assemblage of curiosities, or as Thomas Watling saw it, as a vehicle for picturesque treatment; it is being seen as a whole. And Lewin succeeded not only in portraying the landscape truthfully, but also in capturing something of the adventurous life of the frontier. New themes became prominent in Australian art soon after the Blue Mountains were crossed. By 1825 illustrations of the adventurous lives of early squatters, explorers and bushrangers in the antipodes were beginning to interest British people quite as much as the pictures of the platypus, the black swan, the lyrebird and the kangaroo.[29]

Illustrations of the Australian scene published in England during the 1820's reveal these new interests. Engravers, however, continued to modify Australian scenery according to picturesque and topographic conventions. This is revealed in the work of the convict painter and engraver, Joseph Lycett (*fl.* 1810-25).

Lycett was, like Thomas Watling, a convict strongly addicted to forgery. He was a native of Staffordshire who had resided for some time in the town of Ludlow when convicted at the Shropshire Summer Assizes on 10 August 1811 of uttering forged and counterfeited bank notes. Sentenced to transportation for fourteen years, he arrived in Sydney in the *General Hewitt* on 7 February 1814; among his fellow prisoners was the architect, Francis Howard Greenway. Evidence concerning Lycett's early life is conflicting. The file of indictments relating to his trial describes him as a labourer, but the *General Hewitt*'s list of convicts describes him as a portrait and miniature painter. Lycett certainly possessed skill as an engraver for, sixteen months after his arrival, he was caught in the Police Office, Sydney, where he was employed, forging Commissariat notes. A *Sydney Gazette* notice of 3 June 1815 records how

A Mr Lycett, who, unfortunately for the world as well as for himself, had obtained sufficient knowledge of the graphic arts to aid him in the practice of deception, in which he has outdone most of his predecessors. The bills of Mr Thrupp he has imitated by a means that has not in this colony been before resorted to by the ingenious. The printing type used in such bills has been imitated in copper plate as to deceive the eye upon a slight glance.

For this further lapse Lycett was sent to Newcastle, a place of secondary punishment. Here his abilities were put to better use when he was engaged to paint the altar piece of the new church. It is possible that he was responsible for the plans of the church as well. Mrs Macquarie certainly made use of his services to copy drawings from her books on architecture. Governor Macquarie, too, took an interest in Lycett, employing him between 1819 and 1821 to make drawings of views in New South Wales and Tasmania. In these years he seems to have had a better and happier time. His two daughters came out to Sydney as free settlers and returned with him in 1822 after he had received an absolute pardon from Lord Bathurst, to whom Macquarie had sent three of his drawings. In England, Lycett busied himself with engraving his views, appropriately dedicated to his emancipator, Bathurst, for publication. They were issued in thirteen monthly parts, both plain and coloured, under the title *Views in Australia*, during 1824 and 1825.

If Macquarie intended that Lycett's *Views* should indicate the progress of settlement during his administration, his wishes were certainly realized. For the *Views*, each of which is provided with an accompanying text, provide a graphic survey of the colonies in New South Wales and Van Diemen's Land during his term of office: the chief centres of settlement; smaller towns which had been established or had grown considerably under Macquarie; the residences of wealthier colonists to which were added several picturesque and romantic views. The *Views* also testify to the changing life of the times. The expansion of settlement into the interior wrought considerable changes in colonial life. Until Macquarie's time, Sydney and Hobart had been small penal settlements clinging to the coast and surrounded by hostile bushland. But by 1820 attention was beginning to turn to the frontier. So Lycett's *Views* introduced new pictorial motifs that were to have a long life in Australian art: the hunter chasing kangaroos and emus across the wide grassy plains of the interior; the stockman with his dogs; the sundowner with his swag; the bushrangers—or banditti, as Lycett called them—around their camp fire. The inclusion of such typical embellishments to add local colour was characteristic of picturesque landscape and Lycett's engravings are not, like Lewin's Blue Mountains watercolours, honest transcripts of things seen.

After his arrival in England, Lycett prepared a series of water-colours

18   JOSEPH LYCETT, *Salt Pan Plain, Van Diemen's Land*, engraving,
6¼ x 10⅜, from his *Views in Australia*, 1824

19   JOSEPH LYCETT, *View of the Salt Pan Plains, Van Diemen's Land*,
water-colour, 14 x 19¾, 1824, Dixson Galleries

of his Australian views by way of preparation apparently for his engravings. A comparison of these drawings with their corresponding engravings reveals that in the process of engraving Lycett tended to make the scene correspond to conventional ideas of the picturesque landscape. In the engraving of *Salt Pan Plain, Van Diemen's Land* (18), for example, the eucalypt in the left foreground of the corresponding water-colour drawing (19) has been transformed into two picturesque trees of an indeterminate species, and the open tracery of the foliage has been turned into opaque and laterally-disposed foliage reminiscent of an oak. Figures have been introduced and the engraving as a whole looks more like a piece of English countryside than a land into which Europeans had recently entered. This was due, to some extent, to the sway of picturesque convention in landscape drawing. But the alterations may have been due also in some measure to quite practical reasons. Lycett's was the first important illustrated book to hold out a direct appeal to the prospective migrant to settle in Australia. Such literature has always sought to depict the country in the 'most favourable' light. Lycett was transported to Australia for forging English bank notes. How many migrants he induced, by forging landscapes, to settle freely in the country will never be known.[30]

FOOTNOTES

[1] EDWARD SMITH, *The Life of Sir Joseph Banks*, London, 1911, p. 16

[2] SYDNEY PARKINSON, *A Journal of a Voyage to the South Seas, in his Majesty's ship, The Endeavour*, London, 1773

[3] JOHN HAWKESWORTH, *An Account of the Voyages undertaken by the Order of His Present Majesty for Making Discoveries in the Southern Hemisphere . . .*, London, 1773

[4] Because of a legal injunction granted to Hawkesworth restraining publication of Parkinson's *Journal, see* SIR MAURICE HOLMES, *Captain James Cook*, R.N., F.R.S. *A Bibliographical Excursion*, London, 1952, pp. 25-6, 53-5

[5] See H. N. FAIRCHILD, *The Noble Savage*, New York, 1928

[6] See L. FITZHARDINGE, 'Some "First Fleet" Reviews', *Hist. Stud. Aust. and N.Z.*, ix (1959), 88

[7] Banks was elected President in 1778.

[8] Now better known as Sydney Harbour

[9] The Port Jackson Painter may have been Henry Brewer, *see EVSP*, p. 118 n.

[10] JUVENAL, *Satire VI*, 165

[11] Accounts of the art work of these men will be found in: MOORE, i, 10-11; *EVSP*, pp. 117-20

[12] In the Royal Commonwealth Society Library, London

[13] For Humboldt and nineteenth-century landscape painting *see EVSP*, pp. 151-7

[14] On Westall *see also* the forthcoming publication of the Royal Commonwealth Society. *Drawings by William Westall, Landscape artist on board* H.M.S. *Investigator during the circumnavigation of Australia by Captain Matthew Flinders*, R.N., *in 1801-1803* (ed. T. M. Perry and D. H. Simpson)

[15] On Ferdinand Bauer *see also* W. BLUNT, *The Art of Botanical Illustration*, London, 1950, pp. 195-202, *passim*

[16] For a more detailed account of these reactions *see EVSP*, pp. 133-4, *passim*

[17] WATLING, *Letters from an Exile*, Penrith [n.d.] (1794), pp. 8-9

[18] ibid., p. 9

[19] ibid., p. 26

[20] WILLIAM FOSTER, 'British Artists in India', *Walpole Soc.*, xix (1931), 88

[21] On Watling *see also* HUGH S. GLADSTONE, 'Thomas Watling Limner of Dumfries', *Transactions of the Dumfriesshire and Galloway Natural History and Antiquarian Society*, 3rd ser., xx (1935-6), 70-133

[22] op. cit., p. 225

[23] *See* W. DIXSON, 'Notes on Australian Artists', *Journ. RAHS*, v (1919), 231

[24] On Eyre *see also* EVSP, pp. 162-4

[25] On Evans *see also* article in *AE*, vol. iii

[26] i.e. a lazy method of working

[27] On Robert Barker *see also* article in *DNB*, vol. i, p. 1129 ff

[28] *See* EVSP, pl. 112

[29] On Lewin *see also* PHYLLIS MANDER JONES, 'John William Lewin: a Memoir', *Biblionews*, Sydney (Nov. 1953), 36-46, and bibliography (Dec. 1953); *EVSP*, pp. 158-62, *passim*

[30] On Lycett *see also* article in *AE*, vol. v

CHAPTER TWO

ARTISTS ON THE PASTORAL FRONTIER
1821 - 51

New South Wales is a perpetual flower garden, but there is not a single scene in it of which a painter could make a landscape, without greatly disguising the character of the trees.
BARRON FIELD, *Geographical Memoirs*, 1825

PRIOR to 1821 settlement in Australia was confined to areas around Sydney, Hobart and Launceston. But after the recall of Macquarie, expansion into the unoccupied areas of New South Wales proceeded apace, and under the able administration of Colonel George Arthur (1824-36) the struggling settlements of Van Diemen's Land were transformed into a flourishing colony. From 1820 onwards both colonies, despite a minor slump in New South Wales in 1827, experienced boom conditions, based upon the expansion of the pastoral industry, which continued until the depression of 1843.

The rapid expansion of the pastoral frontier brought a greater variety of scenery to the notice of travellers and artists. In New South Wales men came to realize that Australian scenery was far more diversified than the visual monotony of the Cumberland Plain, in its virgin state, had led the first settlers to believe. They became acquainted with the sub-tropical cedar brush of the Illawarra and Port Stephens districts, the precipitous sandstone scarps of the Blue Mountains, the open forest and savannah lands beyond the Great Divide.

Settlement in the interior also introduced a greater variety of human experience. Before 1821 the main occupation of artists in Australia had been to portray the curiosities of nature, the life of the aborigines and the progress of the small settlements. Indeed the new settlements founded during the period now under consideration, at Brisbane (1824), at Perth (1829), at Melbourne (1835) and at Adelaide (1836), stimulated both amateur and professional artists to recapitulate the graphic interests of Sydney's first artists, each settlement recording its local fauna and flora, its native peoples and its own progress. But in the older colonies a new range of subjects, already foreshadowed in the work of William Lewin and Joseph Lycett, illustrating frontier life, became increasingly popular. Colonials on horseback hunting the emu and kangaroo, bivouacking around an evening camp fire, or attacked by aborigines or bushrangers: these were

25

the themes which came to symbolize the adventurous colonial life and to attract migrants to the country.

During the period Australia began to experience some of the effects of the romantic revival in arts and letters. Certainly, elements of romanticism can be found in Australian work before 1820, but they are exceptional. Distance and isolation from Europe created a noticeable time-lag in taste and fashion, a lag emphasized by the fact that the colonial economy was never affluent enough to support the arts in any but the smallest degree. The neo-classical taste of the late eighteenth century persisted in Australia well after 1820. Barron Field (1786-1846), who claimed, not without justification, to be Australia's first poet, wrote poetry and prose in the 1820's, still governed largely by Augustan conventions; and John Glover's paintings of the 1830's, as we shall see, echo the pictorial tastes of eighteenth-century England.

It should be realized, too, that the Australian colonist was cut off from one of the most important sources of romantic sentiment and inspiration, the veneration of the past, especially the Christian medieval past of the northern nations of Europe. As John Ruskin wrote in 1856:

. . . the charm of romantic association can be felt only by the modern European child. It arises eminently out of the contrast of the beautiful past with the frightful and monotonous present; and it depends for its force on the existence of ruins and traditions, on the remains of architecture, the traces of battlefields. . . . The instinct to which it appeals can hardly be felt in America.[1]

He might equally have said Australia, for Australia as so many at the time remarked, possessed no ruins: she could not dream about her past, only about her future.

There were, however, two sources of romantic sentiment available in the new colonies; the love of the simple and adventurous life freed from the conventions of civilized life, and the closely associated delight in wild, mountainous scenery. The noble savage itself was, at heart, a romantic symbol; and as the century progressed it shed its classical associations. Such a painting as Captain James Wallis's *Corroboree at Newcastle* (20) admirably expresses the romantic interests of the time. Here is that love of primitive man, wild scenery and moonlight which the romantics adored. And yet, for all its romantic interest, the image of the noble savage was quickly replaced in the second and third decades of the century. Even in the eighteenth century, despite a wide currency, it had appealed only to a limited number of educated people. It ill accorded with colonial experience. For the great majority of the colonists the natives represented the lowest condition of human existence. Contact with Europeans debauched their intricate tribal structure and shattered the economic basis of their existence. Clad in old rags to hide their nakedness from the eyes of the newcomers,

20   JAMES WALLIS, *Corroboree at Newcastle*, oil on wood, 28 x 48,
c. 1817, Dixson Galleries

the aborigine became, during the 1820's and 1830's, the butt of a cruel and insensitive colonial humour.

The moral values of the convicts, such as they were, were still largely responsible for determining the moral values of colonial society at large.[2] And for the convicts the aborigines were a species of human being who belonged to a social class lower even than their own. Much of the cruelty which convicts experienced from their masters during the period of their servitude was visited upon natives with whom they came in contact on the pastoral frontier where so many became shepherds and stockmen in the years following their emancipation. T. R. Browne, a convict stationed at Newcastle in the years 1812-13, was among the first to caricature the aborigine. He produced comical silhouettes of well-known natives called by nicknames such as Long Jack, Pussy-Cat, and Hump Back'd Maria (21). Caricaturing the aborigine was carried on into the 1830's by W. H. Fernyhough (1812-49), a surveyor and architectural draughtsman, who lithographed *Twelve Profile Portraits of the Aborigines of New South Wales* in 1836. The grotesque gestures of his *Native Dance* (22) afford a sharp contrast with James Wallis's *Corroboree at Newcastle*. The aborigine is no longer conceived as a romantic figure performing his strange rituals under the light of the moon. He has become the colonial clown. Even more striking is the contrast between John Carmichael's besotted and debauched *Male and Female Black Natives* (23) of 1839 and William Blake's idyllic *Family of New South Wales* (3) of 1793. Such contrasts testify to the decline of the idea of the noble savage, an idea which did much to humanize relationships between Europeans and native peoples during the second half of the

21 T. R. BROWNE, *Hump Back'd Maria, a Female well known about Sydney*, water-colour, 11½ x 9½, *c*. 1819, Nan Kivell Collection, N.L.A.

eighteenth century. In place of the noble savage, the nineteenth century evolved the idea of the ignoble savage, a concept crystallizing largely out of the attitudes formed by evangelists and evolutionists. For, to the thoroughgoing evangelist, aborigines were pagan savages who (saving Christian conversion) were destined to perdition; to the evolutionist they were creatures but one step above the brute creation, destined to extinction by the immutable laws of natural selection.

To replace the eighteenth century's black noble savage the nineteenth century produced a white one: the noble frontiersman. He became the new representative, the new symbol, of a life freed from the restricting conventions of civilized life. His was a life lived close to nature, dangerous, adventurous and often heroic. The image arose in the art of many pioneering communities in the second decade of the century; in America, for instance, in such forms as Natty Bumppo, the hero of several of James Fenimore Cooper's novels. In its Australian context, the graphic image is foreshadowed in pictorial embellishments to Joseph Lycett's engravings, but it is better expressed in the work of Augustus Earle (1793-c. 1838), an artist himself greatly given to a life of wandering and adventure.

Augustus Earle was the son of James Earle (1761-96), and the nephew of Ralph Earle (1751-1801), a well-known American portrait painter. Augustus's father, who was himself a painter, travelled

22   W. H. FERNYHOUGH, *Native Dance*, lithograph, 8½ x 11, 1836

to England as a young man, and his son studied at the Royal Academy. After completing his studies, Augustus travelled in the Mediterranean (1815-17), spent two years in the United States (1818-20) and four more in Brazil (1821-4). In 1824, on his way to India, Earle was wrecked on the south Atlantic island of Tristan da Cunha. After an adventurous eight months on the island he was taken off by the *Admiral Cockburn* bound for Van Diemen's Land, and arrived in Hobart in January 1825. He later visited New Zealand and India, and in 1831 embarked as topographical artist aboard the *Beagle*, where he made the acquaintance of Charles Darwin.

Earle only remained in Australia until October 1828, and there was an intervening visit of nine months to New Zealand. He was, therefore, only a bird of passage; but he worked with great industry and covered a large part of the country. He also became quite well known as a portrait painter in New South Wales. His best-known portrait is the full-length standing figure of *Captain John Piper* (1773-1851), the Naval Officer of Port Jackson (24). Piper is presented in his uniform of office, standing upon a southern

23   JOHN CARMICHAEL, *Male and Female Black Natives*, etching, 4½ x 7, 1839

point of Sydney Harbour, beside a gum tree. His splendid residence, 'Henrietta Villa', the scene of many of the colony's most lavish entertainments during the 'twenties, is portrayed behind him. Earle also painted portraits of Governor Brisbane and Governor Darling, and a number of the notables of New South Wales.

Earle made many excursions into the newly-opened regions of New South Wales, including the Illa-

24 AUGUSTUS EARLE, *Captain John Piper*,
canvas, 75¾ x 47½, *c.* 1826, Mitchell Galleries

warra, Port Stephens, Port Macquarie, the Bathurst Plains and Wellington Valley—at that time the most westerly of all the settlements of the colony. On these excursions he sought to portray natural curiosities of the landscape, especially geological curiosities, the life of the native people and the activities of the regions recently opened up by European settlement. Like many of the roving artists of his time, Earle was anxious to visit regions 'hitherto unvisited by any artist'. In the early years of the century before the invention of photography (1839), when the perfecting of the coloured aquatint and the lithograph was making illustrated travel books popular, there was a great need for illustrations of little-known parts of the world. Earle was only one of a great number of artists who wandered widely about the world seeking to provide them.

Many years after his visit to Australia Augustus Earle, back in England after his work on the *Beagle*, exhibited a painting at the Royal Academy of 1838, made from drawings executed in the Illawarra district of New South Wales. He called it *A Bivouac of Travellers in Australia in a Cabbage Tree Forest, Day Break* (25). The painting seeks to present something of the life of the colonial frontiersman, which was now beginning to impress itself upon the European imagination. The scene is set in a landscape highly exotic to English eyes. A group of travellers, accompanied by their native guides, are seen about their camp fire, which has been kept blazing all night. Around them are strewn saddles, rifles and dogs, and the results of the previous day's kill. Two men are preparing to break camp; another is about to place a quart-pot on the fire in preparation for breakfast. One traveller stretches himself on awakening; another is still asleep. By means of such paintings the image of the noble frontiersman was transmitted. It was just the kind of picture calculated to stir the imagination at a time when migration from the old world to a new was exercising the thoughts of thousands.

The noble savage had inhabited a romantic wilderness. The noble frontiersman entered, like Abram, into a land of sweet pastures. During the 1820's and 1830's, as sheep runs were pushed farther and farther into the interior, the pastoral imagery of the Bible rose constantly in the minds of travellers. It was the land of Canaan. 'O I congratulate you,' exclaimed the Reverend Samual Marsden, as he encountered a family of settlers negotiating the precipitous passes of the Blue Mountains. 'You are all going to the land of Goshen.'[3] And when Barron Field in 1822 rode into the Bathurst Plains (to which Marsden had been referring) he found, as he had never found upon the coast, a country his heart could warm to:

I could hardly believe I was travelling in New Holland this day, so different, so English—is the character of the scenery—downs, meadows and streams, in the flat—no side scenes of eucalyptus. . . . You may see as far as the eye can reach. Stockmen, cattle and sheep occasionally form your horizon, as in old Holland— a Paul Potter or Cuyp effect rare in New Holland. At sunset we saw wooded hills, distant enough to display that golden glow which landscape painters love.[4]

And another traveller a year later wrote:

The fatigue of the journey was now over, and we were really in a Christian country—the climate mild and delightful, the prospect cheerful and extensive— the sheep returning to the fold seemed healthy and happy, and awakened thoughts of abundance—of content—of thankfulness. The gorgeous sun was setting in a robe of gold, over that undiscovered country west of the Macquarie, and the scene was altogether worthy of a Claude.[5]

Throughout the 1820's and 1830's some of the best pastoral land of eastern Australia was opened up by squatters and explorers. Their reports resounded with a note of optimism and hope for the future. In 1836 Major Mitchell found, in the Western District of Victoria, the land of Australia Felix:

As I stood, the first European intruder on the sublime solitude of these verdant plains, as yet untouched by flocks or herds, I felt conscious of being the harbinger of mighty changes there for our steps would soon be followed by the men and the animals for which it seemed to have been prepared.[6]

It is not surprising that the new pastoral country opened up should suggest to some the possibility of a new and independent school of landscape painting in Australia. Dr John Lhotsky, a Polish scientist who made a visit to the Southern Alps in 1834, wrote a few years later:

Australian sky and nature awaits, and merits real artists to pourtray it. Its gigantic gum and acacia trees, forty feet in girth, some of them covered with a most smooth bark, externally as white as chalk; the enchantment—like appearance of forests, the foliage of which is pruinose and mellow, in a way defying description— mornings and evenings so pure and serene that the eye is absorbed as it were, in the depths of the azure of the horizon. . . . All this and more . . . will produce a Daniell, and in succession a Salvator Rosa, and, perhaps, such as will even succeed them.[7]

Lhotsky wrote his comment in 1839. By that time John Glover, a very well-known English artist who knew and revered the work of Claude and Salvator Rosa, had already been working for nine years in Australia seeking to render as ably as he could the characteristic features of the country's landscape. Augustus Earle had been a bird of passage, but Glover (1767-1849), who arrived in Hobart in February 1831, came to stay. He was the son of a Leicestershire farmer who first established himself as an artist and drawing master in Lichfield. In 1805, he began to practise in London and rapidly became one of the most successful artists and art teachers in the kingdom. He was elected President of the Old Water-colour Society in 1807, and exhibited regularly at the Royal Academy and the Society of British Artists, holding one-man shows in London in 1823 and 1824. In 1830, however, at a time when Van Diemen's Land was receiving con- siderable publicity in England as a desirable home for migrants with capital, and when Glover was sixty-four years of age, he decided to leave England to paint the little-known scenery of the new colony and to settle his family upon the land.

In 1832 he obtained an extensive grant of land in north-eastern Tasmania on the northern slopes of Ben Lomond. There he built a fine two-storeyed stone house, and called his property 'Patterdale', after Patterdale in Cum- berland where he had lived for some time before migrating to Van Diemen's Land. Here, as his family proceeded to farm, he continued to paint pro- lifically, as he had done throughout his life, and was able to prepare an exhibition 'descriptive of the scenery and customs of Van Diemen's Land' which he held in Bond Street, London, in 1835.

Glover's style was formed in the last decades of the eighteenth century, and he retained a great affection for those landscape masters, such as Claude Lorraine, Salvator Rosa and Gaspard Poussin, whom the connoisseurs of the time revered. Indeed, he owned two Claudes himself. It is not surprising, therefore, that his interpretations of the Tasmanian landscape should at times recall these masters. Glover's son, John Glover junior, remarked once that the rocks along the Tamar River reminded him of the rocks in Gaspard

25 AUGUSTUS EARLE, *A Bivouac of Travellers in Australia in a Cabbage Tree Forest, Day Break*, canvas, 41½ x 32¾, *c.* 1838, Nan Kivell Collection, N.L.A.

26   JOHN GLOVER, *Australian Landscape With Cattle*, canvas, 30 x 40,
c. 1835, Nan Kivell Collection, N.L.A.

Poussin's paintings;[8] and John Glover's painting of a hunting party on Ben
Lomond (NLA)[9] recalls the banditti scenes of Salvator Rosa and Gaspard
Poussin. This is not to say that Glover was incapable of catching the
character of the local landscape. There need be little doubt that he had
come to the colony with that intention very much in mind. Some of the
remarks which he wrote into the catalogue of his 1835 exhibition are most
perceptive, as when he observes: 'There is a remarkable peculiarity in the
trees in this country; however numerous they rarely prevent you tracing
through them the whole distant country.'

Such observations were also expressed in his drawings and paintings, as
in his *Australian Landscape with Cattle* (26). This fine landscape concedes
nothing to later artists like Louis Buvelot, Tom Roberts, Arthur Streeton
and Hans Heysen in the unmistakable clarity of its vision. Here is no
Englishman painting the landscape with English eyes nor interpreting it
by means of the ideal formula of Claude. The light and open foreground
untidily strewn with fallen logs and branches, the translucent screen of trees
in the middle distance, the pale blue hills beyond: such typical features of
the local landscape are seen and depicted lucidly. In such paintings Glover
established himself as one of the pioneers of Australian landscape painting.
Yet in those optimistic years of the pastoral expansion everything seemed
possible, and the reality often faded imperceptibly into the ideal.

In *My Harvest Home* (27) the old blends with the new.[10] A bountiful
harvest has sprung from what was once an antipodean wilderness. The

27   JOHN GLOVER, junior, *My Harvest Home*, canvas, 30 x 46½,
c. 1840, Hobart

eucalypt forest glows in the mellow light of Claude. It is a vision of a pioneer's paradise. But the sense of plenitude and physical well-being which the painting figures forth is no mere pictorial device, for it expressed the living experience of the Glover family as Australian farmers. North-eastern Tasmania became a granary for the mainland in the early 1830's and played an important part in the growing prosperity of the island. 'We sow, plant, fence and break up new ground in progressive order,' wrote John Glover, junior, to his sister in England, 'and our crops thank goodness turn out equal to most, our wheat in particular often surpasses most of our neighbours . . . Mr Glover continues painting.'[11]

Glover continued painting until the last few years of his life when he became something of a patriarch on his splendid agricultural and pastoral property, surrounded by his children and grandchildren. He impressed all who met him in the closing years of his life with his natural dignity and his strong religious convictions. One of his English pupils wrote of him:

Though he was a very plain man and uncouth in appearance he was one of the most interesting persons I ever met with. He could not, I imagine, have been a highly educated man, but his mind appeared to us as innately elegant, poetical and refined, and when he spoke of the beauties of nature he seemed to conduct his hearers into a world of his own so deeply did he feel and appreciate.[12]

In his deep feeling for nature, Glover was closely akin to the early romantic poets. It is likely that he knew Wordsworth, for they lived less

28   J. ROPER, *Gold Diggings, Ararat*, canvas, 17½ x 29½, 1854,
Dixson Galleries

29   WILLIAM STRUTT, *Bushrangers on the St Kilda Road*,
canvas, 29¾ x 61½, *c.* 1887, Lady Grimwade

than ten miles apart in the Lake District for some years. In several of his Tasmanian landscapes, Glover's lucid observations of natural forms were mingled with a delight in capturing the transient effects of sunlight, mist and cloud. He was the first artist working in Australia in whom the effects of the romantic revival may be observed at work.[13] But others were soon to follow. In 1835, the year in which Glover held his exhibition of Tasmanian landscapes in London, Conrad Martens (1801-78), a pupil of that highly romantic water-colour painter, Copley Fielding, arrived in Sydney.

Martens's early life serves to remind us that the practice of using professional painters as artists upon voyages of survey and discovery, which Joseph Banks had done so much to inaugurate when he travelled with Cook in the *Endeavour,* was still very much alive. Martens was the son of a German who had come to England as Austrian consul and later settled as a merchant. Both his brothers were artists; and when his father died in 1816 Conrad studied landscape painting under Fielding, later making many sketches along the Devon coast after he and his mother had moved from London to live at Exeter. Late in 1832 or early in 1833 he accepted the offer of a trip to India, but while his ship was at Rio de Janeiro, Captain Fitzroy offered him the post of topographical draughtsman on the *Beagle,* as Augustus Earle was about to vacate the position because of ill health.

Martens remained with the expedition from November 1833 until the *Beagle* and the *Adventure* arrived at Valparaiso where, in October 1834, it became necessary to sell the *Adventure* to reduce the expense of the expedition. This forced Martens to leave the expedition; or, as Charles Darwin, who had become a friend of the painter, put it in a letter to his sister, 'to leave our little Martens to wander about the world'.[14] As it happened he only wandered across the Pacific; first to Tahiti, for a few weeks, then to the Bay of Islands, New Zealand, for a few days, and then on to Sydney, where he arrived in April 1835. There he remained until his death in 1878.

Like Augustus Earle, Martens travelled widely in New South Wales shortly after his arrival and it seems that at first he intended to move on as Earle had done. By 1835, however, there was a small but influential circle of people in the colony, including Sir Richard Bourke, the Governor of New South Wales from 1831 until 1837, Alexander and William Macleay, General Sir Edward Macarthur, and Captain P. P. King, all of whom were interested in the promotion of science and the arts in the colony. They were able to provide Martens with some initial support and bought his paintings. Local patronage was fitful and unpredictable, however, and, when the depression of 1843 hit the colony, Martens and his family (he had married in 1837) were reduced to straitened circumstances for several years, though he received a little financial help from his family in England from time to time.

D

Lithographic views of Sydney, the first of which he produced in 1842, also helped to tide him over the worst of his difficulties. Finding it impossible to live on the sales of his painting despite a prolific output, he was pleased to accept the position of Assistant Librarian of the New South Wales Parliamentary Library. In 1843 he had built a cottage at North Sydney, then called St Leonards, and there he lived with his family until his death at the age of seventy-seven.

Martens was the most prolific, if not the most important, of Australia's colonial painters. His early work, as revealed in his Devonshire watercolours, is based on the practice of his master, Fielding, which consisted in broad, fluently-handled renderings of picturesque aspects of sea and shore, moorland and country road, renderings which delighted in making use of accidental effects of light and shadow and the visual drama of storm and rain clouds. The work which he executed during the months aboard the *Beagle* was, and had to be, more precise, documentative and empirical. For he was in the company of men whose capacity for observing the world of nature was penetrating, analytical and precise: not only Darwin himself, whose powers of observing nature have never been surpassed, but also men like Captain Robert Fitzroy, a pioneer meteorologist, from whom Martens clearly learned much of use to him in the observation of clouds and other atmospheric conditions.

The paintings which Martens produced in the years immediately following his arrival in Sydney are still conceived in the traditions of picturesque topography which he had employed while an artist on the *Beagle*. As the years passed, however, he became more interested in the elevation of his themes above the level of topography and sought to capture effects of romantic grandeur (30). His *North Head, Sydney Harbour* (Adelaide, 1854) is still largely a picturesque composition, with its side-screens of trees and its heavy dark foreground. But there is much insistence upon the documentation of foreground detail, and he exaggerates the size of his trees to endow them with dignity and grandeur. All this is most Turnerian. And, like Turner, and the landscape painters of his generation, Martens was fascinated by the problems involved in the depiction of light.[15] Light, as the great romantic painters conceived it, was the most dramatic element in the involved drama of nature. And Martens became a master in rendering vivid effects of light, cloud and storm over Sydney Harbour (30). Entries in his notebooks reveal how he studied the heavens like a meteorologist. He also made water-colour sketches of moonlight and dawn over the sea. From such researches came paintings like *Sydney from Vaucluse* (31). Here the close-up precision of urban topography is replaced by a romantic vision of the city as a small world of man encompassed by the larger world of nature. It is a splendid study in atmosphere and light, highly reminiscent of Turner.

30 CONRAD MARTENS, *View from Neutral Bay*, water-colour, 17¾ x 25¾,
c. 1857/8, Mr K. R. Stewart

31 CONRAD MARTENS, *Sydney from Vaucluse*, water-colour, 17½ x 26,
1864, Dixson Library

Only rarely did Martens reach such heights, and then only in his finest water-colours. He had been trained as a water-colour painter and his oils tend, by comparison, to be heavy in treatment and flat in colour. It was a medium he never fully mastered.

Although Martens will always be remembered for his romantic interpretations of Sydney Harbour, the plains of the interior attracted him as they had Barron Field. In the early 1850's he sailed to Brisbane, travelled across the Great Divide to the Darling Downs, and made his way down the New England Tableland painting landscapes and the residences of squatters. The district had been occupied during the 1820's and 1830's, and Martens found some hospitality (and an occasional patron) in the homesteads he drew and painted. His Darling Downs landscapes have certain similarities with the Mills Plains landscapes of John Glover in the way the pictorial elements are assembled. Foregrounds have a sense of spaciousness, groups of trees tend to be placed in the middle distance, and there is a further emphasis upon treeless spaces in the depths beyond. The emphasis is upon openness, flatness and bigness. But the Australian savannah, which was to prove such a compulsive image to the painters of later generations, was not Martens's true *métier*. At heart a romantic, he was more at home painting the gorges and sandstone battlements of the Blue Mountains, and those foreshores of Sydney Harbour from which there sprouted in Martens's own day many Gothic Revival mansions whose battlemented heads, rising above the gum trees, served to remind their owners in exile of the ancient northern origins from whence they had sprung.[16]

Until the end of the 1820's colonial art in Australia was produced almost entirely for an English audience; though there was always some local demand for portraits and miniatures. The period from 1830 to 1851, however, witnesses the emergence of local patronage in New South Wales and Van Diemen's Land. Artists became aware that a small local market for their work existed. It depended very largely upon the interests of professional people: the higher civil servants, Army and Navy officers, doctors and lawyers, together with some members of the older pastoral families, such as the Macarthurs, as distinct from the newer class of squatters who, during those years, were too fully occupied establishing themselves upon their holdings to have any time or money for the cultivation of the arts.

One indication of the rise of local patronage is the publication from time to time of engraved and lithographic views of Sydney and Hobart. Sometimes these were brought together in book form. Thus Charles Atkinson published his *Views through Hobart Town* in 1833, in which he made some concession to contemporary taste by featuring himself standing before a Gothic ruin. In 1836 J. G. Austin published his *Lithographic Drawings of Sydney and its Environs,* and two years later J. Maclehose published his

Picture of Sydney. Similar publications followed during the 1840's. Such books rarely rose above the level of modest topography but they were produced for a local market not an English one.

Another indication of the growth of colonial taste and patronage is to be found in the emergence of amateur art circles and the organization of the first art exhibitions. In early Victorian England the ability to sketch in water-colours was an elegant accomplishment suited alike to ladies of fashion and gentlemen of taste. And among a small and select circle of Van Diemen's Land society water-colour painting became quite fashionable during the 1830's and 1840's. From the time of John Glover's arrival in 1831 an amateur interest in painting flourished. During the 1840's the amateur painters included G. T. W. B. Boyes, the Colonial Auditor; Dr F. R. Nixon, the first Bishop of Tasmania; George Frankland, the Surveyor-General of Tasmania (1828-38); Lieutenant F. G. Simpkinson, the nephew of Lady Franklin, and Samuel Prout Hill, a journalist, lecturer and poet.

Some of the work possessed distinction, notably that of Boyes, who also wrote an outstanding personal diary invaluable for the study of his life and times, which has never been published.[17] Rallying points for those like Boyes and others who were interested in raising standards of public taste were provided by the establishment of Mechanics' Institutes, first in Hobart in 1827, then in Sydney in 1833. By 1851 the capital of every Australian State had its own institution. These Institutes provided among other things a forum for public lectures and the exchange of ideas concerning the fine arts and standards of public taste.[18]

Art exhibitions also helped artists and potential patrons to come together. An exhibition of his own work which Augustus Earle held in Sydney in July 1826 aroused considerable interest; but little appears to have been done until many years later. John Skinner Prout (1806-76) awakened considerable interest in painting through his lectures at the Sydney Mechanics' Institute when he arrived in 1840. Seven years later a Society for the Promotion of Fine Arts was established under the presidency of Sir Charles Nicholson, and held its first exhibition in the Australian Library, Sydney, in June 1847. In Hobart, which he visited in 1843, Prout's lectures and teaching aroused widespread interest. 'The prevalent fashionable epidemic, instead of betraying symptoms of the ancient Berlin wool influenza or the knitting disorder, had taken an entirely new turn,' wrote Louisa Ann Meredith, 'and that a landscape-sketching and water-colour fever raged with extraordinary vehemence.'[19] The enthusiasm led to the organization by Prout, Boyes, Nixon and others, of the island's first exhibition, which was held in the Legislative Council Chambers in January 1845. An art exhibition in which John Glover participated was held at the Launceston Mechanics' Institute in 1848.

32 JOHN SKINNER PROUT, *Grass Trees, Richmond Road, Van Diemen's Land*, water-colour, 10 x 7, 1844, Nan Kivell Collection, N.L.A.

Apart from Conrad Martens, the two most important artists working in the Australian colonies during the 1840's were John Skinner Prout and George French Angas (1822-86). Both of them, however, like Augustus Earle were birds of passage, and both had gained experience in picturesque travel before arriving in Australia. John Skinner Prout was a nephew of Samuel Prout, an artist greatly admired by John Ruskin for his renderings of medieval architecture. Largely self-taught, he had obtained considerable experience in England sketching ancient buildings, a practice then much in vogue. He could also write with facility about his travels and had experience in handling a lithographic press. Prout published some of his drawings in his *Castles and Abbeys of Monmouthshire* (1838). Early in 1840, however, finding it difficult to obtain a living in England, he migrated with his family to Australia where he threw himself with vigour into the task of promoting an interest in water-colour painting in the colonies.

Like Earle, Skinner Prout travelled widely. His paintings, however, are much less of a documentary and topographical nature than Earle's. For he sought out picturesque effects seeking to capture them swiftly with a few deft washes and telling strokes. His work is much lighter in treatment than the more heavy and finished work of Martens (32). Prout possessed considerable facility and it is clear that he was appealing to that early Victorian taste for breadth, charm and simplicity in water-colour which was to be shattered by the geological, botanical and moral thunderings of John Ruskin. But Prout lacked Martens's capacity to study nature with patience and humility.

Prout, none the less, worked with great industry. After a sojourn in Tasmania he visited the Port Phillip District and sketched there. Before he returned to England in 1848 he had published by means of his own lithographic press: *Sydney Illustrated* (1844), *Tasmania Illustrated* (1844), and *Views of Melbourne and Geelong* (1847). He had, however, arrived in the colonies at a most unfortunate time and lived through the 1841-3 depression in the eastern States. On his return to England he held an exhibition of dioramic views of Australia based on his drawings. The scenes he chose, such as a *Bivouac of Emigrants in the Blue Mountains*, were those likely to interest prospective migrants. After returning to England he lived first in Bristol and then in London, where he was a member of the New Water Colour Society for many years. He died in 1876.[20]

The work of George French Angas is closely connected with the foundation of South Australia and a programme to induce migrants to settle there. He was the son of George Fife Angas (1789-1879), the banker, shipowner and philan-

33 RICHARD READ, senior, *Mrs Macquarie*, miniature on ivory, 3¾ x 2¾, *c*. 1819, Hobart

thropist who did so much to found the colony. George French Angas first studied art under Waterhouse Hawkins, a natural history painter; and, like Skinner Prout, travelled in search of the picturesque, having published some travels before journeying to Australia. At the age of nineteen he made a trip to the Mediterranean and in 1842 published *A Ramble in Malta and Sicily in the Autumn of 1841*. In September 1843 he sailed for South Australia where he travelled widely about the colony, sketching the scenery and the aborigines. Both his art and his programme recalls that of Augustus Earle, and is more documentary and factual in its approach than that of Prout.

From South Australia, Angas visited New Zealand and then paid a short visit to Sydney, returning home to hold an exhibition of his work in the Egyptian Hall, Piccadilly, in 1846. He then set about publishing his travels: *Savage Life and Scenes in Australia and New Zealand* (1847); *The New Zealanders Illustrated* and *South Australia Illustrated* (1847 (15). These books contained large coloured lithographs and were based on the scale and manner of publication of John Goud's *Birds of Australia* (1841-8). Such books and the exhibitions of his work helped to publicize South Australia and New Zealand to prospective migrants. Angas next visited South Africa (1848) and on his return published *The Kaffirs Illustrated* (1849).

34 AUGUSTUS EARLE, *Mrs Piper and Her Children*, canvas, 76½ x 47¾, c. 1826, Vaucluse House, Sydney

He then returned to Australia and for seven years (1853-60) was the Secretary of the Australian Museum, Sydney. By that time he had become as interested in science as in art, and published several papers on conchology and zoology. His work provides yet another example of the close association of art and science during the first half of the nineteenth century. He returned to London in 1861 and died there in 1888.[21]

Early Colonial Portrait Painting

The history of portrait painting in colonial Australia is a field which awaits special investigation, and will only be treated here briefly. The first portrait painter of any standing was Richard Read, senior, who was active in Sydney between 1814 and 1826. Read painted portraits of Governor Macquarie and Mrs Macquarie (33) and local notables such as Dr Bland and Michael Massey Robinson. Read's portraits are of historical interest only.[22] Richard Read, junior, a miniaturist who advertised that he 'had no connexion whatever with any other person in the same profession' was active in Sydney between 1819 and 1849.[23] Other early Sydney miniaturists include T. B. East, Samuel Clayton and Josiah Allen. Charles Rodius made engravings of Paris streets prior to his arrival in Sydney in 1823. Apart from making a number of portrait drawings of well-known citizens he also executed a series of portraits of aboriginal 'kings' and their wives, which were published by J. G. Austin in 1834.[24] The portraits which Augustus Earle painted in Sydney between 1825 and 1828 of such people as Governor

Brisbane, Governor Darling, Mrs Blaxland, Captain John Piper (24) and Mrs Piper and her children (34), though by no means the work of an accomplished portrait painter, are of a better quality than the work of the men before him, and possess a primitive colonial charm.

The first portrait painter to practise professionally in Tasmania was Thomas Bock (1790-1857), born at Sutton Coldfield and probably apprenticed to the Birmingham engraver, Thomas Brandard. Bock practised engraving in Birmingham between 1815 and 1823. In April 1823 he was sentenced to fourteen years' imprisonment at the Warwick Assizes for administering drugs to a young woman. He appears to have been an exemplary convict and received a conditional pardon in June 1832 and a full pardon in November 1833.[25] Bock practised as an engraver in Tasmania, engraving the colony's first bank notes. Apart from drawing and painting (mainly in crayon or water-colour) portraits and miniatures of local citizens, Bock also painted a series of studies of Tasmanian aborigines for Lady Franklin, now in the collection of the Tasmanian Museum.

The second portrait painter to practise in Hobart was Benjamin Duterreau (1767-1851), of French Huguenot descent, who was born in London and apprenticed to engraving there. In 1790 he engraved two colour plates for G. Morland. Later he turned to portrait painting, exhibiting six portraits at the Royal Academy between 1817 and 1823, and three genre pieces at the British Institution. Duterreau, like John Glover, migrated to Australia rather late in life. In his sixty-fifth year he arrived in Western Australia but decided to transfer to Hobart, arriving there with his daughter in August 1832. Miss Duterreau became governess to Governor Arthur's children, and Duterreau himself began to practise as a portrait and landscape painter. In 1835 he etched some portraits of Tasmanian aborigines, probably the first executed in Australia.[26]

In November 1837 Thomas Griffiths Wainewright arrived in Hobart, having been transported for life for forgery. Wainewright was a talented littérateur and artist, a spendthrift, and probably a poisoner. His colourful life has received much attention from many writers, including Oscar Wilde and Mario Praz, and need not be considered here. Suffice to say that Wainewright studied painting under Thomas Phillips and became an associate of that circle of English pre-romantic artists which included Fuseli, Blake, Stothard and Flaxman. During the early 1820's he exhibited at the Royal Academy regularly and contributed to literary magazines like *Blackwood's* and the *London Magazine* for which he wrote art criticisms and literary essays under various pseudonyms. His literary interests gave him access to the literary circle around Charles Lamb. Although in his English work Wainewright echoes the mannerist extravagance and voluptuousness of Fuseli whom he much admired, in Tasmania, as Robert Crossland has

35   THOMAS GRIFFITHS WAINEWRIGHT, *Frances Maria
Brodribb*, crayon, 20½ x 16½, *c.* 1840, Adelaide

pointed out, he produced a series of portraits 'almost monotonous in their
insistence on the domestic virtues of grace, elegance and refinement'. Such
sensitive portraits as *Francis Maria Brodribb* (35) and *Dr Frederick John
Clarke* (G. R. F. Nuttall) reveal him as the most accomplished portrait
draughtsman at work in Australia during the colonial period.[27]

FOOTNOTES

1 RUSKIN, *Works* (ed. E. T. Cook and A. Wedderburn), London, 1903-12, vol. v, p. 369

2 *See* R. WARD, *The Australian Legend*, Melbourne, 1958, pp. 66-99, *passim*

3 MRS HAWKINS, 'Journey from Sydney to Bathurst in 1822', quoted from G. Mackaness, *Fourteen Journeys Over the Blue Mountains of New South Wales*, 1813-41, pt. ii (1950), p.30

4 BARRON FIELD, *Geographical Memoirs on New South Wales*, London, 1825, pp. 430-1

5 Article in *The Australian*, 24 March 1827

6 T. L. MITCHELL, *Three Expeditions into the interior of Eastern Australia . . .* London, 1838, p. 158

7 J. LHOTSKY, 'The State of Arts in New South Wales and Tasmania', *The Art-Union*, London (July, 1839), pp. 99-100

8 John Glover, junior, to his sister Mary, 20 February 1831, Glover MSS., Mitchell Library, Sydney

9 *EVSP*, pl. 133

10 This painting is usually attributed to John Glover but is more likely to be by his son John Glover, junior.

11 John Glover, junior, to his sister Mary, 12 July 1839, Glover MSS., Mitchell Library, Sydney

12 MS. note on the artist by a former pupil, in the possession of Dr W. L. Crowther, Hobart, Tasmania

13 On Glover *see also* B. S. LONG, in *Walker's Quarterly*, xv (1924); FARINGTON, *Diary*, iii, 87 and v, 53; T. S. R. BOASE, *English Art 1800-1870*, Oxford, 1959, p. 42, *passim*; *EVSP* 194-201; Glover MSS. in the Mitchell Library, Sydney

14 NORA BARLOW, *Charles Darwin and the Voyage of the Beagle*, New York, 1946, p. 108

15 Martens acknowledged his debt to Turner in his 'Lecture upon Landscape Painting', delivered at the Australian Library, 21 July 1856, Mitchell MS., C. 338.

16 On Martens *see also* LIONEL LINDSAY, *Conrad Martens the Man and his Art*, Sydney, 1920; M. H. GRANT, *Dictionary of British Landscape Painters*, Leigh-on-Sea, p. 124; *EVSP*, pp. 232-40, *passim;* J. GRAY, 'Conrad Martens', B.A. Thesis, University of Melbourne

17 The Diary of G. T. W. B. Boyes, Royal Society of Tasmania, Hobart. Some extracts from the Diary are printed in the *Papers and Proceedings of the Royal Society of Tasmania*, 1946 (1947), pp. 35-50.

18 On the Mechanics' Institutes and Schools of Art in Australia, *see* G. NADEL, *Australia's Colonial Culture*, Melbourne, 1957; *PTT*, pp. 88-94

19 L. A. MEREDITH, *My Home in Tasmania*, London, 1852, pp. 326-7

20 *See also* J. S. PROUT, *Journal of a Voyage from Plymouth to Sydney, in Australia, on board the Emigrant Ship Royal Sovereign*, London, 1844; W. DIXSON, 'Notes on Australian Artists', *Journal RAHS*, vii (1921), p. 379; MEREDITH, op. cit., pp. 326-7

21 *See also* EDWIN HODDER, *George Fife Angas*, London, 1891; and MOORE, i, 61, *passim*

22 On Read, senior, *see* W. DIXSON, 'Notes on Australian Artists', *Journ. RAHS*, v (1919), 245-7

23 Quoted by DIXSON from the *Sydney Gazette*, in his article on Read, junior, art. cited

24 *See* DIXSON, art. cited

25 Tasmanian State Archives; Report of the Warwick Assizes, *Birmingham Gazette*, 14 April 1823

26 On DUTERREAU *see also* the article in *DAB*; MOORE, i, 37-8

27 On Wainewright *see also* JONATHAN CURLING, *Janus Weathercock*, London, 1938; ROBERT CROSSLAND, *Wainewright in Tasmania*, Melbourne, 1954

CHAPTER THREE

THE LATE COLONIAL ARTISTS
1851 - 85

'. . . in Australia alone is to be found the Grotesque, the Weird, the strange scribblings of nature learning how to write.'

MARCUS CLARKE, Preface to *Poems of the late Adam Lindsay Gordon*, 1880

PAYABLE gold was discovered in Australia in 1851 and wherever it was in quantity a community of tents and shanties sprang up rapidly. Life at these diggings was both vigorous and exacting. A spirit of energy and bustle prevailed which did much in the end to provide Australian life with a new fund of resource and an independence far finer than, though in many ways related to, the dull-spirited and sub-literate modes of resistance inherited from the convict 'founding fathers' of New South Wales and Van Diemen's Land. Life in these new mining communities is expressed with a simple charm in J. Roper's *Gold Diggings, Ararat*, 1854 (28). Nothing is known about Roper, but he was clearly an observant man capable of seeing the amusing and incongruous side of things quickly. How different this painting is from the rural peace of Glover's *Harvest Home* (27); and the contrast provides a sharp indication of the marked difference of life on the old pastoral frontier of Tasmania and the new mining frontier of Victoria. A bearded miner is busily digging for gold while his mate, his hands in his pockets, quietly looks on. The billy is on the boil and the evening's joint of mutton has been securely slung from a tree, where it swings safe from ants, if not from the flies. Below them men are panning and cradling gold by the creek. A team and jinker is halted by a group of stores—the nucleus of the rising town—the cosmopolitan characters of their occupiers denoted by the flags which surmount the buildings. The stores have been roofed with the new corrugated iron then being exported in considerable quantities to Melbourne by such iron foundries as the Clift manufactories, Bristol. In the middle distance, a group of aborigines, dressed in European cast-offs, gaze at the diggings which spread out in the distance into the hills. This painting is the work of an artist with little or no professional training—a primitive painter. It succeeds none the less in conveying a very good idea of life on the Victorian diggings during the mid-'fifties.

48

36   SAMUEL THOMAS GILL, *Overlanders*, water-colour, 13¼ x 23⅛,
c. 1865, Sydney

As the frontiers of settlement moved from the coastal regions to the interior, artists tended to interest themselves increasingly in subjects drawn from life outback. New themes, of great importance in the growth of Australian national sentiment, began to emerge both in literature and art. The life of drovers and stockmen who moved large flocks and herds over vast stretches of arid and semi-arid country provided one such theme. For the open-air life of freedom and adventure, in the saddle by day, and camped out under an open sky by night, held a great appeal especially for city-dwellers. The heroes of the colonial frontier, whether they were honorable men like the explorers Burke and Wills or dishonorable men like the bushranger Ned Kelly, exercised an enormous emotional appeal. The first poet of the Australian frontier to become well known in England was Adam Lindsay Gordon (1833-70), who described the frontier life of the stockrider in glowing terms:

> 'Twas merry in the glowing morn, among the gleaming grass,
> To wander as we've wandered many a mile,
> And blow the cool tobacco cloud, and watch the white wreaths pass,
> Sitting loosely in the saddle all the while.
> 'Twas merry 'mid the blackwoods, when we spied the station roofs,
> To wheel the wild scrub cattle at the yard,
> With a running fire of stockwhips and a fiery run of hoofs;
> Oh! the hardest day was never then too hard![1]

While Gordon was writing his bush ballads, the artist, Samuel Thomas Gill (1818-80), became well known both in Australia and England for his lithographs depicting the open-air life of the Australian diggers and bushmen. Gill had migrated with his parents to Adelaide in 1839 at the age of

37   BENJAMIN DUTERREAU, *The Conciliation*, canvas, 47 x 66,
1836, Hobart

eleven and, as a young man, soon established his reputation as an illustrator
and cartoonist before moving to the Victorian diggings in 1851. For the
next five years he produced many series of lithographic views on various
goldfields. They were widely circulated in England where the desire to
emigrate in search of gold was at its height. Later, Gill turned his attention
to life in the rapidly expanding cities of Sydney and Melbourne. Taken
together, his drawings form a most valuable commentary upon the life of
the times, a commentary which is expressed with much gusto and great
good humour. Gill is the first artist whose work expresses a distinctly Australian attitude to life; the sardonic humour, the nonchalance and the
irreverent attitude to all forms of authority, so frequently remarked upon
by the students of Australian behaviour, are all present in his work.

In his lithographs Gill succeeded in popularizing the image of the
frontiersman, as Gordon had done in his ballads. In his *Overlanders* (36)
two men are sitting 'loosely in the saddle', as they move slowly across a great
flat of semi-arid country with their dogs and pack-horses behind them. One
stockman drains a flask while his companion spins a yarn. The dead and
fallen timber, the stunted grass-trees (favoured by early colonial artists as
the typical emblem of the country's vegetation) had long been used to
stress the melancholy of the Australian scene. And the melancholy is here
increased by a further reduction of the traditional divisions of landscape,
foreground, middle distance and background, to minor components of little
importance. What is perhaps new, however, is the presentation of the

dramatic in a primeval setting: the comical, the banal, and often the tragic being enacted either in a semi-arid desert setting of natural curiosities or an open forest of unrelieved monotony.[2]

Linked with the desire to paint visual records of Australian life was the desire to paint events of historic significance. The conventions of history painting, however, differed from the less elevated conventions of genre painting. History paintings were not normally painted by eye witnesses of the events depicted and they were confined to events of great significance. During the eighteenth century the painting of history was regarded by most artists and critics as the highest form of painting, but for them history was the painting of events from the Bible and classical antiquity; and even when the events depicted happened to occur in more recent times, a classical form of dress and a dignified presentation of heroes noble of bearing and expression were considered essential to this elevated form of art.

The American artist, Benjamin West, who became President of the Royal Academy, was largely responsible for breaking down the authority of these conventions with his painting of the *Death of Wolfe* (1771), which depicted an event which had occurred only twelve years before. West still invested his figures with an air of great dignity and nobility, but he clothed them in their contemporary dress; and his choice of a subject with great patriotic appeal transformed history painting from a highly academic to a highly popular form of art. As a result of West's innovations, nineteenth-century artists adopted a less stylized approach to the painting of history than eighteenth-century artists. Even so, it was still assumed that a history painting should depict an event of major significance, the figures being drawn and composed in a heroic and dignified manner.

It is not surprising that the desire to execute paintings which would record events of national significance was felt by several artists working in Australia during the second half of the century. For the country was expanding rapidly, and social and political events of a decisive nature for the future history of the nation were taking place. How much better it would be to record the events of history as they were enacted under the eyes of the artist, or at least before the actual events had passed out of living memory. In 1869, the Trustees of the Public Library of Melbourne, thinking along these lines, commissioned S. T. Gill to make forty water-colour paintings of the events he had witnessed on the Victorian diggings over fifteen years before.

Such paintings were social documents rather than history paintings in the accepted sense of the word. History painting in Australia had begun, however, over thirty years before when Benjamin Duterreau painted *The Conciliation* (37). It shows George Robinson, the Methodist bricklayer who became a protector of aborigines, conversing with a group of Tasmanian aborigines to pacify them and induce them to leave their wild life and go with him.[3]

History paintings of a much finer quality than Duterreau's *Conciliation* were painted by William Strutt (1825-1915), who migrated to Victoria in 1850, and remained in the colony for eleven years before returning to England to continue his career. Strutt came from a family of artists and received a thorough professional training, first from his father, William Thomas Strutt, a miniature painter, and later in Paris where he studied at the atelier of Michel Drölling (1786-1851) and then at the Ecole des Beaux Arts. There he had the advantage of instruction from, as he claimed, such masters as Ingres, Delaroche and Vernet, and several other well-known teachers. Certainly Strutt became an able draughtsman, and his closely-finished, precise paintings are closely related to the neo-classical manner then favoured by the teachers at the Beaux Arts. Strutt remained in Paris for some time after completing his training and illustrated several books, including Anna Jameson's *Sacred and Legendary Arts* and Ferdinand Seré's *Le Moyen Age et la Renaissance* (1848). This last work strained his eyesight and he migrated to Australia in 1850 bent upon an open-air life. The trip restored his health and he decided not to abandon his profession. When he arrived in Melbourne he began working as a lithographer. Strutt's teacher, Drölling, had been a history painter, however, and it was clearly Strutt's own intention during the eleven years in which he resided in Australia to execute history paintings which would commemorate historic and typical events of colonial life in a dignified and memorable fashion.

William Strutt's largest and perhaps most impressive painting of an Australian subject was his *Black Thursday* (39). In February 1851, soon after he arrived in Victoria, a tremendous bushfire swept across the State. Melbourne was covered in a black pall of smoke and dust that completely obscured the sun, and the temperature rose to 117 degrees. After the fire, Strutt traversed the devastated areas and made many sketches. From these he painted his *Black Thursday* which he worked on for three years. It was first displayed at the Royal Academy, then at the Crystal Palace, and later taken on a tour of the capital cities of the Australian States.

In October 1852, another event occurred which attracted Strutt's attention. Early one afternoon a number of travellers were held up and robbed by bushrangers on St Kilda Road, a short distance from Melbourne. The captives were tied together in twos and threes, a man being posted over them with orders to fire if anyone stirred, the ringleader explaining to him that 'if you miss one, you are sure to hit some of the others'. The bushrangers remained for two hours adding seven more travellers to the original group. Then towards sunset they all galloped off into the bush in the direction of South Yarra.

38 WILLIAM CHARLES PIGUENIT, *The Upper Nepean*, canvas, 35⅞ x 51, 1888, Sydney

In *Bushrangers on the St Kilda Road* (29), Strutt has directed his attention not to the violence of the incident, but to the reactions of the participants. We are presented with a quiet moment at the height of the outrage when the victims are all safely trussed up and the bushrangers are dividing the booty. The prisoners reveal the most varied emotions: fear, defiant disgust, despair, resignation; one handsome young man even seems to be calculating the possibilities of escape. The painting is an admirable social document of the time, revealing the varied types and costumes to be found on the Victorian high-roads during the height of the gold-rushes; for Strutt, like his contemporary, Holman Hunt, was painstakingly accurate in the rendering of detail. The landscape, too, is of interest. Strutt, like Gill, portrays a wide, flat, open expanse, broken only by a few trees. The sun-drenched scene is capably suggested by the high tones used throughout and the lack of cast shadows. Clearly Strutt was not seeking merely to record an incident which had momentarily caught the public's attention. In *Black Thursday* and *Bushrangers on the St Kilda Road*, he was seeking subjects that would typify Australian colonial life as a whole.

Consider Strutt's bushfire theme. Throughout the nineteenth century when virgin forest stretched far more extensively across the country than it does today, and when safety precautions were virtually non-existent, the menace of the bushfire was always present in the minds of settlers. It became a popular subject in colonial literature and the graphic arts. In *Black Thursday* Strutt sought to bring the elevation and dignity of history painting to a theme already well-established in colonial art and life. The

39   WILLIAM STRUTT, *Black Thursday*, canvas, 42 x 135, 1862-4, State Library of Victoria

bushranger theme, too, had become a well-established emblem of colonial life. For the deeds of the bushranger were no less fascinating nor of less romantic appeal because they were outside the law. Joseph Lycett introduced bushrangers into his *Views in Australia* as early as 1824, describing them as 'a sort of banditti who live in the woods', and in the years intervening the bushranger had become a well-known figure in colonial poetry, prose and illustration.

All of Strutt's major works of outdoor Australian life tend to stress the hardships and dangers of colonial life. Holdups, bushfires, droughts, the death of explorers: these themes are in keeping with the strand of melancholy that runs right through colonial art and literature in Australia. Indeed in one of his water-colours painted in 1852, entitled *Martyrs of the Road* (40), Strutt paints the carcasses of horses lying in an open waste of landscape: a painting which both in its theme and treatment foreshadows the drought and erosion scenes of Drysdale and Nolan.[4]

Although William Strutt was essentially a history and portrait painter, his grim interpretations of the Australian environment find fitting contemporary parallels in the melancholy bush ballads of Gordon and the equally melancholy stories of Marcus Clarke (1846-81). It was Clarke who gave the most complete expression to the prevalent attitude of the writers and artists of the time towards nature in Australia: 'What is the dominant note,' wrote Marcus Clarke, 'of Australian scenery?'

That which is the dominant note of Edgar Allan Poe's poetry—Weird Melancholy. A poem like 'L'Allegro' could never be written by an Australian. It is too airy, too sweet, too freshly happy. The Australian forests are funereal, secret, stern. Their solitude is desolation. They seem to stifle, in their black gorges, a story of sullen despair. No tender sentiment is nourished in their shade. In other lands the dying year is mourned, the falling leaves drop lightly on his bier. In the Australian forests no leaves fall. The savage winds shout among the rock clefts. From the melancholy gum strips of white bark hang and rustle. The very animal life of these frowning hills is either grotesque or ghostly. Great grey kangaroos hop noiselessly over the coarse grass. Flights of white cockatoos stream out, shrieking like evil souls. The sun suddenly sinks, and the mopokes burst out into horrible peals of semi-human laughter.[5]

The writers and artists of the 1860's and 1870's found Australia no paradise of sunshine and adventure; it was a weird, grotesque, melancholy land. The convention dominated both art and writing. It is not to be assumed,

E

40 WILLIAM STRUTT, *Martyrs of the Road*, water-colour, c. 1852, Parliamentary Library of Victoria (*Reproduced by permission of the Library Committee, Parliament of Victoria*)

however, that artists and writers adopted the convention in order to express their dislike of the local landscape and to reject it. The best of them, indeed, tended to identify themselves with the weirdness and melancholy they found in the landscape. Marcus Clarke, for instance, in the passage quoted above, continues:

. . . In Australia alone is to be found the Grotesque, the Weird, the strange scribblings of nature learning how to write. Some see no beauty in our trees without shade, our flowers without perfume, our birds who cannot fly, and our beasts who have not yet learned to walk on all fours. But the dweller in the wilderness acknowledges the subtle charm of this fantastic land of monstrosities. He becomes familiar with the beauty of loneliness. Whispered to by the myriad tongues of the wilderness, he learns the language of the barren and the uncouth, and can read the hieroglyphs of haggard gum-trees, blown into odd shapes, distorted with fierce hot winds, or cramped with cold nights, when the Southern Cross freezes in a cloudless sky of icy blue. The phantasmagoria of that wild dreamland termed the Bush interprets itself, and the Poet of our desolation begins to comprehend why free Esau loved his heritage of desert sand better than all the bountiful richness of Egypt.[6]

William Strutt did not, however, identify himself with his adopted country in the way Marcus Clarke did. That is not surprising, for his sojourn in Australia was a comparatively short one, and the large historical paintings of Australian subjects were painted in England and exhibited at the Royal Academy. They were, indeed, very much an Englishman's impression of Australia. Nevertheless they strongly appealed to colonial taste, which is not surprising either, since colonial taste was determined by educated Europeans—British people, mainly, though gold had brought a sprinkling of cultivated Europeans—not by the native-born. William Strutt was not personally involved in the colonial situation. An artist of the time far more involved, though he, too, painted with the Royal Academy in mind, was Robert Dowling.

Robert Dowling (1827-86) was brought to Tasmania by his father, a

41   ROBERT DOWLING, *Group of Natives of Tasmania*, canvas,
60 x 120, 1859, Queen Victoria Museum, Launceston

Baptist minister, in 1831. His first art lessons came from Thomas Bock, and
in 1856 he was able to leave for London where he exhibited sixteen pictures
at the Royal Academy between 1859 and 1882. Like Strutt he was primarily
a portrait, genre and history painter. Though thoroughly trained in the
Academy Schools, the scenes of his boyhood in Tasmania left a deep impression upon him. In his *Early Efforts—Art in Tasmania* (Melbourne), which
he exhibited at the Royal Academy in 1860, an admiring family are gathered
outside a hut set amid sylvan surroundings of Tasmanian bush and mountain. A young artist is seen in the act of painting a group of Tasmanian
aborigines posed statuesquely before him. The choice of subject is significant. After George Robinson had 'conciliated' the Tasmanian aborigines
they were all placed on Flinders Island in Bass Strait where they slowly
pined away and died. When Dowling painted his picture there were only
a few left. Dowling came from a deeply religious family and it is clear that
the tragedy of the Tasmanian aborigines left a lasting impression upon his
mind, for he returned to the subject on several occasions, and he chose it
for his most important work, *Group of Natives of Tasmania* (41).

Dowling handles a subject which might have fallen quite easily into a
sentimental treatment with a fine restraint. He identified himself with the
subject and succeeded in evoking an atmosphere of tragic melancholy
brooding over the doomed race. The natives are seated—emblematic of
their situation—around the dying embers of a burnt-out log near a great
blackened stump, and in the far left corner there is a leafless tree with
shattered branches. The figures themselves are disposed in a closed and
classically-ordered composition but there is no communication between

them; they neither converse nor look at one another, but stare stonily in front of their own faces, like the doomed. Only the fisherman and his wife moving up from the lake show any signs of life, and they seem to be staring with some perplexity at the petrified circle. Dowling worked from drawings made by Thomas Bock. The foreground natives, though with their backs to us, are painted with their faces in profile, a device which brings a frieze-like severity to the foreground. The composition, a history painting in the full sense of the word, not only provides a valuable record of the last members of 'the most primitive people in the world' but also serves to celebrate yet another death of the noble savage—that enduring symbol of civilized man's guilty conviction that he is at heart far more savage than the savages. Two or more years before, Dowling had painted a smaller *Tasmanian Aborigines* (Melbourne) in which many of the same natives are represented. The figures in this painting have a greater sense of community, but the firmly-closed frieze-like composition is already present.[7]

Landscape Painting

The most important landscape painters of the period were Eugène von Guérard, Nicholas Chevalier, William Charles Piguenit, and Louis Buvelot. In the work of the first two we may study late examples of the 'typical' landscape that had been developed during the previous hundred years by artists, travellers, geographers and critics. Typical landscape developed out of the picturesque and topographical forms of landscape. It may be defined as a kind of landscape the component parts of which are carefully selected in order to express the essential qualities of a particular type of geographical environment. The typical landscapist introduced into his paintings rocks, plants, animals, people and so forth that he felt to be most representative of the country or region he was depicting.

Eugène von Guérard (1811-1901) was an Austrian painter whose father had been the court painter to Francis I. Eugene had studied at the Düsseldorf Academy and travelled in Italy. His landscapes, however, owe most to the Austrian Biedermeier School, especially to Ferdinand Waldmüller (1793-1865), whose work von Guérard would certainly have known. Waldmüller sought absolute naturalism in his landscapes, painting detail with a close-focus vision like the Pre-Raphaelites. At the age of forty-two von Guérard emigrated to Australia and made a number of sketches on the Ballarat diggings. Later, in 1870, he was appointed the Curator of the National Gallery of Victoria and Principal of its Art School. He retired in 1881 when he sailed for England. During his twenty-eight years in the country he painted many landscapes, mainly in Victoria.

Von Guérard worked in a highly finished topographical style, seeking to render details of vegetation and terrain with a polished accuracy. He sought to depict plants and rocks with detailed precision. Indigenous animals were often added to further identify a scene. But von Guérard was no colourist; the olive-green of Australian foliage escaped him, and the subtler colours of the atmosphere (42). His great expanses of virgin forest, however, amply convey the depressing effect so frequently mentioned by travellers and settlers.[8]

Nicholas Chevalier (1828-1902), like Eugene von Guérard, obtained a thorough professional training in European art schools prior to migrating to Australia. He was born at Moscow, the son of a Swiss overseer of the estates of a Russian prince, but received his training in painting in Switzerland, studied architecture for a time in Munich, and moved to London in 1851. There he worked as a lithographic illustrator and exhibited paintings at the Royal Academy of 1852. Then followed a period of study in Rome. He appears to have gained some access to Royal patronage for he is said to have designed a fountain for Osborne, and the setting for the Koh-i-noor diamond in the British crown. In 1855 he arrived in Australia to attend to some of his father's investments. In Melbourne he became the first cartoonist on the *Melbourne Punch* (1856-61). Later he visited New Zealand (1867-8), accompanied the Duke of Edinburgh on a world tour (1868), and held an exhibition of his work at South Kensington on his return to London (1871).

Chevalier's large painting, *The Buffalo Ranges* (43), won him a £200 prize offered by the Trustees of the National Gallery of Victoria in 1864 for a local landscape. Its alpine character and geographical grandiosity is characteristic of late romanticism. It also seeks to celebrate the innate dignity of pioneering labour. Such themes possessed an immediate popular appeal and continued to attract Australian artists until the end of the century. But as a painting *The Buffalo Ranges*, with its large areas of unresolved tone, its laboured detail and drab colour is rather pompous and dull stuff. By contrast, the artist himself appears to have been a pleasant and sociable person, always upon the best of terms with the British Royal Family and a keen amateur musician. In the orchestra on H.M.S. *Galatea*, Nicholas Chevalier, it is said, played second fiddle to the Duke. Later, he was commissioned by the Queen to paint historical pictures of her reign and, for the twenty years prior to his death in 1902, was the London adviser to the Trustees of the National Gallery of New South Wales.[9]

William Charles Piguenit (1836-1914) was a native-born Tasmanian of French descent who, like so many of the artists who worked on the American, New Zealand and Australian frontiers, began life as a surveyor. Piguenit received some lessons from Frank Dunnett, a Scottish painter, and in 1872 retired from surveying and devoted himself to landscape painting. His approach to landscape may be compared with Strutt's approach to history painting. Like Strutt, he sought dramatic and exciting subjects which would be typical of the country at large. An explorer by nature, he made long journeys into little-known country in search of natural scenery both sublime and typical. His approach was, indeed, essentially romantic, but it was that late and rather grandiose romanticism of artists like F. E. Church, the American artist who also sought the sublime and dramatic in nature: illimitable plains, snow-covered volcanoes violently erupting, impenetrable tropical jungle. Piguenit himself delighted in mountain scenery (38), especially the central Highlands of Tasmania (44); but he had an eye for the typical, and one of his finest canvases, *Flood in the Darling* (45), depicts floods covering the vast river-flats of the interior of New South Wales. The first Australian-born landscape painter of any consequence, he was also the last of the colonial painters who occupied themselves with painting the Australian landscape in its primeval condition, and an element of desolation and melancholy invests most of his paintings.[10]

The work of Louis Buvelot (1814-88) heralds a significant change in the approach to landscape painting in Australia. Like John Glover, he did not arrive until towards the end of an active painting career. Born at Morges, Switzerland, he studied first under Arlaud at Lausanne, and later with Camille Flers, a landscape painter, in Paris. For eighteen years he lived and painted in Brazil and then returned to Switzerland. In 1858 he visited the East Indies; and it was not until he had again returned to Switzerland that he decided, because of the cold winters, to migrate to Victoria, where he arrived in 1865 at the age of fifty-one. He first set up as a photographer in Melbourne, but the success of his wife as a teacher of French enabled him to give his whole attention to landscape painting until his death in 1888.

It is not at all unlikely that Buvelot's earlier landscape work in Brazil belongs to that class of topographical and typical work favoured by those nineteenth-century artists who travelled about the world a good deal in search of unusual subjects. By the time Buvelot had reached Australia, however, his work bore a close affinity with the landscapes of the Barbizon school: it should be compared with the paintings of Daubigny and Theodore Rousseau. Unlike Chevalier and Piguenit, Buvelot was not ambitious to paint large canvases depicting sublime mountain scenery or the great open spaces of the interior. Like the Barbizon painters themselves, he was attracted by homely, rural scenes usually painted in the warm light of the late afternoon or early evening. He was not a young man, and he did not wander very far afield, but spent most of his time painting in and around the Port Phillip District. Consequently his landscapes tend to portray a settled rural countryside, not a primeval wilderness. It is quite untrue to say of him, as is often said, that he was the first artist to paint the Australian landscape with a clear vision unsullied by memories of European landscape. Indeed the scenes which he painted, having been modified by European

42 EUGÈNE VON GUÉRARD, *Valley of the Mitta Mitta, with the Bogong Ranges*, canvas, 26½ x 41¼, 1866, Melbourne

43 NICHOLAS CHEVALIER, *The Buffalo Ranges, Victoria*, canvas, 51 x 71, 1864, Melbourne

44   WILLIAM CHARLES PIGUENIT, *Mount Olympus, Lake St Clair,*
Tasmania, canvas, 27⅛ x 42⅛, 1875, Sydney

settlement, were in fact more European in quality than many of the scenes
painted by earlier men like Lewin, Earle and Glover; men intensely interested in the curiosities of the landscape and quite capable of depicting its
characteristic forms. Buvelot, much as he enjoyed the eucalypt, saw the tree
against a background of European recollections. 'It is so poetic,' he once
said. 'It can take so many shapes. Sometimes it has the breadth and strength
of a venerable oak and another time it is slight and graceful like the poplar
and birch.'[11] And it may be noted that in his *Summer Evening, Near Temple-*
stowe (46) his taller gums are slightly reminiscent of Lombardy poplars,
and the two large trees in his *Waterpool at Coleraine* (47) give the distinct
impression of being a kind of cross between eucalypt and oak. Nevertheless,
Buvelot's contribution to the evolution of an Australian school of painting
was very great indeed, for he began to work in Australia at a most crucial
time for the development of art here, and his perception of colour, schooled
as he was in *plein-air* methods, was far superior to that of his predecessors.
Before Buvelot very little attempt had been made, despite some interesting
water-colour paintings by Earle and Angas, to analyse the local and atmospheric colour of Australian scenery.

We may gain some idea of the changes which Buvelot introduced from
his *Summer Evening, Near Templestowe,* painted in 1866 (a year after his
arrival) in a district which is now a suburb of Melbourne. Human interest

45 WILLIAM CHARLES PIGUENIT, *Flood in the Darling*
1890, canvas, 48¼ x 78½, *c*. 1895, Sydney

here replaces the interest in nature's curiosities. We are introduced to a
settled countryside of high roads and fenced paddocks. A drover has just
driven his flock across a small bridge and they move up the road slowly
towards us throwing up a golden dust into the warm mellow light of the
summer evening as they come. To the right, a herd of cows has just been
driven into the home paddock of a farm and waits to be milked. In the
distance, men are still at work in the fields. All these details have been
drawn together and unified by the artist's keen sensitivity to tonal values.
Foreground details have been suppressed in the dark shadow which falls
across the road. The people and cattle in the central mid-ground have been
painted with broad patches of colour; the shadows on distant trees are of
purple and grey-blue; blue smoke issues from the chimneys of slab huts
at the right; a rosy afterglow is beginning to rise in the evening sky. Everything in the landscape is for Buvelot a problem in tone and colour. The
characteristic form and colour of the tall eucalypts is, for instance, admirably realized; but it is a homely and rather European scene for all that,
with its flocks and herds, fields and cottages, with none of the forbidding
antipodean melancholy that haunted the vision of earlier colonial artists and
writers. It is in fact a scene of peace and rural plenty, a variant on the
pastoral classical landscape traditional to European painting, and one full
of nostalgia for Europeans exiled like Barron Field in the Antipodes.
Buvelot's *Waterpool at Coleraine* is even closer in spirit to the Barbizon
school with its huge oak-like gums, its lawny meadows, ducks and village
pond all seen by the light of the sunset.

46   LOUIS BUVELOT, *Summer Evening, Near Templestowe*,
canvas, 30 x 46, 1866, Melbourne

Louis Buvelot, through his teaching, wide influence and example may be said to have created a school. For this reason he has been rightly called the Father of Landscape Painting in Australia. The artists who worked before him worked in isolation. Some, of course, like Martens, took pupils. John Skinner Prout established a flourishing art school in Hobart during the 'forties, and made water-colour painting quite popular in fashionable circles. But what influence they had did not last; did not make any permanent contribution to the growth of a local tradition. Many artists, however, who came to play a very important part in the foundation of the Australian school of painting came to know Buvelot during the formative years of their lives. He influenced as a result not only a number of artists who continued to apply the *plein-air* tradition of the Barbizon school to the Australian landscape, but also the men who were to create the Heidelberg School of Australian impressionist painting.[12]

Four painters may be noted here, all of whom were influenced by Buvelot and helped to continue the *plein-air* methods which he had introduced. Two were Englishmen, Julian Ashton and Walter Withers, and two Scots, John Mather and John Ford Paterson. They are typical of the new situation in Australian art. Professionally trained abroad they migrated to Australia in early manhood and made their reputations here. The country was still too young and still not sufficiently interested in the arts to maintain a com-

47 LOUIS BUVELOT, *Waterpool at Coleraine*, canvas, 42 x 60,
1869, Melbourne

munity of professional artists. But there were a number of trades and callings flourishing in Melbourne, and to a lesser degree in Sydney, that could provide some form of economic support for young men interested in the arts, such as photography, printing, lithography, and especially newspaper and magazine illustration. And the newly-formed art schools created a small demand for art teachers. Julian Ashton (1851-1942), who had trained in London and Paris, arrived in 1878 to draw for the *Illustrated Australian News*. Walter Withers (1854-1914) arrived in Melbourne in 1882 to farm, but soon left the land to obtain a position as a draughtsman to a firm of printers. John Ford Paterson (1851-1912), who had attended the Royal Scottish Academy Schools in Edinburgh, arrived in Melbourne first in 1872, stayed three years, and then returned to Scotland. In 1884 he came out and remained.[13] John Mather (1848-1916) also studied in Edinburgh, migrating to Victoria in 1878. He helped to decorate the dome of the Melbourne Exhibition Building and later became well known as a teacher.[14]

The newcomers were not entirely of British origin. By 1885 Melbourne's art community had taken on a continental flavour. The Portuguese artist, Arthur Loureiro (1860-1932) had been awarded the *Prix de Rome* by the Royal Academy, Lisbon, and had studied at Rome and Paris, exhibiting for three years at the Old Salon, before arriving in Melbourne in 1884, where he began to teach and paint. His work became known for its broad, free handling, and fresh out-of-doors feeling which was attributed, by one Melbourne critic of the time, to his French training. Both Ugo Catani and Girolamo Nerli (1863-1926) studied at the art school in Florence under Antonio Ciseri before arriving in Melbourne c. 1884-5. Nerli, an Italian *marchese*, was born at the Palazzo Pieri Pecci in Siena. His mother was the daughter of Thomas Medwin, the biographer of Shelley and the author of *Conversations of Lord Byron.*

Nerli, like Loureiro, became well known for his freer style of painting. Although his Melbourne work does not appear to have been noticed by contemporary critics he began to exercise an influence upon Sydney taste (following his arrival there in 1887-8), according to James Green. Green, who had been a journalist on the *Building News* (London) before he arrived in Sydney, was widely travelled, widely read and a voluminous writer. He exercised a considerable influence upon local opinion both in art and architecture in Sydney during the 1890's. The first of his many articles for the *Australasian Builders' and Contractors' News* was published on 1 January 1890, and he may have been in the country some time before that date. Green, who often signed himself 'De Libra', was an ardent and extremely vocal follower of John Ruskin. His early articles are, not surprisingly, extremely critical of anything slightly savouring of impressionism. But such attacks weakened as his sympathies broadened. He may, therefore, have been recording his own early reactions when he wrote in 1899 that:

The Marchese Nerli, an Italian by birth, and with a thorough European training, was the first to introduce to New South Wales the daring independence of Southern neo-continentalism . . . in its disregard of generally accepted trammels and its frequent substitution of the mere sketch for finished works. . . . His wildly sketchy 'Bacchanalian Orgie', *à la Monticelli*, was 'caviare to the general', and the audacity of his Salome—suggesting, black and yellow symphony, 'Repose', with what a critic called *un tantino troppo di bravura* about it, took the Sydney public's breath away.[15]

During the early 'eighties many of these young artists began to spend their week-ends sketching in the countryside around Melbourne. Favourite sketching-grounds were discovered to which artists returned again and again. The habit of week-end sketching in the open air spread. Buvelot, like most of the Barbizon painters, sketched, but did not paint finished canvases, in the open air. In France it appears to have been the Barbizon painter, Daubigny, who promoted the practice of completing his landscapes in the open. It is difficult to say just when the practice began in Australia. But Julian Ashton[16] claimed that his painting, *Evening, Merri Creek*, painted in 1882 and now in the Sydney Gallery, was the first. In the following year

48 JULIAN ASHTON, *Sentry Box Reach, Hawkesbury River,*
water-colour, 22⅛ x 36, 1884, Sydney

Ashton moved to Sydney where he drew for the *Picturesque Atlas*. During
the early 1880's Julian Ashton, Frank P. Mahony and A. H. Fullwood spent
week-ends painting in the bush around Sydney Harbour at such places as
Sirius Cove, Mosman, on ocean beaches like Coogee, or in the country at
such places as Richmond or favoured spots along the Hawkesbury River.
George Collingridge (1847-1931) and his brother, Arthur, had already discovered the Hawkesbury River District as a sketching-ground in 1879.
Here Ashton worked with A. J. Daplyn (1844-1926) in 1884 and painted
a large water-colour *Sentry Box Reach, Hawkesbury River* (48) which
brings a new feeling for light and space to the treatment of Australian
landscape and points directly towards the spring freshness of his delightful
little *Solitary Ramble* (50).

Daplyn was another pioneer of *plein-air* painting in Australia. Born in
London, he had studied under Gerome and Carolus-Duran in Paris, painted
landscapes at Pont-Aven and exhibited in the Old Salon, before migrating
to Australia in 1881. Here he applied himself immediately to the problems
peculiar to Australian *plein-air* painting and years later brought the fruit of
his researches together in a manual entitled *Australian Landscape Painting*.
In 1882 the *Argus* critic described Daplyn's *Boat Builders* as 'painted in
low tones after the French method and in the style of the "impressionists" . . .'.[17] It is possibly the first occasion on which the word was used in
an Australian context. Not that Daplyn was an impressionist, his *plein-air*

manner consisted simply in a greater truth to tone and a method of handling broader than the landscapes of Piguenit, Chevalier, von Guérard and even Buvelot, all by the 1880's somewhat old-fashioned. Daplyn became the first instructor at the (Royal) Art Society classes in Sydney when they were established in 1885. Nor is it without significance that this French-trained Englishman who had painted landscapes at Pont-Aven was Charles Conder's first teacher.

Meanwhile, in Melbourne, Mather had discovered Healesville as a sketching district, and had worked along the eastern shores of Port Phillip Bay. Such artists drew others about them. Consequently, in the years between 1880 and 1885, we may see a new pattern emerging in Australian art. A number of young migrant artists, some from Britain and some from the Continent, settled in the rapidly-expanding cities of Sydney and Melbourne. The illustrated Press of the day helped in one way or another to support most of them. During the week-ends they sought out picturesque spots in the countryside and made *plein-air* sketches. It was the masters of the Barbizon School and the English water-colour painters whom they most admired. Their works painted before 1885 were still low in tone, generally speaking, and rather like those European scenes to which they were still accustomed. Like the Barbizon painters they preferred the evocative hours: early morning, evening, sunset, twilight. But, like Buvelot, they continued to analyse the true values of colour as seen through an envelope of atmosphere. In consequence they came, despite the lowness of the tones in which they customarily painted, to a more faithful depiction of the colours of the Australian landscape than any of the painters before them.

Study Abroad

The practice of leaving Australia to study art in Europe did not become a feature of Australian cultural life until the 1880's, but began somewhat earlier. The first Australian-born artist to study abroad was Adelaide Ironside; and she was followed by two British-born artists whose families had settled in the country in their youth, Robert Dowling and Edward a'Beckett.

Miss Ironside (1831-67) was a Sydney girl with good connections, delicate health, and a highly nervous sensibility. A citizen's fund enabled her to leave for study in Europe with her mother in 1855. Settling in Rome she became well known for a time as a painter and spiritualistic medium, painting visions she saw in crystal balls. Joseph Severn, the artist-friend and companion of John Keats, took an interest in her. Perhaps it was Severn who brought her to the attention of John Ruskin, for when Miss Ironside settled in London in 1865 she struck up a curious friendship with the critic

49   ROBERT DOWLING, *A Sheikh and his son entering Cairo
on their return from a pilgrimage to Mecca*, canvas, 54 x 96,
1874, Melbourne

who gave her private lessons in drawing, largely confined, it would seem, to drawing shells and the flower of the convolvulus.[18]

Adelaide Ironside's paintings were inspired by the religious paintings popularized by the Nazarenes in Rome and the Pre-Raphaelite Brotherhood in England. She exhibited *The Marriage in Cana* and *The Pilgrim of Art* in the New South Wales Court of the London Exhibition of 1862, and there appears to have been some contemporary interest in her work. Both the Prince of Wales and William Charles Wentworth are said to have bought paintings worth £500 each from her. But though *The Marriage in Cana*, *The Pilgrim of Art* and the *Presentation of the Magi* eventually found their way back to St Paul's College, in the University of Sydney, her work had no influence upon the subsequent development of Australian painting.[19]

In 1856, a year after Adelaide Ironside had left Sydney with the help of a citizen's fund, a similar fund was raised by Launceston citizens to enable Robert Dowling to study abroad. Dowling studied at Leigh's Academy, and exhibited sixteen paintings at the Royal Academy between 1859 and 1882. A large subject painting, *A Sheikh and his son entering Cairo on their return from a Pilgrimage to Mecca* (49), was shown at the Academy of 1875.

In 1851 Edward a'Beckett, a nephew of Sir William a'Beckett, arrived in Melbourne at the age of seven with his parents. After completing his formal education at Melbourne Grammar, he left in 1867 for England in order to study at the Royal Academy Schools. On his return to Melbourne he painted a number of portraits of Melbourne citizens. One of his best is that of Dean Macartney, the first Dean of Melbourne, in the Chapter House of St Paul's Cathedral, Melbourne.

But these three cases were exceptional. It was not until the development of technical education during the 1870's and of art schools in particular, especially the art school of the National Gallery of Victoria, that art students began to emerge who were sufficiently well trained to benefit from study in Paris and London.

FOOTNOTES

[1] From 'The Sick Stockrider', *Poems of the late Adam Lindsay Gordon*, Melbourne, 1880

[2] On Gill *see also* A. W. GREIG, 'Gill, the Artist of the Goldfields', *Vic. Hist. Mag.* (Mar. 1914), pp. 133-42; MOORE, i, 59-61, *passim*; ii, 142-5, *passim*; W. DIXSON, *Journ. RAHS*, ix (1923), pp. 162-3; W. S. CAMPBELL, *Journ. RAHS*, xv, 21; ALAN MCCULLOCH, 'The Art of S. T. Gill', *Meanjin*, x (1951), 27-32

[3] On Robinson *see also* the article in *AE*, vii, 470

[4] On Strutt *see also* GEORGE MACKANESS (ed.), *The Australian Journal of William Strutt, A.R.A. 1850-1862*, Sydney, 1958, 2 vols; A. CHESTER, 'The Art of William Strutt', *Windsor Magazine*, no. 215 (Nov. 1912), 611-26; MOORE, i, 124-5, *passim*. The Parliamentary Library of Victoria possesses Strutt's *Exploring Expedition Sketch Book*, and his *Victoria the Golden Sketches and jottings from nature 1850-62*. The Dixson Library possesses several other sketch-books of a similar nature.

[5] *The Poems of the late Adam Lindsay Gordon* (preface by Marcus Clarke), London [n.d.], pp. iv-v

[6] ibid., pp. v-vi

[7] On Dowling *see also* MOORE, i, 36-7, *passim*; article, *DAB*; N. J. B. PLOMLEY, 'Pictures of Tasmanian Aborigines by Robert Dowling', *Annual Bull. National Gallery of Victoria*, iii (1961), 17-22

[8] On von Guérard *see also* MOORE, i, 52-3

[9] On Chevalier *see also* F. A. FOREL, *Nicholas Chevalier, Peintre Vaudois*, Lausanne, 1908; MOORE, ii, 166; *CAO*, pp. 42-3

[10] On Piguenit *see also* W. V. LEGGE, the *Tasmanian Mail*, 6 May 1915; MOORE, i, 89-90, *passim*; article in *AE*, vii

[11] Quoted by MOORE, i, 88

[12] On Buvelot *see also* S. DICKINSON, *Catalogue of Oil Paintings in the Collection of T. W. Stanford Esq. of Melbourne*, Melbourne, 1892, pp. 20-1; article in *DAB*

[13] On J. F. Paterson *see also* MOORE, i, 91-2, *passim*, ii, 213, *passim*; *Argus*, Melbourne, 1 July 1912

[14] On Mather *see also* the *Argus*, Melbourne, 21 Feb. 1916

[15] DE LIBRA (JAMES GREEN), *Australasian Art Review*, 1 June 1899, pp. 23-4

[16] On Ashton *see also* his autobiography, *Now Came Still Evening On*, Sydney, 1941; The Julian Ashton Book, *Art in Aust.*, Sydney, 1920; *CAO*, pp. 16-17

[17] *Argus*, 25 March 1882. Quoted by V. SPATE, 'Art criticism in the Melbourne Press 1880-1900', B.A. Thesis, Hon. Schools of History and Fine Arts, University of Melbourne

[18] RUSKIN, *Works*, ed. cit., xxxvi, 484-8

[19] On Adelaide Ironside *see also* MOORE, ii, 1-4

CHAPTER FOUR

GENESIS
1885 - 1914

Australian sky and nature awaits, and merits real artists to
pourtray it . . . there is a whole system of landscape painting of
the most striking character, yet available for human art. . . .
JOHN LHOTSKY, 'The State of Art in New South Wales
and Tasmania', *The Art-Union*, July 1839, pp. 99-100

The Formation of the Heidelberg School

BETWEEN 1885 and 1890 a distinctive Australian school of painting sprang
into existence. Its creation was due mainly to the vision, energy and per-
sistence of Tom Roberts (1856-1931) who, with his widowed mother, had
migrated to Australia from Dorchester, England, in 1869 at the age of
thirteen. The family settled in Collingwood, Melbourne, where they lived
for some years in difficult and somewhat straitened circumstances. Roberts
became a photographer's assistant and rose to be senior operator at Richard
Stewart's studio in Bourke Street, Melbourne. On Friday evenings he
attended drawing classes at the old Court House, Collingwood. This was
one of the Artisans' Schools of Design set up in the later 1860's. The evening
classes were the first attempt to provide schools of art in Victoria, and
though instruction was elementary and facilities primitive, they succeeded
in attracting some able men as teachers, such as Thomas Clark and Louis
Buvelot. Clark, who became instructor in figure-drawing at the Carlton
School of Design, had studied at the Royal Academy, and had been a master
of the School of Design, Birmingham, and Director of the Nottingham School
of Art prior to his arrival in Melbourne in 1857. At Birmingham, Clark is
said to have taught Burne Jones. Buvelot was also a master at the Carlton
School. Roberts owed much to both Clark and Buvelot.

In 1875 Roberts went on to the evening classes of the National Gallery
which had been established five years before. There he studied drawing
under Clark (who had become drawing master at the school) and painting
under Eugène von Guérard, the curator of the Gallery and master of the
art school from 1870 to 1881. Clark urged his best pupils to study abroad,
advising Roberts to save in order to study at the Royal Academy, London,
and at Julian's in Paris. Although working as a photographer by day and
an art student by night, Roberts also managed to contribute drawings to

71

50   JULIAN ASHTON, *A Solitary Ramble*, water-colour,
13¼ x 9¾, 1886, Sydney

the local Press. After six years' study at the Gallery he had learnt enough
and had saved sufficiently to sail for England in 1881. There he studied at
the Royal Academy school and continued to draw for newspapers like the
Graphic.

In 1883 he embarked upon a walking tour of Spain in the company of
three Australian friends, John Russell, a Sydney artist, Sydney R. Russell,
his architect brother, and Dr William Maloney. It was planned that the
artists should sketch, the architect study the architecture of Spain seen on
the trip, and that Dr Maloney should keep an account of the tour. They
sailed to Bordeaux, walked through southern France into north-western
Spain, and on to Madrid and Granada.

At Granada, Roberts met two artists, Laureano Barrau and Ramon Casas, whose talk and work appear to have acted as an illumination to him. Both artists had studied in Paris and had gained some knowledge of the aims of the French impressionists.

Casas was a pupil of Carolus-Duran (1838-1917) and, like his teacher, was primarily a portrait painter who adopted a naturalistic and painterly technique. A portrait which Casas made of Roberts at Granada in 1883 makes use of the informal pose, and the 'truth in tone' values so much discussed by students at the time. It may owe something to the influence of Manet; and Casas, a student in Paris during the later 1870's, may have seen some of the work of the French impressionists. Some small oil paintings which Roberts painted in Spain in 1883, though by no means impressionist and painted within the limits of academic naturalism, suggest that during the Spanish tour he came to acquire a keener interest in colour and light, true tones, and the importance of keeping painterly values. It was natural enough, therefore, that the influence of Whistler should appear in some small oil paintings which he executed in London in 1884.

Roberts, nevertheless, had been trained as a portrait painter and always retained an interest throughout life in the subject picture. It is not surprising, therefore, to find that he was also greatly influenced by the work of Bastien-Lepage (1848-84), a great hero of the art schools of the time. Lepage had specialized in the painting of rural and peasant scenes which, though visualized in the *plein-air* manner, were usually tinged with melancholy and sentiment. His *Potato Gatherers* (Melbourne, 1878) is typical. In this way he continued the realist tradition established by Millet and Courbet in French painting during the mid-nineteenth century. It was from such artists as Bastien-Lepage and Courbet that Roberts gained a heroic conception of rural labour.

In 1885 Roberts returned to Australia with his new ideas and some paintings in his new manner. By this time *plein-air* sketching was, as we have already seen, a well-established local practice and, a year after his return, Roberts and Frederick McCubbin, an old fellow-student from the Gallery School, pitched their tent near Housten's farm, Box Hill, and began to paint. Roberts sought to apply the new principles he had learned abroad to painting the light and colour of the Australian bush. At Box Hill in 1886 he painted *The Artists' Camp* (51). There is no attempt to render a large expanse of countryside as there is in the work of the earlier men, Piguenit, von Guérard and Buvelot; nor any attempt at this stage of Roberts's development to dignify a rural theme. The scene depicted is quite small— nearly all foreground—and quite casual in its human interest. Roberts has adopted a palette of richly modulated browns and greens (faintly reminiscent of Manet's landscapes) in order to capture the colour of eucalypt saplings seen in the crisp blue light of morning; 'French methods of land-

F

51   TOM ROBERTS, *The Artists' Camp*, canvas, 17½ x 23¼,
1886, Melbourne

scape painting', a contemporary critic remarked, 'their avoidance of too much definition of form and their disposition to secure striking effects by colour laid on in broad masses.'[1] There was, as yet, no strong critical opposition to the new methods. In 1886, too, he painted *A Summer Morning's Tiff* and, in 1887, *Reconciliation* (Castlemaine), in which a slight human interest is introduced into paintings which are, however, essentially studies in light and colour.

Friends joined Roberts and McCubbin at Box Hill. In 1886 they rented a cottage at Mentone on Port Phillip Bay and there met Arthur Streeton, a young lithographer's apprentice who was studying drawing in the evening classes at the Gallery School. Streeton was out on the rocks painting a free study of the sea and shore. He became a close friend. Then in 1887 Roberts visited Sydney, met Charles Conder (1868-1909) and discussed impressionist painting with him. Like Roberts himself, Conder was born and educated in England.[2] He also learned something about *plein-air* painting from Girolamo Nerli (1863-1926). Nerli's *Wet Evening* (Hinton, Armidale) reveals the broad effects for which he became known. He was also a capable portraitist. Nerli's influence on Australian art was, however, short-lived, for after a four-year sojourn in this country he moved on to Dunedin, New Zealand, to become the director of the art school there and one of the first teachers of Frances Hodgkins.[3]

In 1888 Conder painted *The Departure of the* s.s. *Orient* (52), a work

52   CHARLES CONDER, *The Departure of the* s.s. *Orient,*
canvas, 17¼ x 19¾, 1888, Sydney

similar in its breadth, low tones and subject-matter to Nerli's *Wet Evening.*
Although he was only twenty at the time, this picture is one of the finest
Conder painted in Australia. Its rich low tones embrace passages of
exquisite painting resonant with colour and admirably controlled. When
Conder exhibited it at the annual exhibition of the Art Society of New South
Wales in 1888, local critics remarked upon the quality of the painting and
the Trustees of the National Gallery of New South Wales purchased it for
their collection. It was the first occasion upon which the new school of
Australian painting had received official recognition.

The Departure of the s.s. *Orient* owes perhaps as much to Nerli as to
Roberts, but Conder was greatly impressed by his conversations with
Roberts, and in October 1888 he moved to Melbourne. Roberts's visit to
Sydney indicates a new freedom of handling in his own work. His *Coogee
Bay* (53) reveals the use of colour harmonies more subtle and gradual than

53   TOM ROBERTS, *Coogee Bay*, canvas, 15⅞ x 22, 1888, Sydney

before, more adapted to the expression of distance and light, looser and bolder colour and stronger contrasts of tone.

In 1888 Roberts, Streeton and Conder established themselves in a large weatherboard house at Eaglemont which Streeton had discovered during the previous summer. It was set upon a hill above the Yarra and surrounded by a fine but neglected garden. Here the three artists camped, sleeping on sacks tied between saplings with only candles to light the house at night. To ease the financial strain, Streeton and Conder began a school in landscape and still life, which was attended by about a dozen girls, mostly during the week-ends. Roberts spent several days each week working on portraits in a Collins Street studio. Eaglemont soon became an important rendezvous for many artists who had thrown in their lot with the new movement.

At Eaglemont, Roberts and his friends made many impressionist oil sketches on cigar-box lids, working deftly and rapidly with colour broadly applied. From these experiments came Australia's first impressionist exhibition—the most famous art exhibition in the country's history. It was called the Exhibition of 9 × 5 Impressions and was opened at Buxton's showrooms, in Swanston Street, Melbourne, on 17 August 1889. One hundred and eighty-three paintings were shown: Roberts exhibited sixty-two; Streeton, forty; Conder, forty-six; Frederick McCubbin, five; C. Douglas Richardson, twenty-six (of these six were sculptured impressions); R. E. Falls, three;

and Herbert Daly, one. The exhibition, quite a large one for a group of local artists to stage, was cleverly managed and gained a good deal of publicity. Prices were low and most of the paintings sold. There can be no doubt that it was a direct challenge to prevailing taste which favoured the English and German schools, distrusted French methods and held the moral and didactic values of John Ruskin in high regard. These values had been amply demonstrated in the large Centennial Exhibition held only the year before in which accepted academic values prevailed. The 9 × 5 Exhibition may well have been stimulated by the great success of the Centennial, but it was certainly a local reaction to the values which its pictorial exhibits enshrined.

The 9 × 5 Exhibition appears to have sharpened critical reaction for a time against local impressionist work, which hitherto had been treated tolerantly, being misinterpreted as sketches for more finished work. Indeed the *Age* critic (17 August 1889), in a sympathetic review, still thought of the paintings in the show as charming 'shadows of coming events'. The *Daily Telegraph* critic (17 August 1889), however, whilst admitting the presence of an educated taste and much to admire, complained nevertheless that impressionism left too much to the imagination. 'The lazy artist will be prone to dash off dauby work and expect his admirers to see the production with the mind's and not the body's eye . . . leaving the spectator to do the hard work of detail and elaboration mentally.' It was left, however, to James Smith of the *Argus* to condemn the exhibition in the most trenchant terms. Smith, as much as anyone, embodied the received cultural values of colonial Melbourne. He had written books on Wilton and its associations, on English poetry and rural life, before he migrated to Melbourne in 1854. He wrote plays, including one on Garibaldi (produced in 1860), interested himself in the *Alliance Française* and became President of the Dante Society. He was a Trustee of the Public Library and the National Gallery of Victoria and, for fifty-six years, worked tirelessly for the improvement of local culture. But on 17 August 1889 he made it indubitably clear that he did not like impressionism in any form:

Such an exhibition of impressionist memoranda as will be opened today at Buxton's gallery by Messrs Roberts, Conder, Streeton, and others, fails to justify itself. It has no adequate *raison d'être*. . . . The modern impressionist asks you to see pictures in splashes of colour, in slapdash brushwork, and in sleight-of-hand methods of execution leading to the proposition of pictorial conundrums, which would baffle solution if there were no label or catalogue. In an exhibition of paintings you naturally look for pictures; instead of which the impressionist presents you with a varied assortment of palettes. Of the 180 exhibits catalogued on this occasion four-fifths are a pain to the eye. Some of them look like faded pictures seen through several mediums of thick gauze; others suggest that a paint-pot has been accidentally upset over a panel nine inches by five; others resemble the first essays of a small boy who has just been apprenticed to a house painter; whilst not a few are as depressing as the incoherent images which float through the mind of a dyspeptic dreamer. . . . A few afford something agreeable to the eye to rest upon, but the exhibition, viewed as a whole, would leave a very painful feeling behind it, and cause one to despond with respect to the future of art in this colony, did we not believe with Mr W. P. Frith, R.A., that 'Impressionism is a craze of such ephemeral character as to be unworthy of serious attention'.

To all such criticisms Roberts, Streeton and Conder replied in a joint letter to the *Argus* about a fortnight later (3 September 1889), which reveals that they were aware of the impressionist approach to painting, the perceptual problem involved in it, and were already thinking of themselves as the pioneers of an Australian school:

We will not be led by any forms of composition or light or shade. . . . Any form of nature which moves us strongly by its beauty, whether strong or vague in its drawing, defined or indefinite in its light, rare or ordinary in its colour, is worthy of our best efforts. . . . We will do our best to put only the truth down and only as much as we feel sure of seeing (but) the question comes, how much do we see and how much are our ideas and judgements of works made up by comparison with those we have already known . . .? We believe that it is better to give our own idea than to get a merely superficial effect which . . . may shelter us in a safe mediocrity which . . . could never help towards the development of what we believe will be a great school of painting in Australia.

In 1890 a second artists' camp was established at 'Charterisville', not far from Eaglemont, by Walter Withers (1854-1914), who had returned from study in Paris the previous year. 'Charterisville' was an old stone house with a large barn, gardeners' lodges and stables, and was set in a magnificent but neglected garden. It had been the former home of David Charteris Macarthur, a pioneer banker of Melbourne. Following his death in 1887 the purchaser, a dairy-farmer, let portions of the house and the garden lodges to artists, the collapse of the land boom making it impossible to retain the house in its former state. Many artists lived for a time at 'Charterisville' and many more visited it. In 1893 Phillips Fox and his friend, Tudor St George Tucker, both of whom had returned from Paris the year previously, established a Summer School there as a section of their Melbourne Art School in the city.

From these two Heidelberg camps the new approach to painting spread among a widening circle of artists and students. It is to be stressed that in the years between 1888 and 1893, when they were exercising a most vital influence upon Australian painting, the members of these camps were by no means cut off from a knowledge of artistic developments in Paris. The impressionist painters of the Heidelberg School were not ignorant of the existence of French impressionism, or of the broad principles upon which

54   CHARLES CONDER, *A Holiday at Mentone*, canvas, 17¼ x 23,
1888, Mr and Mrs M. S. Atwill

it was based. John Russell corresponded with Roberts from France from October 1887 and he seems to have had some knowledge of impressionist techniques from at least 1886. Conder discussed Monet's methods in a letter to Roberts from Paris in February 1891 and said that he agreed with those who said Monet was 'the greatest landscapist in his way'.[4] On the other hand, the school was not a provincial attempt to copy the technical methods of Monet and his associates. It was an original attempt to apply impressionist principles to a different set of visual and social conditions.

The close association of Roberts, Streeton and Conder terminated shortly after the 9 × 5 Exhibition though they remained friends and corresponded with one another for the rest of their lives. Conder left for Europe in April 1890, Streeton went to Sydney in the same year, shortly after the National Art Gallery of New South Wales purchased his *Still Glides the Stream* (55), and was followed there by Roberts in 1891. In Sydney, Roberts and Streeton established Curlew Camp on Little Sirius Cove, Mosman, in a picturesque spot on Sydney Harbour. The camp became a well-known rendezvous for artists and their friends during the 1890's when many Sydney artists were feeling the effect of the economic depression. Later, Roberts established a teaching studio in Vickery's Chambers, Pitt Street, Sydney.

Both Roberts and Streeton made many oil sketches and small paintings

55   ARTHUR STREETON, *Still Glides the Stream and shall Forever Glide*, canvas, 32¼ x 60¼, 1889, Sydney

around the coves of Sydney Harbour and at such ocean beaches as Coogee. In these paintings the impressionist aspects of their work were contained and in some ways developed. Streeton's paintings became somewhat higher in key, more summary in handling, and often richer and brighter in colour. His harbour and beach scenes were severely criticized, when he exhibited them in the 1890 Exhibition of the Art Society of New South Wales, by James Green (de Libra), probably the most influential critic of the 1890's in Sydney:

Can Mr Streeton's 'Study for Colour' be characterized as other than a kaleido-scopic nightmare? What of the splotchiness of 'Sunlight Sweet, Coogee', the smudginess of 'From McMahon's Point', or that dab of paint in the left-hand corner of the 'Sunny South' (where probably a tree would grow), like nothing in the heavens above, the earth beneath, or the waters under the earth? . . . I contend that treatment of this kind has no place in an exhibition of finished works of art.[5]

During the same period, however, Streeton travelled inland to the Blue Mountains and the Hawkesbury River to paint on a more heroic scale. The desire to paint landscapes which would suggest the immensity and grandeur of Australian nature never left him. In 1892 he had returned to Melbourne, but it is clear that the idea of painting landscapes of the interior still meant much to him. As he wrote to Roberts in 1892:

I want to stay *here*, but not in Melb. If I can raise the coin I intend to go straight inland (away from all polite society), and stay two or three years and create some things entirely new, and try and translate some of the great hidden poetry that I know is here, but have not seen or felt it.[6]

Now although the interior certainly exercised its fascination, the attraction of London and Paris was, if anything, greater. Indeed the main reason Streeton had not gone earlier was due largely to the fact that he could not afford it. But in 1896 he held a one-man show in Melbourne, from which he did rather well. A letter which he wrote to Roberts c. 1896 reveals his divided state of mind.

I picture in my head the Murray and all the wonder and glory at its source up towards Kosciusko . . . and the great gold plains, and all the beautiful inland Australia, and I love the thought of walking into all this and trying to expand and express it in my way. I fancy large canvases all glowing and moving in the happy light and others bright decorative and chalky and expressive of the hot trying winds and the slow immense summer. It is *immense,* and droughts and cracks in the earth, and creeks all baked mud.

But somehow it's all out of reach, and all sorts of damn'd little things in the way. Two-thirds of the year I have a feeling of dependence on other people, indebtedness, etc. It carries you off your work and holds thought that should play in a good current on to many canvases and be strong. The current gets weakened.

I love Australia (yet have seen so little) and shall be beastly sorry to go away . . .

But I can't sit here thinking, 'tis waste of time. I want to hurry up and *move* somehow. So first opportunity and I'm off . . .

Of course, my troubles are, no doubt, small—we hear of good artists who starve all their lives, and so on. I don't grumble a bit, but it's unfortunate. This country is full of wealth, but somehow can't afford artists yet. Why, dammit, bricklayers, scene-shifters, office boys, all get their work recognized and are able to go on—and if I were recognized more I could *paint more.* Perhaps I'd have the same trouble in Europe, but I must risk it. . . .[7]

The Art of the Heidelberg School

Two main interests may be observed in the work of the artists of the Heidelberg School: their interest in depicting effects of light and colour and their interest in creating a distinctively Australian art. These two interests, as we shall see, were closely related.

Their first interest was clearly expressed in the catalogue which they prepared for the Exhibition of 9 × 5 Impressions.

An effect is only momentary: so an impressionist tries to find his place. Two half-hours are never alike, and he who tries to paint a sunset on two successive evenings must be more or less painting from memory. So, in these works, it has been the object of the artists to render faithfully, and thus obtain first records of effects widely differing, and often of very fleeting character.

It was with this programme in mind that they had already begun to solve many of the problems involved in rendering the effects of light and colour peculiar to Australian atmosphere and vegetation. Although they were most certainly indebted to Europe for the sources of their inspiration these problems were their own, and the technical solutions which they found to them were also largely their own. The Heidelberg School, therefore, is rightly considered as the first distinctive Australian school of painting. That does not mean, as is so often assumed, that little of an Australian character was produced by the men who came before them—rather the reverse. The work of the Heidelberg painters had its roots in an Australian as well as in a European past. It represented the culmination of a century of colonial endeavour. For the colonial painters, as we have seen, had already done much to portray the special qualities of the Australian scene, the shape and form of a great deal of its typical topography and vegetation. Indeed, some of the best of them, like John Glover, Conrad Martens and William Charles Piguenit, had gone farther and reacted sensitively to the moods and sensations which Australian landscape evoked.

To say, as it is so often, that the artists before Buvelot and Roberts saw the Australian scene with English or European eyes is to falsify the history of Australian art. The great contribution which the Heidelberg School *did* make to the history of vision in Australian art was to produce, for the first time, a naturalistic interpretation of the Australian sunlit landscape. They analysed with skill, enthusiasm and sensitivity the appearance of eucalypt and *melaleuca*—and such dominant forest types—in the full blaze of sunlight. They depicted the colour and luminosity of the pale shadows of midsummer—blue, turquoise, pink and rose-violet; the atmospheric effects of dust, heat-haze and afterglow. But they loved most the warm coloured stillness of summer evenings.

This great love of the sun did not spring simply from a desire to state visual facts truthfully, though the desire to be truthful to appearances was certainly there. The image of the sun came to be used increasingly in Australian literature and art during the last two decades of the century as a symbol of Australia itself. The sun, that is, came to occupy a key place in the *mystique* of Australian nationalism, and when, in 1915, the Anzacs stormed the Dardanelles, they wore it emblazoned upon their slouch hats. It had been making its way as a characteristic symbol of Australian life and nature since the 1830's. In the work of writers of that time, John Dunmore Lang and Charles Harpur, for example, the clear, sunny skies of Australia were already seen as emblems of hope beckoning the European migrant. The symbol had been increasing in popularity in the face of that other and quite different attitude to Australian nature which we have already discussed in connection with the work of William Strutt and Marcus Clarke; namely, the conviction that Australian nature was monotonous and melancholy. In order to understand the new sense of optimism, joy, and love of the sun which the Heidelberg School brought to Australian nature we must appreciate the historical conditions in which the school arose.

By the 1880's both Sydney and Melbourne were great cities containing hundreds of thousands of people. The young Heidelberg artists were city-dwellers: Roberts began life as a photographer, Streeton as a lithographer's apprentice, McCubbin as a baker. Conder, who spent two years surveying in the country, was the most urban-minded of the four, and soon found a place as an artist on the *Illustrated Sydney News*. In the week-end they escaped into the bushlands which still, in much of their pristine splendour, surrounded the new cities. The suburban bushlands afforded them refreshment and recreation after their week of routine work in the city; and the new vision of Australian landscape which they brought into existence with such success was a vision of city-dwellers who had chosen to identify themselves with the sunshine and colour of the bush, its vibrating blue hills and rosy skies; a vision which lifted the youthful spirits of the Heidelberg painters far above the lonely, monotonous and melancholy back yards of Collingwood and Carlton.

It must be stressed, however, that they did not give all their attention to landscape painting. Roberts spent only a portion of his time at camps such as Eaglemont and 'Charterisville'. For at the time he was establishing himself, and supporting himself, as a portrait painter in the city. In 1887 or 1888 Grosvenor Chambers, a three-storey building, had been erected in Collins Street East 'expressly for occupation by artists', the whole of the top floor being designed as studios on principles, so it was claimed, 'laid down by Reynolds'. Roberts occupied one of these studios and a number of artist-friends, such as George Walton, the English portrait painter who had studied at the Royal Academy with Roberts and had come out for the sake of his health, occupied others. Conder also rented studios in the city.

It is not surprising, therefore, to find that urban scenes form a significant part of the work of the Australian impressionist painters. Tom Roberts's *Bourke Street* (59) affords an impression of one of Melbourne's main city streets exuding the heat and light of an Australian summer. In its informality and directness of handling—the figures, for instance, are suggested with great breadth and simplicity—it recalls French impressionist composition. But the colours are paler, more opalescent—faint rose-pinks and purples, dusty yellows and the palest of blue skies. Indeed, the Australian character of the work of the members of the Heidelberg School is most apparent in their sensitive apprehension of local colour. The lights and reflections upon city streets after rain were a special interest. Nerli's *Wet Evening* and Conder's *Departure of the* s.s. *Orient* have already been discussed, and Streeton's *Redfern Station* (56) is another fine essay on the same theme.

The new impressionist vision of the Australian city can be traced in contemporary prose writing. To take but one example, the descriptions of Sydney in Ada Cambridge's novel, *A Marked Man*, published in 1891, are

56   ARTHUR STREETON, *Redfern Station*, canvas, 16 x 24,
1893, Sydney

directly inspired by her personal knowledge of Curlew Camp, established
in that year by Tom Roberts at Little Sirius Cove. An evening on Sydney
Harbour is described in terms closely equivalent in colour and feeling to
the oil sketches of the Harbour painted in the early 1890's by Streeton:

The rosy afterglow lingered yet, but the Moon was rising over the North Head
—they turned round to look at it whenever they reached a point that gave them
a clear view. The great cliff was black as the blackest night, but the waters of
Middle Harbour were softly shining and tumbling, every moment growing whiter
and brighter. And the shores were veiled in that exquisite pinky-blue haze which
never seems so ethereal and dreamlike anywhere as in Sydney Harbour at the
close of a sunny day.[8]

It was, however, images of the country and of country life, not of the
city, which finally captured the public imagination and brought the greatest
fame to the members of the Heidelberg School. It could not have been
otherwise. By 1889 (the year of the 9 × 5 Exhibition) the greater proportion of Australians already lived in the cities. But these city-dwellers came
to identify themselves increasingly with the life and attitudes of the
Australian rural worker during the later decades of the century, as Australians sought to fashion a national identity of their own. The frontier
exercised an enormous influence upon the imagination of all Australians.
To some extent this idealization of rural labour was a world-wide phenomenon of the later nineteenth century. As liberalism transformed itself into

democratic socialism and labour parties arose in the European world, the image of the noble peasant invented largely by the romantic writers became an increasingly popular figure in art and literature, and was enshrined in the paintings of artists like Millet, Bastien-Lepage and Van Gogh. In older countries humanists and socialists stressed the patience and the endurance of the peasant. Young countries like Australia had had insufficient time to develop such a noble class of patient plodders. The bushman was the closest type to the noble peasant which the life of the country had produced, but he was characterized by his independence and an egalitarian collectivism which crystallized in the ideal of mateship.

> They call no biped lord or sir,
> And raise their hat to no man.[9]

Thus it was that the outback came to exercise a powerful influence upon the emergence of Australian culture. As Dr Russel Ward has put it:

. . . even as they faded from the workaday world, the value and attitudes of the nomad tribe (that is, the rural workers) were embalmed in a national myth, thence to react powerfully, as they still do, upon thought and events. The extinct bushman of Lawson and Furphy became the national culture-hero on whose supposed characteristics many Australians tend, consciously or unconsciously, to model their attitude to life.[10]

Three of the members of the Heidelberg School, Frederick McCubbin, Tom Roberts and Arthur Streeton, each after his own fashion, made a significant contribution to the growth and diffusion of this national myth.

Frederick McCubbin appears to have been the prime mover in promoting the distinctly national quality of the Heidelberg School. Already at the Box Hill camp, as Roberts recalled years afterwards, he would wax philosophic around the evening camp-fire. For such reasons the others dubbed him 'The Prof'. Doubtless, much of his philosophizing concerned the growth of a national school of painting. McCubbin had studied at the Gallery School under G. F. Folingsby (1830-91), a product of the Munich School. It was Folingsby who transmitted to the young McCubbin that school's romantic interest in the painting of history pieces with a national flavour. The National Gallery of Victoria possesses some of Folingsby's sketches for history paintings, and his *Bunyan in Prison*.

When Julian Ashton arrived in Melbourne in 1878, already an advocate of *plein-air* painting, he found McCubbin engaged upon a *Death of Semiramis*. 'Why bother about a lady so long deceased?' Ashton asked. 'Why not paint the life about you?'[11] The remark probably left an impression for, in 1886, prompted by Roberts's interest in the work of Bastien-Lepage, McCubbin began a series of paintings in which *plein-air* methods were applied increasingly to subjects redolent with local history. The need for a school of Australian *history* painting had been discussed in the *Melbourne University Review*, two years before, in an article which claimed that there were 'some pages of Australian *history* worthy of treatment'.[12] The introduction of European life into new surroundings, the discovery of gold, Eureka, and inland exploration were mentioned. McCubbin began his series of social *history* paintings with a well-known theme. The death of children who wandered away into the bush was one of the most common tragedies of Australian frontier life, and had already found frequent literary expression, notably in Kingsley's *Geoffry Hamlyn* and Marcus Clarke's melodramatic little tale of *Pretty Dick*. McCubbin's *The Lost Child* (58) sought to incorporate this old colonial theme into the new pictorial methods. He followed it with his *Down on His Luck* (57), another well-known folk-image of the unsuccessful gold-digger, and *Bush Burial* (Geelong, 1890). The figures were painted from models posed in the open air and set in grey landscapes undisturbed by changing effects of sunlight and shadow. These paintings were quite different from the small impressions shown at the Exhibition of 9 × 5 Impressions. But that exhibition never at any time summed up the whole programme of the Heidelberg School.

In McCubbin's case, though not in Roberts's and Streeton's, the large national subject picture introduced a note of melancholy into the work of the school, a melancholy in sharp contrast to the sun-drenched optimism and gaiety of spirit which animated the landscape impressions of Roberts

57   FREDERICK McCUBBIN, *Down on His Luck*, canvas,
45 x 60, 1889, Perth

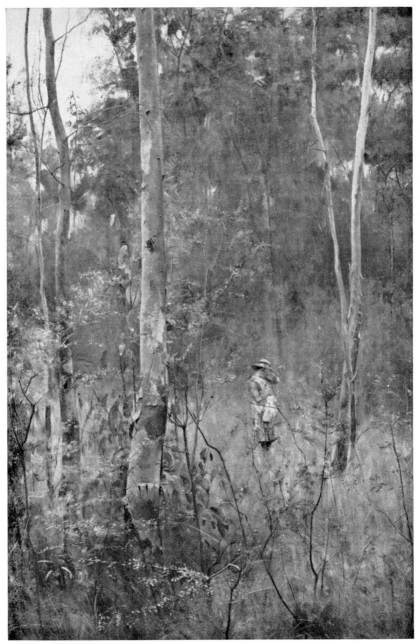

58 FREDERICK McCUBBIN, *The Lost Child*, canvas,
45 x 28½, 1886, Melbourne

and Streeton. It was akin to the older colonial melancholy from which the paintings of the Heidelberg School, in other respects, afforded such a dramatic rupture. Indeed, McCubbin's work forms a bridge here between old and new. He was the means whereby older colonial fears and attitudes were carried on into the new school. Nevertheless, McCubbin's history paintings reveal, after 1890, the impact of impressionist techniques. In his *Bush Burial, Wallaby Track* (Sydney, 1896) and *The Pioneer* (Melbourne, 1904), the figures are covered with loose flecks of paint in which the palette knife has been used freely. By such means McCubbin sought to 'keep' his figures more naturally within their atmospheric space. Thus 'historic genre, Victorian sentiment, open-air realism, and a certain impressionism of technique intermingle in the same work'.[13]

McCubbin had painted his tragic depictions of colonial life in the comparative peace and tranquillity of his surburban home, and at Macedon. Roberts was, by his nature and training, more of a realist. His interest in painting subjects of Australian interest dates, like McCubbin's, from 1886 when he painted his fine picture, *Coming South* (72) based, doubtless, upon drawings he had made on the voyage back from London. It is clearly, with its careful study of different types, an essay on the theme of migration. He hung it in the Indian and Colonial Exhibition, London (1886). It was described by the *Age* critic as 'a very careful and well-drawn work full of character and very tender and harmonious in colour. The influence of the French school is clearly seen as it is evident that he has attained his present proficiency by a careful and exhaustive study of drawing . . .'.[14] Roberts followed this painting a few years later with a fine series of paintings devoted to the pastoral industry.

In order to paint *Shearing the Rams* (60), Roberts visited Brocklesby Station, in the Riverina, New South Wales, during two successive shearing seasons, where he made a large number of sketches and drawings, and set up his easel for a time in the shearing shed itself, later finishing the painting in a city studio. He adopted a similar practice when painting *The Breakaway* (61) and *Shearing at Newstead* (Sydney, 1894). In such paintings, Roberts sought to give a heightened and ennobled expression to the life of the rural worker. It was a subject in which his own feelings were deeply involved. In explanation of his choice of *Shearing the Rams* as his subject, he wrote:

. . . one of the best words spoken to an artist is, 'paint what you love, and love what you paint', and on that I have worked; and so it came that being in the bush and feeling the delight and fascination of the great pastoral life and work I have tried to express it. If I had been a poet . . . I should have described the scattered flocks on sunlit plains and gum-covered ranges, the coming of spring, the gradual massing of the sheep towards that one centre, the woolshed

59   TOM ROBERTS, *Bourke Street*, canvas, 19½ x 29⅜,
1885-6, N.L.A.

59a   TOM ROBERTS, *Bourke Street* (a detail), 10 x 15

. . . the shouts of the men, the galloping of horses and the barking of dogs as
the thousands are driven, half-seen, through the hot dust to the yards . . . but
being circumscribed by my art it was only possible . . . to give expression to
one portion of this . . . it seemed that (in the woolshed) I had the best expression
of my subject, a subject noble enough and worthy enough if I could express the
meaning and spirit of strong masculine labour . . . and the great human interest
of the whole scene. . . . I believe . . . that by making art the perfect expression
of one time and one place, it becomes art for all time and of all places.[15]

Roberts possessed an easy and natural manner and appears to have been
quite at home among shearers. We cannot in fairness say that his paintings
are romantic or that he was painting a world unfamiliar to his experience.
Certainly he may never have himself observed a genuine holdup or breakaway, but such things still happened, though much less frequently, and
Roberts did all he could to reconstruct such situations as realistically as
possible. Both *The Breakaway*, with its informal composition, and *Bailed
Up* (Sydney), with its lack of histrionics, are splendid examples of this. Of
course, Roberts thought out and carefully composed his larger figure compositions. But this is a feature of all large work of this kind, including many
examples by the French impressionists. To come nearer home, a painting
like *Shearing the Rams*, which combines careful formal artistry with a high
degree of realism, may be compared with the similar craftsmanship that
went to the writing of Henry Lawson's short stories.

60   TOM ROBERTS, *Shearing the Rams*, canvas, 47 x 71,
1889-90, Melbourne

61   TOM ROBERTS, *The Breakaway*, canvas, 53½ x 65½,
1891, Adelaide

Unlike Roberts and McCubbin, Streeton was neither a portrait nor a figure painter. But he, too, felt their desire to paint large paintings typical of the Australian scene. In his case, they had to be produced within the limitations of landscape painting. In such works as *Fire's On* (62) and *Purple Noon's Transparent Might* (Melbourne, 1896) Streeton sought to paint his hymn of praise to the Australian sun. And he set about it in the same methodical manner that Roberts adopted when painting his pastoral pictures. In 1891 he painted *Fire's On* at Glenbrook, in the Blue Mountains, New South Wales. A letter which he wrote to McCubbin at the time provides a better insight into his methods and existing state of mind than anything else, and is therefore worth quoting in detail:

I follow the railway line for three-quarters of a mile through a canyon or gully where big brown men are toiling all the hot day excavating and making a tunnel, which will cost thousands . . . but will save wearing out a great number of engines on the first Zig Zag. I've passed the west mouth and now am arrived at my subject, the other mouth, which gapes like a great dragon's mouth at the perfect flood of hot sunlight. There is a cutting through the vast hill of bright sandstone; the walls of rock run high up and are crowned by gums bronze-green, and they look

G

quite small, being so high up, and behind is the deep blue azure heaven, where a crow sails along like a dot with its melancholy, hopeless cry—long drawn, like the breath of a dying sheep. Right below me the men work, some with shovels, others drilling for a blast. I work on the W. colour drying too quickly and the ganger cries, 'Fire, Fire's On'; all the men drop their tools and scatter and I nimbly skip off my perch and hide behind a big safe rock. A deep hush is everywhere—then, 'Holy Smoke', what a boom of thunder shakes the rock and me. It echoes through the hills and dies away 'mid the crashing of tons of rock; some lumps fly hundreds of feet sometimes and fall and fly everywhere among the trees. . . . All at work once more—more drills; the rock is a perfect blazing glory of white, orange, cream and blue streaks here and there where the blast has worked its force!

By the following day Streeton had developed an acquaintance with the men working on the tunnel.

. . . I sit down, drink tea and eat a bit, rest, and then yarn all the afternoon with my friends, the big, stalwart men. Sitting on a gunpowder keg at the tent door, I hand round the ruby twist; we smoke, and I listen to long yarns and adventures —diggers, prospectors, and so on. One old chap, but energetic; tales of coal, gold, and discussions on the present hard 'bullocking' they have to do in the broiling sun. I like these men. They're like a 'roaring camp', big and bronzed. I say 'Good-bye' to my friends and move off. My path lies towards the west, which is a flood of gold. I felt near the gates of paradise—the gates of the west.[16]

In such passages as these Streeton echoes the same feeling of respect for the dignity of manual labour which Roberts sought to express in his paintings of shearers and drovers.

Purple Noon's Transparent Might was another attempt to paint a large landscape under full sunlight. It is, indeed, an interesting essay in the painting of atmospheric colour over the great expanse of a wide river valley. Streeton's sensitive perception of colour values is here remarkably well sustained throughout the whole canvas. There are few paintings, as large as this one, which are so consistently based upon the careful painterly assessment of retinal impressions. In later years Streeton came to rely too greatly upon the tricks and sleight-of-hand of a fluent style; the hand working on from habit when the eye had become lazy. His style, that is, became mannered. But in such early paintings visual perception and painting technique are wonderfully balanced.

The romantic element in the work of the Heidelberg School is present not only in their desire to paint typical Australian life and landscape; it is also to be found in their affection for the lyrical moods of nature. The true impressionist—if there ever was such a person—was an objective painter. He was not concerned with the moods of nature or with literary values. It was his business to depict a fragment of the world in a moment of time with all the conditions of light, atmosphere, temperature, wind and shadow peculiar to the moment. Only upon occasion—and then only in their

62   ARTHUR STREETON, *Fire's On, Lapstone Tunnel*, canvas,
72⅜ x 48¼, 1891, Sydney

sketches in oil—did the Heidelberg painters attain such objectivity. Musical and literary associations are by no means an uncommon feature of their early work. Roberts's *Bourke Street* is realistic enough in its apprehension of light and colour, but it is illuminating to find that he associated its colour values with music and first called the painting *Allegro con brio*. An increasing interest in the ideal as opposed to the real, and in the ways in which poetry and music might be associated with painting, appears in 1889. The new interests are perhaps best revealed in a letter Streeton wrote to Roberts from Sydney in 1890. Already he was waxing nostalgic over the summer of 1889 at Eaglemont, dreaming of the time before Conder had left for Paris, and 9 × 5 Impressions were still being painted. As the years passed, that summer became the lost golden age of their lives to which all three looked back with varying degrees of nostalgia.

The enjoyment of the 'last summer at Eaglemont' was to me more intense than anything I have up to the present felt. It would surprise you how often I think of it, and, oh it is a great comfort. Its suggestion is a large harmony, musical, rose. Fancy if you could grasp all you feel and condense your thought into a scheme which would embrace sweet sound, great colour and all the soft slow movement, sometimes quick with games, and through all the strength of the great warm and loving sun. . . . How we made sketches of the girls on the lawn. The lovely pure muslin, and gold, sweet grass-seeds and the motherly she-oak, with its swing spreading a quiet blessing over them all. Behind this splendid tree was the deep gold of the summer gates of the west sunset, and the whole gem was framed, yes, with oleander on the east with the two tropical sleepy round bushes, and on the south pittosporum, and north the big solemn pine. They seemed to keep guard as the silver dusk of night simplified the group of quiet, happy boys and girls.[17]

Streeton is here writing about an experience which has touched him deeply. Precision of observation is linked with a mood Watteauesque in its ineffable dreaminess. Here nature, Australian nature, is seen as a happy idyll; the mention of a swing even calls to mind a faint image of Fragonard's famous painting. The Eaglemont camp has become a *fête champêtre*— a neo-Rococo vision that will play an increasingly important part in Australian art during the following decades. The dreaminess and air of reflection in the description had already been expressed in one of Streeton's last paintings at Heidelberg, *An Australian Gloaming*. It is the romantic light of the afterglow and moonrise which attracts him. The painting is closer in spirit to Claude and the later paintings of Corot than to the French impressionists. Streeton later changed the title to *Still Glides the Stream and Shall Forever Glide* (55)—a line taken from Wordworth's sonnet, 'After-thought'. Thus he sought to invest the painting with poetic associations. And he was not alone in this. Charles Conder's paintings in the 9 × 5 Exhibition already in 1889 indicated a cleavage between transcripts of nature and an impressionist's dream of ideality. To such works as *Impressionist's Camp, Prince's Bridge*, and *Burning Off* there may be opposed *Arcadia, A page from Herrick, A Dream of Handel's Largo, Old Time is Still A-Flying*. Streeton's descriptions of the Eaglemont camp, his interest in Wordsworth's 'After-thought', which has for its theme the transience of man and the permanence of art, together with Conder's interest in Arcadia as a subject, and in the work of Herrick, all suggest that Streeton and Conder had become interested in transience as a theme suited to artistic expression.

In Conder's work, the movement away from the objective depiction of impressions was heralded by the emergence of a decorative element in his work. Even when painting beach scenes directly from nature with Tom Roberts at Coogee in 1888 it is clear that Conder's interests were more decorative, less realistic than Roberts's. Characteristic was Conder's use of silhouetted foreground figures, reminiscent of Whistler's etchings, and shown in casual but decorative positions, and he also made great play with coloured parasols and gaily-striped costumes to enhance the richness of his colour schemes. Such little masterpieces as *Cove on the Hawkesbury* (78), at once decorative and impressionistic, have a Japanese air about them. There is in this trend away from the immediacy of sensation towards the decorative, the lyrical, and the wistfully melancholic already a suggestion of the *fin de siècle* and symbolism.

Symbolism began to appear in Conder's work in August 1889, in his cover design for the catalogue of the Exhibition of 9 × 5 Impressions (63), in which he sought to express a personal philosophy of art. The figure 9 is shown upon a circular wooden plaque which is cut with the grain, but the figure 5 is depicted upon a plaque cut against the grain. This is a reference to the wooden cigar-box lids on which the 9 × 5 impressions were painted, the length of a lid being normally cut with the grain and the width across it. The grain of the lower plaque, however, bursts forth at its base into curious root-like tentacles. On one side they are connected to the antennae of a dragon-fly and on the other to the root-like forms which sprout from an oddly-shaped figure, the lower half of which is in the form of a tree-trunk and the upper half in the form of a classically-posed female figure. Conder seems to be suggesting how the impressionists draw upon the transient beauty of life (symbolized by the petals which fall from the blossoming tree and the dragon-fly which lives but a day) and embody its variety in the permanent forms of art (symbolized by the classical figure). But art forms are themselves transient. When they cease to draw upon life (symbolized by the broken branch and the figure beside it), they become bound by convention and assume cold, academic forms. Yet even the apparently lifeless traditions of art may give rise to new forms of beauty. An image,

63 CHARLES CONDER,
*Catalogue Cover Design, Ex-
hibition of 9 x 5 Impressions,*
August 1889

64 CHARLES CONDER,
*Catalogue Cover Design, Vic-
torian Artists' Society Winter
Exhibition,* March 1890

long bound by convention, may still hold a living flame to a newer and higher form of beauty. Yet even these new forms must take on conventions of their own (signified by the ribbon of convention as it floats through the blossoming tree) in order to become art.

Such ideas varied in certain important respects from the impressionist programme. It is true, of course, that in many of the great French impressionist paintings we may hear at times beneath the bright harmonies a solemn chorale upon the transience of earthly beauty, but Conder here is making direct use of classical imagery and neo-classical notions about the nature of art. The direction of his thought may be traced also in his cover design for the Catalogue of the Winter Exhibition of the Victorian Artists' Society held in March 1890 (64). Again the dragon-fly and falling petals appear as symbols of transience, and the symbol of art is again shown in the form of a dual image, a female head into which a tree has been incorporated. On this occasion it may signify nothing more than figure and landscape painting but it is, it will be noted, even more closely identified with the notion of transience, being linked by ribbon bands to the symbols of time (stars and sickle) and death (pomegranate and the waning moon).

Conder's growing interest in symbolism is accompanied by a significant change in his style. The 9 × 5 Exhibition catalogue reveals Conder as a pioneer of the *art nouveau* style in Australia. The new linear emphasis which he gives to his design, his use of plant forms, and the lettering which itself suggests plant growth, are all features which foreshadow the *art nouveau* style. The decorative emphasis in his work, his interest in symbolism and the stylistic forms of *art nouveau* all indicate Conder's knowledge of the aesthetic movement prior to his return to Europe. An aesthetic taste in Whistlerian mode is also observable in the furnishings of his Melbourne studio. It was fitted with soft drapes of liberty silks, madras muslin and other light fabrics, and sketches by his Sydney friends Phil May, F. B. Schell, Frank Mahony, B. E. Minns, Nerli and Madame Constance Roth, together with his own pictures, were scattered about the walls among fans and curious odds and ends. Conder probably saw the Whistler exhibited in Sydney in the Anglo-Australian Exhibition of 1885 and it is possible that he gained information concerning the art of Whistler and the aesthetic movement from two young Englishmen: Blamire Young, a schoolmaster from Cambridge who arrived to accept a post as mathematics master at Katoomba College, New South Wales, in 1885, and Phil May who arrived in 1886 to accept a position as a black and white artist on the *Bulletin*.

Young had studied classics and mathematics at Pembroke College, but his artistic interests, both practical and critical, had been roused by his association with the Cambridge Fine Art Society, from which the critic, Roger Fry, had graduated to connoisseurship. At Cambridge, Young had begun to sketch and paint in water-colour. In 1887 he induced the Head-master of Katoomba College to help him to build a studio in the school grounds. This, in imitation of Whistler, he decorated with Mirzapore rugs, a Persian Wilton carpet, and a blue-tiled fire-place. Wrought-iron lamp frames, painted scarlet, hung from the ceiling, and the windows were curtained at one end with silk madras muslin and at the other with floral chintz. It was in this studio that he met Phil May who gave him his first instruction in drawing and painting. The studio became the centre of a little coterie which included May, Theodore Fink and Godfrey Rivers, who had studied at the Slade and emigrated to Australia in 1889. The studio, however, was destroyed by fire. May left for England at the end of 1888. Young resigned his teaching post in 1893 and followed him to London.

Whether or not the proto-*art nouveau* quality in his work was gained from May or Young, by 1889 Conder was making considerable use of symbolism in his painting. In that year he painted two pictures for the Victorian Artists' Society Exhibition: *Hot Wind*, in which a half-nude girl lies full-length upon sunburnt ground blowing upon a brazier; and *Victorian Idyll* (which has disappeared) wherein summer is depicted as a goddess robed in reddish draperies. Both paintings appear to have been inspired by Adam Lindsay Gordon's lines:

> Where with fire and fierce drouth on her tresses
> Insatiable summer oppresses

Sere woodlands and sad wildernesses,
And faint flocks and herds.

And it is probable that the great drought of 1888, one of the worst on record since Australian records began, may have helped to suggest the subject of at least the first painting.

Conder's use of nude and semi-nude female figures to convey symbolic meanings became popular. Aby Altson, for example, who won the Travelling Scholarship of the National Gallery of Victoria in 1890, painted *The Golden Age* (65) about 1893. It is a large, rather immature painting in which slender, lissom *art nouveau* youths and maidens disport themselves with music and dancing in a sunlit landscape; but it catches admirably the spirit of the time. In Sydney in 1894, Sydney Long (1872-1955), while still a student at Ashton's, painted his figured landscape, *By Tranquil Waters* (66), a remarkably fresh and broadly painted canvas with clear lights and bright blue shadows. It was purchased by the Trustees of the Sydney Gallery from the annual exhibition of the Art Society of New South Wales in 1894, and was criticized on moral grounds by a member of the New South Wales Legislative Council. It was the first occasion upon which a State gallery had purchased a painting containing youthful nude figures set in a naturalistic Australian landscape. Such purchases were still likely to create a furore in the Press and Parliament even in 1894.

On such matters Tom Roberts and Julian Ashton often found themselves in public opposition to the prudery prevalent in Australian society. About 1880, Tom Roberts and his friend C. Douglas Richardson, while still

65   ABY ALTSON, *The Golden Age*, canvas, 54¼ x 98, 1893,
Melbourne

66 SYDNEY LONG, *By Tranquil Waters*, canvas, 43¾ x 72⅜, 1894, Sydney

students, succeeded in obtaining permission from Sir Redmond Barry and the Trustees of the National Gallery of Victoria to establish a life class in the Gallery school. Roberts's charming little *Sunny South* (67) must be one of the first, if not the first, studies of the nude in a *plein-air* setting painted in Australia. It is difficult, perhaps, to appreciate fully today the moral issues of the time. Surf-bathing in the open sea was proscribed by law, for example, and rigidly policed until 1902. Among writers and artists, however, the growing opposition to Victorian values expressed itself in an almost neo-pagan interest in nudity, sex and sun-cults, international in scope and significance.

Havelock Ellis's one essay in fiction captures this burgeoning neo-paganism of the time with success. Although not composed until 1885, six years after he had left Australia, his *Kanga Creek: An Australian Idyll* is clearly written from his own experience. In his *Autobiography* Ellis explained that:

In Australia I gained health of body; I attained peace of soul; my life task was revealed to me; I was able to decide on my professional vocation; I became an artist in literature . . . these five points covered the whole activity of my life in the world. Some of them I should doubtless have reached without the aid of the Australian environment, scarcely all, and most of them I could never have achieved so completely if chance had not cast me into the solitude of the Liverpool range.[18]

67   TOM ROBERTS, *The Sunny South*, canvas, 11⅝ x 23⅞,
1887, Melbourne

Kanga Creek is an imaginative reconstruction of those early years. Therein youth, love, a fullness of sensational experience, a pagan delight in mother nature, are the things worth while. On one occasion the young school-master, the hero of the story, 'flung himself down beneath a gum tree with an excess of joy in the presence of that glad warm earth, as though he would kiss the whole world'. Yet the land, for all that, still retained its melancholy emblems: 'the long-drawn cry of the curlew', 'the lagoon, a silent spot with an air of melancholy brooding over it'. The menace and dread of the bush to which Marcus Clarke had given voice is still there but it is now muffled. With Ellis, as with Streeton, the predominant tone is one of sensuous enjoyment linked with an awareness of the transience of earthly beauty. One summer evening the schoolmaster brings the young woman of his heart to Kanga Creek and sits her there naked upon a rock in the moonlight. 'I wanted to bring you here', he said suddenly; 'I wanted to seat you like a queen on this throne. It's been waiting for you thousands and thousands of years.'[19] In such writing the erotic is evoked indirectly, the nude seen idealistically through the diaphanous gauze of neo-pagan senti-ment. It is usually the same with the paintings which employ the nude figure during the last decade of the century.

Not only the nude was aetherealized. During the 1890's it happened to many of the motifs which had become traditional to Australian painting and writing. The bush came to be seen increasingly through a haze of romance. The changing tone of the popular ballad poetry is a clear indication of the new literary fashions of the time. For Lawson, Farrell, Edward Dyson and Barcroft Boake the bush retained a large measure of its traditional malevolence. But for A. B. Paterson, who lived most of his working life in the city, the bush is a pleasant place for the city clerk to escape to during a vacation:

> And I sometimes rather fancy that I'd like to change with Clancy,
> Like to take a turn at droving where the seasons come and go,
> While he faced the round eternal of the cashbook and the journal
> For the drover's life has pleasures that the townsfolk never know.

The bush becomes a place of escape and recreation for the city man. Bush types are idealized. In Roderic Quinn's 'The Camp Within the West' the swagman becomes a Christ-like symbol bearing upon his shoulders the burden of the world's sorrow. A similar apotheosis of the sundowner occurs in J. Le Gay Brereton's *Landlopers*:

> . . . the tramp can appreciate everything, and can find enjoyment even in misfortune. He is not stifled by conventional obligations. He wanders at large in a perfect atmosphere of love. He is on the common level; no social lies raise him to a pedestal or depress him in a cess-pit. He feels his fellowship with Nature. An individual he is yet merged in the universe. He recognizes his union with the Divine. He is a god . . . he is so brimming with exultant joy that he would like to clasp the hand of every man he meets, and kiss the lips of every girl. . . .[20]

Le Gay Brereton, however, was not a professional tramp himself, but a Professor of English Literature who enjoyed bush-walking.

Such then is the temper of much of the painting and writing of the last decade of the century. Sunshine has become a pervading presence enfolding youth and nature in a shimmer of joy. The new sensuousness was not due, of course, entirely to local circumstance. Conder read Whitman, and the poet probably inspired Le Gay Brereton's *Landlopers* in more ways than one. And then it was Verlaine's cult of faded things, not Edgar Allan Poe's melancholy which provided the keynote to Australian nature. A. G. Stephens, the critic, wrote a preface to the *Bulletin Story Book* in 1901 which reads like a reply to Marcus Clarke's preface to Gordon's *Poems*. 'Verlaine's cult of faded things, extolling the hinted hue before the gross colour, finds a natural home in Australia—in many aspects a Land of Faded Things—of delicate purples, delicious greys, and dull, dreamy olives and ochres.'

Through such followers of the Heidelberg School as David Davies and Walter Withers, the fashion for landscapes with luminous yet muted colours became popular. Evening effects, crepuscules, and afterglows provided themes through which nature could be seen in a soft romantic haze (68). Ten years after Streeton had painted his *Still Glides the Stream*, the critic, James Green, was able to write that the poetic note which was first struck as the tone-key of Australian art in 1889 had become by 1899 the strongest element of national individuality. The popularity of poetic landscape was due, he said, to

68   DAVID DAVIES, *Moonrise, Templestowe,* canvas,
46 x 58, 1894, Melbourne

the dire prosaicism of Australian life in general. The landscape of a country is
the distilled aroma of her being, and, when truthfully translated upon canvas,
remains her esoteric own and essentially none others. . . . It is in this poetic
distillation of Australian Nature, apart from mere literal transcription or excel-
lence of technique, that our painters are now learning so specifically to excel.[21]

The new romanticism of faded things was making its own contribution to
the national *mystique.*

One sign of the increasing romanticism in landscape is to be found in
the conversion of the naturalistic nude into classical myth. Roberts's naked
young bathing boys are replaced by images of the god Pan. The transition
is marked in Long's *By Tranquil Waters* where a boy bathing in the foreground plays a pipe. Henceforth the image of Pan in a bushland setting
becomes increasingly common in Australian painting and poetry. Long's
Pan of 1898 depicts two satyrs dancing with two young girls to the tune
of a pipe played by a Pan figure. The design reveals considerable movement away from the decorative naturalism of *By Tranquil Waters* towards
a more purely decorative and *art nouveau* style. Yet Long continued to use
living models for his allegories. From D. H. Souter we learn that 'Pan was
an Irishman as far as the waist; the rest was studied from a Woolloomooloo
goat'. Long's *Spirit of the Plains* (69) is a fine piece of *art-nouveau* decora-

69   SYDNEY LONG, *The Spirit of the Plains*, canvas, 24 x 51,
1897, Brisbane

tion applied to an Australian setting. His attempt to populate the bush with
classical gods was followed by other painters, but had a much wider vogue
among poets. Long's *Pan* found an early parallel, for example, in Christopher
Brennan's poem 'Secreta Silvarum' written about 1901:

> . . . This is the house of Pan, not whom blind craze
> and babbling wood-wits tell, where bare flints blaze,
> noon-tide terrific with the single shout,
> but whom behind each bole sly-peering out
> the traveller knows, but turning, disappear'd
> with chuckle of laughter in his thicket-beard,
> and rustle of scurrying faun-feet where the ground
> each autumn deeper feels its yellow mound.
> Onward: and lo, at length, the secret glade,
> soft-gleaming grey, what time the grey trunks fade
> in the white vapours o'er its further rim.
> 'Tis no more time to linger: now more dim
> the woods are throng'd to ward the haunted spot
> where, as I turn my homeward face, I wot
> the nymphs of twilight have resumed, unheard,
> their glimmering dance upon the glimmering sward.[22]

But the bush could not be easily submitted to classicizing. In 1905 Long,
in a moment of self-criticism, admitted that artists in Australia would never
be able, unlike those of older countries, to people their country with
nymphs, naiads, pans and centaurs. Instead, he suggested, the Australian
artist 'will bid the aborigine blossom out in all his manly vigour, when
sufficient time has allowed us to forget his failings'.[23]

Art nouveau suggested new ways of depicting Australian tree-forms. The thin, graceful stems and feathery branches of young eucalypt saplings and the sinuous lines of the tea-tree lent themselves splendidly to a decorative treatment. They are a feature of landscape and graphic art between 1895 and 1905, notably in the work of Ruby Lind (1887-1919) and Violet Teague (1872-1951). It was D. H. Souter (1862-1935), however, who made the most use of *art nouveau* in graphic art, though it affected the work of most Australian artists, to some extent, during the first decade of the century. In 1902, for example, Walter Withers, possibly influenced by Blamire Young's essays in history painting, executed six panels for the entrance hall of Purrumbete homestead at Camperdown, Victoria, in a fully-fledged *art nouveau* style. The panels depicted stages in the development of the property by the Manifold family. The paintings and sculpture of C. Douglas Richardson (1853-1932) were also strongly influenced by *art nouveau*.[24]

Ernest Moffitt (1870-99) was another pioneer of *art nouveau* in Australia. The pen drawings and woodcuts which illustrate Lionel Lindsay's *Consideration of the Art of Ernest Moffitt* (1899) are among the most delightful examples of the style produced in Australia. There is an echo of *Jugendstil* and the Austrian Secessionists in such woodcuts as his *Bathers* (70), transmitted, no doubt, through the early issues of the *Studio*, a most important vehicle from the time of its first publication in 1892 for the diffusion of *art nouveau* in Australia and elsewhere. Moffitt, who died young and was interested in all the arts, was a spiritual force among the little confraternity of artists at 'Charterisville'. Lionel Lindsay has vividly depicted the man and his time in his *Consideration*:

The old garden at Charterisville, and everybody down the river, either swimming or lying on the rocks in the hot sun. Moffitt, his whole body sunburnt, as bronze as a faun, and some of us climb the bank, and binding flowers and vine leaves about us, dance on the short grass, or chase each other, shouting; and we think of happiness and pagan Greece, before Christianity came to throw its ominous shadow of melancholia and 'purity' upon the blytheness of life.

70 ERNEST MOFFITT, *The Bathers*, woodcut, 4 x 3, from L. Lindsay, *A Consideration of the Art of Ernest Moffitt*, 1899

The movement from impression to romance in Australian landscape was a product of aesthetic attitudes and *art nouveau*. In both Blamire Young was a leading influence. He remained in England for two years after leaving his Katoomba school, married, and developed under the influence of the Beggarstaff Brothers, James Pryde and William Nicholson a consuming interest in the new poster. Returning to Melbourne in 1896, he formed with Harry Weston what may be called a co-operative group for the production of commercial posters. Between them Weston and Young succeeded in producing a series of remarkable *art nouveau* designs which vitalized poster art throughout the country. But Young, a man of varied and original talent, could not confine himself long to the constricting requirements of the commercial world. At that time Roberts and McCubbin were still engaged upon their cycle of social history paintings. Young contributed to the trend with two large water-colour paintings illustrative of Victorian history, *William Buckley* and *Fawkner's Printing Press* (both at Geelong) in the decorative manner of *art nouveau*. They were exhibited at the Exhibition of the Victorian Artists' Society, but their heavy decorative contours and bright flat colours found little favour with the critics. For some years Young and his family lived through the depression years of the 'nineties (like many of his Melbourne fellow-artists) in straitened circumstances punctuated by financial crises.

It was not until 1911 that a series of water-colours painted at Mount Buffalo and exhibited at the Guildhall, Melbourne, brought him, then in his fiftieth year, critical acclaim and public notice. Exhibitions in Adelaide and Melbourne (at the Athenaeum) followed, and Young later visited Tasmania with his family. The holiday left a permanent impression upon him and from it proceeded some of his finest paintings, which he exhibited in Sydney in 1912 prior to departing with his family for Europe. The fascination of Spain had touched him, as it touched many of his generation, and he made his way leisurely to England via the Canary Islands, Lisbon, Oporto, Madrid, Bourgos and Paris. In England he painted only for a few months on the Sussex Downs before the outbreak of war forced him back to his youthful skill with a rifle, as an instructor in musketry and machine gunnery. He did not return to Australia until 1923.[25]

Blamire Young handled water-colour with versatility, grace and, at times, with wit. But his light romantic gift, which gained much from Bonington, Watteau and the later paintings of Corot, often betrayed him into an excessive prettiness of design and sweetness of colour. He was romantic in his love of old buildings, in his devotion to atmosphere and light, and his love of the theatre. One of his plays, *Art for Art's Sake*, was produced in Melbourne in 1911, and another, *The Children's Bread*, was published in 1912. And the stage is never far from his work. Figures are often placed, in the manner of his friend Pryde, against a huge drape, or against the greater curtain of the sky. From Whistler he learned to assemble his tones

71   BLAMIRE YOUNG, *Dry Weather,*
water-colour, 21⅝ x 29½, *c.* 1912, Sydney

and masses in telling decorative areas, and from the Japanese, the value of open composition and bright, flat washes of colour. Young's decorative neo-Rococo manner is in sharp contrast to the *plein-air* realism of Roberts and McCubbin. He played with a dream-world behind the thin veils of his graded and granulated washes, though on occasion a note of mordant satire can appear. But usually even his droughts occur upon the hills of Arcadia (71).

The desire to interpret Australian landscape as a southern Arcadia of sunshine and lyrical colour reached the height of its expression in the later work of Frederick McCubbin. The last and perhaps finest phase of his art was presided over by Turner's genius. We know that McCubbin studied with great interest a special publication of the *Studio* for 1903-4, devoted to Turner's work. Thenceforwards he abandoned his large-scale figure pieces on Australian themes in favour of lyrical landscapes inspired by the later paintings of Turner (83). Colour is now flecked on brightly, loosely, with great freedom. McCubbin no longer seeks to provide a true impression of things seen but to paint a hymn in celebration of Australian light.[26]

Despite McCubbin's personal triumph late in life, the vision which had inspired the painters of the Heidelberg School was fading. J. J. Hilder's[27] slim, lyrical effusions manage somehow to avoid vulgarity (84); the same cannot be said of Elioth Gruner's early work. Trained under Julian Ashton, he combined his master's *plein-air* methods with an interest, then widely current, in the lyrical excursions of the later paintings of Corot. It is said that he made a special visit to Melbourne to study *The Bent Tree.* But there was something mundane about the quality of his imagination that does not fail to reveal itself even in his most lyrical evocations of spring blossom, morning light, or dappled cows and cow-sheds at dawn. True, like Max Meldrum, Gruner analysed tonal gradations with much devotion; but his mood is invariably sentimental, his composition stereotyped, and his colour lacks sensitivity. To compare any of Gruner's early beach scenes or spring landscapes with similar early paintings by Roberts, Conder or Streeton is to realize at once that Australian impressionism had lost the power to inspire creative art.[28]

Norman Lindsay and Hans Heysen

During the first two decades of the present century Norman Lindsay was the most controversial figure in Australian art and letters. His life spans the history of Australian art from its beginnings in the camps at Heidelberg (he spent some crucial early years at 'Charterisville') to the present day. His work represents, among other things, the full flowering of that school of graphic art which gained so much impetus from the *Bulletin* and other illustrated journals in the years between 1880 and 1914. Lindsay revealed himself to be the most talented, imaginative and prolific pen draughtsman in the country, and the effect of his work and thought extended eventually into the whole field of Australian culture.

In his work as an artist, whether in pen and ink, etching, water-colour or oil painting, Lindsay is a magnificent illustrator. Preoccupied, however, from the beginning of his intellectual life with literary, ethical, and technical questions, his art has revealed a complete lack of interest in the formal and constructive elements of design, especially in painting. Not surprisingly, therefore, his influence upon Australian painting has been of no great importance. It is in the realm of letters, especially in poetry, that his ideas and attitudes have found the most responsive audience.

During the first two decades of the century Norman Lindsay became a liberating force of considerable power in Australian culture. Far more than any of his contemporaries, he helped to widen the range and deepen the curiosities and interests of Australian artists and writers. From the beginning he opposed nationalism and brought a most salutary breadth of interest in the masterpieces of European literature, art and music, to the local scene. His own art became a lifelong protest, arising first in his own family, against the strict code of Christian morality. Deeply impressed at an early age by the writings of Nietzsche, he acquired a profound belief in the overwhelming importance of the artist's role in society as a creator aligned against the forces of a Philistine establishment habituated to hypocrisy, wowserism and corruption. The conception of the dedicated artist alienated from society was not familiar to Edwardian Australia; and the spectacle of its enactment in real life created, on the one hand, a series of crises with officialdom and, on the other hand, standards of behaviour for professional artists and writers which involved relationships with the 'art-loving public' less compromising than hitherto.

Norman Lindsay was born in the small mining township of Creswick, Victoria, in 1879. His father, Dr Robert Lindsay, a graduate of Trinity College, Dublin, was a general physician in the town, and his mother was the daughter of the Reverend Thomas Williams, a Wesleyan missionary who had settled in Fiji in 1839 and retired to Creswick in the later 1850's. The Lindsays had ten children, five of whom, Percy, Lionel, Norman, Ruby

72   TOM ROBERTS, *Coming South*, canvas, 24¾ x 19½, 1886,
Mr L. P. Kendall

and Daryl, became well known as artists: Lionel and Daryl also achieved knighthoods for their services to art and connoisseurship in Australia.

Norman's early education and interests owed a good deal to his missionary grandfather who encouraged and criticized his first drawings, read Shakespeare to him, and took him regularly to the Ballarat Art Gallery, where Solomon J. Solomon's painting *Ajax and Cassandra*, with its exciting and dramatic nude, Cassandra, left a permanent impression. A persistent illness troubled his youth and he read widely from childhood. His home provided him with some books of germinal significance: an illustrated Bible with 'embattled hosts and charging charioteers', *Tales from Homer*, and Knight's *History of London*. By the age of twelve he was acquainted with Shakespeare, *Don Quixote, Gil Blas* and *The Three Musketeers*. The Creswick library furnished reproductions of Dürer's prints, and drawings by Edwin Abbey, from *Harper's*. Norman Lindsay first attended the State School and later the Grammar School at Creswick where he revived the school paper, the *Boomerang*. At the age of fourteen he made a series of drawings inspired by *Hamlet* and *The Three Musketeers*. But his drawings soon began to reflect the interests and curiosities of pubescence and he came violently into conflict with his mother's Calvinistic morality.

Meanwhile, Norman's elder brother, Lionel, had obtained employment in Melbourne upon a weekly paper, the *Hawklet*, a kind of police gazette specializing in sensational news; and Norman came to Melbourne at the age of sixteen at his brother's request to help him with his work. Drawing for the *Hawklet* brought Norman into direct contact with the carnal and violent aspects of Melbourne life: prize-fights, the music hall, saloons, brothels, the scenes of murders. He also contributed drawings to the *Tocsin* and the *Freelance*, and became art editor of the short-lived *Rambler*. Black and white illustrations from old copies of such journals as *Once a Week*, *Good Words*, and the *Cornhill Magazine*, containing reproductions of the work of Millais, Frederick Sandys and Whistler, appear to have been the most important influences upon his art at this time. 'We were all', Sir Lionel Lindsay has written, 'ardent collectors of the illustrators of the 'sixties.'

About 1897 Lionel and Norman with their friend, Ernest Moffitt, settled in one of the lodges in the old garden at 'Charterisville'. Norman, captivated by the drawings of Sandys, drew the trunks and branches of the old trees in the garden with the 'fervid care of a Pre-Raphaelite'. Moffitt, who had studied art, and music under Marshall Hall, became secretary of the Conservatorium of Music at East Melbourne. It was Moffitt who transferred to Lionel and Norman his passion for the Greek authors; and at 'Charterisville' Norman began his practice of making sets of illustrations to books that appealed to him, beginning with the *Idylls* of Theocritus, and following with illustrations to *Boccaccio*. He was also reading widely:

H

Rabelais, Balzac, Pepys, Gautier, the letters of Byron, Rossetti and Swin-
burne. About 1898, at the age of nineteen, he read Nietzsche's *Anti-Christ*
and *Zarathustra*, which had appeared in an English translation.

In Melbourne, during the later 1890's, Norman was associated with his
brothers, Percy and Lionel, in membership of the Prehistoric Order of
Cannibals, a club of young artists founded in 1893, which also included
among its members Miles Evergood, Max Meldrum, Will Dyson, Hugh
McCrae, Ernest Moffitt and Harry Weston. The life of the Club later
provided him with material for his novel *A Curate in Bohemia* (1913). At
this time, too, Norman regularly attended life-classes, organized by George
Coates, and there he met Raymond Parkinson, whose sister Kate he married
in 1899.

About this time the *Hawklet* failed and Norman Lindsay, at the age of
twenty-one, succeeded in obtaining a permanent position on the *Bulletin*
staff in Sydney, after J. F. Archibald had been shown his *Boccaccio* drawings. During the following nine years (1901-9) he produced an enormous
amount of work for the *Bulletin*: political cartoons, joke blocks, comments
on national life. He settled in Sydney, at Lavender Bay, with his wife and
son, Jack (*b.* 1900), and opened a studio in Bond Street. A few years later,
in 1903, his brother Lionel, after some years in Spain and England, joined
him in Sydney. Norman continued to feed his imagination upon translations
from the classics: Catullus, Horace, Petronius and Plautus, and on one
occasion wrote a Roman play in the vein of Plautus, which he called *The
Pink Butterfly*.

In Sydney, too, Lindsay gradually freed his drawing from the decorative
elements and precise detail which he had inherited from *art nouveau* and
the Pre-Raphaelites. Contrasts of sunlit flesh and white togas against the
brilliant blacks of foreground shadows and heavy foliage brought a more
tonal and painterly quality to his drawings. His brother Lionel has suggested that the 'deep metallic tones' of the Moreton Bay fig trees at
Lavender Bay inspired him in this new interest in dappled and heavily
contrasted lights. During the next ten years or so Norman made an important series of imaginative drawings expressive of his philosophy of life and
art, the most notable being: *The Scoffers* (1903), which was purchased by
Bernard Hall, the first buyer and one of the earliest admirers and champions
of Lindsay's work; *Pollice Verso* (1904), *Dionysius* (1905) and the *Crucified Venus* (1912). In the *Pollice Verso* (73), nude Roman warriors and
their women gesture violently with their thumbs down at the Crucified
Christ as they surge forward in a Bacchanalian procession inspired by
Titian and Rubens. The influence of the latter, gained first from the book
by Max Rooses, became in the opinion of Lionel the most momentous and
abiding influence upon Norman's art. The Trustees of the National Gallery

73   NORMAN LINDSAY, *Pollice Verso*, pen drawing,
17¾ x 22⅞, 1904, Melbourne

of Victoria purchased *Pollice Verso* from an exhibition held in Melbourne
in 1907, but so great was the public outcry which followed that the painting
was hung for the remainder of the exhibition with its face to the wall.

In 1906 Norman Lindsay turned from line to wash drawing, and began
to illustrate the *Memoirs of Casanova*. In order to gain historical accuracy in
setting and costume he read widely and studied contemporary prints carefully, the task taking him three years to complete. In 1909 he set off for
London in search of a publisher but failed to find one. However, one
hundred illustrations for the *Satyricon* of Petronius, which he had begun
at Naples with Pompeii at hand, were published in a limited edition, with
text and translation. Lindsay remained in London for fifteen months, and
visited Paris several times. Among the European masters he most admired
Rubens, Delacroix, Manet, Goya, Degas and Turner. But London affected
his health and he returned to Australia, suffering from pleurisy, to accept a
new contract on the *Bulletin*. During his convalescence at Leura in the
Blue Mountains the First World War broke out. For the next four years
Lindsay, sharing the current war fever, produced full-page cartoons for the
Bulletin and hundreds of cartoons for Government war posters. They were
critical years for the artist personally. He separated from his wife and three
sons, Jack, Raymond and Philip, who went to live in Brisbane; his health
was not good; his brother Reginald was killed at the Somme in 1916; and

his sister Ruby, married to his friend, the artist Will Dyson, died from pneumonic influenza in 1918. Lindsay became increasingly critical of war-time patriotism, turned away from the carnage of war and became deeply interested in spiritualism. His thoughts on life and art, which underwent a thorough reappraisal at this time, were published in *Art in Australia* in February 1922, and more fully in *Creative Effort* (1924).

Prior to the First World War, Norman Lindsay's art and thought exercised a stimulating and civilizing effect upon Australian culture. The bent of his genius lay not in formal experiment or formal construction, though technical problems and their solution delighted him; it lay in his use of art as a moral weapon to create an apotheosis of the *élan-vital* he believed in, and to belabour orthodoxy. But the war brought to Sydney forms of art with which Lindsay found himself entirely out of sympathy and, during the post-war years, this *enfant terrible* of Edwardian times was gradually trans-formed into a kind of Australian institution himself. His later work is discussed in a later chapter.[29]

As early as 1903 the great majority of Australia's most talented artists were in London or Paris, and exhibitions in the eastern States were domin-ated by minor artists and semi-amateurs who worked for the most part in a sweet and popular romantic-impressionist manner spiced with *art nouveau* sophistication. In South Australia, however, in the same year, an artist of originality and power returned from studying abroad. Hans Heysen (*b.* 1877) did not confine his art to the limitations imposed by impressionism and *art nouveau*. Although he has himself admitted that Streeton's high-tone landscapes came as a revelation to him (and his work may be seen in more ways than one as a development of Australian impressionism), his mature work differs markedly from the painterly impressions of the Heidel-berg School and the colour poems of Young, Hilder and the later paintings of McCubbin.

Born in Hamburg, Germany, Heysen was brought to Adelaide by his parents at the age of six. Early training at Norwood and the School of Design, Adelaide, was followed by four years abroad, during which he studied at Julian's and the Beaux Arts, and painted in Italy, England and Holland. On his return he married and settled at Hahndorf in the Mount Lofty Ranges, amid a rich and beautiful agricultural country first settled by a community of Evangelical Lutherans who had migrated from Prussian Silesia, to avoid religious persecution, in 1839. His early work such as *The Coming Home* (Sydney, 1904), with its soft evening glow, crepuscular effects and emphasis upon decoration, reveals his link with *art nouveau*. But his response to nature was too deep to be long confined to decorative mannerisms.

From the Hahndorf country Heysen fashioned an image of the Australian landscape which has come to occupy a permanent place in the national imagination, to be the delight of ordinary people and the despair of the sophisticated. Yet his vision was not commonplace. It acquired nobility, as did Constable's, through a lifelong devotion to the countryside of his boyhood. He chose, like the Barbizon painters to whom he was undoubtedly indebted, simple rural themes: haystacks, turkeys, barns, and country work such as ploughing and droving. The magnificent charcoal and chalk drawings which he made of such subjects reveal the power and integrity of his drawing. The eucalypt forests of the Mount Lofty Ranges provided him with a subject he made his own, and a generation of Australians came to see the gum tree as he saw it. This creation of a popular landscape convention was not the achievement of a second-rate painter. But, unfortunately for Heysen's reputation, a tangled scrub of little gum tree painters has grown up around the roots of his achievement to obscure the originality of his own work.

Nowadays dislike of the work of his imitators makes an unprejudiced approach to his work difficult. And so it must be stressed here that Heysen's landscapes have never at any time been 'mere imitations of nature'. They are certainly realistic in their firm, disciplined drawing and love of simple things. But Heysen's vision is cast in a heroic mould. There is baroque magnificence in the amplitude of his scale, something of the plenitude of Rubens in his pastorals, and his gum trees achieve a dimension larger than life (74). At times, indeed, they are almost Piranesian in their grandeur. Heysen was perhaps the only Australian painter of the Edwardian years to handle the big landscape with success, though many attempted it. He continued to explore the problem after Streeton and McCubbin had moved on to other interests, and his achievement, all things considered, was more successful than theirs. Streeton's *Fire's On*, to take an example, for all its excitement of colour and light, retains the quality of a sketch. It is essentially a blown-up impression: informal in composition, swift and broad in handling. The figures in McCubbin's rural genre pieces never quite belong to their setting. There is something of the lamp about them, with their studio poses and literary associations. But Heysen's control of breadth and detail in drawing and of figures in landscape was sure, for he drew more thoroughly than either Streeton or McCubbin upon the figure and landscape tradition of the European masters. The echoes of Turner, Constable and Rubens which recur in his work help to give his large paintings the authority of accumulated knowledge which theirs lack. Occasionally, however, in his large oils, his control of colour values deserts him and areas of flat, uninspired painting appear. Such weaknesses do not appear in his water-colours, a medium which he handled with power, clarity and vigour.

74   HANS HEYSEN, *Red Gold*, canvas, 50 x 67½, 1913, Adelaide

Heysen's vision of Australia was his own, but it was not narrow in range. The country was not for him all sunlit plain nor all melancholy desert. He painted the hot summers, the spring mists, the fruits of autumn, and the dry, dead Centre. One of his finest drawings depicts an approaching storm seen through a bushfire haze (75). It is based upon an effect seen near Hahndorf during the great bushfires of 1912, and it possesses the freshness and authority of an old master. He also painted pastorals drawn from the rich farm-lands of the valleys among the Mount Lofty Ranges. But in 1925 he began to travel north into the desert country; and in his drawings and paintings of such places as the Aroona Valley in the Flinders Range, and Oratunga in the Centre (76), he foreshadowed an interest in the desert landscape to be made much of by Drysdale, Nolan and others in the 1940's.

His comments of his experience of Central Australia, written in 1932, carry a prophetic ring.

The far Northern interior of Australia with its stern reality of desert country holds a peculiar fascination for many who have come under its spell, and I must confess to having fallen a victim. I have seen it at various times over a period of years but always when the country was in the throes of severe drought. Yet those who have lived there longer have told me that there are years when its surface is covered with an abundance of grass and wild-flowers and this desert is converted into a veritable paradise. I have not seen it under these conditions. My experience makes this paradise sound like an impossible dream. . . . Again

75   HANS HEYSEN, *Study for Approaching Storm,* pen and
wash, 22½ x 29½, 1913, the artist

I have seen it on calm days of crystalline purity when the eye could travel, as it were, to the end of the world, bringing with it that wonderful sense of infinity that a land of moist atmosphere could never give. There is an undeniable call about this interior which covers by far the greater portion of Australia, and offers, for the artist, a wide field as yet practically untouched.[30]

And where Heysen pioneered, others followed.[31] Rex Battarbee, for example, whose work and enthusiasm has helped to create a Central Australian group of painters grounded upon Heysen's vision: the most notable painters of the group, apart from Battarbee himself, being Albert Namatjira, and the two brothers, Edwin and Otto Pareroultja.[32]

Nationalism, Taste and Patronage, 1880-1900

The Heidelberg School effected a revolution in Australian taste. Here again Tom Roberts was a leader, though his achievement was equalled in Sydney by Julian Ashton, who became an outstanding champion of the new movement for the recognition of Australian art in its own right. One important aspect of the battle for recognition lay in the struggle for power within the existing art societies. The early art societies owed their existence more to enthusiasts for cultural improvement and well-meaning amateurs than to professional artists. When Roberts returned from overseas in 1885,

76   HANS HEYSEN, *The Land of the Oratunga*, water-colour,
19 x 25, 1932, Adelaide

amateurs were in control of the Victorian Academy of Art, the only important art society in Victoria. Largely due to his leadership, a group of professional artists broke with the Academy and formed the Australian Art
Association. It included Roberts, Streeton, Conder, Mather, Ford Paterson,
W. B. Spong, Percival Ball, Arthur Loureiro and Ugo Catani.

The name of the new society was significant, for it implied the recognition of Australian art in its own right. During the 1870's, exhibitions of
local works were invariably called exhibitions of *colonial* art. The New
South Wales Academy of Art, for example, held annual exhibitions of
colonial art during the 1870's to which local professionals and amateurs
alike contributed. Local taste was determined by a more or less cultured
British-born minority who could not bring themselves, for fear of allowing
their standards to become provincial, to take the work of local artists
seriously. They were not well served, however, by their London advisers.
To take but one example: while Sir Charles Eastlake enriched the National
Gallery of London with many fine early Italian masterpieces, he advised the
Trustees of the National Gallery of Victoria to purchase large paintings
from the Royal Academy Exhibitions of the 1860's and 1870's which
possessed no more than a popular and sentimental appeal and are now
comparatively worthless. He can hardly be blamed, however, for the taste
of Australia's educated minority was more provincial than it knew. It

derived directly from the taste of Victorian England in its more popular aspects. Sentimental and narrative genre, grandiose canvases both in history and landscape deriving from the Munich and Düsseldorf schools, and the melodrama and linear naturalism of the Pre-Raphaelites were the order of the day. These values were filtered through to the Australian colonies by means of newspaper reports of exhibitions of the Royal Academy and the Paris Salons and, to a greater extent, by means of the loan works and reproductions shown at those intercolonial and international exhibitions so frequently held in Australia during the second half of the nineteenth century. Paintings were expected to possess an immediate and popular appeal and were improved by the incorporation, either implicitly or explicitly, of a moral message of some kind. After 1880, the evangelical earnestness and high-mindedness of John Ruskin began to dominate local criticism, and is reflected in the writings of the leading critic of Sydney, James Green (de Libra), and the leading critic of Melbourne, James Smith. It was against their popular Victorian values that Tom Roberts and Julian Ashton rose in order to champion art for its own sake rather than for the sake of morality, *plein-air* and impressionist painting rather than Victorian academic painting, and the right to existence of an independent Australian school of painting.

Julian Ashton became President of the Art Society of New South Wales in 1887. From that time he campaigned vigorously for the recognition of Australian art. In 1888 he made the acquaintance of Sir Henry Parkes, then the Premier of New South Wales for the fourth time. Though decidedly mid-Victorian in his tastes, Parkes was genuinely interested in the arts. Ashton became his friend, painted his portrait in 1889, and gained his support in his campaign for Australian art. At the Annual Dinner of the Art Society in 1888, which Parkes attended, Ashton spoke vigorously to the toast, 'Australian art', and criticized the buying policy of the Trustees of the National Gallery of New South Wales. In the following year Parkes appointed Ashton and Bernhard Wise, his Attorney-General, as Trustees. They were responsible for the purchase of Streeton's *Still Glides the Stream* in 1890. As a result of Ashton's tireless advocacy, the work of the Heidelberg School met with greater favour from the Trustees of the Sydney Gallery than it did from those of the Melbourne Gallery.

Meanwhile, in Victoria, the difference between the professional artists and the Victorian Academy was resolved in 1888, mainly through the efforts of Roberts, Streeton and Conder, the Australian Art Association and the Academy amalgamating to form a new society called the Victorian Artists' Society, which still exists today. A similar disagreement between the professional and lay members of the Art Society of New South Wales took place in 1895, when no professional artists were elected to the Selection Committee for the annual exhibition of that year. Under the leadership of

Roberts (then in Sydney) and Henry Fullwood, a new Society, entirely confined to professional artists, was formed and called the Society of Artists, Roberts being elected its first President. These changes in the art societies of Sydney and Melbourne brought a greater measure of recognition to impressionist and *plein-air* painting.

Roberts, Streeton and Conder all exhibited a lively interest in literature, music and the theatre, and won their first friends and patrons from among people actively interested in these associated arts. The Mannington Caffyns, for example, encouraged Charles Conder and introduced him to their friends. Mrs Caffyn, whose portrait he painted *c.* 1888, encouraged him to lead, as he himself put it, 'a fashionable existence'. Both Dr Caffyn (*b.* 1851), the English physician who migrated to Australia in 1881 and practised at Brighton and South Yarra, and his Irish wife, were writers. He wrote two novels, contributed to the *Bulletin* frequently, and wrote articles for the *Pall Mall Gazette*, under the pseudonym, 'The New Philosopher'. Mrs Caffyn contributed to the local Press and wrote A *Yellow Aster* (1894) in Australia, the character of Charles Brydon, the painter, being modelled on Conder. The Caffyns were interested in social and moral reform. In Mrs Caffyn's books there are frequent contrasts between the 'Victorian' woman and the 'new' woman. When the Charringtons produced a series of plays by Ibsen in 1890, 'the new woman' became a topic of cultivated conversation. Conder and Streeton were friendly with Charles Charrington, and his wife, Miss Janet Achurch, who starred in Ibsen's 'Doll's House'. Conder painted Miss Achurch's portrait, and Roberts presented her with his *Coogee Bay*, the first picture he painted in New South Wales.

One of the earliest, and in some ways the most influential and important, patron of the Heidelberg School was G. W. L. Marshall Hall, the London-born musician, poet, teacher and dramatist, who became the first Ormond Professor of Music in the University of Melbourne in 1890. After ten years of inspired teaching during which he established the Melbourne Conservatorium of Music and exercised a deep and lasting influence upon the intellectual and cultural life of Melbourne, the University Council refused to renew his second five-year term appointment to his chair 'because of his blasphemous and mildly sensual poems and utterances'. He thereupon created his own conservatorium and orchestra, both of which he conducted successfully until 1912. Hall became a friend of Roberts and Streeton and many other artists shortly after his arrival in 1890. He associated closely with painters, and was a frequent visitor to their camps in Sydney and Melbourne. It was at the Curlew camp that he wrote his 'Hymn to Sydney', published in 1897.

Another influential friend and patron was Theodore Fink (1855-1942), the politician and educationalist who was born in the Channel Islands and educated in Australia, qualifying as a solicitor at the University of Melbourne. Fink was interested in journalism and was able to provide the Heidelberg School with influential support at a time when it was most needed, through his association with the *Herald* and *Weekly Times* newspapers, of which he became a director in 1889. A keen Federationist, Fink became closely associated with the Australian Art Association during the brief period (1886-8) of its existence, and usually chaired its 'smoke' nights. He remained a lifelong friend of Roberts and Streeton.

Among other early patrons of the Heidelberg School are to be included Dr Felix Meyer and Dr J. W. Springthorpe, who both became well known for their liberal patronage of art; Carl Pinschof, the Consul-General for Austria, whose hospitality was always extended to representatives of the arts; and Sir Baldwin Spencer (1860-1929), the famous English-born anthropologist, who became Professor of Biology at the University of Melbourne at the age of twenty-seven. Spencer formed one of the first large collections of Australian painting and was one of Streeton's close friends.

In Sydney, one of the most valued patrons of the new Australian school was Eadith Walker, the daughter of Thomas Walker, a public benefactor who had amassed a considerable fortune as a general merchant. Thomas Walker was a member of the first elected Legislative Council of New South Wales; his daughter Eadith was created a Dame of the British Empire for her varied philanthropic activities. In 1898, at the suggestion of Julian Ashton and Bernhard Wise, she covered the cost of sending a representative exhibition of Australian art to London. It contained three hundred and seventy-one works by members of the Heidelberg circle of painters and those grouped about Julian Ashton in the Society of Artists, Sydney. Among the exhibits were such representative paintings as Roberts's *Breakaway*, and *Golden Fleece*; Conder's *Departure of the* s.s. *Orient*; Streeton's *Golden Summer* and *Purple Noon's Transparent Might*; McCubbin's *On the Wallaby Track* and W. C. Piguenit's *Flood in the Darling*. It was shown at the Grafton Gallery and was received not unfavourably by English critics.

It may be said, generally speaking, that during its emergence in the decade between 1885 and 1895, the Heidelberg School found its earliest supporters from an educated minority among the artistic, musical and literary circles of Sydney and Melbourne, and from medical men, academics and some journalists. Born and bred in the cities themselves, the Heidelberg painters gained their first support from an urban intelligentsia. The movement was not, at the beginning, considered by the educated public at large or by art critics as a national movement in art; it was seen rather as a minority expression, an *avant-garde* group. And indeed, that is how the artists, despite their strong national sentiments, tended to regard themselves.

For though Roberts, McCubbin and Streeton certainly sought to paint large canvases redolent with national sentiment, this was only *one* aspect of a varied programme. Success in Paris and London was what they all desired most—but such success, as they were all to find, was not achieved easily. They never embraced nationalism as a desirable end in itself. It was not until the 1920's that the Heidelberg School came to be identified by critics and the informed public alike as a purely national expression in painting. The national element was played up at the expense of the purely artistic element in the works of the School. This distorted interpretation of their work was used both as an excuse and a precedent for the highly nationalistic and isolationist tendencies which developed among many Australian artists during the 1920's and 1930's. In reality a genuine expression of Australian nationhood, launched by men who in youth were curious and open-minded to all forms of contemporary artistic expression which came within their ken, the Heidelberg School and its associated derivatives came to serve the pathological nationalism of the 1920's and 1930's—a nationalism which sought, not without success, to insulate Australian art from contact with artistic expression abroad. Created by city-born artists in a thoroughly urban *milieu*, the Heidelberg School came to be accepted by its friends and its foes alike by the late 1930's as a school which specialized in the creation of an up-country *mystique* based upon the apotheosis of the pastoral industry and the gum tree. It was more than that.

None of the leaders of the Heidelberg School committed themselves to political activity. Indeed, the Australian painters of the time were far less closely associated with the Australian Labor Movement than were the writers. Nevertheless, during the 'eighties and 'nineties it is fairly clear that the sympathies of Ashton, Streeton and Roberts lay with the Labor Movement. Such sympathies are clearly revealed in the comments which Roberts wrote concerning *Shearing the Rams* and Streeton wrote concerning *Fire's On*. Julian Ashton numbered William Lane and J. F. Archibald (a fellow-voyager with Tom Roberts on the s.s. *Lusitania* in 1885[33]) among his friends. Dr Maloney, one of the pioneers of the Socialist Movement in Victoria, was one of Tom Roberts's oldest companions. They toured Spain together in 1883. Quite a large number of black and white artists were brought into direct contact with the Labor Movement through their contributions to the *Bulletin*, J. F. Archibald's great radical and republican weekly, which came to be known as 'the Bushman's Bible'. The *Bulletin* between 1880 and 1900 trained a generation of black and white artists, and its regular contributors included Phil May, Frank Mahony, George Lambert, B. E. Minns, Norman Lindsay, Lionel Lindsay, David Low, Will Dyson and many others.

The association of artists and the Labor Movement rested mainly upon broad humanitarian sympathies rather than economic ties. In the years following the economic collapse of 1893 it is possible to trace a certain change of heart and attitude in Roberts's relation to the Labor Movement, and of the artists whose attitudes he influenced. His series of large history paintings of pastoral life came to an end with his *Mountain Muster* (H. O. Vary) painted in 1898. These paintings were essentially gallery paintings and were painted in the hope that they would be purchased by public galleries in Australia. But however well they expressed the Australian *ethos*, they were not easy paintings to sell. Roberts, always a realist, acknowledged that it was desirable that artists should be upon friendly and easy terms with the people from whom they expected support. This side of Roberts was vividly described by D. H. Souter, the brilliant artist and journalist who drew for the *Bulletin* for over thirty-five years.

Tom Roberts had everything. Chief among his sartorial possessions were a crush hat and a dress cape lined with red satin. Neither was new when he brought them to Australia, and they were still serviceable when he took them to England in the early years of the Commonwealth. He was our sole Society Bohemian and wore his crush hat and red cape with more dignity than many a king wore his coronation robe and crown.

He represented the successful artist with the entrée to Government House, and was on the dining list of most people who had over a couple of thousand a year. Before he came we never dreamt of calling on Royalty's representative. We set no store on State levées or gubernatorial garden parties. We possessed no society clothes and were criminally indifferent to the nice distinctions or the etiquette of social functions. Tom Roberts showed us the error of all that: 'There is no occasion, dear boy', said he, 'for an artist to be a boor. A man may be able to paint decently well and also know how to comport himself in good society. Besides, you don't usually sell your stuff to people who rent cottages at seventeen and six a week: Business, my dear boy, business.'

So under the shadow of his tutelary wing we learned to shake Governors-General and State Governors by the hand as if to the manor born; exchange small talk with diamonded dames, and sip champagne and crack jokes with quite a lot of titled personages from Dukes to C.M.G.'s, and form ourselves into a select cult where brains were the only qualification and bluff was a goodly proportion of the entrance fee.[34]

Tom Roberts married in 1896 and during the last years of the century was engaged largely upon portrait painting. At this time he painted portraits of Sir Henry Parkes, Viscount Hampden (the Governor of New South Wales, 1895-9) and Earl Beauchamp (the Governor of New South Wales, 1899-1901). He had long been intending to return to England on a second visit and held a farewell one-man show with that intention in 1900. He was persuaded, however, to accept the commission to paint a picture commemorating the Opening of the First Commonwealth Parliament by the Duke of Cornwall and York in the Exhibition Building, Melbourne, in January 1901. The huge painting (77), which took him two years to com-

77   TOM ROBERTS, Oil sketch for his *Opening of the First
Commonwealth Parliament*, canvas, 12 x 18, *c.* 1901, N.L.A.

plete, was presented to King Edward VII, and hung for many years in
St James's Palace, London. In order to complete his picture Roberts painted
portraits from life of all the most distinguished personages concerned in the
ceremony.

'The Big Picture', as it came to be called, was a turning-point in Roberts's
career. In the fifteen years between his return from Europe in 1885 and
1900 he had been responsible to a greater extent than any other artist for
bringing an independent Australian school of painting into existence. In
his own work he had achieved distinction in painting both rural and urban
landscapes; he had made a reputation second to none in the country in
portraiture; and he had painted the most memorable history paintings of
Australian rural life. His personal influence upon his fellow artists had been
profound. Streeton, Conder and McCubbin all spoke of their great indebtedness to him. He had played a leading and creative role in the politics of the
art societies. In every way he had been a natural leader and a creative artist
in his own right.

'The Big Picture' has sometimes been looked upon as a most unfortunate
aberration in the middle of his career, from which his art never fully
recovered. Yet in one sense the painting is a summing-up of earlier work,
and may fairly be seen as the last of those national and historical paintings
which he began with *The Breakaway* in 1889, in which he sought to embody

what was most characteristic of Australian life. Present himself at the opening of the First Parliament, he responded deeply to this historic movement in the history of his adopted country. And the painting itself represented a personal triumph. 'So it came about', he wrote in a private memoir for his son, 'that this painter came into touch with some of the great ones of the earth, and the incongruity of it was the thought of the early days in Australia, and the poverty and hard times for us . . .'[35] Others, like N. Graves B. Jefferson, who represented the entrepreneurs who commissioned the painting, felt that it would bring him both success and honour. 'Roberts', wrote Jefferson, 'has been brought closely into touch with the Royal Family and the whole of the representative men of Australia and of foreign countries. Under all these circumstances, it is doubtful whether Tom Roberts will ever have to look back, and good luck to him.'[36] His own artist friends, however, were not so confident. '. . . there is a feeling with others and with me', wrote Streeton from London in 1902, 'that you are putting too much time into your big gem of the Opening . . .'[37] Conder was less complimentary: 'I hope the big machine will be a success, but it must be an awful job to do. I should think "Parliamentary Coves" are usually so beastly ugly.'[38]

Early in 1903 Roberts left for England in order to complete 'the Big Picture' in London.

FOOTNOTES

[1] *Argus* (Melbourne), 7 September 1886

[2] On Conder *see* FRANK GIBSON, *Charles Conder, His Life and Work*, London, 1909; JOHN ROTHENSTEIN, *The Life and Death of Conder*, London, 1938; URSULA HOFF, *Charles Conder: His Australian Years*, Melbourne, 1960

[3] On Nerli *see* MOORE, ii, 210, *passim*

[4] Conder to Roberts, 13 February 1891, *Smike to Bulldog*, Sydney, 1946, pp. 133-4

[5] JAMES GREEN, 'Imperfect Finish in Australian Painting', *Australasian Builders' and Contractors' News*, 29 November 1890, vii, 401

[6] *Smike to Bulldog*, p. 40

[7] op. cit., pp. 63-4

[8] ADA CAMBRIDGE, op. cit., p. 172

[9] HENRY LAWSON, 'Shearers', *Poetical Works*, Sydney, 1944, pp. 168-70

[10] R. WARD, *The Australian Legend*, Melbourne, 1958, p. 196

[11] LIONEL LINDSAY, 'Twenty-five Years of Australian Art', *AA*, ser. i, no. 4; quoted by U. HOFF, *Meanjin*, xv (1956), 302

[12] The *Melbourne University Review*, 27 September 1884

[13] U. HOFF, 'The Phases of McCubbin's Art', *Meanjin*, xv (1956), 304

[14] The *Age*, 19 January 1886; quoted by V. Spate, thesis cited

[15] R. H. CROLL, *Tom Roberts*, Melbourne, 1935, p. 340

[16] *Smike to Bulldog*, pp. 21, 23

[17] Streeton to Roberts, c. 1890; *Smike to Bulldog*, pp. 14-15

[18] HAVELOCK ELLIS, *My Life*, London, 1940, p. 139

[19] HAVELOCK ELLIS, *Kanga Creek*, Waltham St Lawrence, 1922, p. 53

[20] J. LE GAY BRERETON, *Landlopers*, Sydney, 1899, p. 25

[21] DE LIBRA (JAMES GREEN), 'The Poetry of our Painting', *Australasian Arts Review*, 1 September 1899, pp. 1, 2

[22] *The Verse of Christopher Brennan* (ed. A. R. Chisholm and J. J. Quinn), Sydney, 1960, p. 112

[23] SID LONG, 'The Trend of Australian Art Considered and Discussed', *Art and Architecture*, ii (1905), 8-10

[24] For several points made in this paragraph I am indebted to E. Thacker, 'Art Nouveau in Australia'; B.A. Thesis, 1961, School of Fine Arts, University of Melbourne.

[25] On Young *see also* J. F. BRUCE, *The Art of Blamire Young*, Sydney, 1921; MOORE, ii, 234, *passim*

[26] On McCubbin *see also The Work of Frederick McCubbin*, Melbourne, 1916; U. HOFF, 'The Phases of McCubbin's Art', *Meanjin*, xv (1956), 301-6; MOORE, various refs.; CAO, p. 137

[27] *See The Art of J. J. Hilder*, Sydney, 1918

[28] *See also Elioth Gruner* (Foreword by N. Lindsay), Sydney [n.d.]; CAO, pp. 79-80

[29] The literature on Norman Lindsay is extensive; two useful sources of biographical information are: *Norman Lindsay's Pen Drawings* (introd. by Lionel Lindsay), Sydney, 1931; *Norman Lindsay Water Colour Book* (with a biog. by Edmund Blunden), Sydney, 1939.

[30] AA, iii, 44 (1932), 19-20

[31] On Heysen *see* various references in CAO, pp. 90-1

[32] *See also* T. G. H. STREHLOW, *Rex Battarbee*, Sydney, 1956; C. P. MOUNTFORD, *The Art of Albert Namatjira*, Melbourne, 1944; and R. BATTARBEE, *Modern Australian Aboriginal Art*, Sydney, 1951

[33] I am indebted to Sylvia Lawson, who is preparing a biography of Archibald, for this point.

[34] Quoted by CROLL, pp. 40-1

[35] op. cit., p. 63

[36] op. cit., p. 60-1

[37] Streeton to Roberts, 7 August 1902; quoted by CROLL, p. 203

[38] *Smike to Bulldog*, p. 137

78 CHARLES CONDER, *Cove on the Hawkesbury*,
panel, 14 x 8¼, c. 1888, Melbourne

CHAPTER FIVE

EXODUS
1881 - 1919

His body dwells on Gander Flat,
His soul's in Italy.
VICTOR DALEY, *Correggio Jones*, 1898

ARTISTS as a distinct social group in the Australian community came into existence during the 1880's. Previously they had worked in isolation from one another and did not distinguish themselves in their manner of living and their social attitudes from the public in general. Indeed, artists like Conrad Martens, W. C. Piguenit, Robert Dowling and William Strutt were highly respected members of the colonial society, and helped to define rather than to criticize Victorian values in Australia. But as young men Roberts, Streeton and Conder, to name only three, differed considerably in their manner of living and personal values from the community at large. The camps established around Melbourne helped to underline this separation of the artist from the community. For the Heidelberg impressionists, as for their contemporaries in France and England, art became a way of life. If in such a painting as *Shearing the Rams* Roberts sought to hold up the mirror to Australian life, it must not be forgotten that he was also in one sense the Australian champion of *l'art pour l'art*.

The revolt of the artists was both timely and essential, for even the most intelligent and educated of the public looked upon art at best as little more than an elegant and polite accomplishment. When, in 1889, Conder's cousin and first love, Margaret Conder, described his art as his hobby, he gently reprimanded her:

. . . you must know that it is more than that, for a hobby is a fad which a man takes up probably to kill time. Unless it were more than a hobby to me I could never hope to do what I hope to. You are rather like my father in your way of looking at art—you don't feel it quite I fancy as many do—almost a religion it is to them and duffers like myself unless we regarded it as such would soon lose heart in it.[1]

Margaret Conder's attitude was one which generally confronted the local artist. It was criticized trenchantly by Sydney Dickinson in 1891:

In painting, as in other refinements, Australian opinion has not emerged from the embryonic condition wherein it is regarded as a light and graceful recreation which, when cultivated in a spirit of dilettantism, may evoke a languid interest, and give to ladies an opportunity to enjoy afternoon tea amongst attractive surroundings. Art for art's sake is an idea that finds little occasion for lodgement in the chinks of our busy day of money-getting; those who practise the cult are asked to amuse merely, and anyone who invades the sleepy circle of decorous self-satisfaction with an original idea, is viewed askance, and with the suspicion of lifted eyebrows. Such criticism as we have is judiciously tempered to these conditions. It babbles gently of commonplaces, and sets forth with an air of originality opinions which have begun long since to grow stale on the other side of the globe.[2]

The more serious artists sought to insulate themselves, so far as they could, from such philistinism. They rebelled against the conventional teaching of G. F. Folingsby at the National Gallery School; they foregathered in painting camps, in favourite pubs and cafes, like Fasoli's and the Maison Dorée in Lonsdale Street; and sought the company of writers, musicians and actors. During the 1880's, those who espoused the Bohemian life supported themselves more or less precariously in various ways. Some painted portraits, others provided drawings for the illustrated Press which flourished splendidly in those years, or were employed as lithographers, like Streeton, or as photographer's assistants, like Roberts. But with the onset of the economic crisis of 1893, the life of the Australian artist became increasingly precarious. 'There was a strange sense of unreality about the art life of those days,' said Harry Weston. 'It was after the land boom had burst; and on the rare occasion you received a cheque, you rushed to the bank, feeling certain that it would be stopped. Living, however, was wonderfully cheap . . .'.[3]

The art life of Melbourne at this time has been described graphically by William Moore:

These bohemians were full of life and their ebullitions often startled the other customers. It was Ernest Moffitt who discovered Fasoli's in Lonsdale Street, whose interior had the rude simplicity of an old-time inn. The dinner, with wine *ad lib*, and *café noir*, cost a shilling. Work was difficult to get, and a frequent change of residence became a necessity. . . . Most of them had read about Bohemian life in Paris, and life's little difficulties never flurried them. The cares of the week were forgotten at the free and easies on Saturday nights, when enough was thrown into the hat to ensure an adequate supply of bread and cheese, and beer. At these functions they were joined by well-known musicians, journalists, and connoisseurs. . . .[4]

The Melbourne Bohemians foregathered in such clubs as the Cannibal Club and the Ishmael Club, both formed about 1893, the year of the collapse of the boom. The Cannibal Club was formed by a sociable and convivial spirit called Leon (Sonny) Pole, and included artists, poets and musicians. The

J

members of the club included Percy and Norman Lindsay, Max Meldrum, Will Dyson and Miles Evergood among the artists; Hugh McCrae, the poet; and Hermann Kühr, the Viennese French-horn player in the Marshall Hall orchestra.

The small Melbourne art market for original paintings barely survived the depression of the 1890's. As late as 1905 Moore wrote: 'The encouragement of art in Melbourne is practically non-existent.'[5] In the event, neglect was seen as an attribute of genius. Had not all the great artists starved in their day? Was it not true that a great artist was a man who could not sell his work during his lifetime? 'Therefore,' said D. H. Souter, 'to accuse an artist of painting pictures which the public really buys during his lifetime, is to place an ineradicable blot upon his escutcheon.'[6] And Norman Lindsay has stated that during his early life he became so accustomed to the public not buying or even wanting to buy pictures, that it became very difficult to alter his original impression that the public was not interested in art.

It is not surprising that local indifference encouraged most artists with outstanding talent to leave the country for England and the Continent. There were only two chapters in the life of a Victorian artist according to Moore—'Genesis and Exodus'. 'No wonder there are so few of them left,' he complained in 1905.[7] But the reasons for the wholesale departure of artists from Australia at the turn of the century springs, of course, from deeper reasons than public indifference.

The fact of the matter was that Paris and London were looked upon as the only cities in which an artist could hope to complete his professional training. To be exhibited upon the line at the Annual Exhibition of the Royal Academy, London, or to receive a *mention honorable* at the Old Salon (Société des Artistes Français) became the ambition of the art students of Melbourne and Sydney. This is not at all surprising, for the art world of Australia contained a large proportion of European-trained or European-born artists. The art schools were staffed almost entirely by teachers born and trained in Europe. Since its inception in 1870, the head of the Gallery School in Melbourne had received a continental training. Eugène von Guérard was trained at Düsseldorf; G. F. Folingsby, his successor, at Munich; and Lindsay Bernard Hall, who succeeded Folingsby in 1892, had been trained at the Royal College of Art, South Kensington, at Antwerp and at Munich, and was an original member of the New English Art Club, the society which pioneered the reception of impressionism in England. Phillips Fox, an Australian, and Tudor St George Tucker, an Englishman, had both studied at the Ecole des Beaux Arts prior to opening their own Melbourne Art School in 1893. In Sydney, the Academy of Art of New South Wales established an art school in 1875. Its two instructors, Giulio Anivitti (1850-81), a painter, and Achille Simonetti, a sculptor, were both Italians trained in the Accademia di S. Luca, Rome. Lucien Henry became instructor at the Mechanics School of Art, Sydney, in 1881. He was a Provençal who had studied under Viollet-le-Duc and at the Beaux Arts. He was transported to New Caledonia for the active part he played in the Paris Commune and settled in Sydney following his release. Julian Ashton, who became instructor of the classes of the Art Society of New South Wales in 1892, and four years later established his own Sydney Art School, had been trained both in London and Paris. It was natural for such people to stress the importance of overseas study.

The emergence of the Australian school of painting is closely paralleled, therefore, during the 1880's by the movement of artists and art students to Europe in order to work and study. Most of them went, naturally enough, to Paris and London. It is true, of course, that isolated cases of students leaving Australia for study overseas do occur from the later 1850's onwards. The work overseas, for instance, of Adelaide Ironside and Robert Dowling, has already been discussed. But overseas training does not emerge as a persisting trend in Australian art until the 1880's. From that time forward it has continued to exercise a continuous influence upon the course of Australian art.

The artists who left Australia to study in Europe between 1880 and 1914 may be divided into two groups. There were, firstly, those who, like Roberts on his first sojourn overseas (1881-5), remained only a few years abroad and made no attempt to exhibit and become known in French and English art circles during their stay. Secondly, there were those who, like Roberts on his second sojourn overseas (1903-19), remained long enough to attempt with greater or lesser success to identify their work and life with the art and life of France or England. The work of the first group, of course, lies entirely within the field of Australian art. But the work of the second group involves a problem both historical and psychological in its implications. For these people became *expatriate* artists. In their desire to find a place in the art world of Europe lay a respect for European tradition and a desire to measure themselves against the most widely accepted standards of the day.

Expatriation, however, involved a withdrawal from direct participation in Australian art and a break, more or less, with their Australian connections. But the break was rarely complete. For expatriate artists tend to return to the scenes of their childhood and adolescence either in the flesh or in the imagination. The break was not complete even in the case of Charles Conder, the one artist on record who, after beginning his career in Australia, succeeded in making a genuine contribution to European art, even though a minor one. Conder retained his connexions with his Australian friends, especially Roberts, intermittent though it was in his later years. But Australia held him, as we shall see, in a more fundamental way. And it is precisely because the expatriate's break tends to remain a partial rather than a complete one that his work retains an importance for the art of his homeland. During the period between 1880 and 1914 (with which we are here directly concerned), expatriate artists maintained a connexion with Australia in various ways. Correspondence with artist friends remaining in Australia created a new and more personal channel by means of which knowledge of current developments in Europe became known to local art circles. Expatriates often sent work back for exhibition; some revisited Australia for short periods for the purpose of holding exhibitions of their work. Finally, most of them after remaining abroad for periods of between ten and forty-five years, returned to Australia permanently, where they exercised an effect upon local art which was often considerable, and was at times of decisive importance for the development of Australian art.

Of the more important artists who departed for Europe during the period between 1880 and 1900, Tom Roberts, C. Douglas Richardson and John Russell left in 1881, Bertram Mackennal, the sculptor, in 1883, Rupert Bunny in 1884, Phillips Fox and Walter Withers in 1887, John Longstaff in 1888, Charles Conder in 1890, James Quinn in 1893, George Coates in 1896, David Davies in 1897, Arthur Streeton in 1898, Hugh Ramsay, Max Meldrum and George Lambert in 1899. Already by 1895 the *Argus* in an editorial was beginning to criticize the practice of awarding overseas scholarships to the outstanding students of the National Gallery of Victoria. 'There can be no doubt that an Australian school is in process of birth. A certain indefinable something runs through the work of Messrs McCubbin and Streeton, Roberts, Withers and Paterson which marks them of the same class of inspiration . . .'. But, the editorial lamented, the Trustees (who awarded the scholarship), 'take away those who have shown their competency to join and lead this school and they send them to Paris to swell the ranks of a huge army who hope by tricks of technique or laborious skill to put new life into out-worn subjects. . . . Thus we observe that our own men who have never left us are each in their own individual manner recording their impressions of nature and humanity as they appear in Australia, while the men sent away . . . become stronger but less original; desert simplicity for mythology . . .'.[8] By 1900, the departure of artists from Australia was so frequent as to attract wide attention. It became a source of some resentment to artists and writers who either preferred to remain in Australia or could not afford to travel. In 'London Calls',[9] Victor Daley (the talented Irish-born poet and champion of national aspirations) criticized this wholesale desertion by painters (and writers) of their own country for what he considered to be nothing more than the flesh-pots of European culture:

> They leave us—artists, singers all—
> When London calls aloud,
> Commanding to her Festival
> The gifted crowd.

And in 'Correggio Jones',[10] another fine satirical poem, Daley created the comic figure of a potential expatriate painter:

> Correggio Jones an artist was
> Of pure Australian race,
> But native subjects scorned because
> They were too commonplace.

and ended his poem with an apt comment on Jones's distressing situation:

> He yet is painting at full bat—
> You'll say, if him you see,
> 'His body dwells on Gander Flat,
> His soul's in Italy.'

That was one way of viewing the situation. But it was not the only way. Australia, as we have already seen, was paying less attention to its artists than to its writers. For most Australians, art was a dubious luxury they could not afford. It was widely suspect as a form of cultivated affectation. The young Australian society of the 1890's was neither rich enough, nor populous enough, nor educated enough to support the fine arts. Closely associated with the desire to leave the country was the growing realization on the part of local artists that the very existence of art had always depended upon the existence of a privileged class. . . . you don't as a rule sell your pictures,' remarked Tom Roberts, 'to people who rent cottages at seventeen-and-six a week.'[11] But the values of Australian society were determined largely by people who did. 'The rich an' educated', wrote Henry Lawson in 1893, 'shall be educated down.'[12] That was no programme for art or artists. It is not surprising that they left the country in large numbers.

A rich and educated Australian became our first important expatriate artist. He was John Russell, the friend and companion of Tom Roberts during his first visit to Europe. Russell, however, had nothing in common with the comic image which Victor Daley created in the person of Correggio Jones. Had Australian artists been able to follow the artistic interests of Russell they would have made contact with the *Ecole de Paris* half a century before they did, and the rich promise so evident in the early work of the Heidelberg School might have flowered magnificently. But as it happened, Russell died unknown in his own country.

Russell, who was born at Darlinghurst, Sydney, in 1858, was the son of John Russell and the grandson of Robert Russell, an ironmaster and engineer of Kirkaldy, Scotland, who had migrated to Hobart in 1832. The business was later transferred to Sydney and carried on by his sons. It flourished for many years and built railways, bridges and ships, including gunboats for the Maori wars of the 1860's. As a young man, Russell discovered a passion for drawing while sailing in the Pacific where the family had many business interests. At the age of eighteen, he visited England to study engineering, and there his interest in art grew. Returning from England three years later on the death of his father, he set up a studio in Sydney and began to paint portraits. Realizing, however, that overseas study was essential, he set off for England in 1881, travelling, it is said, on the same boat as Tom Roberts. Russell settled in Paris and in 1886, seeking at this time to learn more about the methods of Puvis de Chavannes and Fernand Cormon, entered the latter's studio as a student. At the Atelier Cormon he met several brilliant young artists who were at that time engaged upon staging a full-scale revolt against the methods of their master and who were to play, in the years immediately following 1886, an important role in the creation of modern art.

There was Toulouse-Lautrec, the creator of the French *art nouveau* poster whose portrayals of the night-life of the Montmartre cafés are among the masterpieces of French post-impressionist painting; and there was Louis Anquetin, a tall, studious artist who was among the first followers of Seurat in his *pointilliste* experiments. Seurat was, at that time, developing a technique of painting by means of small dots juxtaposed upon the canvas in order to create a mixture of colour in the eye of the observer. This technique sought, by scientific means derived from colour theorists like Chevreul, to preserve the brilliant colours of nature by avoiding the mixture of colours upon the palette prior to painting. In 1886 Seurat was working on his masterpiece, *La Grande Jatte*. Anquetin began to champion *pointilliste* methods among the students at Cormon's, and Emile Bernard, the youngest student at the school but also one of the most brilliant, became his ardent disciple. Russell became a member of the Anquetin-Bernard set as did Vincent Van Gogh, who had also become a student at the school, on his brother Theo's advice, shortly after his arrival in Paris in February 1886.

Thus, in 1886, the year Tom Roberts and Frederick McCubbin were beginning their first essays in Australian impressionism at Box Hill, John Russell was establishing himself among the circle of Parisian painters who were pioneering the break from impressionism, and laying the foundations of modern art. He rented a studio for himself in the Impasse Hélène, in the Clichy quarter, which had become the centre of the *pointilliste* experiments. Cormon's was a select studio containing only thirty to thirty-five students, mostly French; American and English being rarely admitted. A. S. Hartrick, an English painter who gained entrance to Cormon's with Russell's help, describes him in 1886 as 'a big Australian who had become notable among art students in Paris by his athletic prowess in a boxing circle he had formed'.[13]

Fernand Cormon was an academic history painter and was considered an arch-reactionary by the Anquetin-Bernard circle. He was strongly opposed to their experiments. Tension ran high, and when he attempted to dismiss Bernard for painting in the new manner pandemonium broke out in the school. Van Gogh went home to fetch his revolver, threatening to shoot Cormon. The master made off and the school was closed for several months.

About that time Russell met Mariana Antoinetta Matiocco, a young Italian whom Rodin claimed was the most beautiful woman in France. She read extracts from Dante's *Inferno* to him as she posed (1885) for his *Porte de l'Enfer*. Her face reappeared in his *La France* and his *Minerve sans Casque*. She also modelled for Fremiet's *Jeanne d'Arc*, now in the Place des Pyramides. Russell, himself, was at this time developing a select circle of friends among artists in Paris which included Fantin Latour; Guillaumin, the friend and pupil of Camille Pissarro; Paul Gauguin, whom Russell met shortly after Gauguin's return from Martinique in the winter of 1887; Alexander Reid, a Scottish painter greatly interested in the work of Monticelli; Dodge McKnight (*b*. 1860), an American painter; and Fabian de Castro (*b*. 1868), a Spanish painter.

Russell's friendship with Van Gogh lasted for several years. The Dutch painter was a frequent visitor to his studio in 1886 and about this time Russell painted the portrait of Van Gogh now in the Stedelijk Museum, Amsterdam; it was Van Gogh's favourite portrait of himself (79). Then in the winter of 1887 Russell left Paris for Sicily with his wife and baby son and painted landscapes there until the end of the spring. Van Gogh saw these paintings when Russell returned to Paris and they may have contributed to his own decision to leave for the south of France in 1888. Writing to Russell from Arles in the spring of 1888, he recalls them: 'I remain enraptured with the scenery here; am working at a series of blooming orchards. And unvoluntarily I thought often of you because you did the same in Sicily.'[14] He suggests that they exchange work—one of his Arles orchards for one of Russell's Sicilian studies, and continues:

You know I thought and think such a deal of those of yours I don't gainsay that your portraits are more serious and higher art but I think it meritory in you and a rare quality that together with a perfection as appeared to me the Fabian and McKnight portraits you are at the same time able to give a Scherzo the adagio con expressione the gay note in one word together with more manly conceptions of a higher order. And I so heartily hope that you will continue to give us simultanément both the grave and elaborate works and those aforesaid scherzos. Then let them say if they like that you are *not always* serious or that you *have* done work *of a lighter sort*—so much the worse for the critics and the better for you.[15]

This was praise indeed from a man like Van Gogh who always spoke his mind so frankly that he experienced the greatest difficulty in maintaining friendships. Russell agreed to send Van Gogh some of his Sicilian drawings and later received some of Van Gogh's finest Arlesian drawings, including *Le Zouave Milliet*, *Paysage d'Arles* and *Barques aux Saintes-Maries*.

Van Gogh, it is to be noted, wrote to Russell as a painter and as an equal giving full vent to his great enthusiasm for the paintings of Monticelli (gained in part from his conversations with Alexander Reid) and discussing the way in which the neo-impressionist techniques might be applied to paintings in the south.

Surely Monticelli gives us not neither pretends to give us local colour or even local truth. But gives us something passionate and eternal—the rich colour and rich sun of the glorious South in a true colourists way parralel [sic] with Delacroix' conception of the South viz. that the South he represented now by contraste simultané of colours and their derivations and harmonies and not by forms or lines in themselves as the ancient artists did. . . .

In another letter he again speaks of the paintings he is working on:

I have been to the seaside for a week and very likely am going thither again soon. Flat shore sands—fine figures there like Cimabue—straight stylish. Am working at a Sower. The great field *all violet*, the sky and sun very yellow, it is a hard subject to treat. Please remember me very kindly to Mrs Russell—and in thought I heartily shake hands.[16]

Shortly after his return from Sicily in 1887, Russell built a fine house at Belle Ile, Brittany and, in the following years, he invited many of his artist friends there. It became known as the Englishman's castle. It was at Belle Ile that Russell met Claude Monet and a long friendship developed between the two men. It was while staying with Russell that Monet painted the portrait of Hippolyte Guillaume, who was a general handyman and model in the Russell household. Like Van Gogh, Monet had a high opinion of Russell's art, considering some of his landscapes superior to his own. Matisse met John Russell at Belle Ile in 1897. He was then a young artist still painting in a rather conventional manner in the studio of Gustave Moreau. According to his biographer, Alfred H. Barr, it was Matisse's two visits to Brittany in the summers of 1896 and 1897 which set him on the path towards becoming a leader of modern painting. While Matisse was in Brittany, Russell gave him two drawings by Van Gogh. 'His first acquisition of work', writes Barr, 'by a martyr of modern painting.'[17] It seems that Russell played a part in the growth of Matisse's appreciation of modern art. The Russells made many friends among some of the most famous artists of the day, including Sargent and Alfred Sisley, the impressionist. Rodin was also a great friend, and the sculptor held a high opinion of Russell's work.

79 JOHN RUSSELL, *Portrait of Van Gogh*, canvas,
23¾ x 17¾, *c.* 1886, Stedelijk Museum, Amsterdam

Although Russell numbered among his associates some of the most revolutionary artists of France, his own work tended to combine an interest in neo-impressionist techniques with the more traditional approach of a portrait painter. This is especially true of his fine head of Van Gogh. Russell's portrait of Dr William Maloney (86), with whom he toured Spain in 1883, is dated 1887 and reveals the high palette and divisionist technique which the students at Cormon's were then developing under the influence of Anquetin and Bernard. It is, with its light pink and blue tones, a fine sensitive portrait, vibrant with life and full of feeling.

Russell did not entirely lose contact with Australia. He continued, for instance, to correspond with Roberts after the latter's return to Melbourne. It would be interesting to know whether he ever mentioned the neo-impressionist experiments at Cormon's in the years between 1886 and

1889 when the Heidelberg School was coming into existence. That he did indeed discuss painting techniques in his letters to Roberts is clearly suggested in a letter which Streeton wrote to Roberts in 1896. Streeton thanks Roberts for letting him read a letter from Russell, and continues: 'He seems to love the open air very much, and, therefore, must be a fine chap. . . . But he does seem to me to bother too much about the ways and means—really there's not time enough to do that.'[18] Streeton's distrust of theory is here apparent. That he did not employ divisionism in his own work may well have been due not so much to ignorance as to a dislike of methods based on theories. If, however, Streeton disliked the methods Russell had embraced, Russell disliked the lack of interest in art in Australia. 'J. P. Russell, my Australian friend in Paris, told me there was no appreciation of painting there,' wrote Hartrick, 'for its inhabitants were at that stage of culture when thirty shillings would be considered a good price for a portrait; therefore he decided not to return to his native land, but abide in France.'[19]

There were doubtless other reasons why Russell remained in France. He had made many friends, he had married, and he possessed a private income of £3,000 a year. Hartrick tells us too that he had quarrelled with his people in Australia. Yet Russell maintained an interest in his own country. It is clear from his letters that he was contemplating the formation of a collection of contemporary painting to improve taste in Australia, and also advocated, later in life, the formation of a national museum. The idea was already present in his mind as early as 1890, for in January of that year Van Gogh wrote to him from the asylum of St Rémy: 'If ever you come to Paris take one of my canvases from my brother's place if you like, if you go on with the intention of making a collection one day for your country. You will remember that I have already told you that it is my ardent wish to give you one with this end in view.'[20] Russell also seems to have toyed with the idea of lecturing on modern art. But nothing came of these plans.

Russell's wife died before the First World War. He sold the house at Belle Ile, moved to Neuilly, and then to Portofino on the Italian Riviera. Later he moved to England. Then a return to Paris was followed by visits to the Côte d'Azur, Switzerland and Italy. At that time he made some experiments with cubist painting. Then, after the First World War, Russell returned to Australia to establish a home for his second wife, an American; and to settle another son by his first marriage on a farm in New Zealand. Finally, he bought a small house at Watson's Bay, Sydney, and lived there quietly until his death at the age of seventy-three in 1931.[21]

John Russell was the first Australian expatriate artist to live in Paris, and his presence there formed a point of contact for other Australians coming over to study during the 1880's. One of the first to come was Bertram

Mackennal, who left Melbourne in 1883, two years after Roberts and Russell, and he shared a studio in London with Roberts for a time while attending the Royal Academy Schools. Mackennal appears to have become a friend of Russell's even before his visit to Paris in 1884.

In 1888, John Longstaff and his young wife arrived in Paris, after he had won the first travelling scholarship awarded by the National Gallery of Victoria in 1887. Russell had been informed of their coming and booked them in at the Hôtel de l'Univers et du Portugal in the Rue Croix des Petits Champs. This hotel in the late 1880's became one of the small centres at which Australian artists in Paris forgathered. A night or so after the Long-staffs arrived in Paris, Russell had them to dinner with Rodin and his wife, and it was arranged that Longstaff should enrol at Cormon's. There Longstaff met Anquetin and Toulouse-Lautrec, as Russell had done before him. But Longstaff, a conservative at heart and a man who surrendered rather quickly to the chance of academic success, never allowed himself to become too much involved in *avant-garde* experiments. He did, however, make some experiments with impressionism. Not long after they had settled in Paris an epidemic of black influenza broke out and Russell invited the Longstaffs to stay with him at Belle Ile. There Longstaff was able to watch Russell at work on his large impressionist paintings, and painted a number of land-scapes in the impressionist manner himself (92). But the interest did not last. At Belle Ile he painted a number of sunrise studies. On showing one to student friends in Paris, they remarked, 'What a splendid sunset'. There-upon he wrote to Russell: 'After this I paint any dawns I have to paint comfortably at the end of the day instead of the beginning'.[22] He was, however, keenly interested in the visual effects of moonlight (a Pre-Raphaelite rather than an impressionist preoccupation). During his sum-mer holiday at Yport on the Normandy coast in the year following the Belle Ile visit he would rise at two in the morning to watch a late moon rising; and upon one occasion he employed a fisherman to accompany him in order to note the effect of moonlight upon flesh. The knowledge so gained from these studies was used in painting his huge, melodramatic composition *The Sirens* (80), which he exhibited with success at the Salon of 1892 and the Royal Academy of 1893.

Despite the fact that this painting is a typical example of the pseudo-classical manner favoured by French academic artists at that time, it also reasserted those literary tendencies which Longstaff had first expressed in his scholarship-winning picture, *Breaking the News* (Perth) of 1887. Anecdotal, scrupulously faithful to detail in the manner of the Munich school, which Longstaff had derived from his teacher, Folingsby, that paint-ing revealed both his technical dexterity and artistic limitations. It gained far greater popularity at its first showing than any of Roberts's or Mc-

80   JOHN LONGSTAFF, *The Sirens,*
canvas, 118⅞ x 82⅜, 1892, Melbourne

Cubbin's essays in Australian genre. That painting and *The Sirens* indicated
the direction Longstaff's career was to take. A gentle, uncomplicated man
with a sentimentally romantic nature and some talent for drawing, Longstaff was, to all accounts, greatly handicapped by an extremely beautiful
but diffident wife whose personal values were even more banausic than
his own. In Paris she locked herself up in her hotel, refused to learn French,
or entertain Longstaff's student friends. In consequence she found the
French and French life most distasteful. After three years of it, Topsy (as
Longstaff called her), with one son and another on the way, left for home
with an aunt. Longstaff remained in Paris another three years and then
in 1894 moved to London. There he discarded the picturesque clothing of
the Paris art student, discovered a new interest in sartorial decorum, and
began to move in respectable circles. He became a friend of J. J. Shannon,
an American painter well known at the time for his portraits of fashionable
women. Sir Frederick Leighton, the President of the Royal Academy,
invited him to his studio; he became a friend of Frank Brangwyn; and the
Earl of Shaftesbury invited him to dinner. He was a frequent visitor at the
more informal gatherings at the home of Phil May (whom he had known

in Australia). There he met Melba and Tosti; and saw Isadora Duncan 'lolloping about in time to the music'.[23] He did a little teaching to sustain himself, but portrait commissions soon began to grow.

When Longstaff returned to Australia in 1894, Melbourne was in the depths of an economic depression. The times could not have been worse for an up-and-coming young painter of fashion. He was soon reduced to designing trade advertisements, and although one splendid whisky poster did call forth the praise of the Sydney *Bulletin*, that trenchant guardian of the Australian verities, he realized grimly that he should never have left Europe. Even in Australia, however, Longstaff's amiable personality and European training stood him in good stead. He had thoroughly mastered the faculty for catching a likeness fluently and investing it with a dignity or grace that delighted his sitters and often flattered them. So official portraits even in those penurious times were not long in coming his way. His important commissions of the period include: Sir Arthur Snowdon, the Lord Mayor of Melbourne; Sir Frederick Darley, the Chief Justice of New South Wales (1900), and Henry Lawson (81).

In 1886 William Gilbee, a prominent Melbourne surgeon, bequeathed £1,000 to the Trustees of the National Gallery of Victoria for a commission for an Australian history painting. By 1900 interest had accrued and the Trustees commissioned two paintings: one by E. Phillips Fox of *The Landing of Captain Cook*, and the other by Longstaff of the *Arrival of Burke, Wills and King at Cooper's Creek, Sunday Evening, 21st April, 1861* (82). A stipulation of the gift was that the work should be executed in England. With the assistance of an advance payment, therefore, Longstaff left for England in September 1901, taking his wife and fourth son with him. The painting, a huge and most melancholy one, was completed and shipped out to Melbourne towards the end of 1907.

Longstaff's large paintings on Australian themes represent a curious survival into the twentieth century of that melancholy interpretation of Australian life and nature which we have already considered in discussing the work of Thomas Watling, Strutt and McCubbin. For Longstaff Australia was

81 JOHN LONGSTAFF, *Henry Lawson*, canvas, 35⅞ x 28¼, 1900, Sydney

82   JOHN LONGSTAFF, *The Arrival of Burke, Wills and King
at the Deserted Camp at Cooper's Creek*, canvas, 111 x 169½,
1902-7, Melbourne

a land of flood, fire and famine, and he heightened his themes with melodrama. Yet they were always based in part upon personal experience. His
Breaking the News was based on a vivid childhood memory of a mining
disaster in his home town of Clunes; *Gippsland, Sunday Night, February
20th 1898* (Melbourne) was painted after a trip through the country which
the fires had devastated; *The Arrival of Burke, Wills and King at Cooper's
Creek* (1907) contained a landscape background based on sketches of desert
landscape around Port Augusta.

Longstaff did not take long to establish himself as a fashionable portrait
painter following his arrival in London in 1901. From the moment of his
arrival he never looked back. Shortly after landing in England, he had been
commissioned by the Imperial Colonial Club to paint portraits of the
Prince and Princess of Wales for their clubrooms. Then the young Lord
Beauchamp, freshly returned from his Governorship of New South Wales
(1899-1901) commissioned a portrait of Edward VII for the National
Gallery of New South Wales, where he had acted for a short period as a
Trustee. The Trustees of the Gallery, on being informed of the gift
impending, resolved that a companion portrait of the Queen should be
commissioned. In consequence, through the good offices of Sir John See,
then the Premier of New South Wales, the 'Ladies of New South Wales'

humbly begged Queen Alexandra also to sit for Longstaff, and later paid for the portrait. In the event, however, Longstaff found that he was expected to paint the portraits almost entirely from photographs and other data. The King gave him an hour when the portrait was nearing completion; but he had to content himself with mental notes of the Queen's appearance while standing close to her during a court presentation.

It is not at all surprising that, in the circumstances under which they were painted, the two royal portraits are not to be numbered among the finest of Longstaff's work, or that now, suffering considerably from crackle and mould, they are rarely exhibited. Such commissions, however, helped to establish Longstaff quickly in London, and each year found him represented at the Academy. Some notable portraits of this period included: Sir Edmund Barton, the first Prime Minister of Australia; the Australian-born Countess of Darnley (1905); Mrs Breitmeyer, the wife of Louis Breitmeyer, the South African diamond merchant; Marjorie Williamson, a daughter of J. C. Williamson, the Australian theatrical impresario; Mrs Reginald Turner, Mrs Stewart Dawson, Miss Alice MacDonald, and the Countess of Eldon in her Coronation robes.

Longstaff possessed good looks, an easy and pleasant manner, and a punctilious regard for the social conventions of Edwardian England. 'Night after night', writes Nina Murdoch, his sympathetic biographer, 'he spent at dancing clubs, and week-end after week-end saw the successful portrait painter setting forth as one of a gay crowd bidden to one or another of England's country houses.'[24] In his seventies he declared himself that he had never known what it was to feel tired. By 1910, he had thoroughly established himself as a portrait painter of fashion with a large studio in St John's Wood which once belonged to R. W. MacBeth, R.A. In the following year he made a hurried trip to Australia to visit his ageing parents. The dutiful son of an affectionate mother, Longstaff had always written a weekly letter to her during his long years in Paris and London, outlining his experiences and successes. He returned to Melbourne on the *Grosser Kurfürst*, the Nord Deutscher Lloyd Company setting aside for him a five-berth cabin as a bedroom and an adjoining four-berth as a dressing room. On arriving in Melbourne he boarded the train for his parents' home at Shepparton to find, to his surprise—and doubtless to his delight— a cheering crowd awaiting him. The Shire President and Councillors made formal speeches of welcome, and the admiring crowd escorted him home, while the town band in front played 'See the Conquering Hero Comes'. They asked him if he felt glad to be home, to which he replied:

Am I glad to be home again? I cannot tell you how glad. The Australian landscape has always seemed to me the most beautiful in the world as well as the most mysterious. When I first saw the brown, hot earth from the ship's decks at Fremantle I cannot tell you the emotion it gave me—after all that confounded sappy English green![25]

Unfortunately, however, he could not remain home for long. On arriving at Shepparton he found several important commissions awaiting him which he could not bring himself to reject. So, after a day or two with his parents, he was off to Sydney where, during the next two months he completed six portraits. By May he was on his way back to his family and the 'sappy English green'. Portrait commissions continued to flow steadily in England, too, and when the war came, Longstaff became an official War Artist with the A.I.F. in France.[26]

The third artist from Australia to study at the Atelier Cormon was Charles Conder, who arrived in Paris in August 1890. His uncle had agreed, shortly after the Exhibition of 9 × 5 Impressions, to allow him £120 a year in order to study abroad. Conder took a studio at 13 Rue Ravignan, a long low wooden building, high up in Montmartre above the Boulevard de Clichy. It was a centre of Bohemian life and housed many *avant-garde* artists and writers. Some years later Max Jacob christened it the Bateau Lavoir; and it was there that Picasso lived between 1904 and 1909 and executed some of his finest paintings.

Although it is not on record, it is almost certain that Conder knew Russell, who may have been responsible for his enrolment at Cormon's. Conder, however, also spent half his time working at the Académie Julian, where Julian Ashton had studied in the 1870's. Conder, tall and extremely handsome, like Russell himself, soon became a well-known figure in Montmartre. Louis Anquetin and Toulouse-Lautrec became his close friends and companions. Lautrec painted his portrait, and also included it in his painting of *Two Waltzers at the Moulin Rouge*.

Conder's work in France and England belongs to the art of the *fin de siècle* and does not need to be dealt with here. Yet the formative influence of his early years should be stressed.

Conder was a child of the British Empire. Born in London in 1868, he was the third son of a railway engineer who accepted a Government appointment in India two years after his son's birth. Conder's mother followed her husband to India but died when her son was five years of age. He was then sent back to England where he spent ten unhappy years attending, with his brother James, between 1874 and 1876, first a dame's school and then a boy's day school, and later, between 1877 and 1883, a boarding school at Eastbourne. Conder's relations with his father were not happy. He refused to become an engineer and was sent to Australia in 1884 to work under his uncle, William Jacomb Conder, an official in the Lands Department of New South Wales. Eight months in the Department's office was followed by two years (1884-5) in a Trigonometrical Survey

Camp. About 1887, apparently with the help of his uncle, he gained employment as a lithographic apprentice with Gibbs Shallard, and became an illustrator for their paper, the *Illustrated Sydney News*, to which he contributed regular weekly drawings from April to October 1887. It was not long afterwards that he met Roberts and joined the Heidelberg group.

In Australia Conder became an artist. In the survey camp he discovered his passion for landscape painting, and about this time first fell in love— with his cousin, Margaret Conder. The experience meant much to a motherless and homeless youth, and his art became a kind of nostalgic celebration of the transience of love. The *female fatale* symbol, so much a feature of his later work, was already present in his Australian drawings and paintings. It was Roberts who introduced him to impressionism, and Eaglemont which provided him with his first vision of Arcadia and of a life dedicated to art. 'Give me', he wrote to Roberts later from Paris, 'one summer again with yourself and Streeton—the same long evenings— songs—dirty plates—and the last pink skies.'[27] It was his Australian uncle who paid for his early, crucial years in Paris. It was in Australia, too, that he made his first contact with the aesthetic movement, decorating his Melbourne studio with liberty silks and Madras muslins. And it was in Australia, to all accounts, that he contracted the disease which slowly killed him.

Australia fashioned the artist but it could not contain him, for Montmartre was his spiritual home. He was not, in his maturity, in the least provincial like his friends, the Longstaffs. John Longstaff came to Paris to learn how to become a successful painter, Conder came to learn how to live. The Longstaffs, significantly enough, shortly after their arrival in Paris, moved to a *ménage* in the Rue Notre Dame des Champs in Montparnasse, at that time a quarter favoured by English and other foreign students, quieter, more medieval and more academic than Bohemian Montmartre. The difference in personality was reflected in different attitudes to art. Longstaff was attracted to the more conservative art of the Old Salon, Conder to the somewhat more experimental art of the New Salon. This is revealed in Conder's letters to Tom Roberts, on 22 May 1891, for example,

Longstaff has a picture in the Old Salon and it seems popular with most of the students at Cormons I think he may get a mention or medal on it—The Old salon is most uninteresting I think and the New most charming I find so much I like at the latter and the Whistlers—Puvis de Chavannes—Dagnans etc most exciting and make one want to work.

Then, on Thursday 26 May, he continued, '. . . I am glad to say that Longstaff has a mention . . . He was here yesterday and seemed very pleased about it. Longstaff is a nice fellow and I'm glad of his success. I feel little enough sympathy with him on art matters . . .'.[28]

83 FREDERICK McCUBBIN, *Golden Sunlight*,
canvas, 30 x 45½, 1914, Castlemaine Art Gallery

84 J. J. HILDER, *Landscape With Sheep*, water-
colour, 20½ x 17½, 1912, Sydney

From Montmartre Conder moved, with the ease and grace natural to him, into English art circles and became, during the 1890's, one of the best-known artists of the *fin de siècle*. And as he became identified with the circle that included Aubrey Beardsley, Will Rothenstein, Oscar Wilde, James Pryde and William Nicholson, he became increasingly estranged from his Australian connections, and his contact with the colony of Australian artists in London grew more tenuous. The story told by William Moore is revealing. In 1905, at the suggestion of Tom Roberts, the Australian artists in London arranged an annual dinner at the Soho café *Au Petit Riche*, whose proprietor had once managed a café in Melbourne: 'One night Charles Conder appeared. He had been away from the group for some time and for some reason or other he was left alone. "Anyone going my way?" he asked as the party broke up. As no one moved, he went out alone.'[29] A complete and satisfactory explanation of the incident has never been given: but Conder had achieved fame by that time and with it, there need be little doubt, the jealousy of many of his former companions.

Australian artists yearned desperately for European recognition, but those who achieved it risked a double alienation: an alienation from those artists who had never succeeded in fleeing the country to work abroad, and made patriotism the virtue of their necessity; and an alienation from those who, having left their Australian *milieu* had never succeeded in arriving in any other, but remained exiles caught between two societies, cherishing a veneer of Australian anti-culture in Europe and a veneer of European culture in Australia. Conder was perhaps the first to be touched by such jealousies but others, returning to Australia after the First World War, Lambert, Longstaff, Bell, Quinn and Rupert Bunny, were to feel it, too— Bunny perhaps most of all. For Rupert Bunny lived for forty-seven years in France and became, like John Russell, to all intents and purposes, a French artist. Although his work was quite well known to Australian artists through works purchased by public galleries during his visits to Australia in 1911 and 1923, Bunny's work was not widely appreciated in Australia until a few years before his death.

Rupert Bunny (1864-1947), the son of a Victorian County Court judge, was born at St Kilda, Melbourne, and educated first at the Alma Road Grammar School, St Kilda, and later at Hutchins School, Hobart. Although he matriculated and enrolled at the University of Melbourne, he enrolled instead, in 1881, following what appears to have been a family dispute concerning his future career, in the School of Design, under O. R. Campbell, at the National Gallery, later joining the School of Painting under Folingsby in 1883. About a year later he travelled to Europe with his father and remained in England for eighteen months studying at Calderon's, St John's Wood, a preparatory school to the Royal Academy.

There he met Henry Tuke and T. C. Gotch who gave him letters to their former master, Jean-Paul Laurens. Bunny arrived in Paris in 1886 and studied under Laurens for two years. In 1888 he first exhibited with the Société des Artistes Français and, in 1890, became the first Australian to gain a *mention honorable*—for his *Tritons*.

During the early 1890's Bunny became associated with a group of English art students living in Paris. Among them were Alastair Cary-Elwes, a nephew of the Earl of Denbigh, a former Governor of South Australia; Douglas Robinson, a son of Sir William Robinson, who had given up the Navy for art, and Harold Mostyn, the son of a Welsh baronet. At this time his work was still dark in tone, romantic in feeling, somewhat histrionic in gesture. His *Avant L'Orage* (1894) marked the beginning of a change; paint was used more heavily and there was a stronger feeling for volume. But allegorical themes persisted.

Between 1890 and 1910 Bunny made frequent trips to England and exhibited at the Royal Academy regularly. But following his marriage in 1902 to Jeanne Morel, the daughter of a French army colonel, his associations with French art and life deepened. His work became known: Gustave Geffroy, one of the most influential critics in Paris, held a high opinion of Bunny's decorative art. He became a member of the New Salon, the Autumn Salon, and the International Society of Sculptors, Painters and Gravers. The French Government purchased three of his works for the Luxembourg. Nine others were purchased for the French provincial collections. When he visited Australia in 1911 at the age of forty-seven he was at the height of his fame: the Felton Bequest purchased *Endormies*, and the Sydney Gallery bought his large *Summer Morning*. In the same year he exhibited work in the International Exhibition, Rome, and at the Carnegie Institute, Pittsburgh.

Bunny was a talented and sensitive exponent of the more conservative side of French painting at the turn of the century. Early in life he acquired the painterly methods of French realism as modified and developed by the *plein-air* painters. But his temperament, quiet, sensitive and restrained, was predisposed towards idealism. Not surprisingly, his early work contains a strong literary element drawn from classical literature and the Bible. There is evidence of Pre-Raphaelite influence in his earliest works, but more important was the example of artists like Arnold Böcklin, whose landscapes abound with symbols and personify the elements of nature. Bunny arrived as a student in Paris when the influence of Puvis de Chavannes was already at its height, and from his work learnt how to organize large compositions and simplify his forms. Doubtless it was Chavannes, too, who led him away from chiaroscuro and realism towards a more primitivistic, decorative style depending upon bright, flat, dry surfaces and simplified, monumental forms, often drawn directly from classical models. But Bunny, throughout his life, drew upon varied sources. Although deeply responsive to the past he was tolerant of modern innovation when not pressed to excess and extravagance. For a time *art nouveau* strongly affected his work: as in his fine *Rape of Persephone* (93) with its vigorous rhythmical conception, its highly-keyed colour, and freely-flowing forms. Impressionism, *Japonisme* and Gauguin were among the contemporary sources of his style; but it is clear that he also learned much from Delacroix, Rubens and Veronese.

No Australian artist ever painted women more perceptively than Bunny. There was something in his gentle nature that led him to idealize feminine grace and charm with a becalming innocence of mind. Among his most representa-

85 RUPERT BUNNY, *Returning from the Garden*, pulp board, 36½ x 25¾, c. 1895, Sydney

tive works are those conversation and genre studies of women talking intimately among themselves, returning with flowers from the garden (85), enjoying a walk, musing over tea (97) or upon a park bench. In such paintings his rococo love of texture and light, his sensitivity and good taste, are beautifully realized. Bunny indeed belongs in spirit, like Pierre Bonnard (1867-1947), his greater French contemporary, to the Indian summer of nineteenth-century naturalism—an *intimiste* and idealist still in love with surfaces and the appearance of things. The First World War ended his world. Tolerant though he was of modern painting, the post-Cézanne experiments quite clearly meant little to him personally. His late landscapes of southern France and the Pyrenees, for all their formal simplicity and sensitivity of touch and colour, are remembrances of times past. Many were painted after his return to Australia, following the death of his wife in 1933, during the depths of the economic depression. He took a flat in South Yarra and lived frugally and very much to himself, composing music and spurning publicity, until his death at the age of eighty-two in 1946. A few months before his death Sir Daryl Lindsay arranged a retrospective exhibition of his work, at the National Gallery of Victoria, which revealed for the first time to Australians the range and variety of his work. It was this exhibition and the smaller shows held at the Macquarie Galleries, Sydney, during the last decade of the artist's life, and later, that re-established Bunny's Australian reputation. Since his death his work has been held in the highest regard, and rightly so, some critics, Paul Haefliger and Clive Turnbull, for example, considering him the finest of all Australian painters.

Yet, in a very real sense Bunny, apart from the accident of his birth, was barely an Australian painter at all. He was, with John Russell and Emanuel Phillips Fox, one of the three Australian expatriates who assimilated the French tradition thoroughly and gained a modest reputation abroad. His work lies outside the development of Australian art much more completely, for example, than the work of Charles Conder. Bunny proved that the gulf could be bridged: that an Australian art student could become a French artist. But returning to his own country, like Russell, at the end of his life, he found himself an outsider, largely ignored by local artists and critics. In the end he was accepted by the champions of the modern movement as a kind of father-figure.[30] It was, indeed, not Rupert Bunny or John Russell, but the men who did not succeed in thoroughly establishing themselves as artists in Europe: Streeton, Lambert, Norman Lindsay and George Bell, who were, each in his own way, to influence the course of art in Australia in the years between the wars.

The work of Emanuel Phillips Fox (1865-1915) forms a natural comparison with that of Rupert Bunny, for he spent a good deal of his life in France and was attracted to subject pictures of an *intimiste* character; paintings with domestic and garden settings featuring people enjoying themselves, entertaining and relaxing. Fox, however, avoided the classicism, allegory and literary overtones so often to be found in Bunny's work, keeping more closely to impressionist subjects, and devoting himself single-mindedly to the painting of light and colour. Although, like all the Australian painters of his generation, apart from Russell, he refused to involve himself in experiments with broken colour and *pointillisme*, he is the Australian artist who in his best work came closest to the impressionist love of sunlight, colour and the good life. In such a painting as *The Art Students* (96), Fox reveals himself as one of the most sensitive, subtle and natural colourists in the whole field of Australian painting. The composition is splendid, the colour painted with feeling and superbly related to atmospheric and tonal values. But Fox was unequal. At times the clarity of his vision and his sensitivity failed and he produced paintings sentimental and somewhat vulgar in their claim upon popular appeal. Yet Fox's work, at its best, is more crisp, more sentient, more alive with light and colour than Bunny's, upon whom the academic manner often rests heavily.

86   JOHN RUSSELL, *Portrait of Dr Maloney*, canvas, 18½ x 13½,
1887, Melbourne

Phillips Fox was the son of Alexander Fox, a Melbourne photographer. He studied art first under O. R. Campbell and G. F. Folingsby at the Gallery School, and in 1886 went to Paris where he worked first at Julian's and then under Gérome at the Beaux Arts. He first exhibited at the Old Salon in 1890, the year in which he returned to Melbourne, where he held a one-man show in December 1892. In the year following he formed the Melbourne Art School with his friend, Tudor St George Tucker, where *plein-air* and impressionist methods of painting were taught. A summer school section was conducted at 'Charterisville'. In 1901 Fox shared the Gilbee Bequest with Sir John Longstaff and repaired to England, according to the conditions of the will, to paint his history painting, *The Landing of Captain Cook*. In 1905 he married Ethel Carrick, a former Slade student, and settled in Paris where in 1908 he became an associate, and in 1910 a member of the Société Nationale des Beaux Arts. In 1912 he became a member of the International Society of Painters, Sculptors and Gravers, and travelled in Spain and Algeria. Fox visited Melbourne in 1908 and held a one-man show at the Guildhall. He came out again in 1913 and held successful shows in Melbourne and Sydney. The colourful paintings of the south of France which he exhibited on that occasion were well received by young art students, like Roland Wakelin, then becoming interested in the modern movement. The outbreak of the First World War found Fox in Tahiti still in search of sunshine and colour. He returned to Australia in 1915 to organize an art union for the Red Cross, but died on 8 October of that year.[31]

Streeton arrived in London in 1898 and remained for eight years that were the most difficult of his life. The Australian students who had preceded him to Europe, Roberts, Russell, Bunny, Fox, Mackennal and Conder, to name the more prominent, came as young men. They enjoyed the *camaraderie* of the art schools and gained lifelong friends. Furthermore, they were sustained during their early years abroad by scholarships or remittances from Australia. But Streeton arrived in London not as an art student but as a man with a colonial reputation. For much of the time he worked in loneliness and isolation. He had come without introductions, and, as he remarked ruefully to Roberts in a letter written from Hampstead three years after his arrival, 'K (i.e. Conder) was right when he said a long time back that you *must* have friends in London. I came without a letter and I knew only two men—Mackennal and Minns'.[32]

Shortly after his arrival he visited the Royal Academy of 1898 which had rejected one of his paintings, and continued to do so, with a single exception, during the eight years of his first sojourn in England. He found himself admiring the Sargent portraits, 'quite as fine as the great Rembrandt',[33] and the work of Greiffenhagen, Brangwyn and G. F. Watts. The atmosphere of the Academy was, he felt, commercial rather than artistic, and he preferred the International Exhibition at Knightsbridge which included work by Rodin, Whistler, Conder, Rothenstein, Beardsley and Charles Keene. The distinctly romantic nature of Streeton's interests, discernible since the Heidelberg days, revealed itself sharply in London. Constable, Turner, Titian and G. F. Watts were the masters which excited him most. In his Chelsea studio it was Chatterton, the Lake Poets and the Brontës which he read. In 1902 he went to the Wye Valley to paint Chepstow Castle. Compared with Russell, Conder and Bunny there was something quaintly old-fashioned about Streeton's taste. Like Longstaff he possessed a simple transparency of mind, yearned for public success, and was cast down by indifference and loneliness. Certainly there was a lyrical impulse in Streeton's romanticism, but he was not at all drawn, either by curiosity or temperament, to the darker and tragic aspects of romanticism. It was a sweet vision of youth and happiness at Eaglemont which he recalled again and again throughout his life. 'Innocent Streeton' was Conder's description of him. And Streeton in turn, writing to Roberts, said of Conder, 'For me he's not healthy, tho' I like him very much as of old, and his work. He's a fine artist.'[34] Streeton's imagination, in short, did not contain the density and intelligence of Conder's. His rugged determination to show that he could equal the English landscape painters on their own ground reveals his naïvety about the nature of artistic success. In a letter to Roberts he said:

I heard lately that the boss of the New English (Steer, who is always amiable when I meet him) does not like my work: well I'm competing with him. I've been down this summer painting his favourite subject and painting it in my own way, and I begin to feel I'm all right. They'll have to accept me yet.[35]

But neither the New English Art Club nor the English art world as a whole ever accepted Streeton. His letters from London frequently reveal the poverty and isolation of his situation. He wrote, for example, in 1901:

I tried the R.A., New English, and International—with the usual result. I don't mind being hard up for years to come, save for the cursed waste of opportunity. These are my most precious years, and all last winter, spring and summer I was confined here—no coin for models. Just doing my best and hoping for the future, and eating my heart out to think of the sweet passing summer and the hills in the country.[36]

English criticism need not be blamed for its neglect of Streeton. All the best that he ever painted and wrote reveals how greatly he depended upon the Australian landscape for his inspiration. During his London years he sought to emulate Constable, Sargent and Steer to little purpose. The great landscape painters were not tourists in search of culture but men with a deep sense of intimacy with the scenes they painted; and there was little intimacy between Streeton and the English landscape. It is clear from his letters, too, that he was thoroughly homesick. Sensing his misery Roberts, in 1902, sent him some gum leaves to burn in his grate, and Streeton wrote a little later:

Lord, how far back it all seems, yet how clear—every detail and trifle ingrained in my brain for life—the Houstons, the creek, the horehound patch, the black wattle, the messmate, the long open space up to the road, the hurrying up the hill on Sunday evenings with Prof. well to the fore: Heidelberg, the she-oak and sienna dust over all; the straw brown hills; pale Dandenongs; the Old England; College tennis; pines and coppery light; hazels, japonica; Impressionist Exhibition; gorse up the drive; girls; the picnics in the twilight and all the loveliness—all a dream![37]

But by that time Streeton was far from being the only artist in Chelsea with nostalgic memories of Australia. 'They all seem to be here,' he wrote, 'Mackennal, Longstaff, Mahony, Fullwood, Spence, Norman, Minns, Fox, Tudor St George Tucker, Quinn, Coates, Bunny, Altson, K., Sonny Pole.'[38] Indeed, by 1902, the exodus to Europe was at full flood. It was in the Chelsea Arts Club that the Heidelberg School established its last and least distinguished camp.

In 1906 Streeton heard that his *Australian December*, which he had painted in 1887 and sold for £8, had exchanged hands for £75. Deciding that an exhibition in Australia would be timely, he gathered a collection of his paintings and arrived in Melbourne in December. With the help of his friend, Professor Baldwin Spencer, he put on a most successful one-man show at the Guildhall, Melbourne, in April 1907, following it with a show in Sydney, and a third in Melbourne shortly after. But he had no intention of remaining. A letter which he wrote to Roberts from Sydney on 5 October 1907, shortly before he returned to England, reveals his state of mind very clearly at the time:

The harbour and the long promontories look as glorious as ever, and I wish I could settle among it all. But I must get back. What is there for one here? I could paint a couple of years free and then be condemned to get half-a-dozen pupils at two or three guineas a quarter, as all the other chaps here do; and then if I got to London again, I'd have to serve *another* apprenticeship before I got into the shows there.[39]

Tom Roberts had arrived in England with his wife and son in March 1903, the task of completing his picture of the Opening of the first Commonwealth Parliament before him. He was provided with a studio at the Imperial Institute and completed the painting in November. The work had given him, he informed his friend, Alfred Deakin, 'a very happy time . . . and for the first time no anxiety about money'.[40] After completing 'the Big Picture', Roberts entered a difficult phase of his life which his son, Caleb, has called his *black* period. He was uncertain as to the direction his art should follow; he suffered from gout and inflammation of the eyes; the Academy constantly rejected his paintings for four years; and he fared little better at the hands of the selection committees of the New English and other art societies. Roberts suspected that the Royal prerogative which had ensured the exhibition of the big picture at the Academy of 1904 would not endear him to the Academicians. '. . . they can't biff your painter in this effort though doubtless they'll be very careful to do it in others',[41] he prophesied to Deakin at the time. Nor did commissions flow from his contact with 'the great ones of the earth' as Mr N. Graves B. Jefferson had so cheerfully imagined. But in Roberts there was no bitterness and he remained throughout his life as equally loyal to his birthplace as to his adopted country:

England does not really *want* anybody; she has everybody and everything. The supply is in excess of the demand. She has the world to draw upon, and everyone comes here sooner or later. The only thing is to make her want you, and that is difficult, for she only really wants the exceptional in any line.[42]

With this realistic appraisal of the situation in mind he set himself to win a small place in the art world of England for himself.

It was a most modest place that he did win, but it was not failure. For Roberts, as for Streeton, however, the first five years were bleak and difficult. 'The Big Picture' completed, he took a studio first in Warwick Square, then in Harrington Road, South Kensington, while the family lived in a flat in Putney. The summers of 1905 and 1906 were spent in Holland, and of 1907 and 1908 in Mundesley, Norfolk. During that time he felt, knowing that recognition came late in England, that he had arrived ten years too late to gain it. The family was sustained very largely at this time through the efforts of Roberts's wife, who attended L.C.C. classes and became a skilled carver and gilder of frames.

Roberts, however, was not the kind of person to suffer isolation for long. Warm-hearted and sociable, he made friends wherever he went, and his house was open both to his English and Australian artist friends. He became a centre for the Australian artist community in London, which by 1903 was quite a considerable one; was responsible in 1905 for the establishment of an annual dinner among them (gum leaves were set alight with much ceremony at table in a censer); and was the originator of the large reception which Australian artists gave to the Australian and New Zealand Imperial Conference of 1911. He was also a very active member of the Chelsea Arts Club.

With his *Mundesley Barn* of 1908, Roberts appears to have emerged from a period of indecision. He had been more alive than Streeton to the dangers of experimenting promiscuously with a diversity of styles. 'I'll have to stand very firm and be sure,' he wrote to Deakin in August 1904, but referred more than once in the years that followed to the need for a 'new departure'.[43] In this search he was helped by his Australian friends, the portrait painters George Coates and James Quinn. He adopted a restricted palette, making much use of muted tones and subtle greys.

In 1910 Roberts moved with his family to Golders Green and entered upon a period of painting which gave him considerable satisfaction. In the summer of 1913 he worked in Italy and held a one-man show in Walker's Galleries, in February 1914, of paintings done in the neighbourhood of Lake Como and the Splügen Pass. Criticism was, in general, favourable, the *Observer* noting the 'unity of vision, tact in selection, and a certain tenderness, not untinged with melancholy'.[44] Roberts returned to Italy the following summer and was there when war was declared. Back in England, he joined the R.A.M.C. in company with twenty-four other members of the Chelsea Arts Club and was posted to the Third London Hospital, Wandsworth, where he worked with a number of Australian artists including Streeton, George Coates, Miles Evergood, and A. H. Fullwood and the companion of his youth on the Spanish walking tour, Dr William Maloney.

George Lambert, who left Australia to study in Europe in 1900 and returned twenty-one years later, was one of the most talented of the Edwardian expatriates. Lambert's early years were in many ways like those of Charles Conder. Conder was the son of an English engineer employed upon the construction of railways in India; Lambert the son of an American engineer employed upon railway construction in Russia. Lambert spent his early years in Russia and Germany; Conder his first years in India. Conder's mother died when he was five; Lambert's father three months before he was born. Both of them were educated in England; both came to Australia in their youth; Conder at the age of sixteen, Lambert at the age of fourteen. Conder spent two years in the bush on a trigonometrical survey; Lambert spent his early years on his maternal granduncle's property at Eurobla, near Nevertire, New South Wales, where, as a station-hand, he was involved in post and rail fencing, branding and dipping sheep, horsebreaking and droving. Both Lambert and Conder developed their early passion for drawing and painting during their years in the bush, and both were drawn to Sydney in the hope of becoming professional artists with the Sydney illustrated Press. Conder became an illustrator on the *Illustrated Sydney News*, Lambert a regular contributor (of humorous illustrations of bush types and bush life) to the *Sydney Bulletin*.

Physically, too, they had much in common. They were both big men, and both, in their own ways, extremely handsome. But there the similarities

87   GEORGE LAMBERT, *A Bush Idyll*, canvas,
19 x 30⅞, 1896, Sydney

ended. For their temperaments and early emotional experiences were quite different. The motherless Conder grew up to detest a father who had little affection for him and resisted his desire to become an artist, to resist also his father's profession as he experienced it in the rough masculine life of the survey camp. The fatherless Lambert, though always an affectionate son to his widowed mother, was drawn in a family of women (he had three elder sisters) to his maternal grandfather, the only male in the English household. Conder became the ladies' man, indolent, dreamy, highly sensitive and poetic, adding to good looks a charm and graciousness of manner irresistible to women. It was a prodigious indulgence in women and alcohol that destroyed his powerful, athletic constitution and finally killed him at the comparatively youthful age of forty-one. Lambert was the man's man, observant, energetic, realistic in all he undertook, attractive to women by the magnetism of his personality—a 'job-lot Apollo' one of his friends called him—but essentially a talented craftsman who gave his greatest love to his work and his horses.

Lambert's early work belongs to the *Bulletin* school of graphic draughtsmanship, with its incisive line and topical comment. His first oil painting of any consequence, *A Bush Idyll* (87), is painted with that loose breadth and informality of composition to which the *plein-air* manner of Julian Ashton gave currency among Sydney painters, but its muted grey-blue tones still owe much to the wash-drawing techniques favoured by the *Bulletin* school. In this regard the painting may be compared with the illustrations Lambert made for A. G. Stephens's edition of Barcroft Boake's *Where the Dead Men Lie* (1897).

A Bush Idyll was purchased by the Sydney Gallery from the 1896 Exhibition of the Society of Artists. The unexpected tribute encouraged

88   GEORGE LAMBERT, *Across the Black Soil Plains*, canvas,
35¼ x 120¼, 1899, Sydney

Lambert to exchange station work for employment as a grocer's clerk in
the city, a position which enabled him to take the evening classes at Julian
Ashton's studio. Soon, however, he was able to support himself entirely
by means of his graphic work and become a day student. While with
Ashton he painted *Across the Black Soil Plains* (88), a large picture in the
manner of Roberts's heroic paintings of pastoral life. The dependence upon
tone rather than colour reveals the continued influence of his wash-drawing
work, and the lowness of tone that interest in *dark* painting then current
both in Sydney and Melbourne. The broad and rather decorative treatment
of the landscape contains an element of *art nouveau* that Lambert may well
have gained from Ashton's other outstanding pupil, Sydney Long. The
subject painting, *Youth and the River* (1900), painted for the Travelling
Scholarship (first awarded in that year by the Society of Artists) is, with
its strongly allegorical note, even more closely related to Long. Here a
nude youth and girl are both mounted upon horses which are stepping
into a dark river from which dim faces threaten and black swans glide, all
quite in the manner of the *art nouveau* allegories of the time.

Lambert won the scholarship, befriended Hugh Ramsay on the voyage
over and studied in Paris with him, first at Colarossi's and then at the
Atelier Delécluse. He had married shortly before leaving Australia and
both he and his wife settled in the Latin Quarter quite near a studio shared
by the three Australians Ambrose Patterson, J. S. MacDonald, and their
friend, Ramsay.

During these early years abroad, Lambert's work was influenced by
Ramsay's painterly style. Both of them painted *dark* in the current manner
and came under the spell of Velasquez, at that time the idol of the studios.
Lambert's *Equestrian Group* (89), in his Velasquez manner, is one of the
most distinguished and painterly of all his compositions. His son, Maurice,
has been posed in a manner reminiscent of Don Balthasar Carlos. *The
Three Kimonos* (Sydney), painted a few years before, and shortly after
the family left Paris and settled in Chelsea, added a touch of *Japonisme* to

89   GEORGE LAMBERT, *Equestian Group*, canvas,
50¼ x 40, 1905, Sydney

the interest in Velasquez. Lambert was an assiduous worker with a superb
sense of devotion to his craft, and sought to learn from the masters. In
The Bathers (90), for example, the influence of Rubens is also present,
and he himself confessed his deep interest in the work of Botticelli, Gior-
gione, Veronese, Van Dyck and, of course, Velasquez. Among the moderns
Puvis de Chavannes, Manet, Sargent and Orpen attracted him. The
influence of Augustus John, too, is often apparent, as in *The Belle of the
Alley* (Sydney). In the years immediately before, during and after the
First World War a light-toned, crisp and drier style owing much to the
influence of Orpen began to dominate his work. The painterly style of his
Velasquez phase was discarded for a linear style of wit and the studied
gesture. It was this style which he brought back to Australia when he
returned in 1921.

During the early war years Lambert was engaged upon a Home Office project felling timber in Wales, but in December 1917 he accepted a commission which required him to make sketches and drawings which were to serve as visual records of the part played by the Australian Light Horse in the Palestine campaign. He was also asked to paint a large battle piece of the Charge of the Australian Light Horse at Beersheba. This led to an association with Australian War Records which resulted in a very large number of drawings of the Eastern campaigns, many portraits of high-ranking military officers, and three large battle pieces, *The Landing at Gallipoli* (91), *The Charge of the Light Horse at Beersheba* and *The Surrender of Kazimain*. Most of his work for War Records is now gathered together at the Australian War Memorial Museum, Canberra.

His war paintings called forth the best in Lambert. Essentially a man of action and a skilled horseman, he saw the Palestine campaign as a daring and perilous adventure, just as the young troopers of the Australian Light Horse must have seen it. The very first officer he reported to when calling at the base camp at Moascar in Egypt, upon taking up his duties, was none other than Major 'Banjo' Paterson. Truly, it must have seemed as though Clancy himself had brought his horse all the way from the Overflow to drive the infidel out of the Holy Places. But on this occasion there was to be no histrionics, though the flamboyant gesture was by no means uncommon either to Lambert's art or his personality. It was not his business to

90   GEORGE LAMBERT, *The Bathers*, canvas, 36½ x 32, 1907, Adelaide

91   GEORGE LAMBERT, *Anzac—The Landing*, canvas, 78 x 145,
1920-2, Australian War Memorial, Canberra

allot praise or blame, depict the heroics or the tragedy of war. He had been given the task of topographer, one of the most ancient of all commissions, and he discharged it well.

His drawings possess the impersonality and brevity of a good military dispatch. In his large battle pieces he depicts the forms of men and horses in action, and the ground across which they fought and died, with an unswerving grip upon reality. He saw a battle like a general, not like a philosopher or a moralist, and that was what he had been called to do. The dispassion and craftsmanship of such art is deprecated today by some critics for whom art can never be more than the expression of personal attitudes and private feelings. They forget that the artist still owes a duty to the tribe. Lambert was called upon to preserve memories and record events precious to the history of the nation. His own comments would have been an impertinence. He had the good sense not to provide them.[45]

In 1892 Lindsay Bernard Hall (1859-1935) became the Director of the National Gallery of Victoria and Head of its School. Although himself an artist of no great merit he came to exercise during his long years of office, both through his own teaching and through his students, an influence second to none in the history of Australian art.

Born at Liverpool in 1859, Hall took up his post at the age of thirty-three. He had studied at the Royal College of Art, South Kensington, and later at Antwerp and Munich. A foundation member of the New English Art Club (formed in 1886 as a challenge to the Royal Academy), he brought to Melbourne that great enthusiasm for 'values' and the art of

92 JOHN LONGSTAFF, *The Cabbage Plot*, canvas, 10 x 17½,
1890, Castlemaine Art Gallery

93 RUPERT BUNNY, *The Rape of Persephone*, canvas, 21 x 31½,
1925, Mr Brian Johnstone

Velasquez shared by the New English Art Club's early members. Hall was an earnest, meticulous and methodical man, respected rather than loved by his pupils. Under him the Melbourne Gallery School became highly efficient in the training of portrait painters skilled in the art of illusionism. The programme left little place for the arts of design and colour nor were students encouraged to exercise their imagination or express their personality. The programme had its advantages and its weaknesses. It produced a generation of highly-competent portrait and figure painters with narrow sympathies and a great distrust of the intellect and imagination. In a country whose citizens have always feared beauty and men highly endowed with creative gifts more than they fear God, portrait painters who could produce a good likeness have provided a welcome substitute for creative artists, so often eccentric and unpredictable in their productions. Bernard Hall's students, in short, and the students of his students, to the third and fourth generation, became an orthodoxy which closed its ranks firmly against experiment and innovation. Hall did his best work as a teacher during the first ten years of his life at a time when an appreciation of the methods of Velasquez, Manet and Whistler could still arouse in students a genuine sense of visual discovery.[46] During those ten years he produced his most able students: James Quinn, a sensitive portrait painter with a complete command of his craft whose achievement has not yet been fully recognized; Hugh Ramsay, the highly-talented young Scot; Max Meldrum, the teacher and theorist by whose influence tonal realism was transmitted deep into the twentieth century; and George Bell, whose classical instinct alone among all of Australia's tonal painters led him to Cézanne and, late in his life, to the leadership of the modern movement in this country.

James Quinn was awarded the Travelling Scholarship a year after Hall's arrival. In Paris he studied at Julian's and the Beaux Arts, married a French art student and remained in Paris for nine years before setting up in London as a portrait painter. Quinn, fortunately, had completed the greater part of his training before Hall arrived in Melbourne, and thus escaped a thorough grounding in Hall's muddy palette. He developed a technique which influenced the later manner of Tom Roberts—a richly colourful style in which greys were skilfully deployed. His *Portrait of a Young Girl* (1915, Melbourne) is a masterly example of his subdued yet sensitive manner. Quinn received a greater measure of recognition as a portrait painter in London than most of the Australian Edwardian expatriates, and did not return to Melbourne until 1936.[47]

Bernard Hall's most talented student, however, was Hugh Ramsay (1877-1906), a boy from Glasgow who studied at the School from 1895 to 1899 and then proceeded to Paris at Longstaff's suggestion and joined

Colarossi's studio. He spent much time in the Louvre studying the old masters and copying Velasquez but contracted tuberculosis in his Paris lodgings and was compelled to return to Australia in 1902. Back in Melbourne he continued to paint with great energy, feeling and versatility until his death at the age of twenty-nine in 1906.

Ramsay attained a mastery of values and a tonal technique unequalled by any Australian of his generation. But his work, despite its great technical virtuosity, remained that of an unusually gifted student. There was still much of the art school about his carefully arranged compositions with their studied posing, lighting and dress, nor had he emancipated himself entirely from the powerful influence of his teachers, Bernard Hall, Velasquez, Manet, Whistler and Sargent. At times his technical precocity betrayed him, and his surfaces developed an oily glitter, as in his *Sisters* in the Sydney Gallery. But he could paint with sensitivity, feeling for character and great beauty of tone. His portrait of *Jeanne* (94) reveals a Whistlerian mastery of rich and closely related greys.[48]

Arthur Streeton's successful exhibition at the Guildhall, Melbourne, in 1907, not only made the purchase of Australian paintings fashionable; it also stimulated a taste for paintings of European subjects by Australian painters. Local collectors maintained strong ties with Britain; the majority had probably travelled on the Continent. It must not be supposed that the emergence of a distinctly Australian art during the 1880's led to a subsequent decline in the demand for European views which had been present in Australia since early colonial days. For many a buyer, and for many an artist, England was still 'home'; and views of London, Paris, Florence and Venice, for example, recalled the joys and adventures of the European journey. Interest in such views grew in the years before the war, reached a peak during the 1920's and has persisted down to the present day. Although, of course, many Australian artists returning from Europe have found a ready

94   HUGH RAMSAY, *Jeanne*, canvas, 50 x 34, 1902, Mrs J. Wicking

local interest in pictures of European cities and the European countryside (the late work of Rupert Bunny has already been noted in this connexion), this continuing factor in Australian taste is best illustrated in the life and career of Will Ashton.

Will Ashton (*b.* 1881) was the son of a drawing master of the York School of Art who settled in Adelaide two years after his son was born. Will was educated at the Prince Alfred College, Adelaide, where his father had secured a post as a teacher of drawing. After leaving the College in 1897 he entered his father's studio for four years and was then sent abroad by his parents to study at St Ives under Julius Olsson and Algernon Talmage. There Ashton developed a liking for marine subjects rendered in free, vigorous impasto in an impressionist manner. From St Ives he went to the Académie Julian to work under Marcel André Baschet and François Schommer. In 1905, after exhibiting with the Cornish painters in London, and in the provinces, he returned to Australia, holding his first Australian exhibition in 1906. A show at the Guildhall, Melbourne, in 1907 established his reputation as a painter of European subjects. Henceforth, a great deal of Ashton's life was spent coming and going between Australia and Europe. After winning the Wynne Art Prize for an Australian landscape in 1908 he returned to England, coming back to hold exhibitions in 1912, and returning to England in 1913. The following year found him in Australia again; but the outbreak of war delayed his embarkation for Europe. Sailing for England, Ashton served for a time with the Y.M.C.A. and returned to Adelaide to enlist in the A.I.F., but was rejected on medical grounds. For five years after the Armistice he made his home in Sydney, returned to Paris in 1923 and came back the following year to hold highly successful exhibitions in Adelaide, Melbourne and Sydney. In 1925 he was back again in France but returned the same year to hold exhibitions in the three capitals that were even more highly successful.

Ashton was a robust, uncomplicated, out-of-door landscape painter with a firm masculine touch. His paintings, often of spots hallowed by generations of tourists—Notre Dame and the bridges of the Seine, Florence and the Ponte Vecchio, the canals of Venice, French and Mediterranean watering places—are picturesquely set down with a firm grasp upon fact and atmospheric colour (103). Ashton's popular and picturesque impressionism became quite a vogue in Australia during the years between the wars when *avant-garde* painting was regarded by most collectors with the deepest suspicion. Ashton himself, as an art adviser to the Commonwealth Government and a Director of the Art Gallery of New South Wales (1937-44) became, like so many of his generation, a sturdy and influential opponent of the post-Cézanne developments in contemporary painting.[49]

George Bell (*b.* 1878) studied under McCubbin and Hall at the Mel-

95 GEORGE BELL, *Portrait of Daryl Lindsay*, canvas, 40 x 30, 1924, Melbourne

bourne Gallery School from 1895 to 1903 and in the Parisian studios of Julian, Colarossi, Castelucha and La Grande Chaumière from 1904 to 1906. In 1906 he visited Italy where the paintings of Titian and Tintoretto claimed his greatest interest. Then in 1907 he worked at St Ives at a time when the English painters, Stanhope Forbes, Algernon Talmage and Julius Olsson were at work there. In 1908 he settled in Chelsea, began to practise as a portrait painter, and became a member of the Chelsea Arts Club where his closest friends were the Australians, George Lambert and Fred Leist, and the English painters, Walter Russell, Philip Connard and Wilson Steer. In 1908 he became a foundation member of the Modern Society of Portrait Painters which included Glyn Philpot, Gerald Kelly, J. D. Fergusson and Lambert. At this time his portraits, such as his *Lady in Black* (Sydney), are still in the dark tonal manner favoured by so many portraitists at the time. Between 1908 and 1914, Bell exhibited work in exhibitions held in Munich, Düsseldorf and Paris, but it was not until he had lived in London for eleven years that the Royal Academy accepted one of his paintings. About 1910 his work became more colourful, more direct in handling, more assertive of planal construction, and his interest in composition grew. His *Lulworth Cove* (Melbourne, 1911) is typical of the new manner, and this is continued and developed in bright, flattish genre paintings of gypsy life painted in 1914. On visits to Italy in 1912 and 1914 he became increasingly interested in Boticelli and Piero della Francesca. During the war Bell taught in a boys' preparatory school, worked in Munitions, and was appointed an official war artist to the Fourth Division of the A.I.F. in 1918. This required the painting of the portraits of high-ranking officers and winners of the Victoria Cross.

After the Armistice he returned to Australia to complete his large battle picture, *Dawn at Hamel 4th July 1918* (War Memorial, Canberra). Unlike other battle pieces painted by Australia's war artists, it studiously avoids the depiction of dramatic action. In a calm but desolate landscape the wounded are being brought in after a fierce engagement. The painting also reveals the beginnings of a tendency in Bell's work towards that cubic reduction of form which English war artists like C. R. W. Nevinson had already developed considerably. The incipient classicism of this work was prophetic. Certainly Bell's friend, Lambert, adopted a liberal attitude to the modern movement, but it was Bell alone among the Edwardian expatriates who came to reject academic realism wholeheartedly, to the distress and dismay of most of his former colleagues, and to reconstruct his art and aesthetic position in the light of Cézanne and what had followed. Trained in the old dispensation he became, having passed the age of fifty, the leader of the new. This phase of his career is discussed in the following chapters.

But of most of the expatriates Victor Daley spoke with the insight of a true poet. None of the artists who left Australia in those Indian summer years of the nineteenth century before the First World War achieved in their art either lasting worldly success or enduring artistic value. Correggio Jones did not reach the Promised Land of art either in the flesh or in the spirit. The history of modern European art can be written, apart perhaps from a passing reference to Conder, without mentioning the men who created the Australian school of painting. Nor are they forgotten only in Europe. Their failure was most fully realized in their own country. If the Edwardian excursion brought little or nothing to European art neither did it bring back much of lasting value to Australia. For the present generation of Australian artists, apart from Roberts and Bunny, perhaps, whose work can still arouse perfunctory gestures of respect from the young, the expatriates might never have lived at all. As to their failure to reach the highest achievement in art there can be no doubt, but the causes are not easy to assess. In refusing to be satisfied with the provincial and second-rate standards prevailing in Australia around 1900 their instincts were soundly based and their years abroad bravely asserted the fact that the world of art, at its best, is always an international community. Perhaps their failure lay in the motives which caused them to leave the country. Perhaps the European venture ceased too quickly from being part of a lifelong process of self-discovery and became, for most of them, a step on the road to success and public acclaim. In the end many of them did achieve success of a sort in the years after the First World War, but only by clinging to the image of a world that was quickly passing.

FOOTNOTES

[1] J. ROTHENSTEIN, *The Life and Death of Conder*, London, 1938, pp. 29-30
[2] SIDNEY DICKENSON, 'Wanted: A Standard in Art Criticism', *The Australasian Critic*, i (1891), 217
[3] Quoted by MOORE, i, 166

L

[4] op. cit., i, 166-7

[5] W. MOORE, *City Sketches*, Melbourne, 1905, 13

[6] D. H. SOUTER, 'J. J. Hilder, Water-Colourist', *Art and Architecture*, vi (1909), 142

[7] MOORE, *City Sketches*, p. 13

[8] *Argus* (Melbourne), 24 August 1895, *see* V. SPATE, thesis cited

[9] *See Creeve Roe* (ed. M. Holburn and M. Pizer), Sydney, 1947, p. 43

[10] ibid., pp. 41-3

[11] D. H. SOUTER, 'Tom Roberts, Painter', *Art and Architecture*, iii (1906), 37

[12] In his poem 'For'ard', *see In the Days when the World was Wide*, Sydney, 1896

[13] A. S. HARTRICK, *A Painter's Pilgrimage Through Fifty Years*, Cambridge, 1939, p. 39

[14] H. THANNHAUSER, 'Van Gogh and John Russell: some Unknown Letters and Drawings', *Burl. Mag.* lxxiii (1938), 96

[15] ibid.

[16] op. cit., p. 98

[17] A. H. BARR, *Matisse, His Life and Art*, New York, 1951, p. 35

[18] *Smike to Bulldog*, p. 63

[19] HARTRICK, op. cit., p. 21

[20] THANNHAUSER, art. cit., *Burl. Mag.*, lxxiii (1938), 103

[21] This account of Russell's life is drawn from the article by Thannhauser, cited above; from letters and conversations with Thea Proctor, the artist's niece; and from letters between Miss Proctor and the artist's son, Alain Russell.

[22] Quoted from NINA MURDOCH, *Portrait in Youth*, Sydney, 1948, p. 102, a book to which this account of Longstaff's life is greatly indebted.

[23] op. cit., p. 159

[24] op. cit., p. 198

[25] op. cit., p. 210

[26] *See also The Art of Sir John Longstaff*, AA, iii, 37 (April 1931) and *CAO*, pp. 128-9

[27] *Smike to Bulldog*, p. 128

[28] ROTHENSTEIN, op. cit., pp. 65, 68

[29] Moore, ii, 10

[30] *See also The Art of Rupert Bunny*, Sydney [n.d.]; and *CAO*, pp. 35-6. I am indebted to Mr L. Course for several points made here.

[31] On Fox *see also* D. H. SOUTER, 'E. Phillips Fox', *Art and Architecture*, v (1908), 88; and *CAO*, p. 68

[32] Streeton to Roberts, 8 January 1901; CROLL, p. 200

[33] *Smike to Bulldog*, p. 65

[34] op. cit., p. 71

[35] Streeton to Roberts, 27 December 1902; CROLL, p. 207

[36] *Smike to Bulldog*, p. 73

[37] CROLL, p. 207

[38] ibid.

[39] *Smike to Bulldog*, p. 90

[40] Roberts to Deakin, 17 November 1903, Deakin Papers. I am here indebted to Professor R. M. Crawford's study of the Roberts-Deakin correspondence to be published in the forthcoming volume of papers in honour of Sir Daryl Lindsay.

[41] Roberts to Deakin, 4 February 1904, Deakin Papers

[42] CROLL, p. 99

[43] Roberts to Deakin, 4 August 1904, Deakin Papers

[44] CROLL, p. 102

[45] On Lambert *see* AMY LAMBERT, *Thirty Years of an Artist's Life*, Sydney, 1938; and *CAO*, pp. 104-5

[46] On Hall *see also CAO*, p. 84

[47] On Quinn *see also CAO*, p. 166

[48] On Ramsay *see also The Art of Hugh Ramsay*, The Fine Art Society, Melbourne; and *CAO*, pp. 168-9

[49] On Ashton *see also CAO*, pp. 21-2

CHAPTER SIX

LEVITICUS
1913 - 32

If we so choose we can yet be the elect of the world, the last of the pastoralists, the thoroughbred Aryans in all their nobility.

J. S. MACDONALD, 'Arthur Streeton', *Art in Australia,*
October 1931

THE modern movement is a vague but useful term. It is here taken to mean the movement which developed out of French impressionism under the influence of Cézanne, Seurat, Van Gogh, Gauguin, Matisse and the artists associated with their respective circles. Artists no longer sought to imitate nature—an ideal the nineteenth century had cherished. Some supporters of the modern movement maintain that the *avant-garde* artists of the early twentieth century gave up attempting to imitate nature because that was a simple matter having little to do with art. Today we know that such arguments are naïve and indeed untrue. The impressionists did not break with nature because its imitation was easy or irrelevant to good painting. They gave up because they came to realize that it is not possible to separate entirely what we see from what we know and what we feel. 'The "Egyptian" in us', as Dr Gombrich has wisely put it, 'can be suppressed, but he can never be quite defeated.'[1] All art, even the most naturalistic, is to some extent conceptual. The artists of the modern movement became increasingly aware of this. They also placed greater emphasis upon the expression of the artist's personality in his work. Paintings were to express the artist's moods and feelings. They also placed great emphasis upon form, especially the arrangement of line, colour and mass in effective artistic structures. Tone, the handmaiden of illusion, fell into disrepute.

In Australia the modern movement may be divided into two phases. The first phase began in Sydney on the eve of the First World War and ended in Melbourne on the eve of the Second World War, when the second phase began and continued down to the present time.

During the first phase of the movement a group of artists, whose numbers increased as the years passed, became influenced to a greater or lesser degree, at times directly and at times indirectly, by the work of such artists as Cézanne, Seurat, Van Gogh, Gauguin, Matisse and their associates. For this reason they may be called Australian post-impressionists. But they remained a minority ranged against an academic establishment. This establishment, in the years between the wars, was led by the Edwardian expatriates and their wide circle of friends and patrons. Returning to Australia one by one after the Armistice the expatriates found to their surprise and joy a flushed economy and a receptive public awaiting them. For most, expatriation had meant years of struggle and disappointment, tempered by limited academic success. But the war brought them, often as official artists, in contact with the Commonwealth Government and they were welcomed back as artists who had achieved some measure of success in Europe and knew, in all things artistic, what was what. They became critics, connoisseurs, gallery directors, and advisers to the Government on art matters. Longstaff and Streeton received knighthoods. When news was received that Lambert had been honoured with an associateship of the Royal Academy, that carefully guarded preserve of English artistic ortho-doxy, he and his friends received the news with as much éclat as if he had been awarded the Order of Merit or the Nobel Prize. Australian society still had little knowledge or understanding of the life of the artist and scant respect for his integrity. But it was now rich enough to corrupt; and it did corrupt as it yearned for culture. The expatriates became the aesthetic mentors of this economically flushed but artistically naïve society, for they had earned by the fact of their expatriation the right to know.

But the irony of it was that they did not know. They rejected Cézanne, and what sprang from Cézanne, almost to a man. Most of them had seen original examples of modern art in Paris and London in the years before the war. It was, they said, the work of incompetents seeking fame through notoriety; a conspiracy among Parisian dealers, a Bolshevik ruse to under-mine the foundations of society. And they clubbed together to prevent the virus spreading to Australia.

Ironically, too, the erstwhile exiles, their wander years over, became champions of the Australian tradition. The expatriates became patriots. But the new nationalism of the 'twenties and 'thirties differed markedly from the nationalism of the 'eighties and 'nineties. Then, nationalism had been closely linked with revolt and innovation. Roberts and Streeton had fought as young men for the recognition of an Australian school of painting against a colonial establishment whose artistic notions, such as they were, were dominated by the moral exhortations of Ruskin and the history painting and didactic art of the English and German academies. But now nationalism allied itself with reaction. The achievements of the Heidelberg School, fostered by the ageing Streeton and his ageing friends, became a national legend. They alone had discovered how to paint the Australian landscape. Before them came the primitives who saw with English eyes

96 EMANUEL PHILLIPS FOX, *The Art
Students*, canvas, 72 x 45, 1895, Sydney

97 RUPERT BUNNY, *The Cosy Corner*, canvas, 23 x 29,
1908, Dr Norman Behan

and after them came the decadents who saw with French eyes. Young Australian artists were exhorted to build on the sound foundations laid by Roberts, Streeton and Heysen, and eschew the decadent forms of contemporary art.

In consequence, stereotyped and debased forms of the Streetonesque and Heysenesque landscape proliferated at the exhibitions of the art societies. Portrait painters, with few exceptions, remained faithful to the tonal illusionist tradition which Bernard Hall continued to disseminate unceasingly at the Melbourne Gallery School from his arrival in 1892 until his retirement in 1934. And under the influence of his pupils, and the pupils of his pupils, the illusionist portrait lived on in declining vigour into the second half of the twentieth century. Melbourne, at the antipodes of the growing points of Western culture and highly conservative and orthodox in all cultural matters, became a stronghold of nineteenth-century values where the traditions of representational painting, however degraded, persisted.

Not all the expatriates became howling reactionaries. Rupert Bunny, long domiciled in Paris, was perhaps the most tolerant, but even he at the beginning was cautious enough. As he remarked in a newspaper interview during a short visit to Australia in 1911:

Van Gogh and the rest simply revolted against the deadness of work that was merely a clever repetition . . . of work that had all been done before, and they wanted to express their own individuality . . . some of them really succeeded. Others did not, because they forgot that unless individuality itself is interesting neither is the expression of it.

And to emphasize his point he added, 'I cannot consider Matisse, for one, anything but a humbug.'[2]

But for the most part the Australian Press paid little attention to the modern movement. Even the local cultural journals, such as *The Lone Hand* and *Art and Architecture*, were mostly indifferent. True, the latter reprinted a brief but sympathetic account by C. Lewis Hind of Roger Fry's exhibition, Manet and the Post Impressionists, held at the Grafton Galleries, London, in December 1910,[3] and a year later (when renamed the *Salon*), featured an article by Fred J. Bloomfield (probably Broomfield) in which the art of Van Gogh, Gauguin, Matisse, Picasso and others was discussed sympathetically.[4] But this was exceptional. Neither books nor coloured reproductions concerned with the art of the post-impressionists were yet available in Australia, still less original works. The first original painting by a French impressionist to be purchased by an Australian gallery on Bernard Hall's recommendation was Camille Pissarro's *Boulevard Montmartre*, in 1905. But beyond the impressionists, public and private buyers were not prepared to move.

The Beginnings of the Modern Movement in Sydney

In Australia, the influence of post-impressionism first appears in the work of a group of Sydney art students trained by Dattilo Rubbo (1871-1955). Like Nerli, who did much to prepare Sydney for impressionism, Rubbo was an Italian. He had studied at Rome and Naples before migrating to Sydney in 1897. A year later he opened an art school in Bligh Street and also became an instructor in painting at the Royal Art Society's School in Vickery's Chambers.

Rubbo was a colourful personality greatly loved by his students and, through his own school which flourished for forty-three years, brought a new interest in colour to art teaching in Sydney. His own work was devoted largely to portraiture and genre painting, much of it being sombre in tone and mood, for he was sensitive to poverty, destitution and the loneliness of old age. Yet his paintings could also be, like his own volatile personality, bright in spirit and highly colourful. Not surprisingly, he encouraged an experimental attitude in his pupils. One of them, Norah Simpson, introduced post-impressionist painting into Australia. She had begun her studies with Rubbo in 1911 at the age of sixteen, and left Sydney on a trip to Europe with her parents in the following year. During the few months they spent in London she attended the Westminster School of Art where Harold Gilman, Spencer Gore and Charles Ginner were teaching. All three were leading members of the Camden Town Group which had been formed early in 1911 and pioneered post-impressionist painting in England. Gilman and Ginner had been influenced by Van Gogh, Gore by Cézanne and Gauguin. Proceeding to Paris, Miss Simpson was able to see a considerable number of impressionist and post-impressionist paintings, including work by Cézanne, Gauguin, Matisse, Picasso and other members of the Ecole de Paris in the collections of Paris art dealers to whom she had received introductions through Gilman. In Paris and London she collected photographs and books dealing with post-impressionist and cubist work and brought them back to Sydney when she returned in 1913.[5]

Norah Simpson possessed, by all accounts, a bright, independent and attractive personality; and upon returning to Rubbo's classes in 1913, succeeded in influencing the work both of her teacher and some of his pupils, notably Roland Wakelin, Grace Cossington Smith and Roy de Maistre. She continued to work in Rubbo's classes until her return to England in 1915. The strong, simple forms and heightened, stippled colours of her Studio Portrait, Chelsea (98), painted about 1915, testifies to her links with post-impressionism and the Camden Town Group, especially Gilman; while the carving in the background reflects the interest in primitive sculpture then widely current in avant-garde circles in Europe.

98   NORAH SIMPSON, *Studio Portrait, Chelsea*, canvas, 20 x 16, *c.* 1915-17, Sydney

Norah Simpson's influence upon Australian art, though crucial, was brief. In 1915, the year she returned to London, Australian paintings revealing the influence of post-impressionism were first publicly exhibited in Sydney by Roland Wakelin and Grace Cossington Smith, in the Annual Exhibition of the Royal Art Society of New South Wales. Wakelin (*b.* 1887) was a New Zealander who had studied at the Technical College, Wellington, under Henri Bastings and had exhibited in 1910 at the Academy of Fine Arts, Wellington, before coming to Sydney in 1912. In the following year he joined the Royal Art Society's classes conducted by Dattilo Rubbo and Norman Carter. His first interest in modern art was aroused upon seeing a reproduction of Marcel Duchamp's *Nude Descending a Staircase* in a Sydney newspaper, the painting being reproduced widely at that time as the most controversial work in the New York Armory Show (February 1913), the first exhibition of modern art to make a major impression upon the American public. Shortly afterwards Wakelin became interested in Miss Simpson's coloured reproductions and began to develop a deep interest in the work of Cézanne. An exhibition of Phillips Fox's work held in Sydney in 1913 after his return from southern France, high-keyed in colour and broadly handled, also affected Wakelin's style at that time.

Grace Cossington Smith studied at Rubbo's studio in Rowe Street from 1910 until 1912 and travelled abroad during 1912-14, studying first at the Winchester Art School and later at Stettin in Germany. It was not, however, until her return to Sydney and Rubbo's classes in 1914 that she, too, under Norah Simpson's influence, became interested in modern painting.

In 1915, with Dattilo Rubbo's encouragement, Wakelin exhibited three, and Grace Cossington Smith one painting at the annual exhibition of the Royal Art Society of New South Wales. Wakelin's *Fruit Seller of Farm Cove* (99) made use of stippled brushwork and a studied and blocky arrangement of the forms in the manner of Seurat. Grace Cossington Smith's sensitive colour sense is already apparent in her *Sock Knitter* (106), in which stippled brushwork is applied to flattish decorative forms reminiscent of Matisse.

Roy de Maistre (then de Mestre), the third and youngest member of the group, was a member of an old pastoral family of southern New South Wales. His father's horses won the Melbourne Cup five times, but the son's interests turned to music and art. In 1913 he came to Sydney to study the violin and viola at the Conservatorium and painting at the Royal Art Society classes under Carter and Rubbo. Here he struck up a friendship with Wakelin and Miss Simpson and started to work in the modern manner.

99 ROLAND WAKELIN, *The Fruit Seller of Farm Cove,*
canvas, 36 x 46, 1915, The Commonwealth Government

100 ROLAND WAKELIN, *Down the Hills to Berry's Bay*, canvas, 26¾ x 48, 1916, Sydney

By 1916 the students in Rubbo's classes who were experimenting with neo-impressionism and post-impressionism had begun to arouse considerable local opposition and Rubbo had to defend their right to exhibit their works in the Royal Art Society exhibitions. This he did successfully, and Wakelin exhibited *Down the Hills to Berry's Bay* (100). Its greens, ochres and terracotta pinks reflect Cézanne; and the massive simplicity of the design Seurat. So enthusiastic was Wakelin for Cézanne's work at this time that he called his own house at Carr Street, Waverton, 'Cézanne'. Local critics were still not quite sure how to react to the new tendencies. One wrote: 'Mr Dattilo Rubbo has joined the pointillists . . . and has dragged two students at least, Mr Wakelin and Miss Tempe Manning, after him. The three of them splash merrily with spots of crimson and green and vermilion and yellow, and the results are certainly amazing.'[6] In the same exhibition Grace Cossington Smith exhibited *The Reader* (the author), more *pointilliste* in manner than her work of the previous year.

Between 1914 and 1916 Wakelin and Miss Smith had been concerned largely with heightening colour, strengthening and simplifying forms and experimenting with pure pigment applied with stippled brushwork. During 1917 and 1918, however, Wakelin, Grace Cossington Smith and Roy de Maistre abandoned *pointilliste* effects in favour of flat, unbroken surfaces. This is apparent in Grace Cossington Smith's war-time paintings of crowds and troop-embarkation scenes which are somewhat reminiscent of C. R. W. Nevinson. Massive, cubic effects dominate Wakelin's *White House* (101), and a flat, posterish manner of composing prevails in de Maistre's *Water-*

101 ROLAND WAKELIN, *White House*, cardboard, 10 x 11¾,
1918, Mr A. J. McDonnell

front on Sydney Harbour (102). These paintings foreshadowed the first
Australian essays in abstract art.

In 1916 de Maistre joined the A.I.F., but he was discharged nine months
later suffering from tuberculosis. During convalescence he returned to
painting and met Dr Moffitt of the Gladesville Mental Hospital, Sydney,
who awakened his interest in the psychological effects of colour. At that
time mental patients were often placed in wards painted in colours intended
to stimulate or soothe. De Maistre persuaded the Red Cross to allow him
to experiment with colour in the treatment of shell-shock cases and became
so interested in his results that he raised sufficient money to establish the
Exeter Convalescent Home; Moffitt became the Medical Director. Rooms
were painted in colour-keys designed to provide the benefits of colour
treatment without the retinal exhaustion and monotony of single colours.

Meanwhile two books, *Cubists and Post-Impressionists* by Arthur Jerome
Eddy (1915), and *Modern Painting, its Tendency and Meaning* by Willard
Huntington Wright (1915), had become available in Australia. The books
were illustrated with works by Matisse, Picasso, Kandinsky, Boccioni and
others, and there were colour illustrations of the work of such artists as
Gleizes, Duchamp, Gris, Villon, Kandinsky and Picabia. Wright included
in his book a long chapter on synchromism, a form of painting based upon
the generation of form by pure colour. It had been developed during 1913
and 1914 by two American painters, Morgan Russell and MacDonald

Wright. Synchromism, said Huntington Wright, was 'the last step in the evolution of present-day art methods. . . . It now remains only for artists to create. . . . The era of pure creation begins with the present day.'[7] Eddy's book included a chapter on colour theory and had a good deal to say on the relation between painting and music, an aspect of aesthetics to which many of the early abstract painters, Kandinsky especially, devoted much thought and experiment. It also provided a detailed description of a colour organ invented by A. W. Rimington, a Professor of Fine Arts at Queen's College, London. Wakelin and de Maistre read these books. They became intensely interested in synchromism and in the possibility of painting pictures according to a chromatic notation analogous to musical notation. De Maistre, of course, had some knowledge of music and he and his friend Adrian Verbrugghen, the son of Henri Verbrugghen, the Director of the Sydney Conservatorium of Music, invented a colour music scale in which the spectrum colours were related to the notes of the diatonic scale. De Maistre and Wakelin also invented a colour disc which was designed to assemble colour schemes from a chromatic scale based on standard principles. It was patented later and used by de Maistre for producing harmonic colour schemes for interiors.

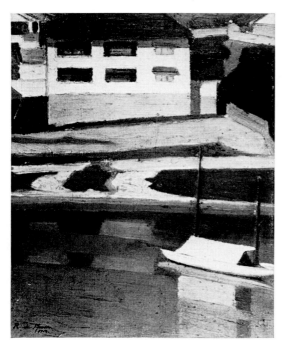

102 ROY DE MAISTRE, *Waterfront on Sydney Harbour*, cardboard, 12¼ x 10, *c.* 1918/19, Mr Daniel Thomas

In August 1919 Wakelin and de Maistre held an exhibition of synchromies at Gayfield Shaw's Gallery, Sydney, Wakelin showing six paintings and de Maistre five, together with exhibits illustrating the application of his colour theory to interior decoration (111). De Maistre also delivered a lecture on colour music at the exhibition, which was well attended, and aroused considerable discussion.

The synchromies exhibition, however, helped to alert and sharpen the reaction to post-impressionist painting. De Maistre's ideas were strongly criticized by Julian Ashton, the President of the Society of Artists and then still the most influential man in the art world of Sydney, and also by Henri Verbrugghen. But the most vociferous critic of all was Howard Ashton, the son of Julian Ashton, a landscape painter and journalist who acted as art and music critic on the Sydney *Sun*. Ashton castigated the exhibition in an art review as 'elaborate and pretentious bosh'.[8]

Such adverse criticism was not without effect. By 1921 the impetus of this first phase of the modern movement in Australia was beginning to lag. In that year Max Meldrum visited Sydney and his tonal theory of painting, discussed below, influenced de Maistre and Wakelin for a time. By February 1922, Norman Lindsay, whose ideas were setting firmly against modernism, could see in the temporary eclipse of the movement reason for faith in the future of the Australian civilization:

Primitivism as an expression of mind has failed to get even a hearing here. Efforts have been made to introduce it, by a few idle busybodies, who think art is merely some 'new idea', some just invented fancy, something to entertain leisure in cultured gabble, but a little derision applied in time withered this noxious growth before it could take root.[9]

In Melbourne, Meldrum was attacking modernism quite as vehemently.

Meldrum and Tonal Realism

Like Roy de Maistre, working away assiduously for some years on the relation between painting and music, Max Meldrum was consumed by the desire to invent a rational theory of painting. Born in 1875, he arrived in Melbourne at the age of fourteen, and studied at the Gallery School under Hall from whom he acquired a preference for dark painting, a lifelong concern with tonal values and a predilection for the artfully designed lights of studio interiors. In 1899 he won the Travelling Scholarship and proceeded to Paris. There a dislike of the 'ineptitude and academic conventions of the schools' compelled him to study in 'the school of nature' which he found in the village of Pacé in Brittany. He exhibited frequently in Paris, however, and in 1908 was elected an Associate of the Société Nationale des Beaux Arts.

Meldrum lived in France at a time when the fauvist and cubist experiments were creating considerable excitement in art circles, and there he developed a violent dislike for modern art. After much study in the Louvre he came to the conclusion that great art had always been impersonal and concerned essentially with the objective depiction of appearance.

Meldrum returned to Melbourne in 1911, and in 1917 established a school in which he developed, practised and taught his theory. Painting, he claimed, was a pure science: the science of optical analysis or photometry. The artist's aim was to transfer to his canvas an exact illusion within the limitations of painting (wider, he asserted, than photography) of the objects present in the act of perception. This was the central problem of painting as revealed in the work of Leonardo, Velasquez, Rembrandt, Canaletto and Corot. Art, said Meldrum, evolved, its advance depending upon the improvement of knowledge concerning the nature of perception. It followed that much academic teaching was quite irrelevant. Both classicism, with its preoccupation with unity and harmony of parts, and romanticism, with its emphasis upon the artist's individuality, were to be discarded in favour of a naturalism grounded in the objective analysis of tone.

Meldrum linked his theory of painting with a criticism of society. Social decadence, he claimed, brought with it a slackening interest in tone and proportion and an increasing interest in colour: modern art with its distortions and excessive interest in colour was a supreme example of social decadence. Meldrum owed much of his power and influence over two decades to thus linking a painting theory with a social theory. Whereas the great majority of the Australian artists of Meldrum's generation identified themselves with the establishment as they grew older, Meldrum remained a critic of society throughout life. When most of his colleagues were enlisting in the services, 'doing their bit' in military hospitals, or being enrolled as war artists, Meldrum, like Cézanne before him, held that the artist had no business with war. It was the only thing they had in common. His strong pacifist views had much to do with the success of his school. With the country split from top to bottom over the conscription issue many young art students preferred to study under Meldrum in a congenial atmosphere than risk being given white feathers at the Gallery School where an atmosphere of high patriotism prevailed.

In seeking to reduce painting to a science Meldrum chose to ignore the fact that the masterpieces of painting have always expressed the personality, temperament, ideas and attitudes of the men who painted them and of the times in which they were painted. He chose, in other words, to ignore the personal and social function of art and to explain art entirely in terms of the painting techniques evolved over the centuries to create pictorial illusion. Yet his theory, it must be stressed, cannot even be considered as an entirely satisfactory account of his own practice, for it was based upon an inadequate theory of perception. Meldrum maintained that the eye perceived tonal relationships 'naturally'; whereas illusions created by lines alone required mental translation. But he did not take into account the fact that tone, too, is an abstraction for it occurs to the normal eye only in association with colour and can only be realized by a mental dissociation of tone from colour. Meldrum himself created highly artificial studio methods to aid these processes of dissociation. Further, there is an infinite number of tonal gradations in nature but the artist, because of the limitations of his medium, must reduce them to a very small number and *construct* his painting out of them. A Meldrum painting is, in short, like all painting, conceptual and constructive. Meldrum's method, however, made it possible for his students to become skilled in capturing a likeness quickly and was greatly favoured by potential portrait painters, and the practical-minded common-sense type of student temperamentally suspicious of imaginative activity.

Among his pupils Meldrum's theory became something of a cult and craft mystery. The adulation of their teacher became uncritical. Some acclaimed Meldrum as the greatest among the masters; the man who had discovered the scientific laws underlying the age-old practices of his craft; the man who had once and for all placed painting upon a scientific basis. As Newton to physics and Darwin to biology, so Meldrum to painting. Such adulation found graphic expression in an odd device invented by Percy Leason, one of Meldrum's most influential followers. Western painting, argued Leason following Meldrum closely, rose and declined as certain factors expressed themselves in art. In order to explain what he had in mind Leason made use of a triangle; the left and rising side of which, holding the numbers 1 to 6, signified growth; the right and falling side, with the numbers 6 to 12, signified decline. Number 6 at the apex of the triangle represented the high point of art: the achievement of objective tonal truth. Some masters during certain phases of their careers, Rembrandt, Velasquez, Corot and Whistler, for example, had managed to achieve 6 during certain moments of their lives, but Leason also gave them less flattering numbers for concerning themselves with such things as expression, colour, and feeling, less important to good painting, in his view as a staunch Meldrumite, than tone. To Meldrum alone he awarded 6 during the whole of his career. In the history of painting Meldrum was the great cock of the roost. The master, like his devoted pupils, seemingly believed it, for he wrote a preface to the book in which his supremacy was so graphically demonstrated.[10]

Such pride and arrogance of mind was, perhaps not unnaturally, associated with intolerance. Meldrum could appreciate few forms of painting but his own and the masters he appealed to in order to justify his theory. The impressionists, for example, by turning to irrelevant scientific theories and by asserting their individuality through colour, had inaugurated the decline of modern art. In his teaching he rejected as useless the study of anatomy, composition, rhythm and the study of colour for its own sake. Meldrumism became an exclusivist doctrine: its truths could be revealed fully only to professional artists. Laymen were able to criticize and enjoy finished paintings but were not in a position to judge theories and methods of painting. Only painters, said Meldrum, could 'define the rhythm and order of ocula sensa'.[11] As so often in such cases, the pseudo-science became

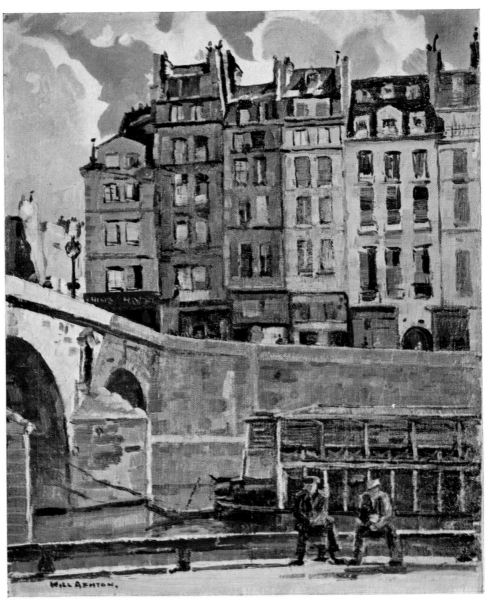

103 WILL ASHTON, *Le Pont Marie, Paris*, canvas, 16¾ x 13¼,
c. 1930, The Rt Hon. R. G. Menzies

a craft mystery, the truths of which revealed themselves only to the initiated.

Yet Meldrum possessed the courage of his convictions. The loyalty he inspired in his pupils sprang as much from his personality as from the deceptive simplicity of his theories. For many his single-mindedness and resistance to personal corruption by social and financial success made him a symbol of artistic integrity in a philistine community where the idea of art as a way of life was a poor joke. In his own art he was a capable and honest but not an inspired craftsman. Much of it has the air of pedantry one finds in his writings. But an early portrait of his mother (104) reveals a precocious mastery of his craft and a truly superb impersonalization of sympathy reminiscent of the young Rembrandt. The latent humanism of such early works, however, did not survive the intellectual rigour which his arid theory imposed upon his own painting. In one sense, however, Meldrum's theory is of considerable interest: it is probably the last of those attempts, so characteristic of the nineteenth century, to deduce a naturalistic theory of painting from scientific or pseudo-scientific presuppositions. And yet, oddly enough, in his later work the very breadth with which Meldrum painted his planes of tones, and his refusal to add detail and polish, had the effect of introducing into his art a kind of tonal, cubic reduction akin in many ways to the modified post-impressionist methods adopted by many painters during the 1920's (115). Even Meldrum's art, despite the practice of a discipline designed to produce impersonal painting as rigorous and thoroughgoing as any in the history of art, was responsive to the imperceptible pressures of period style.

Meldrum exercised a strong influence upon painting in the years between the wars and his ideas were also diffused widely by his pupils, several of whom established schools of their own, notably: Archibald Colquhoun who, following a period of study overseas, established a school in Melbourne in 1927; Hayward Veal, who ran a Meldrum School of painting in Sydney between 1938 and 1950; and Percy Leason, who took Meldrum's ideas to America and taught them with modifications at the Staten Island Institute of Arts and Crafts, the Wayman Adams Summer School in the Adirondacks, and later at his own Summer School at Westport, Lake Champlain. Meldrum himself had done something to make his ideas known in America, however, in a lecture tour in 1931.

Compromise and Reaction

In Sydney, as we have seen, by 1920 the initial energy of the *avant-garde* movement which had begun in Dattilo Rubbo's art classes seven years before was beginning to flag. Wakelin and de Maistre failed to gain sufficient support from their fellow artists and local patrons in order to estab-

lish synchromism or any of the advanced forms of contemporary painting
as viable artistic movements. Indeed, their concern with abstraction, though
pursued with keen enthusiasm at the time, was a passing interest. De
Maistre after his brief experiments with Meldrumism, reverted to a stylized
form of representational painting based upon the formal analysis of figures
and objects after the Camden Town manner. Wakelin, too, returned to less
experimental painting. His *Conservatorium*[12] reveals a curious compromise
between Meldrum and Seurat. In later work he came to combine an interest
in design with a desire to express romantic feeling in landscape, and never
returned to pure abstraction. Indeed, pictorial taste and technique in Sydney
was not to be led during the 1920's by youthful *avant-garde* experimenters
but by those Edwardian expatriates trained in the pre-war academies who
returned to Australia in the years following the end of the war. Still deeply
respectful of Royal Academy tradition, they nevertheless reflected the post-
war interest in bright colours, crisp painting and decorative emphasis given
currency by such British painters as Augustus John, Sir William Orpen, Eric
Kennington, Gerald Kelly, Algernon Talmage, William Strang and Dame
Laura Knight. The work of these artists was brought prominently before the
Australian art public in an exhibition of European art brought out by
Penleigh Boyd and exhibited in Sydney and Melbourne in the second half
of 1923. But the man who did most to popularize the 1920 academy mode
was George Lambert.

Lambert became the arbiter of 'progressive' taste. When he returned in
1921 to complete his war art commissions he was, at the age of forty-seven,
at the height of his career, a man of unusual energy and great personal
charm. His style, under the influence of Orpen and others, had become thin
and dry in texture, pastel-like in colour, firm, and yet somewhat affected in
manner and gesture. Although a skilled exponent of academic methods he
saw himself as a champion of youth and was not intolerant of modernist
experiments providing they were not 'excessive'. Hence his work and
influence provided a compromise between the *avant-garde* and the old
guard: bright enough to be daring, it was yet solid enough in constructive
drawing to be eminently respectable. In 1921, the year of his return, he
exhibited *Important People* (105) at the annual exhibition of the Society of
Artists. Its dry paint surface, decorative manner and enigmatic subject-
matter evoked widespread comment by no means unfavourable, and it
marks a sharp break in Sydney taste from the flaccid tonal romanticism
which had prevailed during the war years in genteel circles. Hilder was on
the way out and Lambert on the way in. The power of the old gods of the
art schools, too, was declining. The inspiration behind *Important People* was
to be found not in Velasquez, Raeburn or Corot, but in the Italian primitives.
Lambert's advice to students underlines this change from tone to design and

104   MAX MELDRUM, *Portrait of the Artist's Mother*, canvas,
23 x 18⅞, 1913, Melbourne

105   GEORGE LAMBERT, *Important People*, canvas,
53 x 67, *c.* 1914-20, Sydney

construction. They should observe closely, he said, and work hard at drawing. 'Get your machinery first, learn how to do the tiresome, uninteresting
foundation work thoroughly.'[13] His influence upon the art students was
immediate and direct: upon Douglas Dundas, for example, who built his
art upon Lambertian lines; and Arthur Murch, who worked as Lambert's
assistant from 1928 to 1930.

Lambert's influence was increased by the support of his friend Sydney
Ure Smith, another Ashton student who had graduated to art publication
after establishing a successful practice in commercial art. In 1917 Smith
established the journal, *Art in Australia*, remaining its editor until 1938; this
was an achievement in art publication in Australia which has never been
equalled. Indeed Ure Smith's tireless devotion to the cause of Australian art
is comparable only to that of Julian Ashton and the young Tom Roberts.
He replaced Ashton as the President of the Society of Artists in 1921, and
as a result of his work the Society became the most influential circle of
artists in the years between the wars. In 1923 Ure Smith was largely responsible for organizing an *Exhibition of Australian Art* held at the Royal
Academy, London. Although his own work was traditional, consisting largely
of topographical studies of old buildings in Sydney and its environs which
he etched, drew, or painted in water-colour with loving care, his policy as
President of the Society of Artists was tolerant and forward-looking. Under
Julian Ashton (1907-21) modernist tendencies of any kind had not been

106 GRACE COSSINGTON SMITH, *The Sock Knitter*, canvas,
24 x 20, 1915, Sydney

encouraged. Under Ure Smith, the influence of post-impressionist painting, although modified and diluted in its passage from Paris via London to Sydney, began to appear with decorous modesty in the annual exhibitions of the Society.[14]

Closely associated with Lambert and Ure Smith in the Society of Artists circle at this time were two women, Thea Proctor and Margaret Preston, whose drawings, paintings and designs evoke the peculiar quality and flavour of Sydney taste during the 1920's more vividly than the work of any of their contemporaries. Miss Proctor studied under Ashton prior to leaving for London where she became a close friend of the Lamberts, and was for a time his pupil. While abroad she fashioned an attractive decorative style out of her interest in Conder's fan designs, the Japanese print, and the drawings of Ingres, expressing it in elegant line drawings (107), tinted water-colours and woodcuts. Although by no means a modernist in her training or methods, an abiding interest in colour and form made her sympathetic to the aims of artists like de Maistre and Wakelin. It was the votes of Thea Proctor and Lambert that gave de Maistre the Society of Artists' Travelling Scholarship for 1923 and three years later she formed with him the (Sydney) Contemporary Group.[15] This exhibiting group brought together those Sydney painters who had been influenced in one way or another by post-impressionist doctrine. Margaret Preston, Thea Proctor, Vida Lahey, Adelaide Perry, Grace Cossington Smith, Aletta Lewis, George Lambert, Elioth Gruner, Roland Wakelin, Roy de Maistre and Kenneth Macqueen were among the earliest exhibiting members of the group which still exists.

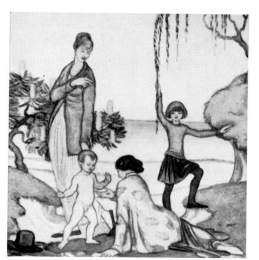

107   THEA PROCTOR, *The Shell*, pencil and wash, 11 x 9½, *c.* 1923-4, Professor E. G. Waterhouse

Margaret Preston was a South Australian who had received a thorough continental training. From the Adelaide School of Design she had graduated to Bernard Hall's studio in Melbourne and thence to Munich and Paris. Her early work, tonal and realistic in the manner of the times, was exhibited at the Royal Academy, the New Salon, the International Society of Painters, Sculptors and Gravers and the New English Art Club. But she was a woman of great independence of mind, volatile in temperament, ardently patriotic and consumed by a passion for experiment-

ing in painting media and all kinds of graphic techniques. After she settled
in Sydney following the First World War, she had discarded the tonalism
of the schools and began to devote herself to colour design in strong, simple
and blocky shapes (117), first only in oils, later in woodcut, lino-cut,
masonite-cut, silk-screen, and monotype—and indeed almost anything else
that could be cut and printed.

Margaret Preston has travelled widely about the world but no one, oddly
enough, has advocated the creation of a distinctive national art in Australia
more ardently both in her own work and in her writing and lecturing. It
became the cause to which she dedicated her life. Much of her work in the
early 'twenties, springing from such interests, was concerned, like Lucien
Henry[16] before her, in arousing interest in the decorative qualities of Australian flora. Then she became aware of the aesthetic beauty of aboriginal
art and sought to gain from it a better insight into the nature of art itself.
Her article, *The Indigenous Art of Australia*,[17] pioneered the appreciation
of aboriginal art among local artists, and she became the first of many
practising artists to champion aboriginal art as an independent art form,
and to be influenced by it herself. She has, therefore, a fair claim to have
been the first champion of the aesthetic quality of an art today known and
admired throughout the world.

Elioth Gruner, another prominent member of the Society of Artists, was
the typical Australian landscape painter of the period between the wars just
as Lambert was the typical portrait painter. But his talent was smaller than
Lambert's. Although he certainly possessed a keen and discriminating eye
for fine tonal gradations, there is a neat and sweetly fastidious refinement
about his work that lacks character. Many of his landscapes might not
unfairly be described as Meldrum taken in the open air with milk and sugar.
He had already, as we have seen, made a pre-war reputation painting spring
blossom and misty mornings *au contre jour* in a sentimental *plein-air* style.
In 1921 he spent four months painting *The Valley of the Tweed*, a large
work which he executed as a commission from the Trustees of the National
Art Gallery of New South Wales for a typical Australian landscape. It was
painted entirely in the open air. In this commission for a landscape at once
big and typical there lay a nostalgic desire to return to the past glories of
the Heidelberg School. But the painting, despite its technical competence,
is a pretty lifeless thing with none of the vitality and sense of visual discovery that characterizes Streeton's *Fire's On*. Sir William Orpen strongly
criticized *The Valley of the Tweed* to Gruner himself while the latter was
acting as manager of the Australian Exhibition in London in 1923, without
knowing that Gruner had painted it. Though Gruner resented the attack,
Orpen's advocacy of thin, dry paint and pastel-like surfaces was not
altogether lost upon him. He did not attempt the big landscape again; and

M

108   ELIOTH GRUNER, *On the Murrumbidgee*, canvas,
40 x 48½, 1929, Sydney

later paintings such as *The Pines* (1926, Sydney) and *On the Murrum-bidgee* (108) contain less sentiment, more drawing, and a greater concern with composition and the anatomical structure of the countryside depicted. But even these later works still possess something of the prim tidiness of a coloured photograph.[18]

The new emphasis upon broad patterns, strong contrasts and sharp con-tours so characteristic of the painting of the time is reflected in changing fashions in the graphic arts. In this Sir Lionel Lindsay was a pioneer. In 1907 he had pioneered the local interest in etching. In the early 'twenties he awakened interest in wood engraving, organizing in 1923, at Tyrrell's Art Galleries, Sydney, the first exhibition in Australia devoted entirely to the medium. Lindsay's own cuts exploited to the full the rich tonal possibilities of the medium by his detailed elaboration of simple designs (109). The rendering of textures, such as the petals of flowers and the feathers of birds, fascinated him.[19] Other artists, like Margaret Preston, Thea Proctor, Adrian Feint and Raymond McGrath, more closely affiliated to the new movement in painting than Lindsay, made greater use of sharp contrasts and bold designs. Associated with wood engraving was the lino-cut, pioneered by Napier Waller about 1923. Both media were admirable for the production of bookplates which became very popular during the 'twenties, Adrian Feint developing a considerable reputation in this field.

The artists associated with the Contemporary Group and the Society of Artists represented progressive and fashionable taste respectively. The Royal Art Society, however, became after 1920 increasingly the centre of conservatism and reaction. In 1922 it was reconstituted for the purpose of creating Fellows and Associates as in the Royal Academy, but it lacked social prestige and its standards of professional competence steadily declined. Under W. Lister Lister, a painter of huge uninspired studio-painted 'plein-air' landscapes, who

109 LIONEL LINDSAY, *Goat and Rhododendron*, wood engraving, 6¾ x 6, 1925

was the President for forty-one years from 1900, a group of ageing professionals increasingly irritated by contemporary forms of expression, joined with aspiring but inept amateurs to champion exhausted forms of naturalism inherited from Bernard Hall, Julian Ashton, Arthur Streeton and Hans Heysen. The leaders of the Society claimed to be champions of sanity in art in a world of artistic decadence, and their paintings sold well.[20] In Melbourne optical realism based upon tonal values, introduced by Bernard Hall into the Gallery School in 1892, continued to dominate taste. Meldrum had codified it into a system during the war years. But in the hands of John Longstaff and W. B. McInnes, a pupil of Hall, it became a popular portrait style. Longstaff had returned in 1919 and his career moved inevitably towards its climax: the President of the Victorian Artists' Society, 1924-5; a Trustee of the National Gallery of Victoria, 1927; and knighted, 1928. For twenty years he became the hearty and complaisant embodiment of art officialdom in Australia. McInnes's portraits were often more flattering and oleaginous than Longstaff's, though he could produce a competent and characteristic likeness, as in his fine study of Sydney Ure Smith (110). Between them they virtually dominated official portraiture for a decade.

In 1919 J. F. Archibald, the sardonic and mercurial editor of the *Bulletin*, a man who had spent a lifetime exposing hypocrisy, pretension and status-seeking, died leaving a portion of his estate for an annual prize to be awarded for the best portrait 'preferentially of some man or woman dis-

110   W. B. McINNES, *Sydney Ure Smith, O.B.E.*, canvas, 37⅜ x 33⅛,
(before 1929), Sydney

tinguished in Art, Letters, Science, or Politics, painted by an artist resident
in Australasia during the twelve months preceding'. The notion implicit in
the will of a Pantheon, a Gallery of Great Australian Men and Women was
in perfect accord with the slightly sour nationalism of the time. McInnes
and Longstaff shared the prize between them nine times during the first
ten years of the award, McInnes winning it five times and Longstaff four.
And as it began so it continued. The Archibald Prize became the last stronghold of tonal illusionist painting in the country; a sleek, flattering, oleaginous

111 ROY DE MAISTRE, *Rhythmic Composition in Yellow Green Minor,*
cardboard, 34 x 45¾, 1919, Sydney

manner having been favoured by the Trustees of the Art Gallery of New
South Wales (who administer the award) down almost to the present day.
The most successful competitor of all has been William Dargie (116) who
has won the competition eight times. Dargie was the pupil of Archibald
Colquhoun, who had been the pupil of Max Meldrum, who had been in
turn the pupil of Bernard Hall. It is quite surprising at first to think of the
number of Australian portrait painters who have continued decade after
decade to hold Bernard Hall's old, dark mirror up to nature and man in
order to reduce them both to so many cream and brown patches: but it
is a levelling mode of portraiture which a society deeply egalitarian in its
sympathies and prejudices seems to have found curiously satisfying for the
portrayal of its most distinguished sons and daughters.

Post-Impressionist Painting in Melbourne

French post-impressionist painting began to influence art in Melbourne
about ten years after it had begun to influence art in Sydney. Although
the work of the gifted New Zealander, Frances Hodgkins, was favourably
received by critics as brilliant and daring examples of French modern
painting when she exhibited in Melbourne in November 1912 and in Sydney
in April 1913, she was at this time relying entirely upon a free, decorative
but quite impressionistic use of colour for her fluent effects.[21] The work of

112   HILDA RIX NICHOLAS,
Grand Mere, canvas, 31⅞ x
25¼, *c.* 1919, Sydney

Hilda Rix Nicholas, however, shown in Melbourne and Sydney in 1918, was indirectly influenced by Van Gogh and Gauguin. Miss Nicholas spent a good deal of time at Etaples during her years of study in Europe between 1909 and 1918, and there, doubtless, learned much about the new modes (112). Her paintings, though received favourably enough, do not appear to have had any effect upon Melbourne art, then still dominated by the teachings of Hall and Meldrum.[22]

In 1918, however, Dr Esmond Keogh, returning home from the Western Front, brought back to Melbourne with him some books he had obtained in France containing illustrations of paintings by Cézanne, Van Gogh and others. Keogh was acquainted with Marriott, whose *Modern Movements in Painting* appeared in 1920, and subscribed to early issues of Wyndham Lewis's *Blast*. In 1920 a friend brought back a book of Picasso's drawings. These books Keogh showed among his circle of friends who included Patrick Harford (who later married Keogh's sister, the poet, Lesbia Harford) and William Frater, who was at that time still much influenced by Max Meldrum.[23]

William Frater (*b.* 1890) had studied at the Glasgow Art School under Legros, Greiffenhagen and Anning Bell while serving his articles as a stained glass craftsman and designer. In 1910 he migrated to Melbourne and obtained employment with Brooks Robinson's Stained Glass Studios in Elizabeth Street, where he gained a high reputation as a craftsman and designer. During 1911-12 Frater attended evening classes at the Victorian Artists' Society. The vigorous *alla prima* methods he was adopting at the time are to be seen in his fluent and sensitive *Portrait of a Girl* (113). In 1912, having resolved a family difference, he returned to Europe, studied for a short period in Paris and London and then for two further years at the Glasgow School. Then, in 1914, he returned to Melbourne and to his former post with Brooks Robinson's. Max Meldrum, who had returned the year previously, was developing his tonal theory at the time, and the two Scots became firm friends. Frater's portrait of his wife reading (the artist, 1915) and his *Self-Portrait* (the artist, 1916) reveal Meldrum's theory increasingly. A small portrait of his son, *Arthur* (*c.* 1922, A. Frater), however, reveals the beginnings of his interest in Cézanne.

Harford worked with Frater at Brooks Robinson's, where Arnold Shore was also serving his articles as a stained glass craftsman between 1911 and 1917, at the same time attending evening drawing classes at the Gallery School under McCubbin and Hall. In 1917 Shore transferred to Meldrum's evening classes. The post-impressionist movement in Melbourne came into existence as a result of the discussions between Frater, Shore and Harford. Frater became a champion of Cézanne's methods. Shore was drawn to Van Gogh's magnificent colour and expressive freedom. Van Gogh liberated him from the constrictions of Meldrum's realism. Both artists began to exhibit their first essays in post-impressionism with the Society of Twenty Melbourne Painters, a group founded in 1917, consisting largely of painters who worked in the Meldrum manner. Their efforts were so different from the rest of the Society that they were hung on an end wall and ignored by Melbourne critics for some years.

Both Frater and Shore have spoken of the stimulating effects of Pat Harford's questioning of the view then generally accepted in Melbourne that art was an imitation of nature. It was Frater, however, who provided some leadership to the small group of modernists in Melbourne during the early 1920's. In 1925 he delivered a lecture in the Queen's Hall in reply to one by Bernard Hall attacking modern art. 'Copying nature', he asserted, attacking Meldrum's position, 'is not an art; the cult at present is to copy effects of light' which, he added, 'tends to destroy form and colour.' Thinking artists organized form and colour. If they help their construction they are used, if not, they are ignored.[24] By 1923 many of Meldrum's former pupils were beginning to question his theory. On 16 March Percy Leason, an ardent disciple of his master, wrote to Frater:

With the wholesale repudiation of Meldrum that seems to be going on amongst his past pupils there is a serious possibility and a very good likelihood that the

113   WILLIAM FRATER, *Portrait of a Girl*,
canvas, 24 x 20, 1910, Melbourne

great school of art which Australia could develop is to become a hopeless ruin, and it is all being pulled down because each individual wants to gratify selfish desires.[25]

Both in Sydney and in Melbourne during the 1920's knowledge of the modern movement was obtained largely by means of coloured illustrations. John Young recalled how the early Sydney post-impressionists around 1919 consulted illustrations in the magazine *Colour*;[26] Frater has expressed his indebtedness, prior to 1925, to colour illustrations of the work of Van Gogh, Matisse and Cézanne in copies of *The Dial*;[27] Shore has described how the last fortnightly issue of Orpen's *Outline of Art*, to which he and Frater were subscribing, with its illustrations of work by Cézanne, Van Gogh, Gauguin and Matisse, came as a revelation to him.[28] But good colour reproductions were difficult to acquire until the establishment by Gino Nibbi, an Italian from Rome, of a book and curio shop in Bourke Street in 1928, materially altered the situation. Nibbi was keenly interested in the modern movement and began to import large Piper prints from Munich of the work of post-impressionist masters. From Nibbi, Frater purchased the large print of Cézanne's *Peasant in a Blue Smock*; and Shore bought copies of *Cahiers d'Art* and *Formes* in which he studied reproductions of work by Modigliani,

Soutine, Picasso, Dufy, Rouault, Chagall and so on. By 1930 Nibbi's book shop had become a rendezvous of artists and laymen interested in European contemporary art and literature. As a result of Nibbi's active advocacy the Melbourne interest in contemporary painting began to widen appreciably. In Geelong shortly afterwards, H. Tatlock Miller began to publish *Manuscripts* (1931-5), a little magazine which championed *avant-garde* thought in literature and art. It was, it would appear, the first Australian magazine to discuss cubism and surrealism without prejudice.

Meanwhile George Bell had become increasingly interested in the principles underlying post-impressionist painting. He saw its insistence upon form and design as a return to the basic principles of good art. His knowledge of the Italian masters had made him increasingly dissatisfied with the tonal illusionism taught by Hall and Meldrum. Settling in Toorak after his return to Melbourne in 1920 Bell had built himself a house and studio, and had begun to paint and take private pupils. In 1922 he taught drawing for a year while McInnes was abroad. By 1925 he had become dissatisfied with his own work and the principles upon which it was based. His interest in modern art grew and brought him in touch with Frater, Shore and others of their circle. Bell had already become respected as a leader of opinion for the prompt action he took when it appeared that the work of Victorian artists would be inadequately represented in the Exhibition of Australian Art organized in Sydney in 1923 by the Society of Artists for exhibition at the Royal Academy; and as art critic on the *Sun News-Pictorial* from 1923 he helped to encourage a sympathetic approach to the work of the younger and more experimental painters.

The Post-war Time-Lag and Reaction

Generally speaking, the decade from 1920 to 1930 was not a particularly creative period in Australian art. It is true that in those years the influence of the modern movement was first felt in the country: but post-impressionism did not bring the same sense of discovery and liberation to the artists of the time that impressionism brought to the men of Roberts's generation, or that expressionism, surrealism and abstract art were to bring to the artists who began to work in the years preceding the Second World War. William Moore called the years before 1900 the Genesis of Australian art, and the years after, the Exodus. And he might well have called the 1920's the Leviticus; for it was then that the old men of the tribe, their years of exile over, began to lay down the law for the guidance of the young. Let us keep Australian art healthy and sane, they said, and not allow the madness going on in Europe to sap the vitality of the true Australian art which we began.

The air was heavy with the arrogance and respectability of old men, old and tired in spirit and in the handling of paint, if not yet quite old in years. When Tom Roberts, the best of them, returned to Australia in 1923 to end his life here he was sixty-seven. The long years he had spent in London seeking for a place on the line at the Academy had taken their toll. An honest and sensitive craftsman he remained, for he was not the kind of man to compromise his values for the sake of cheap success. But the energy, freshness and finer perception of his early work had gone, and he spent the last years of his life painting pale grey-green and saffron landscapes in which the sun never quite shines and the light is like cold steel. The paint is handled in a close, introverted way, and a wistful air hangs over the work. Roberts did not realize the promise of his youth: but neither did Streeton, nor Meldrum, nor Norman Lindsay.

Streeton returned in 1924 to find himself at the age of fifty-seven already a national legend, a legend which he began at once to document, embroider and consolidate. He began to prepare the Streeton history of Australian art designed, he told Roberts, to 'put everybody in their proper place'.[29] The project arose, it appears, partly out of jealousy of Julian Ashton whom some-one had dubbed to Streeton's chagrin 'the father of Australian art'. Later he set himself the task of preparing the *Arthur Streeton Catalogue*. He handled his own exhibitions with the uninhibited assurance of a dealer handling a protégé's work. Melba opened the 1924 one-man show at the Fine Arts Gallery which announced his return to his homeland, and he prefaced his catalogue liberally with business puffs. Sales were splendid and continued to be so. Settling in Toorak and purchasing five acres in the Dandenongs he became more and more engrossed in painting and tending his suburban and country gardens. But he also travelled widely throughout the country painting for his one-man shows, visiting one tourist resort after another: Mount Buffalo, The Grampians, The Blue Mountains; the Barron Gorge in Queensland, to paint the beauty spots of Australia. The two most influential critics of the time, Lionel Lindsay and J. S. MacDonald, vied with one another in praise. His method, said Lindsay, was plastically finer than that of the French landscape impressionists; he had fixed the character of the Australian landscape for all time; he was one of the few great painters of landscape left to the world.[30] Indeed, Lindsay found in Streeton's work piercing beauty which stirred his patriotism to almost mystical depths. So, too, did James Stuart MacDonald. 'They point', he said in an ecstatic survey of Streeton's art, 'to the way in which life should be lived in Australia, with the maximum of flocks and the minimum of factories. . . . If we so choose we can yet be the elect of the world, the last of the pastoralists, the thoroughbred Aryans in all their nobility.'[31] That was written in 1931. By that time Streeton had become the great father-figure of Australian art and his paintings the manifest symbol of a pathological nationalism that had been growing in the country since the Anzacs had stormed the Dardanelles. D. H. Lawrence quickly sensed it during his visit in 1923.[32]

But Streeton's later work did not receive universal approval from the critics. M. J. McNally, the art critic for the *Age*, in his review of Streeton's 1924 show wrote: 'Streeton's art, instead of its old-time dignity . . . now echoed with the boom and bustle of arrogant commercialism'.[33] But already Streeton was something of a national institution; the *Age* editor did not approve and the criticism was not published. Blamire Young, with the discernment and discrimination so characteristic of his criticism, picked out the early Australian paintings and the small English landscapes painted under the influence of Constable as the best work shown in the Streeton Loan Exhibition held in 1932 at the Art Gallery of New South Wales. One of the few critics of the time who had some respect for international values, he concluded his comments with a timely warning: 'It is a problem whether the world of Art will ever again accept wholeheartedly an artist who has kept aloof in his work from the main stream of the tendencies of his time.'[34]

And as with Streeton so with Norman Lindsay. The prodigious energy and facility remained but contact with the living art of his time was lost. Life at Springwood, after the war and his second marriage, brought to his art a world full of satyrs and pirates, sailing ships and lovely ladies. In his *Garden of Happiness* (1920), a series of twenty pen drawings; his *Idyllia* (1920), a series of twelve etchings; his *Man and Hyperborea* (1927); and his illustrations to the poems of Leon Gellert and Hugh McCrae, Lindsay entered a realm of rococo-pagan fantasy. In the Nietzschean and neo-platonic philosophy of life expressed, in an odd kind of aphoristic turgidity in his *Creative Effort* (1924), the artist became, as his son Jack has put it, 'a member of a sort of Apollonian secret-society or blood-brotherhood spread over the ages and redeeming the hungry chaos of matter by the stabilizing Image.'[35]

After the war Norman Lindsay had turned to water-colour, following Blamire Young's methods, and in 1934, at the age of fifty-five, began to work in oil. The colossal output continued, but the paintings, like the pen-drawings before them, were dominated by deep-bosomed, heavy-hipped nudes luxuriating in exotic and bacchanalian settings. As illustrations they are technically superb but possess little, if any, aesthetic merit. Doubtless, Norman Lindsay's women are idealizations; the agents and progenitors of his life-force. But the conception was greater than the accomplishment: his *femme ideale* is quite unconvincing beyond the realm of adolescent erotica. After the war his critical writings, published in *Vision* (1923-4) and elsewhere became increasingly reactionary and he fulminated violently against modernism in literature and art; against the work of Pound, Eliot and Joyce; Cézanne, Van Gogh and Gauguin. His prestige among writers and some

artists undoubtedly assisted in creating the highly conservative and reactionary temper of the time.

It is revealing to find, when one looks at the record, how much liberal
and progressive thought in the arts Australia owed during the 1920's to
women. There were, of course, talented artists like Ethel Stephens, the
portrait painter, and Alice Muskett, the flower painter, at work long before
the First World War and a few achieved some notice while studying overseas. But women, perhaps because of their status in Victorian and Edwardian
society and other reasons that need not be discussed here, did not figure
prominently in Australian art prior to the First World War. This was not
so in the 1920's. The introduction of post-impressionism to the country owed
much to women: Norah Simpson, Grace Cossington Smith, Thea Proctor,
Margaret Preston, Isabel Tweddle, Dorrit Black, Ada Plante, Aletta Lewis,
Vida Lahey and Mildred Lovett, to name only the more prominent. Indeed,
the contribution of women to post-impressionism in Australia appears to
have been corporately greater than that of men; and in individual achievement in every way comparable. This is unusual, for women do not normally
figure as prominently in the visual arts as do men. They have not found
painting, it seems, as congenial a form of expression as the novel. In the
visual arts they have achieved distinction more as patrons than as prac-
titioners. The reason for their unusually important contribution to Australian
art during the 'twenties and early 'thirties is to be found probably in the
occurrence of the First World War.

In this regard it is not without significance that the greatest figure in
Australian art in the period between the wars was Max Meldrum, a pacifist
who believed, like Cézanne and Picasso, that war was a soldier's business
not an artist's. Like the dadaists he opposed not only the war but also the
teaching of the academies. But, unlike the dadaists, Meldrum worked out a
theory of painting based upon a rational and personal reading of the achievements of the past. Had his opposition to the war and the French academies
taken the explosive and irrational form that gave birth to dada and surrealism, the history of Australian art would certainly have been different. For
Max Meldrum, like Tom Roberts and George Bell, possessed the gift of
leadership, and might have led a successful revolt, had he so chosen, against
the values of the smug decade. But Meldrum chose to be rational and place
his faith in the past; and became a reactionary. Had he chosen to be
irrational and place his faith in the future he would have come much closer
to the spirit of the twentieth century.

All this is admittedly speculative but will serve to throw a sharp light on
the time. Meldrum's education as an artist was not interrupted by the First
World War, for he had already discovered by 1913 the position that he was
to maintain intractably throughout his life: but the education of a whole

generation of Australian artists certainly was. Australia sent 330,000 soldiers overseas and casualties totalled 226,000, of whom 60,000 were either killed in battle or died of wounds. Professor Crawford has recently pointed out that 60,000, though a small number beside the millions killed in the war, was not a small proportion of the Australian youth of that generation, and has suggested that 'there is reason to believe that it included a high proportion of those young men of promise who might have been expected to supply the new generation with its leaders'.[36] Just how many of those who enlisted were either intending to be or were art students, and were killed or did not return to the pursuit of art after the war has not been ascertained, and probably never will be. But the figures might well be revealing. It was no easy matter (the official war artists excepted) to turn, or to turn again, to art after the war. Rehabilitation made little provision (as it did after the Second World War) for ex-service training in the arts. And those who nevertheless did turn to art were in no position, as late starters, to influence art until the end of the decade. One typical case will serve to illustrate the position.

Rah Fizelle, born in Goulburn, New South Wales, in 1891, drew and painted from nature from an early age, but had no opportunity of entering an art school or of obtaining any tuition until 1919, following his demobilization. From 1919 to 1921 he attended the Sydney Teachers' College, taking a special course in art; and became, on winning a third scholarship in 1921, a day student at Ashton's. Then from 1922 to 1926 he continued as an evening student at Ashton's while teaching art at a demonstration school. During this period he became a regular exhibitor with the Society of Artists and a member of the Water-Colour Institute in 1924. About this time, while not quite understanding it, he became interested in cubism. He left teaching in 1927 for Europe, studied for a time at the Regent Street Polytechnic, then changed over to the Westminster Art School where he was taught by Bernard Meninsky and Walter Bayes, and gained from them ideas on composition and the solidity of form. Then he travelled in Spain, where he was deeply impressed by El Greco and Titian, and proceeded to move about over southern France and Italy during the next three years devoting his attention to museums, churches, palaces, Etruscan tombs, and finding his greatest interest in the *Quattrocento*. Returning to Australia in 1931 he held one-man shows in Sydney and Melbourne; and from 1932 to 1937 conducted an art school with Grace Crowley based on modern principles, becoming increasingly interested in the geometrical organization of form (114).[37]

Meldrum had arrived in France at the age of twenty-four to study art in Paris; Fizelle arrived at the same age to serve in the trenches. Meldrum began to influence the course of Australian art in 1913 at the age of thirty-

114   RAH FIZELLE, *Morning*, canvas,
39 x 26, 1941, Sydney

eight; Fizelle, at the age of forty-one, in 1932. That Meldrum exercised a far deeper influence than Fizelle is, of course, indisputable. But what is significant in this context is that his work did not begin until 1932 and that probably no other artist who spent his student years on active service exercised as much influence as Fizelle, through his school and his presidency of the Contemporary Art Society of New South Wales, in introducing contemporary art to Australia. Sir Daryl Lindsay certainly played a part in developing a better appreciation of post-impressionist values in Melbourne but his essential contribution to Australian art has lain in the art museum field. It would seem, therefore, on the evidence at present available, that due to the First World War the impact of a whole generation of art students upon Australian art was tragically thin and long delayed. This generation might have been expected, in the normal course, to have introduced cubism and futurism to Australia: those movements so crucial to the evolution of the pictorial language of the twentieth century. But Australian art did not experience cubism, futurism and non-figurative art until about 1935; and even then, not deeply. The First World War isolated Australian art from its sources in Europe far more effectively than the economic depression of the 1930's or the Second World War.

It was not until about 1924 that a new generation of students was beginning to leave the country for study abroad: and by that time the old association with Paris had weakened. Students now tended to study at the Slade, the Regent Street Polytechnic and the Westminster Art School, and contented themselves with shorter periods of study in Paris, often confined to gallery visits, in contrast to the three or four years in a Paris art school that was usually considered minimal to students of the 1890's, even after several years of training in Australia. In this regard the Travelling Art Scholarships did not yield the promise that might have been expected of them. In New South Wales the system broke down after sending Lambert abroad in 1899, and was not revived until de Maistre won the second scholarship awarded in 1923. In Victoria the triennial awards have been continuous down to the present day, but since Meldrum won his scholarship in 1899 no subsequent winner has returned to play an outstanding role in Australian art; a few have become reasonably well known as exhibitors in the annual shows of various societies, but most not even that. It would appear, furthermore, that the great majority of those students who were abroad between 1920 and 1930 had become too dominated by Ashton and Lambert in Sydney and Hall and Meldrum in Melbourne to make fruitful contact with the sources of twentieth-century painting during their years abroad.

The fact that post-impressionism made such a slight impact, and cubism and futurism no impact, upon Australian art and culture during the 1920's and early 1930's cannot, however, be explained entirely in terms of the solid resistance of the older generation, the heavy toll of the war itself, and the comparative failure of the student-body of the 1920's to make contact with *avant-garde* art in Europe. Until the 1940's the modern movement in Australia simply did not bring forth artists of stature sufficient to produce work that, regardless of time and taste, will stand comparison on its own merits with the best work of the Heidelberg School. Nor did it produce a leader of the calibre of Roberts with enough drive and creative ability to break through the thick rind of artistic complacency that encrusted the decade. One of the reasons for this must be found in the nature of post-impressionism itself. As a movement it was as much English as French. The term itself, which has little currency in French criticism, was invented at short notice by Roger Fry as a title to his Grafton Gallery Exhibition of 1910, 'Manet and the Post-Impressionists'. Moreover, as it was defined in the work of the Camden Town and London Groups, and the criticism of Roger Fry and Clive Bell, much of the aestheticism of Whistler and the New English Art Club hung about it. Post-impressionism and fauvism are essentially *fin de siècle*. It is true that extreme simplification, distortion and bright 'toneless' colour aroused the anger of critics whose approach was grounded in realism. But in Australia, Wakelin's and de Maistre's experiments of 1919 apart, post-impressionism never strayed far from the world of appearances. The post-impressionist innovators in Australia were perhaps too cautious; they did not push their experiments far enough to make a complete break with naturalistic painting. Nor is it surprising that in their insistence upon form and lack of interest in subject-matter for its own sake they were iconographically conservative. The still life, the interior, garden and back-yards, landscapes and portraits, a little figure-painting: the range of subject-matter made no advance upon that already treated with distinction by the impressionists. Consequently a great deal of post-impressionistic

115   MAX MELDRUM, *Portrait of John Farmer*, canvas,
30⅛ x 38½, 1936, Sydney

116   WILLIAM DARGIE, *Portrait of Mrs Behan*, canvas,
30 x 24, 1957, Dr Norman Behan

work in Australia tends to be on the light side in terms of real achievement: colourful, well-constructed, eminently decorative, but with an inherent tendency to revert to impressionist modes. Cézanne, Van Gogh and Gauguin were not aesthetes: and had Australia's post-impressionist painters been able to study their work in the original and at its source they might have come to realize that these three artists and their most intelligent followers were beginning to strike at sources of inspiration which had little to do with the polite world of significant form, classical or otherwise. As it was, they were most at home in the world of good taste: that moving limbo between the silent hell of creation and the catchpenny paradise of popular success.

FOOTNOTES

1 E. H. GOMBRICH, *Art and Illusion*, New York, 1960, p. 395

2 *Sydney Morning Herald*, 19 September 1911

3 *Art and Architecture*, viii (1911), 278

4 FRED J. BLOOMFIELD (probably Broomfield), 'The Modern Tendency of Art', *The Salon*, i (1912), 18

5 *in litt.* Mrs Norah Cockren, 11 August 1960, 5 September 1960

6 The *Sun* (Sydney), 1 September 1916

7 W. H. WRIGHT, op. cit., pp. 276, 333

8 ROLAND WAKELIN, 'The Modern Art Movement in Australia', *AA*, iii, 26 (December 1928), and verbal information from the artist; *see also* R. WAKELIN, 'Some Personal Recollections', *Art Gallery of N.S.W. Bull.*, January 1962; on de Maistre *see* JOHN ROTHENSTEIN, *Modern English Painters*, London, 1956, pp. 246-59, and R. DE MAISTRE, *Retrospective Exhibition of paintings and drawings from 1917 to 1960*, Whitechapel Art Gallery, London, May 1960

9 NORMAN LINDSAY, 'The Inevitable Future', *AA*, ii, 1 (February 1922), 38

10 *The Science of Appearance as formulated and taught by M. Meldrum* (ed. by R. R. Foreman), Sydney, 1950

11 op. cit., p. 219. On Meldrum *see also Max Meldrum: His Art and Views* (ed. by C. Colahan), Melbourne, 1917

12 Illustrated in *AA*, ii, 1 (February 1922), 70

13 'A Painter's Advice to Students: A talk by G. W. Lambert to the Students of the Sydney Art School on his Return to Sydney recently', *AA*, ii, 1 (February 1922), 9-13

14 On Sydney Ure Smith *see also Sydney Ure Smith, Memorial Exhibition*, 1950 (Mitchell Library of New South Wales); and *Sydney Ure Smith, Memorial Catalogue*, Sydney, 1950

15 *See also Thea Proctor Number, AA*, iii, 43 (April 1932)

16 On Henry *see* MOORE, ii, 186, *passim*; and R. T. BAKER, *The Australian Flora in Applied Art*, Sydney, 1915; and *Art and Architecture*, i (1904)

17 *AA*, iii, 11 (March 1925). For a list of Margaret Preston's writings and further references *see CAO*, p. 164

18 *See also Elioth Gruner*, Sydney [n.d.], and other references in *CAO*, p. 80

19 On Lionel Lindsay *see also* MOORE, ii, 194, *passim*

20 On the history of the Royal Art Society of New South Wales, *see* G. GALWAY, *Fifty Years of Australian Art*, Sydney, 1929

21 On Frances Hodgkins in Australia *see* E. H. McCORMICK, *The Expatriate; a study of Frances Hodgkins*, Wellington, 1954, pp. 144-60; *The Works of Frances Hodgkins in New Zealand*, Auckland, 1954, pp. 88-91; 247

22 *See The Art of Hilda Rix Nicholas. Exhibition of Paintings and Drawings*. Fine Art Society's Gallery (Melbourne), 1922; *Exhibition of Pictures of Life and Landscape of Australia and France*, Athenaeum, Melbourne, 1928

23 *in litt.* 6 October 1960

24 From a typescript of Frater's notes for the Lecture in the author's possession

25 Holograph letter in the author's possession

26 In his evidence before the High Court in Equity, New South Wales, in the case arising from the 1943 Archibald Prize award; *see* typescript, Art Gallery of N.S.W., p. 70

27 From conversations with the artist

28   A. SHORE, *Forty Years Seek and Find*, Melbourne, 1957

29 *Smike to Bulldog*, p. 112

30 LIONEL LINDSAY, 'Arthur Streeton', *AA*, iii, 40 (October 1931), pp. 9-11

31 J. S. MACDONALD, 'Arthur Streeton', *AA*, iii, 40 (October 1931), p. 22

32 In *Kangaroo*, 1923

33 Quoted in *Smike to Bulldog*, p. 112

34 BLAMIRE YOUNG, 'The Streeton Exhibition', *AA*, iii, 42 (February 1932), p. 19

35 J. LINDSAY, *The Roaring Twenties*, London, 1960, p. 67

36 R. M. CRAWFORD, *An Australian Perspective*, Melbourne, 1960, p. 62

37 From notes supplied by the artist

CHAPTER SEVEN

CONTEMPORARY ART ARRIVES
1930 - 39

One does not necessarily go out and weep because our beliefs
have been betrayed. The love-birds die in the cage, the rose
mildews in the bud, but we live on. Forward the Rebels!
BLAMIRE YOUNG, the *Herald*, 17 August 1932

DURING the 1930's Australian art began to show signs of new vitality. Contact with contemporary European art was firmly established; the reactionary opposition in painting and criticism was challenged and defeated by a new generation of artists who broke completely with the traditions of academic naturalism; and a lively curiosity among artists and the public began to replace the complacency that had prevailed during the preceding decade. This curiosity revealed itself in many ways: in the great interest shown in exhibition work from overseas; in the formation of new art schools, centres and societies, in the sense of excitement and interest in experiment prevailing among local art students; in the return of a new generation of students from abroad keenly interested in contemporary work; and in the arrival of artists and scholars from Hitler's Europe.

Exhibitions from Overseas

During the 1920's anyone interested in modern art in Australia had to depend largely upon books and colour reproductions, and even these were scanty enough. During the 1930's, however, original work by contemporary European painters began to appear in loan exhibitions from abroad or in loan exhibitions from private collections in Australia. Following Penleigh Boyd's exhibition of 1923, which reflected the Royal Academy taste of the time, very little work from overseas, apart from gallery purchases, was exhibited for a decade. Critics, private collectors, and gallery purchasing tended to follow Royal Academy modes and reputations. Even the purchases made by Sydney Ure Smith and Sir James MacGregor in 1933 for the National Art Gallery of New South Wales were considered rather modern at the time by local critics, with paintings by John, Epstein, Duncan Grant and Spencer Gore, and drawings by Eric Gill and John Skeaping.[1]

However, the drift from academic taste, gradual during the early 1930's, quickened as the years passed. Probably the most 'advanced' works in the collection brought out to Australia by Mrs Alleyne Zander in 1933 were paintings by Ben Nicholson, John and Paul Nash, Mark Gertler, Christopher Wood, Edward Wadsworth, Duncan Grant, Vanessa Bell, Stanley Spencer and Matthew Smith.[2] Noting public interest in modern work the Society of Artists began to include contemporary work by overseas artists in their annual exhibitions. In 1935 an Etretat landscape by Matisse, a portrait by Derain, and paintings by Pissarro, Utrillo and Dufresne were exhibited.[3] On the other hand, the Loan Exhibition of Contemporary British Art arranged by the Empire Art Loan Collections Society of London, which was shown in Australia and New Zealand in 1934-5 and was drawn mostly from private English collections, retained a strongly academic flavour.[4] July 1936, however, saw the opening in Sydney of a large Exhibition of International Art drawn partly from local collections and partly from work obtained by Sydney consulates from overseas collections, a good deal of conventional and academic work, paintings by Matisse, Marquet, Utrillo, Vlaminck and Munch. By this time the Press was becoming increasingly interested in the public response to contemporary work and the exhibition drew large attendances.[5] In Melbourne, the Loan Exhibition of Works of Modern Art by Artists Outside Australia, organized by George Bell for the National Gallery of Victoria from October to November 1937, was of considerable importance. This little exhibition of fifty-two items included a Picasso lent by Lady Casey, paintings by Van Gogh and Utrillo lent by Sali Herman, a Kisling lent by Gino Nibbi, a Marie Laurencin lent by Alan Henderson, and a Christopher Wood lent by Isabel Tweddle. Assembled at a time when interest in contemporary art was running high in Melbourne but little original work was yet available, this small exhibition aroused far more interest than its size might suggest.

The loan collections shown in Australia between 1933 and 1938 consisted mainly of contemporary British academic work, and even the advanced work, such as it was, came mostly from Britain. The first, and indeed the only exhibition at all representative of the work of the masters of the modern movement ever to be shown in Australia, was the Exhibition of French and British Modern Art shown in Australia during the second half of 1939. Assembled by Basil Burdett in Europe for Sir Keith Murdoch, the Managing Director of the Melbourne *Herald*, it contained over two hundred works, including paintings by Bonnard, Braque (four), Cézanne (seven), Chagall, Chirico, Dali, Derain, Dufy, Ernst, Friesz, Gauguin (seven), Gris, Laurencin, Léger, Lurcat, Marquet, Matisse (eight), Modigliani (two), Picasso (nine), Rouault (five), Seurat, Signac, Soutine, Toulouse-Lautrec, Utrillo, Valadon, Van Dongen, Van Gogh (eight), Vlaminck, Vuillard, Ben Nicholson, Graham Sutherland, Christopher Wood and Edward Wadsworth. The exhibition created great public interest wherever it was shown and exercised an influence upon Australian taste in the visual arts difficult to exaggerate. It ended the dominance of the Royal Academy of London as the official arbiter of pictorial values in Australia, and was one of the first of three major events which led to the collapse of the authority of the academic establishment in art in Australia; the other two being the struggle against the Australian Academy of Art which led to the formation of the Contemporary Art Society and the lawsuit arising from the award of the 1943 Archibald Prize to William Dobell.

New Schools, Centres and Societies

In Melbourne the economic depression decreased the amount of work available to craftsmen and designers at Brooks Robinson's Stained Glass Studios and, in 1931, Arnold Shore, after discussing the matter with William Frater, approached George Bell with the idea that the two of them should start a new art school in Melbourne to teach the principles and practice of modern art. Bell, who already had a number of private pupils interested, agreed to the proposal. Frater found premises and the new school was opened in February 1932. The partnership between Bell and Shore continued until 1934 when Bell, feeling the need to study modern art at its source, travelled abroad for two years, working for a time with Iain McNab, at the Grosvenor School, London, and visiting France and Spain.

After Bell returned in 1936 the partnership with Shore lasted another year and then broke up, Bell continuing the school alone. Between 1936 and 1939 a group of unusually gifted and intelligent students, with a lively interest in all forms of contemporary art, attended the school. Among the more prominent were Wolfgang Cardamatis, Russell Drysdale, Sali Herman, Geoffrey Jones, Peter Purves Smith, David Strachan, Alan Sumner, Alan Warren, Frances Burke, Maie Casey, Frances Derham, Mary Alice Evatt, Anne Montgomery and Louise Thomas.

The influence of this important school runs parallel to the influence of the Contemporary Group of Melbourne. In 1931 Gino Nibbi wrote a frank and trenchant criticism of the work exhibited in the annual exhibition of the Australian Art Association (a body of professional artists founded in 1912) and of Australian art in general, which was published in the Melbourne Herald[6] and sparked off a Press controversy. Sir Keith Murdoch suggested an exhibition of colour reproductions of modern masters which was held in December 1931 in the Assembly Room of the Herald building, and opened by Mr Theodore Fink (aged seventy-six), the man who in his thirties had been such a staunch supporter of the Heidelberg School. Apart from colour reproductions of work by Cézanne, Van Gogh and Gauguin, the exhibition included original work by Matisse, Picasso, Utrillo, Dufy and Modigliani, all obtained from private owners. Lectures were given by Bell,

117   MARGARET PRESTON, *Implement Blue*, canvas, 16¾ x 17,
1927, Sydney

Frater and Shore. The wide public interest in the exhibition played a part
in the creation of the Contemporary Group of Melbourne which was formed
by George Bell, the following year. Its first exhibition, in August 1932, included work by William Frater, Arnold Shore, George Bell, Adrian Lawlor,
Daryl Lindsay, Eric Thake, Isabel Tweddle, Ada Plante and Eveline Syme.

The work of most members of the new group was well known from their
participation in other exhibitions, but the group itself helped to make the
modern movement an articulate force in the Melbourne art community.
Critical reactions to the first exhibition varied. To Arthur Streeton, now aged
sixty-five and a critic on the *Argus*, the exhibition represented retrogression
rather than progress. His review traced what he believed to be the true
progress of Australian art from Buvelot through Roberts, McCubbin, Mel-

rum and others, to Ernest Buckmaster. 'Mr Buckmaster', said Streeton, 'is taking the lead . . .' But concerning the exhibitors in the first Contemporary Group exhibition he wrote: 'Some . . . seem to hide their gifts with misshapen representations of humanity, flowers, trees and architecture. . . . Much of this painting is done just to attract attention. . . . This exhibition expresses no fresh direction.'[7] But not all the artist-critics of the older generation had joined the ranks of reaction. Blamire Young, then aged seventy-eight and the art critic on the Melbourne *Herald*, wrote a sympathetic and discrimating review, and his concluding remarks are worth quoting in full.

We have been indifferent, and now the anaesthetic of indifference has been overcome, and we are on our way. Under the drug of academism we have perhaps painted with the mindlessness of the sleep-walker, but that is over. One does not necessarily go out and weep because our beliefs have been betrayed. The love-birds die in the cage, the rose mildews in the bud, but we live on. Forward the Rebels![8]

Four years later Young died having helped not a little in his quiet way, since his arrival in 1885, to civilize his adopted country.

The first exhibition of the Contemporary Group was devoted chiefly to work based on post-impressionist principles. Intimations of surrealism, however, appeared in some still life paintings by Eric Thake (118); Blamire Young in his review noted the influence of Chirico and Wadsworth. Thake was one of George Bell's most talented pupils and possessed a splendid sense of design, firm and lucid, sensitive in tone and colour. Australia has not produced a graphic artist with a finer feeling for pure line. His surrealism was predominantly English in its derivation and restraint; its light airy fantasy providing a delicate foil to the firm sensitive economy of his designs.[9]

A sense of adventure and experiment in art had arisen in Melbourne. Already in December 1930 Adrian Lawlor held a one-man show at the

Riddell Gallery in Little Collins Street. He had arrived from England in 1910, studied drawing at the Gallery School and painting with A. D. Colquhoun, Frater, and later George Bell. The paintings, considerably more *avant-garde* than anything shown in Melbourne before, drew publicity,

118 ERIC THAKE, *Bluebells, Blue River, Upper Murray*, water-colour, 16 x 20, 1932, Miss Leslie Henderson

N

119 SAMUEL ATYEO, *Organized Line to Yellow*, canvas, 26¾ x 21¼, *c.* 1934, Museum of Modern Art of Australia, Melbourne

quickened interest and were adversely criticized by Streeton. At the Gallery, where Bernard Hall's long reign as Director, Head Teacher and Felton Bequest Adviser for forty-odd years was drawing slowly to an end, students were beginning to question the authority of tonal naturalism. In 1932 Samuel Atyeo, an able Gallery student expected to win the Travelling Scholarship, dramatically renounced academic art by submitting a painting of nudes in the modern manner. Hall, breaking an old tradition, refused to hang it in the Gallery with other entries. Atyeo thereupon had it displayed in a Little Collins Street shop window, where it aroused much discussion and Press publicity. Having broken with academic art Atyeo experimented in turn with Cézanne, Van Gogh and Picasso, moving increasingly towards non-objective art. His *Organized Line to Yellow* (119) was one of the first truly non-objective paintings produced in Melbourne. Atyeo left Australia a year or two later, making no further contribution to contemporary art in Australia. One of his fellow-students, Moya Dyring, also broke with her Gallery training and was, perhaps, the first artist in Melbourne to experiment with cubism. Her first one-man show was opened at the Riddell Gallery by Mr Justice Evatt, of the High Court of Australia, who was to become one of the most prominent and persistent supporters of *avant-garde* art in the country.

In Sydney an art school devoted to the principles and practice of contemporary art was also opened in 1932. It was run jointly by Grace Crowley and Rah Fizelle. Miss Crowley had been a student and later an assistant at Julian Ashton's school. Between 1927 and 1931 she studied abroad mostly in France under André Lhote and Albert Gleizes, from whom she gained some understanding of cubism and the post-cubist trends in painting (120). The Crowley-Fizelle school was more constructivist in its approach, more interested in the geometric organization of form and in dynamic symmetry than the Bell-Shore school. It was more *avant-garde*, but less influential in the training of artists and the formation of taste in Sydney than the Bell-Shore school in Melbourne. But it did provide facilities for students seeking an introduction to the principles and practice of contemporary art. The establishment by Dorrit Black, a South Australian, of the Modern Art Centre in Margaret Street, Sydney, in the early 1930's, also helped to promote the abstract-cubist-constructivist trend in contemporary art in Sydney. Dorrit Black, like Grace Crowley, had studied under Lhote and Gleizes. The first exhibition of Ralph Balson, one of Australia's early abstract painters, was shown at the Centre (121). During the early 1930's, too, the exhibitions held at Ball Green, Turramurra, the home of Ethel Anderson, a writer and poet, also helped to widen the circle of interest in modern work.

120 GRACE CROWLEY, *Woman*, canvas, 29½ x 21½, *c*. 1936, Dr and Mrs H. V. Evatt

Exhibitions of work by Roland Wakelin, Grace Cossington Smith and others were held. Frank Hinder and his wife, Margel, became members of the circle of artists interested in cubism, constructivism and abstract art when they arrived from America in 1934. By that time it included Grace Crowley, Rah Fizelle, Dorrit Black, Frank Weitzel and Eleonore Lange. Frank Hinder, after two years at the East Sydney Technical College (1925-7), studied at the Art Institute of Chicago in 1927 and then between 1927 and 1929 at the New York School of Fine Arts and the Master Institute of Roerich Museum, where he was taught by Howard Giles and Earl Bistram. Through these two teachers both Hinder and his wife were brought into contact with cubism, futurism, Kandinsky, the Bauhaus, and the murals of Rivera and Orozco. About 1934 the Sydney constructivist circle became deeply interested in relating movement to design; and was stimulated by such books as Jay Hambridge's *Dynamic Symmetry, The Greek Vase* (1920) and Irma Richter's *Rhythmic Forms in Art* (1932). They were, of course, as much interested in sculpture and three-dimensional construction as in painting, and Eleonore Lange's investigations into the problems of dynamic sculpture and light were closely related to the central interests of the circle. Miss

121   RALPH BALSON, *Painting*, wood panel, 30 x 40,
1954, University of Melbourne

Lange was a sculptor and art educationist from Frankfort-on-Main. During
the 1930's and early 1940's she lectured and wrote a great deal, apart from
her own work, bringing a keen, perceptive sympathy to her subject. She
did much to raise the level of understanding in art in Sydney by asserting
international values and the aesthetic equality of style, and played a most
significant role in creating an informed audience for contemporary art,
especially abstract and non-figurative painting and sculpture.

In 1937 Frank Hinder held a one-man show at the Grosvenor Galleries,
Sydney, which reflected his New Mexican experience, his interest in
dynamic symmetry, and contained a number of non-objective paintings.
Then in August 1939, at Miss Lange's suggestion, the circle held an exhibition of work called Exhibition I at the David Jones Galleries, Sydney. It
included paintings by Ralph Balson, Grace Crowley, Rah Fizelle, Frank
Hinder and Frank Medworth; and sculpture by Margel Hinder, Eleonore
Lange and Gerald Lewers. The exhibition, opened by Mr Justice Evatt,
contained in its catalogue a foreword by Miss Lange. In neo-classical art,
she asserted, colour was determined in area, tone, value and line by its
capacity to suggest dimension, and the system of composition was fixed by
the use of vanishing points. The impressionists used an order based on
atmospheric perspective. It was Matisse who first offered a new system of
order which replaced vanishing points and atmospheric perspective by the
picture plane itself. Modern painters, Miss Lange added, 'used a scene or

122 ARNOLD SHORE, *The Vegetable Garden*, canvas, 19½ x 23½,
1939, Melbourne

123 FRANK HINDER, *Fishermen Hauling Nets*, egg tempera,
17 x 24, 1939, Dr and Mrs R. Stiel

a posed model only to elaborate its inherent colour sensations into an artistic theme of colour relations', and were 'abandoning the representation of objects in order to establish a new realm of visual existence'.

It was intended to follow Exhibition I with others annually but, with the formation of a northern division of the Contemporary Art Society and the outbreak of war, the idea was abandoned. Individual members of the circle continued their researches into geometric and abstract form. In 1944 Grace Crowley, Frank Hinder, Gerald Ryan and Ralph Balson held an exhibition of *Constructive Paintings* at the Macquarie Galleries, Sydney. Another exhibition of abstract paintings was held at David Jones Gallery in 1948; but group exhibitions of abstract work were infrequent prior to 1956.

The modern movement developed later in Melbourne than in Sydney, and in Sydney it revealed a greater tendency to experiment in constructivist and abstract or semi-abstract form. But in Melbourne the course of modern art through the 1930's became more of a public matter, was more fraught with disputation than in Sydney, and in Melbourne, too, it developed greater independence and greater vitality. When, in the late 1930's, the authority of reaction to determine the course of Australian art was successfully challenged, it was in Melbourne that the crucial battle was fought. That this was so is due perhaps more than anything else to the differing personalities of Sydney Ure Smith and George Bell. Ure Smith, friendly, cautious, and tolerant by nature, the statesman of the Australian art world as he was called by William Moore, did not allow his interest in new work to ossify or his taste to harden. As the President of the Society of Artists he was determined that it should not lose touch with progress, experiment and change. As the editor of *Art in Australia* he gave cautious but continuous support to the modern movement, and was more tolerant of *avant-garde* thought than the Sydney Press prior to 1938. He maintained a friendly liaison between the Contemporary Group and the Society of Artists; and during the 1930's artists who had contributed to the growth of the modern movement, Arnold Shore, Roland Wakelin and John D. Moore, for example, were elected to membership of the Society of Artists. Indeed the Society became under his presidency an Academy, the door of which was never completely shut to innovators who found the prestige of its status not unacceptable. This process of electing artists possessed of originality to membership of the Society was speeded up during the 1940's when the principles of the modern movement had become widely accepted by critics and the informed public. It prevented the emergence of influential individuals and groups likely to challenge the status of the Society. The Sydney constructivist circle of artists, absorbed and preoccupied by their experiments with form and design had, of course, no such intention. Had they done so, they would doubtless have been invited to become members of the Society.

That the Australian Academy of Art failed, as we shall see, was due in no small measure to the fact that it was superfluous. When the Australian Academy was founded in 1937 the Society of Artists had been operating as the *de facto* Australian Academy of Art for many years.

In contrast to Sydney Ure Smith, George Bell was more the artist, teacher and man of principle who had worked out his own aesthetic position, not without difficulty, during a lifetime. He was less of a tactician, less ready to compromise than Ure Smith, and more ready to challenge established views, whatever their authority, if he thought they were wrong. Like Meldrum, and the professional artists of his generation, he possessed a profound distrust of laymen claiming to be well-informed critics of art. Perhaps it is not surprising if, therefore, under Bell's leadership during the 1930's, the youthful modern movement in Melbourne developed a greater independence, a greater sense of adventure and more vitality than the corresponding movement in Sydney.

The Formation of the Australian Academy of Art and the Contemporary Art Society

The contemporary movement did not emerge as a force strong enough to challenge the authority of academic naturalism until 1937 when it united all elements opposed to the formation of the Australian Academy of Art. The Academy was formed at a meeting held in Canberra in 1937 at which Mr R. G. Menzies, then the Commonwealth Attorney-General, presided. The expressed aim of the Academy was 'the recognition of art in Australia as something significant for the whole of the Commonwealth and knowing no State boundaries'. It claimed to be a national institution with the sole purpose of furthering art appreciation and art education, and set itself up as a 'champion of the rights of individual and associated artists'.[10] Fifty foundation members from the leading art societies were appointed and a council of ten elected, five representing the northern division embracing New South Wales and Queensland, and five representing the southern, embracing Victoria and the other States. The inaugural exhibition was held in Sydney in April 1938 and the second in Melbourne a year later, in the National Gallery of Victoria.

The creation of the Academy created a sharp division among artists. It was felt by many that the real purpose of the Academy was to strengthen the power of the establishment and stifle contemporary forms of expression. Apart from this many, including several well-known academic painters, opposed the Academy on the principle that academies by their very nature stifle originality and progress in the arts.

There were strong grounds for suspecting that the Academy would be no friend to contemporary art. Its Council was composed of men who had written sharp criticism of the *avant-garde* styles beyond post-impressionism, and included some moderates who spoke of including in academy exhibitions 'any and every point of view that was reasonably sound'.[11] But the Academy was, of course, to decide what was sound and what was not. It failed, however, to become a truly representative body even of the older and more conservative artists. Its membership did not include, for example, Julian Ashton, Sir Arthur Streeton and Norman Lindsay and it did include a large number of popular portrait and landscape painters who had made no creative contribution to Australian art whatsoever. Among well-known artists who were invited to join and refused were: Rupert Bunny, George Bell, Daryl Lindsay, Charles Wheeler and Napier Waller.

The key to the situation lay, to a large extent, with the leading post-impressionist painters who, by 1937, had become widely accepted by the older generation of Australian artists and the critics as 'sane' modernists, and were at the same time held in respect by the *avant-garde* as artists who had pioneered the break with academic naturalism. Most of them, however, together with artists once associated with Lambert and the Sydney Contemporary Group, accepted invitations to join, including Douglas Dundas, Adrian Feint, William Frater, Vida Lahey, Kenneth Macqueen, Arthur Murch, Margaret Preston, Thea Proctor, Arnold Shore, Grace Cossington Smith and Roland Wakelin. None of the pioneers of post-impressionism, however, was represented on the Academy's first Council. In April 1937, some months before the Academy was formed, James Quinn, then the President of the Victorian Artists' Society, an artist of the older generation who brought a tolerant mind to modern painting, asked Mr Menzies to open the Annual Exhibition of the Society, and on that occasion Mr Menzies said:

You all know of the proposal to form an Academy of Art in Australia. I must admit that I was the prime mover in this idea. I feel definitely that some authority and body should be formed here as in other countries. Every great country has its academy. They have set certain standards of art and have served a great purpose in raising the standards of public taste by directing attention to good work. This exhibition indicates that the Victorian Artists' Society is encouraging people in every type of painting. Experiment is necessary in establishing an academy, but certain principles must apply to this business of art as to any other business which affects the artistic sense of the community. Great art speaks a language which every intelligent person can understand. The people who call themselves modernists today talk a different language.[12]

Now James Quinn had invited members of the Melbourne Contemporary Group to exhibit, an entire wall was hung with their paintings and many were present in person. Mr Menzies's remarks naturally enough aroused considerable consternation among them and their friends. Quinn, who had himself been invited to join the Academy, publicly dissociated himself on the spot from Mr Menzies's remarks on modernism. But the challenge had been given, and it was accepted.

The opening speech gave rise to a Press controversy. Norman MacGeorge, a landscape painter of the older generation who had long possessed a lively interest in contemporary art, began it by expressing the opinion in the *Argus* that Mr Menzies intended the Academy to be a disciplinary measure aimed at those whose conception of art was not his.[13] 'I realize', Mr Menzies wrote in a reply two days later, 'that an academy should find room in its membership for all schools of artistic thought, provided they are based on competent craftsmanship.'[14] Thereupon George Bell entered the lists:

What does a layman know of craftsmanship or draughtsmanship . . .? Just as it would be ludicrous for an artist to argue a knotty point of law, so it is ludicrous for Mr Menzies to lay down what is good drawing and good art. . . . Academies have been, throughout history, reactionary influences. Art is always growing. An Academy sets out to standardize art. As soon as that is done art is dead. An Academy sets out to be conservative in its very essence. It sets its face against a furthering of knowledge gained by experiment. Every great artist has been a 'rebel', as an experimenter is always called.[15]

To this Mr Menzies replied:

. . . Mr Bell cannot have it both ways. If the artists of Australia expect the educated public to display some interest in their work they must expect the same public to form some opinion of that work, and to express it. . . . As to the reactionary influence of academies, I can only repeat what I said when opening the Victorian Artists' exhibition last week. That was that the Royal Academy in London numbered among its members since 1778 Reynolds, Gainsborough, Hoppner, Turner, Sargent, Raeburn and Augustus John. I will be surprised to learn that these painters whose work is intelligible and, indeed, exciting, even to an individual like myself, are to be regarded as the reactionaries of British art during the last one hundred and fifty years.

I am sorry that Mr Bell should have been so angry as to forget his customary good manners. No doubt he is quite correct when he says that I am not myself a painter. He might be right when he says that I have a pedestrian mind. But in spite of these disabilities the fact remains that I am a typical person of moderate education, I hope reasonably good taste, and a lifelong interest in the fine arts.

In other words, with all my individual defects, I represent a class of people which will, in the next one hundred years determine the permanent place to be occupied in the world of art by those painting today.[16]

The Press controversy continued vigorously for weeks, with Mr Menzies, Max Meldrum, J. S. MacDonald and Harold Herbert ranged on one side, and Norman MacGeorge, Adrian Lawlor, Basil Burdett, Sali Herman and Mr Justice Evatt on the other. Evatt, in opening one of Moya Dyring's exhibitions, made a plea for modern art. 'The Australian galleries,' he said, 'should be induced to buy or borrow modern pictures.'[17] The Director of the

National Gallery of Victoria, J. S. MacDonald, a most vociferous opponent
of modernism, attacked the suggestion. 'I don't think,' he said, 'we should
have modern art in the gallery at all. It is not liked by the art galleries of
Australia.'[18]

The controversial atmosphere of the time was splendidly captured by
Adrian Lawlor. Possessing wide interests in all the arts and an admirable
contempt of self-appointed experts, Lawlor had opposed isolationism and
provincialism in Australian culture since the days when he had written in
Vision in the early 1920's. His pamphlets, *Arquebus* (1937) and *Elimina-
tions* (1939), attacked the idea of an Australian Academy of Art with an
explosive mixture of learning, buffoonery, pastiche and wit. They have
become landmarks in the history of Australian taste.

The Contemporary Art Society

In July 1938 George Bell began to organize opposition to the Academy.
He addressed a printed leaflet, entitled *To Art Lovers*, to a large number of
sympathetic artists and laymen proposing the formation of 'a society which
will unite all artists and laymen who are in favour of encouraging the growth
of a living art, who are determined both to prevent any dictatorship in art
and to nullify the effect of any official recognition acquired by a self-con-
stituted Academy'. He suggested also that the new society should stimulate
public interest in living art, broaden national policy to ensure the purchase
of contemporary masterpieces, seek the removal of customs duties on art
works, provide lectures and hold an annual exhibition of contemporary
work by artist members. An inaugural meeting was held at the Victorian
Artists' Society rooms on 13 July 1938 at which a new society, the Contemporary Art Society, was founded, with George Bell as the President, Rupert
Bunny as the artist Vice-President, John Reed as the lay Vice-President, and
Adrian Lawlor as the Honorary Secretary.

The Society proclaimed that its primary and paramount object was to
encourage and foster contemporary art:

By the expression 'contemporary art' is meant all contemporary painting, sculpture, drawing and other visual art forms which is or are original and creative or
which strive to give expression to progressive contemporary thought and life
as opposed to work which is reactionary or retrogressive including work which
has no other aim than representation.[19]

The new Society, which brought together all groups of opinion in Melbourne opposed to the formation of the Academy, was a heterogeneous
body from the beginning, and soon developed three main groups of opinion.
First, there were those who looked to George Bell as their leader. Their
approach to modern art was based primarily upon post-impressionist prin-

124   WILLIAM FRATER, *Portrait of Adrian Lawlor,*
canvas, 29¾ x 17⅝, 1930, Sydney

ciples. Most of them would probably have agreed with Bell's definition of modern art as 'an artist's personal experience expressed on a surface in terms of his material—that is design in form—reinforced by colour, and presenting a perfect balance of opposing forces which produces a work satisfying an eternal instinct in the aesthetically receptive mind'.[20] Most of the artists to join the Society first, many of them Bell's students, belonged to the group.

By 1938, however, the post-impressionism which George Bell stood for did not represent the most advanced form of contemporary art in Australia. Lively *avant-garde* groups influenced in various ways by dada, naïve painting, surrealism, cubism, social realism, expressionism and abstract art were beginning to make their appearance in the years immediately prior to the outbreak of war. They found a patron and champion in John Reed (*b.* 1901), a law graduate of Cambridge and Melbourne who began to take a deep interest in the promotion of *avant-garde* art from the time he settled in Melbourne in 1925. He and his wife, Sunday, assisted, encouraged and bought the work of many young and virtually unknown artists; and in so doing established an *avant-garde* circle of Melbourne painters, the most prominent of whom were Albert Tucker, Sidney Nolan, Arthur Boyd and John Perceval.

A third group in the Society, consisting of social realist painters, included Noel Counihan, V. G. O'Connor, Josl Bergner, Harry de Hartog and others. Sympathetic to socialism and communism they sought to engage the Society where possible in Popular Front political and cultural activity. During the early years of the Society's existence they maintained an uneasy alliance with John Reed and his circle (most of whom possessed left-wing sympathies) against George Bell and his supporters who were strongly opposed to the intrusion of politics into the Society.

Conflict arose early between Bell and Reed and their respective supporters over the question of the rights and powers of lay members. George Bell, like Max Meldrum, held no high opinion of laymen as critics or judges of art. The issue came to a head over the appointment of a selection committee. Some opposed the idea of any selection committee as being alien to the broad principles of the Society. Bell and his supporters desired a selection committee composed entirely of artists. This was agreed to, with the proviso that the laymen be allowed to submit any *one* picture rejected by the committee for reconsideration. Under this provision a painting by Sidney Nolan entitled *Rimbaud*, at first rejected, was hung in the first exhibition.

The exhibition which was held in the National Gallery of Victoria in June 1939, and opened by Mr Justice Evatt, gave rise to considerable controversy. It was also important in introducing a new generation of artists to the public; a generation that was passing beyond post-impressionism. Among the more prominent artists who exhibited some of their earliest work were: Sidney Nolan, James Gleeson, Russell Drysdale, Peter Purves Smith, Sali Herman, Albert Tucker, Noel Counihan, V. G. O'Connor and David Strachan. The success of the exhibition encouraged the Contemporary Art Society to establish branches in other States; and later in the year Mr Peter Bellew, a lay member of the Society, visited Sydney and helped to establish a branch there, with Rah Fizelle as the President.

Meanwhile, conflict over the rights of laymen in the Society continued. The constitution provided that not more than two-thirds of the Council of twelve should be artists, but no restriction was placed upon the number of laymen who might serve. Bell, disturbed at the possibility of an entirely lay Council, called a special general meeting to alter the constitution; but was defeated by John Reed's circle acting with the social realists and their lay followers. Bell, increasingly distressed by the growth of lay influence and communism within the Council and among the Society's members, resigned, first from the Presidency, and (at the annual general meeting of 1940) from the Society itself, together with eighty-three artists.

The division that thus rent the Contemporary Art Society so soon after its foundation was not due entirely to a difference between personalities or to disagreements about the rights of laymen and the place of politics in the Society. Beneath the disagreements lay a fundamental difference concerning the role of the artist in society. The post-impressionists abhorred politics in art. But to the dadaists, expressionists, surrealists, and social-realists, artistic revolt against established values tended to be viewed as but one part of a more general revolt that possessed psychological, social and political aspects. In one sense the departure of the George Bell group from the Contemporary Art Society foreshadowed the artistic character of the war years. During the 1920's and 1930's the modern movement in Australia tended to be classical and impersonal in its manifestations, preoccupied with the achievement of significant form in one way or another. It did not believe that the artist should involve himself too closely with the problems of life, religion, society and politics. But during the war years the tenor of art and life changed remarkably. The temper of the contemporary movement in art changed from one of classical impersonality to one of romantic involvement. Post-impressionism and the burgeoning experiments with cubism, geometric and abstract form were overshadowed in the new situation by romantic forms of contemporary art such as surrealism, social-realism, realistic expressionism and neo-romanticism that were to dominate the 1940's. The change was foreshadowed in the work of Danila Vassilieff.

Vassilieff (1897-1958) was born in Kagalinitskaia, Rostov-on-Don, into a family of Cossack farmers. At the age of twelve he entered a military academy at St Petersburg and fought on the Eastern Front during the First World War. The October Revolution found him in Denikin's army in which he attained the rank of Lieutenant-Colonel. Captured by the Bolsheviks with the remnants of his regiment in 1921, he was imprisoned at Baku but later escaped and lived for a time with nomadic Tartars in Azerbaijan, and later in Persia. From thence he made his way through India, Burma and Manchuria to China; living for a time in Shanghai. In 1923 he decided to come to Australia. In Darwin he gained a Government contract to construct fourteen miles of railway line near Katherine. From this venture he was able to buy some land near Tully in northern Queensland and clear it for sugar-cane and bananas.

In Australia in 1923 Vassilieff had begun to paint as a hobby, and in 1929, wishing to learn more about art, he left the country for Rio to join an old friend, Dmitri Ismailovitch, who had served in his Cossack regiment and later made a name for himself as an artist in Brazil. Vassilieff shared his friend's studio for two years, painting from plaster casts and

125   DANILA VASSILIEFF, *A Street in Fitzroy,* plywood
panel, 14⅞ x 17¾, 1937, Museum of Modern Art of
Australia, Melbourne

still life groups and learning to glaze, while employed as an engineering draughtsman with the Anglo-Persian Oil Company. Becoming increasingly dissatisfied with Ismailovitch's conventional approach to painting, he began to experiment with more direct and expressive techniques that would bring him into closer contact with life. He wrote later:

I worked like a slave . . . day and night, in every spare moment. And then I realized after two years of nothing but apples and bananas and pumpkins and plaster casts, that it was all a waste of time, it was meaningless to me, it was not what I wanted to do at all. That was dead life and I wanted to paint living life, life and nature and people in action and movement.[21]

He went on a painting excursion along the Amazon, and in 1932 painted in British Guiana, Dutch Guiana, and Venezuela, holding his first exhibition in the palace of the Bishop of Guiana at Georgetown. In 1934 he toured the West Indies; Trinidad, Jamaica, Haiti, Santo Domingo, Puerto Rico, Martinique and Barbados, painting landscapes, seascapes, street, market and slum scenes in a direct, lively and colourful manner. His exhibitions were very well received and, encouraged by Alfred Mendes, a collector and connoisseur, he proceeded to London where he held an exhibition of West Indian paintings at the Albany Gallery in 1934. The following year he visited

Spain and Portugal. On returning to London he exhibited at the Wertheim Gallery, and six months later at Prince Galitzin's Gallery. Here his work was favourably received by several critics including Jan Gordon of the *Observer*.

Then he decided to return again to Australia. Arriving in Sydney in 1936 he worked as the foreman of a gang laying pipe-lines for the Water Board, and painted street scenes around Woolloomooloo and Surry Hills. He held two exhibitions of his work at the Macquarie Galleries in that year.

In 1937 Vassilieff moved to Melbourne, lived for a time in Fitzroy (125) and held an exhibition in September at Riddell's Gallery. It was opened by John Reed, who became a close friend and patron. Then he took up his post at the Nield School, Warrandyte, where he remained until it closed in 1946. Vassilieff continued to hold annual exhibitions in Melbourne until his death in 1958.[22] During the last eight years of his life he produced some notable sculpture.

Vassilieff possessed the prodigal creative energy and vitality of a natural expressionist and his work moved inevitably towards expressionism from the time he began to follow the bent of his own genius. He was passionately fond of Byzantine art, epitomized for him in the work of his compatriot, Rublev; and he held the work of Goya, El Greco, Turner, Rembrandt, Rubens, Soutine and Chagall in high regard. But he had little time for Constable, the impressionists (except Renoir) and the non-objective tradition represented by Kandinsky, Mondrian and the Bauhaus School. These artists represented for him what he called 'ghastly good taste'. His exhibitions in Sydney and Melbourne were always well attended by younger artists and students and there can be no doubt that he was a pioneer of expressionist painting in Australia. His painting of street scenes in Sydney and Melbourne also foreshadowed a theme prominent among social realists in Australia. The freedom, verve and immediacy which he brought to his painting exercised an influence upon Australian art, especially in Melbourne, which it is difficult to estimate. The fact that *avant-garde* art in Melbourne developed during the war years a character more thoroughly expressionistic than Sydney, tended to be more immediate in execution, lay greater score upon vitality and less upon the post-impressionist tradition, was probably due not a little to his work and example.

The 1930's were years of transition between one phase of Australian art and another. From the time Norah Simpson brought back some knowledge of the paintings of the *Ecole de Paris* to the art students of Sydney, local academic art had been modified by a steady intrusion of contemporary ideas. But the modifications did not penetrate deeply enough to influence the public taste profoundly. The art-buying public still remained, for the most part, faithful to the older ideals: Streeton, Heysen and Gruner continued to supply most Australians with the image of the country they had come to

126   NOEL COUNIHAN, *Portrait of William Dolphin*, hardboard,
40¼ x 34¼, 1945, the artist

love, an heroic or Arcadian idyll into which neither tragedy nor any dark passion of the spirit had entered. It was not until the eve of the Second World War that a new generation, and the artists who were to speak for it, found the Heidelberg dream out of touch with the reality of their lives. It was from their quite different, and perhaps deeper, experience of life that Australian art was reborn.

FOOTNOTES

[1] SYDNEY URE SMITH, 'Recent Purchases for the National Art Gallery of New South Wales', *AA*, iii, 55 (May 1934), pp. 8-12

[2] *See AA*, iii, 48 (February 1933), p. 46; and iii, 49 (April 1933), pp. 6-8

[3] As illustrated in *AA*, iii, 60 (August 1935)

[4] LIONEL LINDSAY, 'The Loan Exhibition of Contemporary British Art', *AA*, iii, 58 (February 1935), pp. 60-2

[5] ELEONORE LANGE, 'The International Art Exhibition at the National Art Gallery of New South Wales', *AA*, iii, 64 (August 1936), pp. 29-36

[6] The *Herald* (Melbourne), 7 November 1931

[7] The *Argus* (Melbourne), 17 August 1932

[8] The *Herald* (Melbourne), 5 August 1932

[9] *See also* GEORGE BELL, 'Eric Thake', *AA*, iii, 64 (August 1933), pp. 39-40

[10] Catalogue of the Second Exhibition, National Gallery of Victoria, April 1939

[11] 'The First Exhibition of the Australian Academy of Art', *AA*, iii, 71 (May 1938), 13-24

[12] The *Argus* (Melbourne), 28 April 1937

[13] The *Argus*, 1 May 1937

[14] The *Argus*, 3 May 1937

[15] The *Herald* (Melbourne), 3 May 1937

[16] The *Herald*, 4 May 1937

[17] The *Herald*, 3 June 1937

[18] The *Sun* (Melbourne), 5 June 1937

[19] Extract from the C.A.S. Constitution published in the inaugural exhibition (1939) catalogue

[20] Quoted from LAWLOR, *Arquebus*, Melbourne, 1937, p. 55

[21] From 'Soldier into Artist' (f. 21), notes in typescript for a biography of the artist by Elizabeth Vassilieff, the artist's wife, to which this account is mainly indebted

[22] *See also* 'Daniel [sic] Vassilieff', *AA*, iii, 62 (February 1936), p. 70

CHAPTER EIGHT

REBIRTH

1939 - 50

*This is a period of transition; we are at the beginning of a
new cycle, and ours is a new spring.*
PAUL HAEFLIGER, *Angry Penguins*, December 1944

DURING the 1940's Australian painting reached a level of achievement it
had not previously attained. The Second World War, unlike the First, in-
vigorated the arts. The country was, it is true, cut off to some extent from
direct contact with Europe, but at this stage of the nation's development the
five years of partial isolation were profitable. Under the pressure and challenge of war Australian artists, like the nation as a whole, were thrown
more upon their own resources and were quickened in spirit by the events
they lived through. In Sydney a new generation of artists, fully trained and
with years of European experience behind them, began to work. In
Melbourne a group of young *avant-garde* artists brought vitality and a sense
of adventure to the art of a city noted during the present century for its
conservatism in matters of taste. Contact with the art world abroad, re-
opened during the previous decade, was sustained through books and the
movement of service personnel but most of Australia's leading artists were
at work in their own country. Artists and writers came to mean more to the
nation in this war than they had meant in the First World War or in the
peace between the two. Magazines like *Meanjin* and *Angry Penguins*,
indicative of the intellectual ferment of the time, sprang up and flourished.
Noting the decline in art publication in Europe, *Art in Australia* announced
in March 1941 with brave and touching ambition that it would now embrace
the art of the whole world. 'Art cannot die, and we in Australia can and will
carry on our efforts to preserve, encourage and foster the culture our enemies
would destroy.'[1] Art did not die; but *Art in Australia* did, after five more
issues in the year following, having overreached itself in a pyrotechnic dazzle
of luxury publication that covered everything from Masaccio and Sung
porcelain to Moore and Sidney Nolan. But after two decades of isolation
such ambition to reach international standards quickly was characteristic
of the intellectual adventuring of the time.

Though for most Australians the arts were still exotic curiosities of the mind, there was, none the less, a widespread interest in all the arts among servicemen. *Salt*, the fortnightly magazine of the Army Education Service, did something to satisfy this interest and maintain contact between the arts and the services. Official war artists were not, as in the First War, chosen so largely from the ranks of the conventional portrait painters and illustrators, nor were visual war records confined to the portrayal of officers, war heroes, and the glorification of martial sacrifice. Life in the services and the industrial face of the nation at war was also included and produced some of the best work. Furthermore, despite the inevitable tragedies, irritations and frustrations of the time, most artists managed to draw and paint their way through the war years. The war, in short, brought with it a serious threat to the nation's independence which with the aid of its allies it met successfully: the challenge was great enough to stimulate, not great enough to suppress, artistic expression.

127   ERIC WILSON, *Stove Theme*, canvas, 36½ x 21, 1942, Brisbane

New Arrivals in Sydney 1938-40

Between 1938 and 1940 the whole climate of artistic opinion and practice in Sydney was affected radically by the return of a new generation of students from abroad, and the arrival of a number of important artists, teachers and designers from England and the Continent. During the 1920's and early 1930's Julian Ashton, towards the end of a long lifetime of distinguished teaching produced, together with his faithful partner, Henry Gibbons, a highly talented group of students. Among the most prominent were Grace Crowley, Rah Fizelle, William Dobell, John Passmore, Jean Bellette and Paul Haefliger. Crowley and Fizelle returned, as we have seen, during the early 1930's, to play a significant role in the early history of the contemporary movement in Sydney. Passmore did not return until 1950. But Dobell, Haefliger and Jean Bellette all returned in 1939. Dobell had studied at the Slade, Jean Bellette and Haefliger at the Westminster School under Bernard Meninsky and Mark Gertler. The Westminster School had acquired a reputation for its teaching, was looking very much to Paris, but was also paying great attention to classical composition and the achievement of 'volumes'. The school attracted other Australian students, too, such as Eric Wilson, who had studied at the East Sydney Technical College and won the New South Wales Travelling Scholarship for 1937; and Donald Friend, who had studied under Dattilo Rubbo and Sydney Long. Wilson, a pioneer in Sydney of cubist and abstract painting, returned in 1939 (127); Friend returned in 1940, after he had worked for two years in Nigeria. Students from George Bell's school also moved to and settled in Sydney: Sali Herman in 1938, Russell Drysdale in 1940, Wolfgang Cardamatis and David Strachan a little later.

And there were others; artists, teachers and designers, who returned or arrived in the city on the eve of the Second World War. Desiderius Orban, a Hungarian artist and art teacher, and a foundation member of the group, *Nyolcak*, established in Budapest in 1908, settled in Sydney in 1939, and later opened an art school in which the role of the creative imagination in the practice of art was given first place. Frank Medworth, an English art master, engraver and painter, took charge of the East Sydney Technical College in 1939; and worked unceasingly both in the school and the city to introduce a more tolerant approach to contemporary forms of expression. Hal Missingham, a former student and teacher at the London Central School of Arts and Crafts, a graphic artist, designer, and water-colour painter, settled in Sydney the following year. Carl Plate, after several years abroad, arrived and opened the Notanda Galleries, a print and book shop intimately associated with the growth of the contemporary art movement in Sydney. Elaine Haxton, trained at East Sydney, returned after some years abroad in 1939, full of enthusiasm for the murals she had seen in Mexico on her way home. Dahl and Geoffrey Collings, R. Haughton James and Richard Beck began the slow and difficult process of introducing the principles of contemporary design into Australian industry.

Almost every one of these arrivals in Sydney was a professional artist, and most had received a complete academic training but had come to understand the broad principles upon which contemporary art was based. During the early 1940's, whether serving in the Forces or not, they were able to effect a radical change in the theory and practice of art in Sydney. An international outlook replaced a provincial one, while the pressures and urgencies of war brought a maturity and depth to art in Sydney that it had not experienced before. Two broad trends are observable during the 1940's,

128 RUSSELL DRYSDALE, *Two Children*, canvas, 23½ x 19½,
1946, Melbourne

trends that sprang from the diverse interests and temperaments of the new arrivals. One trend might fairly be called realistic expressionism, and the other neo-romanticism. The realistic expressionists, who were equally if not more prominent in Melbourne, brought an expressionistic idiom to the interpretation of life about them. The neo-romantics, more prominent in the immediate post-war years, explored historical styles; especially the Byzantine, the *trecento*, the *quattrocento* and Persian art, with a new freedom deriving from contemporary principles.

Surrealism

The Sydney branch of the Contemporary Art Society was established late in 1939, and the new arrivals in Sydney joined it in force, so that oddly enough, despite the resignation of Bell and his eighty-two artist supporters, the second (1940) exhibition of the Society, which was held both in Melbourne and Sydney, was one of the most representative and important exhibitions the Society ever held. The exhibition introduced to the art public of Sydney a generation of artists who were to determine very largely the standards and taste of the city in the visual arts during the 1940's, and it represented a landmark in the history of Australian art in that the contributors both from Melbourne and Sydney revealed beyond all doubt the existence in both cities of a generation that had moved beyond post-impressionism.

129   ERIC THAKE, *Salvation from the Evils of Earthly Existence*, cardboard, 16 x 20, 1941, Melbourne

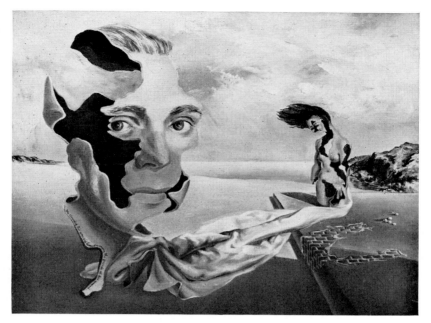

130   JAMES GLEESON, *We Inhabit the Corrosive Littoral
of Habit*, canvas, 15¾ x 19½, 1941, Melbourne

Abstract work from Gordon Andrews, Dahl and Geoffrey Collings and
Leonard Crawford was included; and the exhibition was notable also for
its recognition of surrealism. An anonymous donor provided a £50 prize for
the best picture 'showing new expression of thought in art'. Gino Nibbi, the
judge, awarded the prize equally between Eric Thake's *Salvation from the
Evils of Earthly Existence* (129), and James Gleeson's *We Inhabit the
Corrosive Littoral of Habit* (130).

The two paintings were presented by the Society to the National Gallery
of Victoria. Both artists had exhibited surrealist works before; Thake's being
inspired by the more restrained English surrealism of Wadsworth, Paul
Nash and John Tunnard, Gleeson's by Salvador Dali. Gleeson had studied
at East Sydney and under May Marsden at the Sydney Teachers' College,
who encouraged an experimental attitude in her students. Surrealist trends
appeared in his student work in 1937, and he is the only Australian artist
who has sought to develop his art pretty much upon surrealist lines. Possessed of poetical and critical interests he lectured and wrote a good deal
during the early 1940's to make surrealism better understood. Gleeson first
exhibited surrealist paintings in the inaugural exhibition of the Contemporary Art Society in June 1939; but it was the presence of Salvador Dali's
L'Homme Fleur in Sir Keith Murdoch's exhibition of *French and British
Modern Art* that brought surrealism fully to public notice in Australia. It

o

131   ALBERT TUCKER, *The Futile City*, cardboard, 17½ x 21½,
1940, Museum of Modern Art of Australia, Melbourne

was the most discussed and publicized painting in the exhibition. The
Cézannes were studied and respected but they did not arouse the same
excitement among the younger artists. The 1940's were to be, in essence,
romantic.

By 1940 quite a vogue for surrealist painting had arisen. It appeared in
the work of Adrian Lawlor, always ready to experiment with *avant-garde*
ideas; in the work of Herbert McClintock (Max Ebert), who held one-man
shows of his surrealist work in Perth and Sydney but later turned to social
realism; and in the work of Geoffrey Graham. It appeared in the work of
Albert Tucker, in such paintings as *The Philosopher* (1939) and *The Futile
City* (131). Tucker was also experimenting with social realism; and was to
turn later to a more expressionistic style.

Following its brief period of popularity in the early 1940's surrealism did
not, except in Gleeson's work, continue as a distinctive form of expression
in Australian art. But it played an important part in the formation of the
styles of Purves Smith, Russell Drysdale, Albert Tucker, Sidney Nolan,
Arthur Boyd and the theatre designer, William Constable. Though not
programmatic surrealists they have used surrealist and quasi-surrealist
devices considerably in their work. The influence of surrealism was felt
more strongly in poetry than in painting. *Angry Penguins*, the *avant-garde*

journal edited (1941-6) by Max Harris and John Reed, and *Comment*
(1940-7), edited by Dorothy Crozier, published a good deal of surrealist
and quasi-surrealist verse by Max Harris, Alistair Kershaw, James Gleeson
and others. The much-publicized success of the Ern Malley hoax (1944)
probably reduced the influence of surrealist *vers libre* in Australian poetry.[2]

Social Realism

Following the departure of George Bell and his supporters, the influence
of social realism became more prominent in the councils and the exhibitions
of the Contemporary Art Society. Social realism can be defined simply as
the depiction of contemporary life from a left-wing point of view, and its
prominence in Australian art during the early 1940's was due in large
measure to the success of the Communist Party's united front against
Fascism, and the entry of the U.S.S.R. into the war in 1941. But it must be
stressed that the social realist painters were artists who believed that art
and politics cannot and should not be separated. They were artists in
politics, not politicians. If they found themselves, on the one hand, ostracized
continuously by artists and critics who could not bring themselves to believe
that it was possible to be involved in politics and paint good pictures at the
same time, they also found themselves, on the other hand, continuously
involved at one level or another in theoretical disputes with the members
of the local Party hierarchy for whom the pronouncements of Zhdanov, and
other leading communists, on cultural matters provided endless ground for
discussion but none for disagreement. At its best social realism is a cathartic
and moral art embraced by artists acutely aware, either through personal
experience or imaginative feeling, of the existence in society of cruelty,
injustice and suffering. By depicting the depressing, horrifying or squalid
the artist seeks to alleviate his own sense of guilt and sharpen the feelings
of others against social evil.

Social realism began in Australia as an interest in depicting street scenes
and life in the inner industrial and slum areas of Sydney and Melbourne.
It is foreshadowed in Danila Vassilieff's paintings in the back streets of
Surry Hills, Sydney, during 1936 and 1937; and of Fitzroy and Carlton in
Melbourne between 1937 and 1940. Slums and factories were the subjects
mostly chosen by the short-lived Windsor Group (1938-9), Sydney, a circle
of Fred Leist's ex-students.

Social realism flourished most strongly in Melbourne during the war years
among a group of artists who were members of the Contemporary Art
Society, the most prominent being Josl Bergner, V. G. O'Connor and Noel
Counihan. Bergner was a member of a Viennese Jewish family who was
taken by his parents to Poland at an early age and grew up among artists
and writers. He migrated alone to Melbourne in 1937 and lived in a Carlton

attic where he began to paint street and market scenes, such as *The Pumpkin Eaters* (133), in a sombre, painterly style that owed not a little to his passion for Daumier, Van Gogh and the Picasso of the blue period. Bergner followed his street scenes with a series based on his reminiscences of life in the Warsaw ghetto and an important series of paintings of Australian aborigines which he completed in 1942 while employed with other aliens in an employment company. In 1947 he left Australia for Israel where he still paints.

Victor O'Connor qualified as a lawyer just prior to entering the Army in December 1941 and his training in art was confined to a short period in Bell's studio. During 1941-2, when the Melbourne social realists were producing some of their best paintings, O'Connor painted a splendid series of pictures in red-browns with a great sensitivity of touch, *The Refugees* (134), for example, on the theme of the Nazi persecutions. For another of the series, *The Dispossessed* (1942, the artist), he shared the Society's anonymous prize with Donald Friend.

Noel Counihan, the third member of the group, was a Press cartoonist and caricaturist for many years before he began to paint in 1941. He is a draughtsman of unusual skill and firm, masculine power and, though his art does not possess O'Connor's sensitivity of touch or Bergner's air of brooding tragedy, his painting has become a highly expressive instrument shrewd in its statements, deft and assured in handling. Some of his portraits, such as his magnificent portrait of the violin-maker, *William Dolphin* (126), possess great distinction.

A social realist, Harry de Hartog, succeeded George Bell as President of the Contemporary Art Society in 1940, and he was succeeded in turn by Victor O'Connor. It was at the suggestion of Noel Counihan that the Society decided upon an exhibition of anti-Fascist art, which was held in the Athenaeum Gallery, Melbourne, late in 1942 and opened by J. D. Blake, the State Secretary of the Communist Party. It was intended to present a popular front among artists against fascism and ranged, therefore, from representational to abstract work. Sidney Nolan's contribution to the exhibition, *Dream of the Latrine Sitter*, created considerable consternation among some visitors who found difficulty in deciding for themselves whether an image of a private in a water-closet was a fascist or an anti-fascist gesture.

The Anti-Fascist Exhibition was also held in Adelaide by the South Australian section of the Contemporary Art Society, which had been formed in June 1942 as the result of a split between the Council and the Associates of the Royal South Australian Society of Arts on the question of contemporary art, which had culminated in a highly successful Associates' Contemporary Exhibition held in July 1942. The first annual exhibition of the South Australian C.A.S. was held in October 1943; and early exhibitions brought the

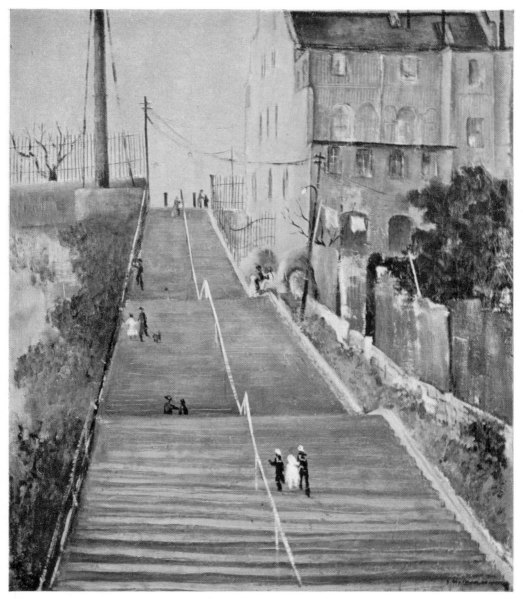

132 SALI HERMAN, *McElhone Stairs*, canvas, 26½ x 22, 1944,
Dr and Mrs H. V. Evatt

work of David Dallwitz, Douglas Roberts, Jacqueline Hick, Ivor Francis (135) and Jeff Smart to notice in other States.

Until the Anti-Fascist Exhibition, co-operation on matters of broad policy had been maintained in Melbourne between John Reed and his circle of artists and the social realists led by O'Connor and Counihan. But the exhibition deepened a rift already growing between the two groups. Reed took his stand on the fact that the Society had been brought into existence to oppose work which had no other aim but representation and disliked the inclusion of purely naturalistic work in the exhibition. The social realists, on the other hand, were highly critical of the very personal and expressionistic character of some of the work, especially Tucker's and Nolan's. Theoretically they had come increasingly to believe that most *avant-garde* art was expressive of the decadence of capitalist culture, and were seeking to unify artists against fascism whether they worked in naturalistic modes or not.

The rift became a public matter in the fourth issue of *Angry Penguins*, which appeared early in 1943 in a new format under the joint editorship of John Reed and Max Harris. It contained an article by Tucker entitled *Art, Myth and Society*. In the process of discussing the role of myth in society and the nature of the artist's freedom, he launched a trenchant but impersonal attack upon the Communist Party's approach, both in theory and practice, to art and artists:

The artist must be free from violence, regulation, coercion, want, and moral blinkers. If, in his role as a social being, he is to co-operate with any political movement, he must be assured of creative freedom at all times. Rest assured, his interpretations and beliefs will assert themselves through his work.[3]

Rejoinders, from Counihan and de Hartog, were published in the September issue of *Angry Penguins*; and the controversy which followed produced a complete break between the Reed-Harris group, which included the artists, Nolan, Boyd, Tucker and Perceval, and the social realists, Counihan, O'Connor, Bergner and de Hartog and their followers. The latter group turned increasingly to popular front activity and was largely responsible for the organization of the Australia at War Exhibition (1945) which sought to unite all artists, irrespective of their differences, in patriotic, anti-fascist activity.

A circle of realist painters that included James Cant, Roy Dalgarno, Herbert McClintock and Roderick Shaw became active in Sydney a little later than the Melbourne group. James Cant (*b.* 1911), after some art training in various Sydney studios, went to London in 1934, worked for a time with the London surrealist group associated with Roland Penrose, and painted in France and Spain before returning to Australia in 1939 to join the Army. Cant tends to take his themes from the simplest and least promising of things and paint them with a lucid spareness of vision. Street

133   JOSL BERGNER, *The Pumpkin Eaters*, hardboard,
31⅛ x 37½, *c.* 1940, Museum of Modern Art of
Australia, Melbourne

134   V. G. O'CONNOR, *The Refugees*, cardboard,
16 x 20½, 1941, the author

135   IVOR FRANCIS, *Schizophrenia*, canvas, 32½ x 24½,
1943, Adelaide

scenes, massive and vacant; aboriginal art; stray bits of landscape closely
scrutinized and painted with a primitive sharpness of focus, as in *The
Yellow Hill* (136), are characteristic of a style which is flexible and still in
a process of development. It was Cant who suggested the formation of the
Studio of Realist Art (Sora), established in March 1945 as an art school and
artists' centre in Sydney. The other foundation members included Hal
Missingham, Dora Chapman, Roy Dalgarno and Roderick Shaw. Dalgarno,
who had trained at the Melbourne Gallery School, was commissioned by a
group of trade unions to paint industrial life and activities; Roderick Shaw,
an original member of the Windsor Group, was also a designer and book
illustrator of ability who later turned to high-quality printing.

The Sydney realists were less doctrinaire, but did not achieve the
painterly quality or emotional depth of the Melbourne group. For the most

136   JAMES CANT, *The Yellow Hill*, hardboard, 36 x 48,
1959, Adelaide

part they confined themselves to industrial themes avoiding direct political
comment.

Although individual artists like Counihan have continued to produce
sound if not always inspired work, social realism as a creative trend in
Australian art barely survived the war. In its programmatic form it has, like
surrealism, ceased to interest the *avant-garde* or the post-war generation of
students. The reasons are not far to seek. Social realists often begin as good
artists and end as poor politicians; by putting more of their energy into
politics than into painting they burn themselves out. Much more important,
however, is the fact that the outlook of the post-war years did not favour
a realistic approach to art.

Realistic Expressionism and Post-Impressionism,
mainly in war-time Sydney

The realistic note in Sydney art during the war years was rarely associated with politics. The search for themes in the daily life of the city and
the nation, foreshadowed in Vassilieff's street scenes, was augmented by the
arrival in Sydney of Sali Herman in 1938 and Russell Drysdale in 1940—
both Bell students. Bell admired Vassilieff's work and encouraged his pupils
to find their subjects in the life about them. Realistic and satirical commentary on life is observable in the work of Peter Purves Smith, another
of Bell's students. Indeed a frank observation of life combined with elements
of surrealist fantasy, humour, dry and sardonic wit, and at times pure
whimsy is often to be found in the work of Purves Smith, Russell Drysdale,
Sali Herman, Donald Friend and William Dobell. These artists, together

with the more expressive and primitivistic *Angry Penguins* group in Melbourne, were largely responsible for establishing the mood and character of art in Australia during the war years. It is most desirable therefore to consider their work individually.

Peter Purves Smith (*b.* 1912), after leaving Geelong Grammar School, spent a few years at the Jervis Bay Naval College but, with its reduction and transference to Westernport, Victoria, turned for a time to jackerooing in the country. When he decided to study art he left for London and worked first under Iain McNab at the Grosvenor School and then with Bell in Melbourne. Apart from his teachers, Modigliani, Henri Rousseau, Christopher Wood, Utrillo and surrealism appear to be the main contributors to his highly personal style, a style strong in formal organization yet droll, whimsical and, at times, sharply satirical. The elongated type of figure which he used with such expressive effect appeared in early student works such as *French Café* (1936, Mrs Purves Smith), as did the influence of surrealism in *New York* (137). His most important paintings belong to the two years he spent in Paris and London prior to joining the British Army in 1940. To this period belong his poetic *Early Morning in Paris* (1939) and *Promenade* (1939, Mrs Purves Smith), with its thinly scumbled and luminous blues and greens. A direct and refreshing awareness of life is present both in such colloquial observations as *The Park* (1938, Mrs D. Tooth) and *The Pond* (1939, Mrs D. Tooth), and in the political satires, *The Nazis, Nuremberg* (1938, Brisbane) and *The Diplomats* (1939, Lady Casey).

Purves Smith was thirty-seven when he died in 1949 after being invalided out of the British Army in Burma, where he had served with Wingate's Chindits. Despite the small amount of work which he left, it is of more than usual importance both for its own intrinsic quality and the fact that it foreshadowed a quite new approach to the interpretation of the Australian landscape, which his friend and fellow-student, Russell Drysdale, was to explore and develop. Purves Smith and Drysdale worked closely together both in Melbourne and in Paris, and learned much from one another. Two small drought landscapes by Smith (138), painted in 1940, anticipate in more ways than one the new approach to the Australian rural scene which Drysdale was to announce in his Albury paintings a year later. Writing in 1939, Gino Nibbi remarked of Purves Smith's work, with considerable perception:

He aspires to decorative effects curiously hallucinatory, and utilizes some primordial visions . . . as he did Rousseau le Douanier for whom the word *naïveté* was synonymous with high knowledge. Purves Smith seems one of the most qualified at the present time to give some allegorical interpretations of the virgin appearance of the Australian land.[4]

137   PETER PURVES SMITH, *New York*, canvas, 30 x 20,
1936, Sydney

138   PETER PURVES SMITH,
Drought, water-colour on paper,
18½ x 15, 1940, Lady Casey

But Purves Smith died young, and the allegories and primordial visions rose in the work of others.[5]

Russell Drysdale was born at Bognor Regis, Sussex, in 1912, into a family possessing Australian associations since the 1820's. The Russells, originally from Fife, Scotland, pioneered as pastoralists first in Tasmania, then in the Western District of Victoria, the Riverina and northern Queensland. Anne Drysdale, also from Fife, took up land near Geelong in the 1840's. Drysdale spent his early years in England but visited Australia with his parents twice before the family settled here in 1923. After completing his secondary education at Geelong Grammar School between 1923 and 1929 he spent a year in northern Queensland acquiring a knowledge of the sugar industry, in which the family was interested, and then returned to 'Boxwood Park', the pastoral property they had acquired in the Riverina. Here he acted as an overseer while his parents were abroad in 1931, joining them in England for some months before they returned. Drysdale had always assumed that, in the family tradition, he would follow a life on the land, though drawing had been a hobby since his school days in England. During an illness in Melbourne in 1932 Dr Julian Smith, impressed by the quality of his draughtsmanship, introduced him to Sir Daryl Lindsay who advised him to study art under George Bell. The artists most discussed in the Bell-Shore school at the time were Cézanne, Gauguin, Van Gogh, Matisse and Picasso; and Drysdale, brought up to admire the Australian impressionists, at first found Bell's ideas and methods difficult to accept. During a second visit to England and the Continent in 1932, however, he was able to see for the first time original works by the impressionists and post-impressionists and the School of Paris; as well as painters such as Utrillo and Rouault less familiar to him. He began to think seriously of becoming a painter.

In 1935 he married Elizabeth Stephen, also of Scottish descent, and with the full support of his parents, decided to become a painter. He enrolled as a student at the Bell-Shore school, studying first under Shore while Bell was abroad in England, and then under Bell after his return in 1936 and Shore's resignation. At the school he met Peter Purves Smith, reviving a school friendship that was terminated only by Purves Smith's death in 1949.

Drysdale's early works were painted between 1936 and 1938 under the influence of Bell and the talented group of students which Bell attracted to his classes after his return in 1936. Their tonal key is high, the paint crisp in handling and dry in texture. A light palette of pinks, pale greens, blues and yellow-reds prevails, and the design tends to be flat and decorative. His early drawing of the figure, in rhythmical arabesques, owes something to Modigliani, Kisling and Ian Fairweather—all strong influences among Bell's students at this time.

Drysdale's skill and perception as a draughtsman underlies and fortifies the expressive power of his paintings. Not surprisingly, therefore, figure subjects —usually associated with manual labour in the city or country—appealed to him from the beginning. In one early painting of 1937 he depicts men mixing concrete in a city street, in another a group of figures symbolizing several aspects of farming. Appealing, too, was the life and architecture of the built-up inner suburbs of Melbourne. In one painting a young guitarist sits on a doorstep and plays to his friends, in another the decorative ironwork of hotel verandas and terrace houses is already beginning to exercise its picturesque appeal. But urban imagery soon gave way to those images of country life which were to form the staple of his style. No early painting is more revealing than *The Rabbiter and His Family* (139), where the random influences of the art school are already being put to the service of personal expression. The folksiness and sophisticated primitivism of Christopher Wood is its point of departure, but already present is Drysdale's abiding interest in the pose, air and gesture characteristic of country types.

He returned to Melbourne in June 1939, a few months before the outbreak of war, and worked in George Bell's private studio for a year where he became increasingly interested in themes concerned with life on the land. In 1940, unable to enlist because of defective vision in one eye, acquired in 1929, unwilling to become involved in the art-politics of the Contemporary Art Society, and interested in working on rural themes, he moved from Melbourne to Albury where he acted for a time as overseer for shearing at a friend's property. Then, late in the year, he settled in Sydney and began to exhibit at the Macquarie Galleries.

1940 was for Drysdale a transitional year. His student work had been bright and decorative—essentially post-impressionist in structure, feeling and subject-matter. But as the war opened and deepened the mood of his art changed; and the reaction of people to hard and hostile environments aroused his interest increasingly. Soutine and the early Picasso might well have been partly responsible for those little studies in isolation or loneliness, such as *Study 1940* (Dr and Mrs H. V. Evatt) and *Newspaper* (Lord and Lady Casey), which he painted in that year; and they owe something perhaps, too, both in technique and style, to Dobell.

In 1941 Drysdale's personal style began to assert itself when he began to paint a series of studies of country life as he had experienced it in the Riverina at various times, but more especially during the previous year when the district had been hit by one of the worst droughts of the century. At once realistic and expressive, these paintings constitute a complete break with the naturalistic landscape which the Heidelberg School had established sixty years before and from which the local post-impressionist painters of the 1920's and 1930's, attached as they were to a structured and stylized naturalism, had never entirely departed. He began to formulate a new set of conventions grounded not upon naturalism but upon ideas drawn from realistic, expressionistic and surrealistic sources. But though he discarded the naturalistic element in post-impressionism, he retained its classicism. The classic quality is to be found in his preference for horizontals and verticals and the ordered, static quality of his compositions; the expressionist quality in his colour and figuration; the surrealist in his use of such devices as deep perspective, vacancy and disjunctive images to create absurd, whimsical or disquieting effects.

Drysdale's art does, in a general way, provide a parallel to the work of such American artists as Thomas Hart Benton and Grant Wood who, in the 1930's, rejected the formal adventures of the School of Paris and returned home to paint the American scene. Its sources, however, are not be found

139   RUSSELL DRYSDALE, *The Rabbiter and His Family*,
canvas, 24 x 30, 1938, Lord and Lady Casey

140   RUSSELL DRYSDALE, *Sunday Evening*, asbestos cement,
23⅝ x 29⅞, 1941, Sydney

in such work but, as we have observed, in contemporary European painting.

Drysdale's interpretations of the Australian outback have often been criticized as ugly and grotesque. Certainly he does not seek beauty-spots in the manner of Elioth Gruner and the later work of Streeton. But the creative artist, it must be remembered, discovers and expresses the truth as he sees and feels it. He is not a manipulator of known and received forms of beauty. Drysdale revealed aspects of country life which the impressionists and their followers chose to ignore. As we have seen, the Heidelberg painters did not for long hold up the mirror to Australian nature with a steady hand. When their visual integrity and the enthusiasm which accompanied it failed them they began to idealize rather than to see. The hard edge of reality was softened by romance. So it was that Drysdale's art became an implicit criticism of Streeton's golden visions and Gruner's sweet pastures.

Although Drysdale's art has its source in twentieth-century European painting, it does not follow that it is unconnected with local tradition. There was, as we have seen, a long-established alternative to the fashionable convention of 'sunny Australia'. It arose from the experience of colonials as they subdued the land and occupied it. Australian nature, the older convention proclaimed, was monotonous, unpicturesque, idiosyncratic, alien and hostile to man, inducing either loneliness and melancholy or nonchalant resistance. It had already been asserted to some extent in the art of such

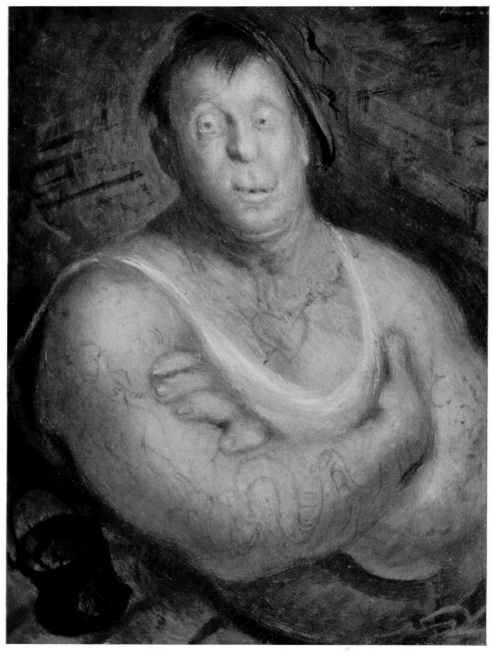

141   WILLIAM DOBELL, *The Billy Boy*, canvas, 28 x 21, 1943,
Australian War Memorial, Canberra

men as S. T. Gill, William Strutt and Frederick McCubbin. But its real strength lay in the literary tradition. Writers from Charles Harpur to Patrick White have not ceased to emphasize the tough, unyielding qualities of the environment. It was this alternative convention that reappeared with renewed vitality in Australian contemporary art in Drysdale's 1941 Riverina paintings (140).

Henry Lawson had first expressed the older convention realistically; and Drysdale finds his true literary parallel in Lawson; he is, indeed, a kind of twentieth-century Lawson of painting. He possesses Lawson's compulsion to tell the truth as he sees it, his sense of the absurd, his humour, his craftsmanly respect for form, his humanity and, though Drysdale restrains it more thoroughly, Lawson's sentiment. Like Lawson he has sought to cut down the over-romanticized and over-glamorized image of the Australian bush to true size. 'Draw a wire fence and a few ragged gums, and add some scattered sheep running away from the train. Then you'll have the bush all along the western line from Bathurst on,'[6] Lawson wrote in his essay, 'In a Dry Season'. He might well have been describing a Drysdale painting half a century later. Drysdale, too, recalls Lawson by the economy with which he visualizes a scene. 'I have left out the wattle—because it wasn't there. . . . I have left out "the sad Australian sunset" because the sun wasn't going down at the time,' wrote Lawson, in 'The Union Buries its Dead'.[7] Drysdale reveals a similar desire to reduce his imagery to essentials. Consequently, like Lawson, he was able to establish a convincing relationship between his 'characters' and their back country setting.

From 1941 the face of the nation at war began to occupy his attention increasingly. *The Medical Examination* (1941, C. F. Vine-Hall) and *Local V.D.C. Parade* (142) are still Lawsonesque in their search for the characteristic and their enjoyment of the absurd. But as the war crisis sharpened the humour and anecdotal element declined. Partly as the result of the influence of the work of English artists such as Graham Sutherland, John Piper, Paul Nash and, above all, Henry Moore, his compositions became more formalized and monumental and his colour deeper in tone, mottled in texture, sharper in its contrasts and edges, and began to free itself from constructional form. The mood also changed. It became far more dramatic, at times threatening and somewhat hallucinatory. Such changes are to be noted in his gouache (Miss C. Belbridge) and his oil studies of *Albury Platform* (1943, Melbourne), *Bushfire* (1944, Brisbane) and *Airport at Night* (1944, Melbourne). The likely influence of Dobell continues in his *Portrait of Donald Friend* (1943, James Fairfax) and his *Nude* (1944, Miss J. Stephen), in which a new interest in the painting of flesh appears.

During the severe drought of 1944, the *Sydney Morning Herald* commissioned Drysdale to record its effects in the Western Division of New

142 RUSSELL DRYSDALE, *The Local V.D.C. Parade*, wood panel,
17½ x 22½, 1943, Adelaide

South Wales. The series of paintings which he exhibited in 1945 based on his drawings at that time are conceived in a mood quite different from the Riverina paintings of 1941. Sheets of iron distorted by fire and twisted in the wind became symbols of the futility of human achievement. Dead trunks of trees, thrown at times into grotesque male and female forms, simulated life. In such country no fence divided the organic from the inorganic or the living from the dead. Oddly enough, however, the dramatic element in his work began to give way to a quieter, more classical mood, and was accompanied by a change of technique. In place of the mottled and sharp edginess of the early war paintings there appeared a manner based upon even transitions of tone and close modelling of forms over thick, white grounds. The mannered eccentricities of his earlier work, such as excessive figural elongation, were modified in order to achieve monumentality. What once appeared ludicrous began to acquire a heroic quality. The change both in mood and technique was revealed in *The Drover's Wife* (143), an image of fortitude, devotion and survival. Children began to appear frequently in these landscapes of drought and desolation, with the loneliness and melancholy of the landscape stamped upon them. Drysdale had begun his studies of loneliness in such paintings as his fine little *Two Children* (1941, University of New England) and his Picassoesque *Mother and Child* (1942, George Bell), and the theme runs continuously through his work. At times it is the nostalgia

143   RUSSELL DRYSDALE, *The Drover's Wife*, canvas,
20 x 24, 1945, Mr Kym Bonython

of migrants, as in *Ennui* (1944, C. Swanton); at times it is the native-born who are alone. The theme appears in another painting of *Two Children* (128), one of the finest of his paintings and one of the few in the history of Australian art—so consistently romantic at heart—in which form and content achieve a classical ideality. By virtue of its formal perfection and profound but controlled feeling, the small painting reaches beyond the individual and the regional to express the consuming loneliness of human-kind.

In thus seeking to express universal values, Drysdale did not wander far from common life. His country town paintings are an example. It is not the contemporary Australian town with its naïve faith in cantilevered awnings and chromium plate which has exercised his imagination, but tumble-down, half-deserted gold towns like Hill End and Sofala (144). In some ways these paintings are like de Chirico's metaphysical paintings; but Drysdale has brought the metaphysics down to earth. In place of massive Roman arcades he substitutes the cast-iron verandas of boom-time Australia. Thus the fantastic element, not being forced, gains power as a threat dimly felt beneath the surface of the commonplace. Here we are confronted with one of the basic qualities of Drysdale's imagination. He seeks continually for what we might call a realistic correlative; in other words forms in real life which correspond to those more abstracted evocative forms given cur-

144   RUSSELL DRYSDALE, *Sofala*, duck on hardboard,
28¼ x 36½, 1947, Sydney

rency by *avant-garde* painters abroad. This matching of ideographs to reality is often found in the work of artists who have retained respect for the rational presentation of the visible world. Realistic correlatives are present, for example, in Rembrandt's work; as when he places the body of Christ before a candle to suggest, but not assert, a divine radiance without infringing—by baroque haloes—the laws of optics.

Between 1946 and 1950 Drysdale produced a series of paintings classical in mood and structure which he has not surpassed; but in 1950 he entered upon a period of uncertainty and indecision marked by an increased interest in technical experiment and greater receptivity to influences from the work of his contemporaries. In that year he began to prepare for his first London exhibition. Held at the Leicester Galleries in December 1950, it brought together some of his finest paintings, but included others repetitious of early work with a feeling of haste and tiredness about them. It may have been, therefore, the desire to avoid repeating himself that caused him to enter upon a phase of increased technical experiment during the early 1950's. At times it is the influence of Graham Sutherland that reappears; at times the primitive quality of early colonial work, or the equally primitive effects to be seen in some amateur snapshots. Then, in 1951, Drysdale visited Cape York and painted a series of studies of aborigines: the first time he had entered that dangerous iconographical territory. It cannot be said, in all conscience, that he has come through it unscathed. He adopted a highly realistic treatment both of pose and expression in the rendering of his aborigines that is at times out of keeping with the abstracted landscapes into which they are set. In some ways these paintings are a compromise not altogether satisfactory between the realism of the 1941 Albury paintings and the classical landscapes of 1949. On the other hand, as the result of technical innovations, his colour has achieved greater luminosity and is handled with new freedom. In recent paintings of Melville Island natives, Drysdale has tended to simplify and abstract his forms, and further heighten his colour (146). Backgrounds are often reduced to flat decorative areas; and an off-focus figuration has appeared; so too has the influence of aboriginal art itself. At present it is the romantic, hallucinatory and somewhat surrealist side of his work which is predominant.

Drysdale is among the most original of all Australian landscape painters. Few contemporary Australian painters of landscape have been able to escape entirely from the broad terms of reference that his Albury paintings of 1941 began to lay down: a landscape alien to man, harsh, weird, spacious and vacant, given over to the oddities and whimsies of nature, fit only for heroes and clowns, saints, exiles and primitive men. It was a radical break with anything that had been painted since the days of the Heidelberg School, but it also testified to the survival of an old vision of antipodes that had long since sunken deeply into the European imagination.[8]

In sharp contrast to Drysdale's work, the art of Sali Herman transmits a radiant and sensuous enjoyment of common things. Born in Zurich in 1898, Herman was an art dealer in Europe before becoming an artist in Australia. He thus brought a well-informed mind to his own art when he began to study under George Bell in 1937. Although he learnt much from Bell, his sense of control and his painterly quality owe not a little to a close and extensive association with painting in Europe.[9]

None of those artists who have migrated from Europe in recent decades has ranged so widely over the country for his material, drawing upon city life, the beaches, the interior and the tropics. His colour, fine and subtle in quality, is more French than Australian, and classical in its control. Although he can be sombre in mood and occasionally dramatic, his work is for the most part joyously full of the zest of living. There is a physical luxury of form and colour in his best paintings that recalls the impressionists; and his paintings, oddly enough, recapture in a contemporary idiom the sense of visual adventure that animates the early work of the Heidelberg School. Even when he paints the slum dwellings of Sydney there is a sense of bounty: the tenement buildings are rich in colour, monumental in form, and the people active and vigorous (132). It is a land filled not with old fears

145   WILLIAM DOBELL, *Portrait of Anne Hamer*, hardboard, 30 x 24,
1956, Dr Norman Behan

146   RUSSELL DRYSDALE, *Man and Woman, Melville Island,*
50 x 40, 1960, Mrs R. Drysdale

but new promise. His art is not, as it is in the case of so many migrants from
Europe, a study in the nostalgia of exile.

Donald Friend (*b.* 1915), Russell Drysdale's close associate and companion for many years, was one of the most inventive and talented artists to
become known in Australia during the war years. A magnificent draughtsman and the master of a fine, dry, facetious manner, he succeeded in

P

147   DONALD FRIEND, *Boy with Fetish*, panel, 20¼ x 24½,
c. 1946, Melbourne

assembling in his drawings, paintings and war diaries a splendid personal
record of the war years. He studied first with Dattilo Rubbo and Sydney
Long at the Royal Art Society's school, and later in London at the Westminster School. In 1936 he held an exhibition at the Redfern Galleries,
London, before spending two years in Nigeria where he painted and acted
as adviser to Ogoga of Ikere. In 1941 he returned to Sydney with a series of
superb wash drawings and paintings of West Africans (147), and joined
the Army in 1942. His *Gunner's Diary* (1943) and *Painter's Journal* (1946)
record the experiences and reflections of the war years. In 1945 he was
made an official war artist. After his discharge from the Army, Friend
worked for a time in the Torres Strait area, then for a time at 'Merioola', a
picturesque old Victorian house in Edgecliff Road, Sydney, before settling
at Hill End, near Bathurst. At present he lives in Ceylon. As a painter
Friend is experimental in technique and style, brilliantly allusive, and never
dull; and his feeling for colour and decorative construction is of high quality.
But a facility, both of mind and hand, has hindered rather than helped the
full flowering of an art which, nevertheless, at its best reveals a combination
of pictorial intelligence, vitality and good taste unusual in Australian art.[10]

The post-impressionist student work of Purves Smith, Drysdale, Herman
and Friend developed, as it matured, realistic, satiric or colloquial trends
in marked contrast to the dry and brightly decorative post-impressionist

art of the 1920's and early 1930's. No better testimony can be found to the changed spirit of the times, to which, however, no one contributed more profoundly than Dobell.

William Dobell (*b*. 1899) was the son of Robert Dobell, a building contractor of Newcastle, New South Wales. His great skill in drawing revealed itself at an early age, and he was encouraged to develop it by John Walker, one of his teachers at Cooks Hill School. At seventeen he entered into articles with the Newcastle architect, Wallace L. Porter; but his interest lay in art, and in 1924 Dobell settled in Sydney where he attended Julian Ashton's evening classes while employed as a designer for Wunderlich Ltd, manufacturers of building materials. In 1929 he won the Society of Artists' Travelling Scholarship and went to London, where he studied at the Slade under Henry Tonks and Wilson Steer, and received private tuition in drawing from Sir William Orpen. In 1930 Dobell shared at the Slade second prize for drawing with a German student, and received first prize for figure painting. In 1930, too, he visited Holland to study the Dutch masters. Visits to Belgium and France followed where he also studied the work of modern masters. He found himself attracted among the old masters to Rembrandt above all, but also to Goya, Tintoretto, Mantegna and El Greco; and among the moderns, Daumier, Renoir, Van Gogh and Soutine began to exercise an influence. But, possessing a profound receptivity both to art and to life, Dobell was able to absorb and assimilate a wide range of influences without compromising the emergence of his own style. In 1933 his work was exhibited at the Royal Academy. He later exhibited with the New English Art Club, and in 1938 with the London Group.

Dobell's early paintings are executed entirely within the conventions of naturalism. The small landscape, *Village in Somerset* (1930) and *Canal Bruges* (1933, C. Gheysens) are intimate and tranquil in feeling; reticent colour schemes in grey, ochre and muted yellow heightened by small touches of red. Occasionally, as in *St Paul's from Waterloo Bridge* (1931), dramatic hatching in the manner of Van Gogh is noticeable, but more frequently the brushwork of his student days recalls both the fluency and the precision of Tonks.

The tranquil sensitivity of Dobell's early work is seen at its best in his little genre piece, *Boy at the Basin* (148). The brushwork is precise, the lighting soft, and the colours, though low in key, rich and resonant. The studied arrangement of the composition and its intimate setting owes much to the Dutch. With its fine impersonality, even texture and lovely colour it summarizes the achievement of Dobell's early years better perhaps than any other painting. It was singled out for praise by P. Konody, the critic on the *Observer*, when exhibited in the Academy Exhibition of 1933.[11]

About 1933 Dobell's painting acquired greater freedom of conception

148　WILLIAM DOBELL, *Boy at the Basin*, wood panel,
16⅛ x 13, 1932, Sydney

and more assurance in handling. The somewhat self-conscious air of his
early work disappeared and he began to draw extensively upon life and
personal experience, finding his material in odd corners and out-of-the-way
situations. This new phase is heralded by his fine little *Woman in Café*
(150). The handling is broad, preserving the immediacy of a sketch, and
the subject realized with sensitivity, the large area of the dress with its
warm shadows being counterpoised against the reds and yellow-greens he
favoured so much in his early landscapes. The influence of Sickert is
apparent; but there is an intuitive response to the subject which is Dobell's
own, and quite unlike Sickert's flair and painterly assurance.

By 1936 the new free manner was fully fledged. But it was still used
to record impressions. Indeed, a painting like *Park Lane* (1936, N.
McEacharn), with its delightful evocation of an early spring day in London,

149 WILLIAM DOBELL, Finished oil study for *Portrait of an Artist*, canvas, 48 x 32, 1943, Mr Warwick Fairfax (The original, formerly in the possession of Sir Edward Hayward, was destroyed by fire.)

150 WILLIAM DOBELL, *Woman in Café*, plywood, 9 x 9, 1933, Lady Murdoch

and the decorative charm of its terraces, street lamps and red chimney pots, owes much to impressionism. Likewise, many of his little genre scenes, such as *Woman Watching a Funeral* (1938, R. M. Crookston), and *Film Crowd Workers* (1937, C. Gheysens), are no more than incidents, closely observed and recorded without comment. Their handling is not dashing and assertive like Sickert's, but exploratory; and the subjects are observed off-guard; drawn into themselves by thought or mood. It is a kind of passive, introverted impressionism. The passive observation of life, however, did not wholly suit either the personality of the artist or his time. In life, Dobell has remained a modest and somewhat diffident person to all but his circle of close friends; a quiet man who can, none the less, hit back at the slightest hint of pretence or humbug with a cutting remark: and London in the midst of the economic depression of the 1930's was a different place from the London of Sir John Longstaff's day. Not surprisingly, therefore, Dobell's little slices of life began to acquire sharp edges; and he has left us a superb portrait gallery of London characters of the time. He began to paint women looking out of windows, maids and tired waitresses, film extras, charladies, costermongers at work and play, with a sense of kinship and affection; though there has never at any time been the slightest trace of sentiment in his nonchalant observations. On other occasions, however, his vision could be acidulous. The figure in the sketch for the *Duchess Disrobes* (1936, Sir E. W. Hayward) is like a great fat bird; a strange comment upon vanity. *Mrs South Kensington* (151) may be taken as an example of his satirical technique. It is a small, rapidly-painted impression in light pigment on a dark ground; the swirl of the brushwork portraying the pallid lips and flesh and narrow eyes has a venomous, ironic vigour. But he is rarely so savage. In *A Lady Waits* (152) there is little bitterness but a huge sense of the absurd. Indeed, Dobell's satire is but one aspect of his direct grasp upon life. Other paintings, such as his splendid interpretations of costermonger picnics, recall the robustness and jollity of Rowlandson.

The satirical paintings of 1937 are social comments, public utterances. Memorable though they are, it is not in those that we encounter Dobell at his best, but in another group of paintings which includes *The Sleeping Greek* (1936, Sydney), *The Charlady* (1936, R. Pennicuick) and *The Irish Youth*, in which his native insight and sensitivity combine with the penetrating observation of the satires. Some indication of the development of Dobell's style may be obtained by comparing *The Sleeping Greek* with his early portrait *Consuelita* (1933, Sir E. W. Hayward). The firm contours of *Consuelita* are, in *The Sleeping Greek*, broken and softened by delicate modelling and hatched brushwork. The head is placed diagonally not vertically, as in *Consuelita*, and has become more a part of the pictorial composition and less an independent image.

151 WILLIAM DOBELL, *Mrs South Kensington*, wood panel, 15⅛ x 13⅛, 1937, Sydney

The colour, too, has become warmer, and the light, smooth surfaces of the early picture have given way before deeper tones and modulated colours; the handling is freer, and the textures more painterly. *Consuelita* possesses an objective, impassive composure, *The Sleeping Greek* a subjective, palpable, moody composure. What is revealed is not only an increasing mastery of technique but a deepening interest in people. In his *Charlady*, for example, a study in scraping technique emerges as a portrait rich in characterization and understanding. Its technical virtuosity is masterly; and that is not all. The painter has been able to approach his subject as an equal: no latent sense of superiority reveals itself, no air of patronage has come between artist and subject to cloud with sentiment the perceptive clarity and technical brilliance of the image. In such paintings the passive sensitivity of his early work is united with greater technical command and deepening powers of observation. *The Irish Youth* (153) is another masterly portrait of an anonymous individual encountered one day among the unemployed upon the Thames Embankment. There is a Hogarthian vitality in the painting of the emaciated head and the dull, questioning eyes. In these portraits Dobell reached a peak of perfection which, in characterization and vitality at least, he has not surpassed.

   In or about 1937 Dobell painted *The Red Lady* (Sir Colin Anderson). It was inspired by his growing admiration for the portraits of Soutine and is a landmark in his development. By contrast with the realistic immediacy of the portraits preceding it, *The Red Lady* is a return to organized composition. But the consciously controlled lines and volumes are not, as in *Consuelita*, used to attain impersonality and objective form but to achieve expressive power. The painting also reveals a new freedom in colour released by his interest in expressionism.

When Dobell returned to Sydney in 1939 both Sydney Ure Smith, the President of the Society of Artists, and Julian Ashton, his former teacher, then aged eighty-eight, praised his work enthusiastically. Its high quality was realized immediately by many artists and he acquired a small circle of discriminating patrons who began to buy his work and, in some cases, commission portraits. He was appointed to the staff of the East Sydney Technical College, was commissioned to design a mural for the Australian Pavilion at the Wellington Exhibition, became an exhibitor in the Society of Artists from 1939 and sent work to early exhibitions of the Contemporary Art Society.

After his return to Australia the satirical edge and swift brevity of statement that had characterized his London work of the later 'thirties declined. Dobell began to pay great attention to technique, widening and deepening the range of his tones, heightening the intensity of his colours, and experimenting with glazes; so that his paintings often achieved a jewel-like surface

152 WILLIAM DOBELL, *A Lady Waits*, board, 7⅛ x 9⅛, 1937, Melbourne

and miniaturesque finesse of touch. A newly-found elegance began to appear in his first portrait commissions. In the portrait of *Jacqueline Crookston* (154), for example, the intimacy and curvilinear grace of the rococo appears: the interplay of line between girl, chair and dog is as delightful as any in his work; and the pale greens, reds, and soft yellows surrounding the figure herald his experiments with colour. Nevertheless, there is in this painting an element of tension and a noticeable attenuation of form present also in his conversation piece, *Mrs Blaxland and Toni* (1941, G. Blaxland). These incipient mannerist traits are much more prominent in his Bronzino-like *The Cypriot* (155) and *The Strapper*

153 WILLIAM DOBELL, *The Irish Youth*, canvas, 21½ x 17, 1938,
Miss Mitty Lee Brown

154   WILLIAM DOBELL, *Jacqueline Crookston*, canvas,
13 x 10¼, 1940, Miss J. Crookston

(156), two of his greatest portraits. In *The Cypriot* Dobell created a most
effective counterbalance between form and content; between, that is, firm,
almost geometric organization of the volumes, and the alert air and uneasy
pose of the sitter. By contrast *The Strapper* is relaxed; but it, too, is given
monumental expression by the reduction of volumes to large simple units
and the skilled modelling of the surfaces. In these two paintings, as in so
many of his finest portraits, the figure is virtually anonymous and casually
dressed, the pose informal.

Despite Dobell's mannerist phase of the early 'forties, the influence of the
eighteenth century remained. It is present in his highly rococo *Carnival*
(1940, Teachers' College, Armidale), wherein he sought, not entirely with
success, to convey the atmosphere and colour of a Sydney surf carnival and

so faced once again the problem so well known to the Heidelberg painters, of rendering a great deal of detail in a high tonal key. It is present in his elegant *Portrait of a Boy* (1943, G. Blaxland), and in the Gainsborough-like *Elaine Haxton* (1941, Lady Lloyd Jones). It is also present in the rhythm and gusto of his *Tattooed Lady* (1941, Crookston), wherein he re-creates the brilliance, cheap sensuality and slightly ludicrous vulgarity of a side-show. In this last painting he achieved, by means of glazes and a *pointilliste* technique, a gem-like lustre of colour. The painting of tattooed flesh was a virtuoso feat which he demonstrated in a masterly fashion later in his *The Billy Boy* (141), one of the greatest of his war-time paintings.

In 1943 Dobell was commissioned by the Allied Works Council to paint pictures of the Council's war-time activities and was attached to the Civil Construction Corps for the purpose. What might be called the Australian bent of his genius now began to reveal itself fully. There had always been something characteristically Australian in his portraiture from the beginning; a direct, quizzical and somewhat deprecating approach to his subjects irrespective of rank and prestige, and during the war it grew in strength and power. The series of paintings which includes *The Billy Boy, Brian Penton, Concrete Construction Worker* (War Memorial, Canberra) and *Professor L. F. Giblin* (University of Melbourne) constitutes a gallery of recognizable Australian types unequalled in the history of the nation's art, and for painterly quality and brilliance of characterization unparalleled in twentieth-century portraiture. In these paintings a complete mastery of the traditional techniques of draughtsmanship and painting are united with a personal gift for characterization equally responsive to the vanity, ugliness, charm, stupidity, sensuality, beauty, obesity, vitality or arrogance of his sitters. On the whole it is a tough and unpleasant vision of humanity that he presents, but one, for all its implicit pessimism, never far short of the truth. It is not often in his work that any inner grace or spiritual beauty shines through the fatty imprisonment of the flesh. And though he renders the substance of flesh in his mature work with superb skill he does not paint it, as Titian and Renoir did, with deep sensual pleasure, but as if he were painting the skin of a grub not long out of the earth. If such a view of the surface of life is distressing to those who cherish a sentimental view of human nature it does perhaps explain the objectivity and clarity of a vision which makes it possible for Dobell to paint the arrogance of a statesman as naturally as he would paint the arrogance of a builder's labourer. In his ability to ignore the idealization so often associated with the portrayal of important personages Dobell reveals what is perhaps one of the better sides of the Australian character. By means of such insights he has been able to raise the art of portraiture in this country—during a century that has tended to ignore it—to the dignity of a great art. Australia, as we have seen, produced good portrait painters in Roberts and Lambert before Dobell, but they followed British practice and British habits of mind. Dobell has brought to his portraiture attitudes of mind that are his own. In achieving this he has not gone out in search of national character or local colour. Indeed, in seeking to depict men and women as they really are he is in no way unique, but the quality of his vision is Australian; as Rembrandt's is Dutch, Goya's Spanish, and Hogarth's English. In being Australian he is being himself. Thus he has done for Australian art what Hogarth did long ago for the art of England; he has shown that it is possible to attain a mastery of his craft and pursue it—despite the constrictions, intimidations and servility of a provincial society—without abasing himself before the false prophets of culture.

In January 1944 Dobell was awarded the Archibald Prize for the preceding year by the Trustees of the (National) Art Gallery of New South Wales for his *Portrait of an Artist* (149). This was a portrait of Joshua Smith, the friend and fellow-artist with whom he had shared a tent while serving in the Civil Construction Corps. Smith was a thin, bony man with prominent features and Dobell produced a portrait which, though not unsympathetic, adopted a manneristic attenuation of form and an expressionistic intensity of colour more vigorous and thoroughgoing than anything he had attempted previously. There was an expression partly of wonder and partly of self-pity upon the face but the figure sat erect with a natural if uneasy dignity. It was as if one of Drysdale's Albury stick-figures had suddenly blossomed in a burning bush and glowed with spiritual fire; and it was one of his finest paintings.

The award, however, aroused intense opposition and joined the battle between the ancients and moderns in New South Wales just as the foundation of the Academy had done in Victoria some years before. Two members of the Royal Art Society who had entered for the prize, Mary Edwards, a painter of picturesque South Sea Island exotica, and Joseph Wolinski, a conventional portrait painter, moved the Supreme Court of New South Wales to set aside the award on the ground that the painting was not a portrait as required under the terms of the Archibald award. This claim was worded as follows:

It is alleged that the picture is not a portrait but is a caricature of Joshua Smith, bearing a certain degree of resemblance to him, but having features distorted and exaggerated. Joshua Smith is a man of normal human aspect and proportion, and is not misshapen or deformed, but the picture is a representation of a person whose body, limbs, and features are grotesquely at variance with normal human aspect and proportions. It is apparent that the picture does not represent any attempt on the part of Dobell to make a likeness of Smith, but on the contrary, represents the result of an endeavour to depict him in a distorted and caricatured form.

155 WILLIAM DOBELL, *The Cypriot*, canvas, 48 x 48,
1940, Brisbane

The case was heard between 23 and 26 October 1944 in the Supreme Court
of New South Wales in Equity before Mr Justice Roper, Mr Garfield Barwick
appearing for the plaintiffs, Mr Kitto for the Trustees of the Art Gallery of
New South Wales and Mr Dwyer for William Dobell.

Mr J. S. MacDonald, the first witness for the plaintiffs, and formerly the
Director of the National Art Gallery of New South Wales (1928-36) and the
National Gallery of Victoria (1936-41), claimed that portraiture was a well-
defined category, as distinctive to art as a sonnet to literature. A portrait,
he said, should be a balanced likeness, objective in featural details and
proportions, though a certain amount of subjectivity was permissible. He
held little respect for the portraiture of recent times and asserted that the
last good English portrait painter was Sir Thomas Lawrence (1769-1830).
Questioned by his counsel, MacDonald asserted that the painting of Joshua
Smith was not a portrait but a 'pictorial defamation of character'. It was a
fantasy, a satirical caricature. When pressed in cross-examination, however,
MacDonald could provide no generally accepted definition of a portrait,
asserted that painters were not in the habit of 'reducing to formulae the

meanings of their art', and finally agreed that the question whether a picture was a portrait or not was a matter of the individual opinion of those considering it.

John Young, the second witness for the plaintiffs, a man who had done much in earlier life to champion the work of the first post-impressionists in Sydney, said that the portrait painter worked under specific limitations; a portrait was a compact between artist and sitter, and they created a work of art shared equally between them. He proceeded to describe Dobell's painting as a biological absurdity with sub-human proportions. The witness who followed Young, Dr Vivian Benjafield, was much more specific. 'I would say,' he testified, 'that it represents the body of a man who had died in that position and had remained in that position for a period of some months and dried up.'

When Paul Haefliger (for Dobell and the Trustees), the art critic of the *Sydney Morning Herald*, was called to the box, he pointed out that old and modern masters alike have painted their portraits within distinguishable types arising from their personal styles. There was, for instance, a Leonardo type and a Picasso type of portrait. Portraits were also painted, he added, within the idiom of the school to which the artist belonged. Dobell was an expressionist; so, too, were Goya and Rembrandt. *The Red Vest*, today acknowledged as one of Cézanne's greatest paintings, contained more distortion than Dobell's *Joshua Smith*. Yet it can only be described as a portrait. Portraiture, Haefliger concluded, was a branch of art, and changes that take place in art also take place in portraiture. This was all very much to the point and Douglas Dundas, the head teacher of painting at the Sydney Technical College got even closer to the heart of the matter under dispute. He began by saying that in his view there were, generally speaking, two basic methods of portrait painting. The first method was to pose the sitter, set up the canvas and proceed to make a visual record of the shapes of light, shade and colour presented by the sitter to the artist's eye. This method, he said, was derived in large measure from Velasquez and Raeburn. It had had a great vogue in Australia, especially in Melbourne. The second method was through drawing in the constructive and not in the imitative sense, when the artist might work from drawings or from the sitter direct. And he continued:

The early Flemish artists did not work nearly so much by light and shade as the artists of the seventeenth century. The development towards visual facts, as revealed by light and shade, was a steady one from the time of Giotto onwards. Roughly the first one hundred or one hundred and fifty years of Italian painting after the beginning of the Renaissance was marked by paintings which relied less upon the extent of light and shade than upon the artist's conception of the form of his subject. Anyway there is a purer understanding of form in those works than there is in the later works where artists became enamoured of the

156 WILLIAM DOBELL, *The Strapper*, canvas,
35 x 26, 1941, Newcastle City Art Gallery

effects of light and shade, of the drama of light and shade as it fell upon their subject-matter.

The portrait painter has to bring about a co-ordination between many different elements. He has the sitter. He has, first of all, a blank canvas, and from those two elements, by his own skill, he has eventually to produce a work of art which will be known as a portrait. I would say that he has to consider the likeness of his sitter. By likeness I don't mean only a likeness to the features of the head of the sitter, but to his general physical bearing as well. If he feels that he wishes to stress certain characteristics, he will do so, but first of all he has to have all the problems of creating on this blank canvas an image—an image which will be satisfactory as a portrait and as a work of art, and to create that image he has to consider the physical fact of the sitter and the material facts of the canvas, paint and brushes, and the intellectual fact or factors of the

157   LLOYD REES, *Omega Pastoral*, canvas, 31¼ x 42⅝, 1950, Melbourne

design, by drawing or characterization, by tonal values of recession and of envelopment of the sitter, his position in space with air surrounding him. He has to consider the illumination of the picture and he has to consider the colour. Now all these various elements are very difficult to combine satisfactorily in the work of art. A great many portraits I think are painted without taking a great deal of account of some at any rate of those elements. They may achieve a certain likeness or resemblance to the sitter, but they will be lacking in that profundity which comes to a work of art which is produced by a man who is capable of co-ordinating all those different elements in his picture. Just getting a likeness alone would not altogether constitute portraiture in my opinion.

Finally, Dobell himself was called to the box. *Joshua Smith*, he told his counsel, was a serious portrait painting. He had known Smith for four or five years, meeting him casually from time to time.

I did not then really know him. I respected him and I still respect him, but I always regarded him as a rather diffident type of person and one who naturally seems to call for people's sympathy, but when I worked with him as a camou-flage labourer, I had to share the same camp with him for almost twelve months, and I got to know his real character. I found that there was a determination that amounted to stubbornness. . . .

Mr Dundas spoke of two methods of portrait painting. One was the light and shade method; the other was the construction method. Mr Barwick seemed to give the impression that the second method was the ethereal one which needed no basic construction. You will find that it is the only one of the two that has a basic construction, because you have to know the figure and you have to draw the figure, no matter what the position is that the light is putting. At the Slade School we began drawing in the morning a figure of a person with the light on one side and to prevent us getting cheap imitation by light, another light was switched on, on the other side of the room later on, and off on the earlier part. This prevented us getting cheap light and shade effects as a camera does. We had to know the figure thoroughly. The first method is light and shade and you don't really have to know your figure. You copy the light and shade that is in front of you. If the light moves, that is just your hard luck.

. . . I selected a colour scheme for my picture. I just wanted to show a man in a warm night light setting—so I built up as a sculptor builds up any form, and I glazed my colours on to it, to obtain that. Had I used a dark colour, or a blue suit or dark brown suit for instance to put over the sculptural building up of the figure, it would have destroyed my form and my design in the picture. It would have made just a single head in the centre of the picture and would have lost my effect of light. That is the reason for the light colour.

(Both MacDonald and Young had maintained that colour was, strictly speaking, irrelevant to portraiture.)

Q. What particular influences are manifested in your painting?

A. My particular love in the art, as you may put it, is Rembrandt. I studied his methods in Holland and in London. I have had a close acquaintance with them—not only, I mean, copying his brush strokes or his technique . . . but his aims.

Q. We have heard various expressions of opinion as to how you would judge your own work. Is it modern work or academic work in your opinion?

A. I would say classic tradition. I do not like the word academic as applied to a great artist like Rembrandt . . . I was not called a modernist until I came to Australia. In London I was regarded amongst artists and art students as academic.

The hearing had obtained the widest publicity and made an artistic question a popularly debated issue throughout the country. A week later Mr Justice Roper announced a judgment which, because of its importance in the history of Australian art, needs to be quoted at some length.

After setting forth the nature of the suit, the terms of the will and the responsibilities of the Trustees of the National Gallery of New South Wales in regard to it, the judgment proceeded:

In this suit the award has been canvassed not upon the ground that the picture in respect of which it was made was not the best portrait but upon the ground that it was not a portrait at all. In my opinion, however, the question whether any competing picture is a portrait is as much a matter upon which the judgement of the Trustees is invoked as is that of whether it is the best portrait . . . the answer to that question depends on the formation of opinions by the observer to whom it is propounded. I think that the testator in this case has submitted that question to the Trustees of the Art Gallery for decision just as he has required them to decide which among competing entries is the best portrait. . . . In these circumstances I think that before this Court should interfere in the administration of the trust it must be satisfied that as a matter of objective fact and not mere opinion the picture is not a portrait, so that the opinion formed by the Trustees to the contrary is founded upon a wrong basis of fact and is not truly an opinion upon the question to which the minds of the Trustees should have been directed.

If this is the proper test, as I think it is, it is not necessary to interpret the word 'portrait' in order to come to the conclusion that the suit fails, because the evidence is overwhelming, in my opinion, that at least there is a proper basis for forming an intelligent opinion that the picture in question is a portrait. . . .

. . . The word is used in a will which was made in 1916 and came into operation in 1919. In my opinion on the evidence there has been no change in its meaning up to the present time. Having heard the evidence of eight persons all highly qualified to express an opinion on the meaning of the word as it is understood by artists, I am satisfied that it has not among artists a technical meaning different from its meaning as an ordinary English word in current use among laymen. Even if it had been found that it had such a technical meaning, it has not been shown that the testator was a member of the class which uses the word in the technical sense. The word is an ordinary word of the English language and its meaning has to be ascertained accordingly. . . . With the assistance of dictionaries and the many works to which I have been referred by Counsel in this case, I think that the word 'portrait' as used in this will, incorporating in its meaning the limitations imposed by its context, means a pictorial representation of a person, painted by an artist. This definition connotes that some degree of likeness is essential and for the purpose of achieving it the inclusion of the face of the subject is desirable and perhaps essential.

The picture in question is characterized by some startling exaggerations and distortion clearly intended by the artist, his technique being too brilliant to admit of any other conclusion. It bears, nevertheless, a strong degree of likeness to the subject and is, I think, undoubtedly a pictorial representation of him. I find as a fact that it is a portrait, within the meaning of the word in this will and consequently the Trustees did not err in admitting it to the competition. . . .

Finally, I think that it is necessary to state my opinion on the claim that the picture cannot be included as a portrait because it is proper to classify it in another realm of art or work—as caricature according to the information or as fantasy according to a witness for the informant. It is, I think, unnecessary to consider whether the picture could be properly classed as a caricature or a fantasy. If it could be so classed that would only establish to my mind that the fields are not mutually exclusive because in my opinion it is in any event properly classed as a portrait. In the result I think this suit must be dismissed.[12]

Portrait or caricature: the fields were not mutually exclusive. Towards the end of his judgment Mr Justice Roper veered close, surely, to the heart of the matter, but did not state it: the portrait was a caricature and the caricature a portrait. For if the word 'caricature' has any meaning at all in normal English usage Dobell's painting of Joshua Smith was most certainly a caricature, but a caricature which was also a portrait of the highest artistic quality. But having regard for the state of artistic taste in Australia in 1944 and the specific circumstances of the case it is to be appreciated

that the judgment contained no such assertion while pointing to its possibility. To say that the painting was both caricature and portrait would
have been taken as equivocation, and satisfied the single-minded partisans
of neither side. As it stood the judgment succeeded in giving a legal sanction
to those who wanted the limitations of portraiture as an art form to be
interpreted with sufficient tolerance to enable an artist to work within it
according to the requirements of his personal style and the nature of his
genius. Consequently the judgment was rightly heralded as a significant
victory for the modern movement in Australia, regardless of whether Dobell
was a classic, academic or modern painter. As a result, expressionist painting acquired some status at law and the angry voices of the old prophets
for whom portraiture would always mean tonal matching in the manner
of Velasquez and Raeburn, Hall and Meldrum, were heard less in the land.
Indeed, the modern movement in Australia was well on the way towards
creating its own prophets and its own establishment.

Apart from Dobell, Australia produced during the 1940's one other portrait painter of note in the Tasmanian, Jack Carington Smith, who developed
a personal style of refined distinction from a grey, tonal, neo-Whistlerian
manner. Carington Smith studied first at East Sydney, and later at the
Royal Academy Schools, returning to Australia, like so many others, in 1939.
In his portraits painterly values and formal construction have always been
given pride of place.

The work of Dobell, Drysdale, Friend and Herman gave a special quality
to the art of war-time Sydney. Crowded with American servicemen, a
major base in the Pacific campaign, the life of the city was quickened by
the international urgency of events. Life was absurd: but it was also
exuberant and worth living. If the temper of the art was often deprecatory
and sardonic, that was but an aspect of its vigour and grasp upon life; and
it was not narrow in its sympathies. Its quality is also to be found both in
the elegant and yet uproarious, piquant and dexterous art of Cedric Flower
(b. 1920), and in the fine, decorative and colourful work of Elaine Haxton.

Neo-Romanticism in Sydney

The war years brought to Sydney not only a deeper interest in the
portrayal of contemporary life; it also brought a renewed interest in the
masterpieces of the past. This interest fed the stream of neo-romantic art
that flowed so freely through the decade. It must be stressed that the ways
in which Australian artists have received and assimilated the European
tradition have never been closely examined. Certainly, Australian art has
repeated in many ways the experience of other nations. But transmission,
like invention, is a personal and selective process carried on largely by
artists and teachers. The response to an old master, for example, however

158   JEAN BELLETTE, *Electra*, paper on hardboard,
23½ x 29¾, 1944, Sydney

universally fashionable at any given time, will differ in impact and diffusion
from one country to another. What an artist or a nation borrows is as much
a part of personal or national character as what it creates or rejects.

Some aspects of the process we have examined: the influence of Velasquez
and Raeburn in Melbourne, diffused by Hall and Meldrum; the influence of
the Rococo, more literary and less influential, diffused by Norman Lindsay;
the influence of Rembrandt and Goya upon Dobell—to name only three.
During the war years many artists in Sydney found help and inspiration in
the primitive and formative phases of Western art in both its Christian and
classical manifestations. Archaic Greek art and the *quattrocento*, Byzantine
and Medieval art excited them as they sought to endow their own work
with the new authority of the primitive and monumental that had replaced
the older authority of the academic and naturalistic. This return to tradition,
despite the considerable use it made of classical forms, was at heart
romantic. Early evidence of the new interests is to be found in a number
of short appreciative articles written by Jean Bellette and Paul Haefliger
during 1941 and 1942 for *Art in Australia*. Miss Bellette wrote on the
fifteenth-century Suabian wood-carvings purchased by the Felton Bequest
in 1941, on Masaccio, Piero della Francesca, and Maillol, Haefliger upon
Giotto and Titian. Both artists brought a warm, sensuously romantic approach reminiscent of Elie Faure, to their material. These articles served to

159   SIDNEY NOLAN, *Kyata*, synthetic enamel on hardboard, 24 x 36, *c.* 1943, Mr John Sinclair

160   SIDNEY NOLAN, *The Trial of Ned Kelly*, synthetic enamel on hardboard, 36 x 48, 1946-7, Museum of Modern Art of Australia, Melbourne

introduce the role both artists, man and wife, were to play in painting and criticism in Sydney during the 1940's and early 1950's.

In the art of Jean Bellette, as Dr Hoff has put it, classic form is instilled 'with a decidedly poetic and romantic feeling'.[13] The classical problem of composing figures in a landscape occupied her attention for many years, and she sought to banish the particular from her vision as firmly as any neo-classical painter of the eighteenth century, but its depth and gravity is romantic. The atmosphere of impending tragedy that broods over her paintings does not depend upon literary allusions which she expressly avoids, but upon the way she conceives and relates her figures to their ominous settings (158). Monumental, generalized in the classical manner, they are held together only by formal order and assert their existence by the loneliness that clings to them like the faded aureole of a god and gives them their pathetic dignity. 'I have tried', she has written concerning her work, 'to paint groups of figures in landscape, using mythology as a pretext; my main preoccupation was to try to order space and colours in a certain way, so that they would suggest to me some atmosphere I recognized, possibly a place I had seen. . . .'[14] In some respects her work recalls that of Henry Moore in the way she achieves emotional tension by using massive, classical forms to express the isolatedness of the individual. Her work, too, may be usefully contrasted and compared with that of Drysdale. Both artists make use of monumental figures and austere landscapes; both use a restricted palette and deep tones. But Drysdale's landscapes are constructed from his experience of the actual. They seek the universal by elevating the particular. Jean Bellette's landscapes are universal from the beginning, constructed out of the classical landscapes of art itself, elemental settings for timeless dramas of the heart. Certainly, stray wisps of her own memories have floated into them and she has made them her own, but the personal character of things can no longer be seen in the melancholy twilight that, *sub specie aeternitatis*, blurs and softens her human monuments.

The neo-romantic trend of the early post-war years is also to be seen at its height in the splendidly controlled but sombre pastels and paintings of Desiderius Orban. The element of mystery in his work never forced or sentimental, is the gift of a style precisely tuned to a temperament (161). The paintings—usually small and jewel-like in colour—of David Strachan (*b.* 1919), who studied first with Bell and later in Paris, were touched at times with a *naïveté* in homage, one felt, to early Italian masters like Piero di Cosimo. They are most typical of the time (162). So too, is the draughtsmanship of Francis Lymburner: broad, fluent and romantic, encompassing all things within lyrical arabesques, dark and swift-running (163). In the work of such artists temperament and style came wonderfully together.[15]

Although Lloyd Rees (*b.* 1895) belongs to an earlier generation and has not been subjected to quite the same influence, in art or thought, as the circle of painters around Jean Bellette and Paul Haefliger, his paintings are nevertheless wholly characteristic of the neo-romantic taste. His art matured slowly. It began with impressionist pen drawings reminiscent of Hilder and developed into a style almost obsessive in its close analysis of geological structure and surface vegetation. On these foundations Rees erected a handsome, conservative style with a restricted palette, broad and dark, of

161 DESIDERIUS ORBAN, *Rueil, France*, canvas, 19¾ x 25⅝, 1925, Sydney

brown, grey and green tonal masses (157). His compositions are always well built despite an interest in the portrayal of detail that has never left him, and his textures preserve the crisp precision of the Lambertian generation of the 1920's but his dark, evocative tonalism is the hall-mark of his romanticism.

In 1945 the neo-romantics formed 'The Sydney Group': Jean Bellette, Paul Haefliger, David Strachan, Francis Lymburner, Eric Wilson, Wallace Thornton, Wolfgang Cardamatis, Justin O'Brien, Geoffrey Graham and the sculptor, G. F. Lewers, exhibiting in the inaugural exhibition. In the years that followed the group was expanded to include other artists with established reputations, such as Drysdale, Nolan, Arthur Boyd, Friend, Passmore, Kmit and Gleeson; so that realistic comment, expressionism and abstract paintings came to figure in annual exhibitions predominantly neo-romantic in flavour. Despite the neo-romantic predispositions of its founders, the Sydney Group was concerned not so much with a point of view as with quality; and it succeeded in establishing itself, with the assistance of the criticisms of Haefliger, as a prestige group at the expense of the older Society of Artists from which it drew several of its most prominent members. The later exhibitions of the Society revealed the Byzantinesque vogue of the late 1940's and early 1950's quite strongly together with the growing strength of abstract and non-figurative art.

162 DAVID STRACHAN, *Young Girl on a Terrace*, canvas, 16 x 24, 1946, the artist

Q

163   FRANCIS LYMBURNER, *Near Circular Quay*, pen and wash, 11⅛ x 7⅜, c. 1945, from *Fifty Drawings of Francis Lymburner*, 1946

The work of those artists who resided between 1945 and 1947 at 'Merioola' also testifies to the neo-romanticism of this time. Although linked more by friendship, propinquity and shared interests than by a common attitude, the art of the 'Merioola' group was, in general, neo-romantic, decorative and merrily eclectic. Persia, Byzantium, the Pacific, the colonial picturesque, costume, theatre and the ballet alike contributed to the 'Merioola' merry-go-round of pattern and whimsical comment. Loudon Sainthill worked for a time there; so too did Donald Friend, Justin O'Brien, Jocelyn Rickards, Edgar Ritchard, Peter Kaiser and the sculptor, Arthur Fleischmann. One group exhibition only was shown, that held at the Macquarie Galleries in 1947, prior to the departure of most of the members overseas.

Melbourne's Angry Penguins

Following the break with the social realists, a new group of painters associated with John Reed and Max Harris and their journal, *Angry Penguins*, came into prominence in the exhibitions of the Contempory Art Society. It included Sidney Nolan, Albert Tucker, Arthur Boyd and John Perceval. Although each artist developed a distinctive personal style they shared some attitudes and beliefs that distinguished them from any other group of artists in the country at the time.

In the first place they rejected all forms of academic training, irrespective of whether they were based upon the tonal naturalism taught at the Gallery School, or upon the post-impressionism favoured by Bell and Bell's pupils, Alan Sumner and Alan Warren, for example, or upon professional training in the abstract form of the post-cubist tradition. In this they differed from the leading contemporary painters of Sydney. Drysdale, Dobell, Herman, Friend, Bellette, Haefliger and Rees had all received professional training of some kind and maintained strong links with the art of the past, and most of them were drawn into the orbit of the Society of Artists which stood for a continuous tradition of professional practice in Australia going back to the days of Roberts and Ashton. In their break with tradition the Angry

Penguins group had more in common with the Sydney abstract and semi-abstract painters, but were not prepared like them to submit their art to intellectual principles of formal construction.

In the place of tradition the Angry Penguins painters laid the greatest emphasis upon vitality in art. All forms of training, they felt, were professionally inhibiting. Writing in 1944, Sidney Nolan remarked that 'A painting is generally the result of an underground disturbance; when the disturbance is an almost biblical moving of the bowels one can only trace the convolutions by oblique means. And in the end as with most things, one backs a hunch.'[16] This approach owed much, of course, to the cardinal importance given to 'pure psychic automatism' by the surrealists. Of importance, too, was the significance the group gave to the work of primitive and untutored painters. In December 1944 *Angry Penguins* published seven paintings by an unknown Australian primitive, 'H.D.' In his article on the work, Tucker stressed the advantage of the natural painter over those professionally trained. 'With the natural artist problems of style and technique matter little, the sustained intensity of his vision solves them for him.'[17] Closely associated with these views was the belief that spontaneity and creative activity should be given pride of place in the educational process itself. In the same issue of *Angry Penguins* Janet and Clive Nield, educational reformers (quoting D. H. Lawrence extensively), stressed the overwhelming significance of giving aesthetic education first place in the primary school.

Other local contemporary groups had, of course, stressed the importance of spontaneity in artistic creation, but none with such emphasis as the Angry Penguins. In another respect, too, they stood somewhat apart from other Australian contemporary artists. From the time of its first glimmerings in Sydney in 1913 the Australian contemporary movement found itself opposed to a tradition that was naturalistic, conservative and above all, nationalistic. Not surprisingly, the movement developed strong anti-nationalistic sentiment from the beginning. By contrast, however, the war years developed national feeling and national sentiment considerably. In literature the *Jindyworobak* group, championing an extreme form of nationalism, gained considerable support during the war years. The word was aboriginal and meant 'to join', the leaders of the movement expressing the desire that Australian culture should draw extensively upon aboriginal culture for its inspiration. They sought to 'link Australian thought with its natural environment', and 'treat as alien everything that owes its being directly to origins in other cultures—English cultures, Irish cultures, Dutch or American'.[18] Australian artists, they declared, should follow the tradition established by Streeton and Heysen.

Although the Angry Penguins were strongly opposed to such a conservative and self-consciously nationalistic outlook they did believe that Aus-

164   ALBERT TUCKER, *Images of Modern Evil*, wood panel,
14 x 21, 1944, the artist

tralian art could achieve distinctive and characteristic features. 'We do ourselves believe,' wrote John Reed and Max Harris in an *Angry Penguins*
editorial (September 1943), 'that Australian art is developing at an aston-
ishing rate and that its growth will inevitably (if that growth is not artificially stimulated) mature into a form of expression which will be unique
and in the truest sense of the word indigenous.' And Albert Tucker, com-
menting upon exhibitions of the work of Sidney Nolan and Danila Vassilieff
in the same issue of the journal, expressed the opinion that in their work 'we
glimpse for the first time since Roberts, McCubbin and the early Streeton,
the return to an authentic national vision on a higher and more independent
level'.[19] Let us consider now the work of the principal members of the group.

Albert Tucker (*b.* 1914) was in many respects the intellectual leader of
the group. Possessed of great, almost ruthless, independence of mind and
considerable mental courage, Tucker succeeded in fashioning a distinctive
style, vital, edgy and tough, from his personal involvement in the art and
left-wing politics of Melbourne during the years around 1940. His earliest
work, painted between 1936 and 1939, consisted mainly of street scenes and
portraits in the post-impressionist manner of George Bell with whom he
studied for a very short period. The influence of de Chirico, surrealism and
T. S. Eliot's poetry appeared in such paintings as *The Philosopher* (1939)
and *The Futile City* (131). Then followed a period in which social realism
and German expressionism together made a strong impact: typical are his
Spring in Fitzroy (1941) and his fine little *Children of Athens* series (1942).

Tucker's social realism was, from the beginning, more individualistic and

165   JOHN PERCEVAL, *The Merry-go-round*, cheesecloth on cardboard,
24½ x 16, 1943, the artist

anarchic than the social realism of Counihan, Bergner and O'Connor,
deriving much of its aggressive vitality from German expressionists like
Beckmann. Indeed, Tucker was probably the first Australian artist to turn
to the German expressionists for inspiration, Australian expressionism deriving for the most part from French or French-inspired sources, such as
Van Gogh, Soutine, Chagall and Rouault. In 1943, following his ideological
break with social realism, Tucker began to paint a series of pictures entitled
Images of Modern Evil (164). This series marks the end of the formative
phase of his work and the emergence of a personal style. It made much use
of recurrent and obsessive symbols: inchoate protoplasmic forms, lip images,
electric light bulbs, city trams; pig-like and snarling monsters are juxtaposed
in night and nightmarish settings. Personal to the point of autobiography,
these paintings also record disgust and despair at the brutalization of the
person by the blind authority of the mass. The life of the modern city
becomes an allegory of evil: soulless, mechanical, stupid; peopled by crim-
inals, prostitutes, clowns and psychotics. (A group of expressionistic
portraits painted in 1946 was based upon the physiognomy of criminal

types.) Tucker returned at that period again and again to the theme of
loneliness, here anticipating, among Australian artists, Dickerson and others;
and during this period he also painted a number of distinguished expressionistic portraits of friends, notably Sidney Nolan and Arthur Boyd. In
1947 Tucker visited Japan for four months and, after returning to Melbourne, left for Europe later in the year. His work overseas is discussed in
the following chapter.

Sidney Nolan, the best-known artist of the group, was born in Melbourne
in 1917 into a family which, like Russell Drysdale's, had been settled in
Australia for several generations. But where Drysdale's forebears were Scottish and members of the pioneering pastoral aristocracy, Nolan's were Irish
and working-class. His grandfather was a policeman in the days of the Kelly
gang; his father a tram-driver for the Melbourne and Metropolitan Tram-
ways Board.

After completing his education at a Victorian State School, Nolan became
an enthusiastic racing cyclist and worked at various odd jobs, picking
asparagus, cooking hamburgers, mining gold and so forth. Then in 1938,
following upon some art school training and work in commercial art during
the mid-1930's, he turned to painting; becoming a member of a confraternity
of Bohemians and artists who inhabited a ramshackle, Chinese-owned, tenement house situated behind the Museum, State Library and National Gallery
of Victoria building in Swanston Street. In the circle which included Boyd,
Tucker, and Perceval, Nolan began to paint pictures, clear, bright and
primitively vivacious, with something of the gaiety and charm of Raoul
Dufy about them. Subjects were taken direct from life and personal experience: swimmers in the St Kilda baths, street scenes, Luna Park, large
studies of heads in a flattish, childlike manner.

It is false, however, to think of Nolan as an artist working outside of
tradition, a bush primitive. True, his work possessed from the beginning a
remarkable directness of statement, a superb sense of space, a bright freshness of feeling and an unusual capacity for creating a memorable image.
But it was not the product of an 'innocent' eye, and can only be understood
in the light of what he gained from the School of Paris, from literature, and
from the highly explosive local situation in which his art emerged. Such
paintings as *Woman and Tree* (1941) reveal what he gained from Picasso's
1932 series of nudes in flowing arabesque; and he himself acknowledged an
indebtedness to Henri Rousseau. Meanwhile he was reading widely: Rimbaud, the French symbolists, Blake. In a sense, too, Nolan's early paintings
were programmatic with much of dada about them, designed, in their
impertinent simplicity, to shock the art-loving public out of its wits. *Boy
and the Moon*, exhibited in the second exhibition of the Contemporary Art
Society (1940) consisted entirely of a great yellow blob against a deep raw

blue background. Attacks upon the exhibition in the Press singled out this painting both in Melbourne and Sydney to attack contemporary art in general, for it cocked a jaunty and colourful snook at conventional art. It irritated the local post-impressionists as much as it irritated the latter-day followers of Roberts and Streeton. Artists like Bell, Herman and Lawlor, who still sought for traditional craftsmanship and formal design, strongly opposed exhibiting the painting in the 1940 exhibition of the Society. But it was John Reed and the group of laymen and young artists committed to expressive vitality above all else who carried the day.

Nolan became a close friend of Reed and his wife, Sunday, and spent much time with them during the early 1940's. They bought the greater part of his paintings, helped him in many ways, and played a most significant role in Nolan's growth and development as an artist. In 1941 Serge Lifar, who had come to Australia with the De Basil Ballet, commissioned Nolan to design the sets and costumes for his ballet, *Icare*. Lifar had been impressed by a painting of Nolan's inspired by lines from Blake. Then in 1942 Nolan entered upon service in the Army and began to paint a series of landscapes while stationed at Dimboola, in the Wimmera District of Victoria (159). Nolan's Wimmera paintings did not make so decisive a break with the local *plein-air* tradition as Drysdale's Albury landscapes had done the year before. He still sought, as the Heidelberg painters had done long before to create a direct and vivid impression of the thing seen. His landscapes were, of course, more startling, rudimentary and immediate, but the colour and the approach to the subject remained essentially visual: a remarkable short-hand poetry of the eye; but something of the hand and vision of older men still lingered. Even in the landscapes of his Kelly paintings (1945-7) there are echoes of the Australian *plein-air* landscapists.

By 1944 Nolan's work was beginning to receive favourable critical attention beyond the Angry Penguins circle. The first critic of standing to react wholeheartedly to his work was Paul Haefliger. In December 1944, Haefliger commented upon Nolan's splendid feeling for spacing and happy colour combinations:

He is a gay adventurer, and lives, in his paintings, entirely upon his sensations. He can be very good and also the reverse. He plagiarizes when he follows too closely in the footsteps of Picasso. . . . But he is also, on occasion, most original and certain of his passages are of rare subtlety. He appears possessed by a light-heartedness which seems to deny real seriousness, but follows the way of his whimsical nature. It scarcely matters; his lyrical impulse, his natural talent, assure moments of realization which are as spontaneous a delight as anything in Australian art.[20]

After Nolan left the Army in 1945 he was associated for a time with the publishing firm of Reed and Harris, illustrated a number of books of poetry and fiction and led an active literary life. Then, about 1946, he read J. J. Kenneally's *The Inner History of the Kelly Gang* and a transcript of the Kelly trial. Encouraged by Sunday Reed, he decided to paint a series of pictures based upon the exploits of the gang (160). Following a hitch-hiking tour of the Kelly country in northern Victoria with Max Harris, he painted the whole series in rapid succession. There had been a good deal of talk about the role of myth in art among the Angry Penguins. As early as 1942 Tucker had discussed in a political context the connexion between myth and art in his article, *Art, Myth and Society*. Arthur Boyd was already developing a personal mythology out of his interest in Brueghel and Bosch; introducing rams, crocodiles and curious lusting dwarfs into his Australian landscapes. Having regard for their interest in 'an authentic national vision' expressed in contemporary idiom, it is not surprising that an attempt to depict a national myth should emerge within the group at this stage.

In turning to Kelly—criminal or no criminal—Nolan turned to a folk-hero still lively enough, as Max Harris has put it, in the minds of 'the St Kilda lads, *and* the countryman *and* the pub raconteur'.[21] Man and myth, Ned Kelly maintains too lively an existence in the Australian imagination to be honestly denied: and it is a measure of Nolan's genius that he should create a Kelly of just the right size, neither a grandiose hero figure nor a proletarian outsider filled with self-righteousness and self-pity, but a kind of absurd relative, an eccentric brother, a joking saint who appears at odd moments merely to assert his eternal, if subterranean, existence in the Australian mind.

The paintings, themselves, bright and colourful, with that light and dexterous lyrical grace so characteristic of Nolan are executed in a kind of sham folk-art style indebted, as the artist himself has said, to 'Rousseau and sunlight'. The wit is eager, the spacing delightful and the mock-heroic sentiment disarmingly charming. But the paintings are not, like Dobell's best portraits, outstanding achievements by any standard and have been praised, perhaps, beyond their true worth. They do, however, represent none the less a significant achievement. Nolan revealed in these works that it was possible to create a witty, decorative and sophisticated art by turning to local history for his sources of inspiration.

In 1947 Nolan spent a year roaming in Queensland and lived for a time on Fraser Island, where he painted out-back and tropical landscapes, and a series based on the story of Mrs Fraser, a Scottish woman, who was ship-wrecked on the Barrier Reef in 1836, and lived for a time among the abor-igines. Then in 1948 he married Cynthia Hansen, John Reed's sister, and settled in Sydney. During the next two years he concerned himself with paintings based on Australian history and legend: Ned Kelly, Mrs Fraser, paintings on glass of the Eureka Stockade and landscapes based on travels in Central Australia. His work during the 1950's is discussed in the following chapter.[22]

Arthur Boyd (*b.* 1920), the third member of the group, was born into a family long associated with the arts in Australia. His grandfather, Arthur Merric Boyd (1862-1940), was a landscape painter who was born in Dunedin, New Zealand, and came to Australia in 1886 where he married Emma a'Beckett, the granddaughter of Sir William a'Beckett (1806-69), the first Chief Justice of Victoria. After travelling in England and the Continent, A. M. Boyd and his wife settled in Brighton, Victoria, where they painted landscapes and seascapes. Both exhibited at the Royal Academy and their work was included in the 'Exhibition of Australian Art in London', held at the Grafton Galleries in 1898. One of their sons, Penleigh Boyd, became a talented landscape painter who worked in a lyrical and atmospheric manner comparable with the early paintings of Gruner. Following his return from Army service in France, he became one of the best-known landscape painters in the country. In 1923, as we have seen, he brought out to Australia an important collection of European paintings, but was killed in a motor accident the same year. A second son, Martin Boyd, remained in England after service with the R.F.C. and became a well-known novelist. A third, Merric Boyd, Arthur Boyd's father, also remained in England for a time after the war to study pottery and kiln construction in Staffordshire and established a pottery at Murrumbeena, Victoria, upon his return in 1919.[23]

At an early age Arthur Boyd gained instruction in the art of ceramics from his father and was taught to paint landscapes in the Heidelberg tradition by his grandfather, but he did not receive formal training in art or technical schools. The Boyd family was a devout one, and Mrs Boyd brought up her children in an atmosphere in which art and religion occupied pride of place. In this family the desire to be an artist was not regarded as an eccentricity but as the acceptance of a calling with rights and responsibilities. Behind the art of Arthur Boyd and his brother David (*b.* 1924), there lies a family tradition of art, craftsmanship and Christian humanism.

During the later 1930's Arthur Boyd came into contact with the modern movement from reproductions and books available at Gino Nibbi's Leonardo Book Shop. Rouault, Van Gogh, Gauguin and Christopher Wood left their impression. About 1938 he made a set of illustrations in the style of Rouault to *The Brothers Karamazov*. Dostoevsky's tragic view of life and his concern with the elemental passions helped to liberate corresponding qualities in Boyd's own imagination. In 1939 Boyd joined the Army Survey Corps where he met John Perceval who later married his sister, Mary. Albert Tucker brought Boyd and Perceval into touch with the Contemporary Art Society, the two painters exhibiting work in the C.A.S. 1942 Annual Exhibition and the Anti-Fascist Exhibition that followed a few months later. The influence of the social realist painters, Josl Bergner especially, exercised a deep influence upon both painters at that time.

In *Progression* (1941, Mus. Mod. Art, Melbourne), a characteristic feature of Arthur Boyd's work emerged for the first time: a tension between distorted and grotesque forms and the tenderness with which they are expressed. There is here already an identification of artist and theme, a humanism all pathos, that reaches beneath the levels of sentiment and political assertion. Following his social realist phase Boyd turned, about 1943-4, to paintings that embodied figures in landscapes. He continued to use a dark, restricted palette, but adopted freer and more expressive brushwork, breaking his canvases into textured expressive surfaces. These figured landscapes afford a parallel with those Albury landscapes painted by Drysdale in 1941. Boyd's work derived little if anything from Drysdale directly; but the publication of a large number of Drysdale's early landscapes in *Australian Present Day Art* in 1943 made his work, and a new orientation to Australian landscape, widely known throughout the country. Both Drysdale and Boyd moved from the light-toned, blue and gold palette and air of optimism traditional since the Heidelberg days towards a dark palette and pessimism. Surrealism and expressionism contributed to the emergence of both styles. But Drysdale's work clung to a more realistic path and was predisposed to the heroic and classical; Boyd's was more personal and allegoric. There is a turbulence and violence about his figured landscapes quite different from Drysdale's ordered composition. Boyd's scruffy bushland of grass trees and stunted eucalypt harks back to early colonial work, but the approach is new. The bush is a dark, primordial wood inhabited by those dwarfs and demons that once populated the medieval imagination, a St Anthony's wilderness full of strange devils. They sprout up from the earth, ride on monstrous animals, copulate, or crouch in loneliness, grief and despair. It is a vision of life heightened to a pitch of agonizing energy in which generations pass like generations of flies. It is curious how Boyd's work, like Drysdale's, testifies to the continuity of thought. In Drysdale the Australian landscape became once again what it was for Barron Field and several generations of pioneers, a 'barren wood', stark and intractable: Boyd's imagination recovered an old medieval vision of antipodes that had survived the rationalism of two centuries and the abstractions of a third. When, in 1793, Captain John Hunter, the second Governor of New South Wales, described in the language of the Enlightenment the novel forms of life he had met with in Australia, he anticipated curiously the surrealist monsters that confront us in Boyd's bush paintings and ceramic sculpture:

It would appear from the great similarity in some part or other of the different quadrupeds which we find here, that there is a promiscuous intercourse between

166   ARTHUR BOYD, *David and Saul*, canvas, 35 x 36¾,
c. 1946, Dr A. M. McBriar

the different sexes of all those different animals. The same observation might be made also on the fishes of the sea, on the fowls of the air, and I may add, the trees of the forest.[24]

In Boyd's paintings and ceramics this ancient vision of lusting antipodean monsters appears in a contemporary idiom.

In 1945 Arthur Boyd and John Perceval turned to a study of the masters of the past, especially to Bosch and Brueghel, in the desire to widen their artistic vocabulary and learn more about expression and composition. Mr Franz Philipp has pointed out how Brueghel's influence enabled Boyd to express the monstrous horrors of the war-time concentration camps with complete detachment.[25] For some years after 1945, religious themes occupied a prominent place in his work. In such paintings as *The Mockers* and *The Mourners* (1945-6), a religious subject-matter was given contemporary pertinence and universal significance. A little later Boyd turned to an intense and prolonged study of Rembrandt, a study that has since entered deeply into the mood and spiritual texture of his own work (166). The religious paintings culminated in a series of murals for his uncle, Martin Boyd, the novelist, painted in 1948 at 'The Grange', Harkaway.

While occupied with his religious paintings, he continued to paint his own highly individual interpretations of the Australian scene. Many were executed in an egg-tempera technique which provided him with rich, enamel-like colours and fine tonal transitions. Some years before Tucker had introduced Boyd to Max Doerner's *Materials of the Artists and Their Use in Painting* (1934), which stimulated his interest in painting techniques and led to his decision to grind and prepare his own pigments.

In 1944 Boyd, Perceval and Peter Herbst, a University friend, founded the Murrumbeena pottery; and, during the later 1940's and early 1950's, both artists turned to pottery and ceramic sculpture with highly rewarding results. Ceramics, long practised in the Boyd *ménage*, provided both artists, after their release from the Army, not only with some economic support for themselves and their families but a new medium which they mastered with skill and imagination. During the early 1950's Arthur Boyd produced some of his finest and most memorable works in ceramic sculpture.

John Perceval (*b.* 1923), the youngest member of the Angry Penguins circle, began to paint from prints of Van Gogh and other modern masters during an attack of poliomyelitis. Closely associated with Arthur Boyd from the beginning, both artists have developed in a partnership of interests and influences. But Perceval has always been an artist in his own right; never at any time a mere disciple of Boyd. His first paintings, exhibited in the 1942 Exhibition of the Contemporary Art Society and the Anti-Fascist Exhibition which followed, were large in scale, combining social realist themes with forceful expressive techniques.[26] At this time he was strongly influenced by Orozco and Rivera. His paintings occupied themselves, at the beginning, with the problem of the individual in society.

The early work consisted of broad, massively constructed tonal paintings, but in 1943 he turned to a more painterly technique using a wider range of colour and more expressive brushwork. In night scenes, spiritually akin to Tucker's work at this time, boys with cats, and jack-in-the-box paintings, the confrontation of innocence and evil were symbolically presented (165). Later Perceval worked with Arthur Boyd, painting in tempera and resin, when both artists were occupied with the problem of painting crowd scenes in landscapes and with the work of Bosch and Brueghel.

After the foundation of the Murrumbeena pottery, Perceval turned his attention increasingly to pottery and, for a time, ceased to paint. His most important achievements, both in ceramic sculpture and in painting belong to the 1950's and are discussed in the following chapter.

By 1947 the Angry Penguins had, as a group, virtually ceased to exist. The last *Angry Penguins Broadsheet* appeared in 1946 and, late in 1947, the Melbourne Section of the Contemporary Art Society collapsed. In 1947 Tucker left for Europe and Nolan spent a nomadic year in Queensland. Boyd and Perceval became increasingly involved in the development of the

Murrumbeena pottery. But though the group ceased to exist, the individuals continued to be as active as ever.

Australian society discovered contemporary art just when it had to face the challenge of war. The unusual degree of vitality which emerged is a clear indication of the vitality of the nation when forced to rely upon its own resources. By 1947, however, with the war over and the battle for the recognition of contemporary art won, there are indications of a slackening of the ebullient vitality of the war years. Peace, and the acceptance of the contemporary idiom in art, brought its own problems. After years of comparative isolation, most practising artists wanted to get away to Europe if only for a time, and a new generation of artists had not yet emerged. It was still, delayed by the war, in the art schools.

Peace, too, brought a marked change from the expressive extroversion of the war years. Art became, in the hands of the most creative, a more private matter, concerned far more with the individual than with society. Many were drawn to religion and became fascinated by medieval styles of one kind or another; others, like Nolan and Boyd—black swans upon alien waters—sought identification by turning to myths and legends which had already for many years provided Australian society with a sense of its own independence among the nations. But ten years of peace brought the triumph neither of religion nor of nationalism in the visual arts, but the victory of those informal kinds of abstraction which flowed for the most part from contemporary American experience and gave sanctity to nothing but the physical activity of painting itself.

FOOTNOTES

[1] *AA*, March-May 1941, p. 9

[2] On the Ern Malley hoax *see AE*, vii, 66; and *Ern Malley's Poems* (int. by M. Harris), Melbourne, 1961

[3] *Angry Penguins*, iv (1943), p. 53

[4] *AA*, iii, 76 (August 1939), p. 18

[5] On Purves Smith *see also Australian Present Day Art* (ed. S. Ure Smith), Sydney, 1943, pp. 109-12; 1960 Acquisitions, Art. Gall. of N.S.W., pp. 28-9; 1960-61 Acquisitions, Queensland Art Gallery

[6] 'In a Dry Season' in *The Prose Works of Henry Lawson*, Sydney, 1935, p. 61

[7] 'The Union Buries its Dead', op. cit., p. 59

[8] *See also Russell Drysdale, a Retrospective Exhibition of Paintings from 1937 to 1960*, Sydney, 1960, which contains detailed biographical notes and an extensive bibliography

[9] On Herman *see also* DANIEL THOMAS, *Sali Herman*, Melbourne, 1962; and B. SMITH, 'The Art of Sali Herman, *Meanjin*, vii (1948), 172-6

[10] On Friend *see also Australian Present Day Art* (1943), Sydney, 1943, p. 70; and *Present Day Art in Australia* (ed. S. Ure Smith), Sydney, 1945, p. 33

[11] *See* UTHER BARKER, 'The Boy at the Basin', *AA*, iii, 76 (August 1939), pp. 46-8

12 This summary is derived from a typescript of the evidence given in the Supreme Court in Equity, New South Wales, H.M. Attorney-General for the State of New South Wales v. The Trustees of the National Art Gallery of New South Wales and William Dobell, in the library of the Art Gallery of New South Wales; on Dobell *see also The Art of William Dobell* (ed. S. Ure Smith), Sydney, 1946; *CAO*, pp. 55-6

13 U. HOFF, 'The Art of Jean Bellette', *Meanjin*, xi (1952), 358-60

14 Quoted by DR HOFF, art. cit., p. 359

15 On Lymburner *see also Fifty Drawings by Francis Lymburner*, Sydney, 1946; D. CLARKE, 'The Art of Francis Lymburner', *Meanjin*, ix (1950), no. 2

16 *Angry Penguins*, Autumn 1944, p. 104

17 *Angry Penguins*, December 1944, p. 25

18 VICTOR KENNEDY, *Flaunted Banners*, Adelaide, 1941, p. 40

19 A. TUCKER, 'Two Melbourne Exhibitions of Paintings', *Angry Penguins*, September 1943

20 P. HAEFLIGER, 'The Contemporary Art Society Exhibition', *Angry Penguins*, December 1944, p. 94

21 'The Young Master', *Nation*, 2 July 1960, p. 12

22 On Nolan *see also Catalogue to the Exhibition of Paintings from 1947 to 1957*, Whitechapel Art Gallery, London, June 1957, and *Sidney Nolan*, London, 1961

23 *See* J. YULE, 'Merric Boyd', *Modern Art News* (Melbourne), i (1959), 15

24 J. HUNTER, *An Historical Journal of the Transactions at Port Jackson and Norfolk Island*, London, 1793, p. 68

25 F. PHILIPP, *Present Opinion*, ii, 11, 1947. I am also indebted here to U. HOFF, 'The Paintings of Arthur Boyd', *Meanjin*, xvii (1958), 143-7

26 On Perceval's early work *see* JOHN REED, 'Introduction to John Perceval', *Angry Penguins*, September 1943; and M. GARLICK, 'John Perceval', Hon. B.A. essay, School of Fine Arts, University of Melbourne, 1961

CHAPTER NINE

FIGURATIVE AND NON-FIGURATIVE
1950 - 60

It sets out to show the direction in which abstract art is heading in that country. . . . It is heading, as elsewhere, right away from the visual image to the point where all that is left is a gesture.

LAURIE THOMAS, reviewing the *British Abstract Painting* exhibition. The *Sun* (Sydney), 17 March 1959

We want to say, finally, that we are more directly concerned with our own art, more involved in it, than in anything else. This is not escapism. It is simply a recognition that the first loyalty of an artist is to his art. Today that loyalty requires, beyond all else, the defence of the image.

The Antipodean Manifesto, August 1959

AFTER the war Australian society entered a new phase. A series of good seasons, a comprehensive migration policy, rapid industrial growth and expanding overseas markets had created by 1950 a society still small in numbers but rich in material wealth. The first post-war decade (1945-55) was not, however, a period of great vitality in Australian painting. Although some of the leading painters of the contemporary movement, Drysdale, Nolan and Arthur Boyd, for example, were widening and deepening the range of their experience and maturing as artists, the initial impetus of the movement itself was spent. The Melbourne Branch of the Contemporary Art Society collapsed in 1947, its first revolutionary phase over; the Sydney Branch was sustained largely by a faithful circle of abstract painters and sculptors, but its influence was marginal. The more successful painters graduated to the Society of Artists and within the C.A.S. itself little was done to encourage discussion and controversy. There was a tendency to assume that the problems of contemporary art had been solved, that the society's business was now primarily to educate laymen. Emphasis upon lay education in the arts was widespread, and sundry bodies arose to perform the task. In rural areas the Council for the Encouragement of Music and the Arts, Adult Education, and travelling exhibitions organized by State galleries were active. In the cities, societies on the American model, designed to stimulate interest in the collections and activities of the State art galleries, were formed, first in Melbourne, then in most other capitals. Such activities widened public appreciation of the arts considerably, but

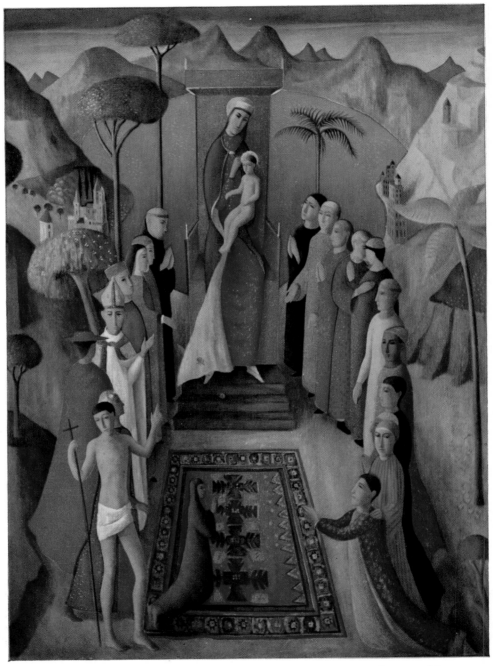

167   JUSTIN O'BRIEN, *The Virgin Enthroned* (central panel of a triptych),
canvas, 44½ x 32, 1951, Melbourne

appreciation was often thin and superficial. There was a dearth of discussion about fundamentals, little real clash of opinions. Serious art publication virtually ceased during the post-war decade. *Art in Australia*, a war casualty, had ceased publication as early as 1942, *Angry Penguins* and its *Broadsheet* in 1946. For two years (1947-9) the Victorian Artists' Society, with their *Australian Artist*, bravely attempted to provide a journal, under the editorship of R. Haughton James and others. Books fared no better. From the death of Sydney Ure Smith in 1949 until the appearance of Kym Bonython's *Modern Australian Painting and Sculpture* (1960), no books of any great consequence dealing with contemporary Australian painting appeared.

Art ceased to be treated in the Press as it had been treated prior to and during the war, as a controversial matter and was featured increasingly, especially in Sydney, as social news and gossip. Paintings were now very rarely reproduced for their own sake, but appeared vicariously behind the heads and hats seen at exhibition openings. Art was rarely considered to be a criticism of life or even of other art and was thought of as culture, an adjunct to 'gracious' living. In Sydney the National Gallery Society became well known for its buffet banquets and candlelight concerts in which the consumption of art was subordinated to the public consumption of food.

The standard of art criticism in the Press continued to be poor. Inadequately paid, committed more to cliques than to principles and written, not as in highly civilized countries by professionals trained to their discipline, but for the most part by ageing painters soured by lack of recognition or very vocal young ones clamouring for it, what passed for criticism was, like the life of Hobbes's first men, 'nasty, brutish and short', given more to taunts and sneers than to enjoyment; hopelessly vitiated by jealousy, hidden loyalties and personal vendettas. Few critics, if any, ever ventured from the shallows of their Press columns into the deeper waters of criticism. None made important contributions to the criticism of European masters, past or present. Exhibitions from abroad were never really criticized, nor welcomed as a chance to test local standards of judgement upon different material. At the very sight of anything from over the water, local art critics were to be seen genuflecting everywhere. The 'cultural cringe'[1] became an occupational disease, a permanent stoop, among the confraternity. Australian art, at least, was better than its critics.

Material wealth and the desire for culture also fostered the art prize. Many local government bodies, in country towns or city suburbs, prompted by citizens anxious to bring a measure of sweetness and light to their localities, provided moneys for annual art prizes. In the cities the new affluence promoted the growth of private galleries and the consequent increase of one-man exhibitions at the expense of the older group or Salon-type exhibitions of the established societies. During the 1950's the annual exhibitions of such societies as the Royal Art Society, the Society of Artists, the Victorian Artists' Society and the Contemporary Art Society became of less significance than they had been in preceding decades. Young artists found it easier than ever before to arrange one-man shows of their work. The private gallery prepared the way for professional dealing in contemporary Australian art, which became increasingly prominent during the later 1950's.

Beneath the stale froth of culture, art pursued its way more or less concealed. Younger artists turned steadily away from all forms of realism; and contemporary life, if portrayed at all, was usually accompanied by an air of wistfulness. The surface of life was no longer interesting; some of the most creative writers and artists of the decade turned to the consolations of religion. For the first time religious painting flourished in the country. The desire to revive religious art was international in its ramifications and due in no small measure to Catholic intellectuals seeking a religious art suited to the spiritual needs of the century. The work in France of the Dominicans, Père Régamy and Père Couturier, through their journal, *Art sacré*, has been of great importance in this regard. But the mood and temper of the time were propitious. Hiroshima and the nuclear arms race that followed, the intransigent power politics of communism and the cold war, the debauchery of intellectual, moral and cultural standards by commercial mass communication in the West, eroded faith in scientific progress and materialistic thought. Those who respected themselves and others withdrew if not into religion, then into the practice of art itself. The artists most honoured by the young, like Godfrey Miller, John Passmore and Ian Fairweather in Sydney and Roger Kemp in Melbourne, lived in comparative seclusion; men alone with their art. They became the local forerunners of the non-figurative revolution which transformed art in Sydney five years ago and has spread throughout the country since.

The Revival of Religious Painting

In Sydney the revival of religious painting centred upon the work of Justin O'Brien (*b.* 1917), who studied and taught painting in Sydney prior to serving in the Army. Taken prisoner in Greece, he began to paint again as a prisoner of war in an Austrian fort on the Vistula, finding a new source of inspiration in Byzantine art. After returning to Australia at the end of the war he held a joint exhibition with Jesse Martin at the Macquarie Galleries in 1944. His work at that stage was still immature and somewhat self-consciously designed; but the burning depth of colour, solemnity and hieratical splendour of Byzantine art had left a permanent impression. O'Brien's art, however, does not belong in spirit to the severe 'expressionistic' Syrian Byzantine but to the delicate transitional art of the Sienese *trecento.* It is a religious art softened by opulent colour, elegant arabesque and sometimes a touch of folk whimsy; owing more to Persia and Matisse than to Rouault and the 'dark night of the soul'; an art devout in its good taste but not militant with evangelical intensity (167).

O'Brien's paintings did much to promote a richly colouristic and neo-Byzantine type of decorative art very popular in Sydney during the late 1940's and early 1950's. Medieval Christian art, Persian and Indian painting and the décor of the Russian ballet all contributed to the mode. Some of the best work of this kind was produced by Loudon Sainthill, a talented theatre designer with a refined yet generous feeling for colour. The Byzantinesque trend was, in a sense, a late development of the neo-romanticism inaugurated by Jean Bellette and Paul Haefliger during the war years. O'Brien's work, especially that based on secular subject matter, reveals the continuing influence of Bellette. In such paintings slender, effeminate nudes rendered in graceful arabesques inhabit a wonderland of magic colour. Jeff Smart (*b.* 1921), a South Australian who later settled in Sydney, has also painted a good deal in this mode.

Neo-Byzantinism was augmented for a season or two in the work of Michael Kmit (*b.* 1910), a native of the Western Ukraine who studied and taught at the Fine Arts Academy in Cracow and worked in Italy, Paris and Vienna before arriving in Australia in 1950. Kmit's Byzantinism was freer and more expressionistic than O'Brien's, and though rapid and uneven in execution could rise at times to work of unusual beauty and distinction (168), as in his fine painting, *The Evangelist John Mark*, which was awarded the Blake Prize for 1953.

In Sydney the interest in a contemporary religious art was sufficiently widespread by 1951 to make possible the establishment of an annual prize and exhibition devoted to religious painting. The idea came originally from Mr Richard Morley, who believed that an annual prize for a religious painting similar to those awarded in many European countries would stimulate both art and religious life in Australia.

William Blake's name was chosen because it was felt that his intensely personal art and religious life would transcend the denominational problem and suggest the type of religious art the committee wished to champion. The catalogue of the first exhibition (1951) pointed out that the award was unique in that two standards were involved—one artistic and the other religious.

We ask of all work that it should be both religious and beautiful. It must be religious in the sense that it has its inspiration in a mind that is not only capable of seeing the inner spiritual meaning of its subject but also the ability to convey that essentially universal reaction to others. It must be beautiful, not in any slavish, photographic way, merely copying nature, but in the sense that by a

168   MICHAEL KMIT, *The Three Wise Men*, canvas,
31 x 25, 1954, Melbourne

new creation the artist has produced that 'something' which, being seen, pleases
—pleasing the whole man, his senses as they ought to be pleased and his mind
as it ought to be pleased.

Many artists found the challenge to interpret traditional religious themes
in a contemporary idiom salutary, and the awards were made, for the most
part, with good judgement and maintained from year to year a reasonably
wide range of sympathies. Justin O'Brien, not inappropriately, won the first
Blake Prize with a splendid *Virgin Enthroned* (167); and Frank Hinder
won the second, with his *Flight into Egypt* (1952), an interesting essay in
dynamic symmetry, if not in religious experience. As the years passed and
critical values changed, the judges of the award became increasingly
tolerant of abstract forms of expression. But they set their face from the
beginning against any use of religious themes in the criticism of contemporary society. Arthur Boyd's magnificent paintings, *The Golden Calf* and
The Mockers, exhibited in 1951, for all their beauty of paint and vitality of
expression, cut too close to the bone of the affluent decade. In the minds

of most of the judges it is clear that religious experience was identified with personal illumination, ritual piety and the sacraments. The prize symbolized not only the religious aspirations of the decade but also its quietism.

The rapid movement in Sydney towards a predominantly non-figurative style in painting, which is discussed later in this chapter, created problems for the Blake Committee. It was committed to support innovation: but it was doubtful to what extent a purely non-figurative art could be deemed religious. 'Religious art must be didactic' asserted the foreword to the 1957 catalogue, 'and it must relate to specific theological truths which have their reality quite apart from the mind of the artist.' How far could a purely non-figurative art be didactic and reveal specific theological truths possessing a reality apart from the mind of the artist? Was the Committee obliged to see God in every artist's burning bush of colour? To what extent was the non-figurative painter an iconoclast helping to destroy the traditional imagery of the Church? To what extent was he glorifying in his own creative power rather than glorifying God? On the other hand, did the new informal modes of abstraction reveal the personal but none the less genuine spiritual experiences of the artists who painted them? Such questions were not easily answered. The judges of the award, however, increasingly favoured abstract work until, in February 1961, Stanislaus Rapotec was awarded the Blake Prize for his *Meditating on Good Friday*, an entirely non-figurative painting.

The Recognition of Australian Art Abroad, 1950–60

Exhibitions of Australian art, such as the Grafton Galleries exhibition of 1898 and the Burlington House exhibition of 1923, had been shown in London from time to time; Australian artists had exhibited continually at the Royal Academy and the Paris Salons from the end of the nineteenth century; but before 1950 critics overseas assumed and often had good reason to assume, that Australian art was for the most part a provincial expression of British art, the inspiration second-hand, the quality second-rate. During the 1950's, however, exhibitions of work by Drysdale, Nolan and Tucker gradually produced a revision of these assumptions. It was observed that Australian art possessed qualities of its own, that it was drawing not only upon European art but also upon Australian experience and attitudes, and upon Australian history. It is not surprising that the recognition of Australian art overseas was long delayed. The men who created the Australian school of painting towards the end of the last century revealed themselves as soon as they left the country to be colonials at heart. They not only failed to make any creative contribution to twentieth-century European art; they also failed in Europe to maintain the level of their youthful achievements. The local tradition was too young, too thin, too ill-nourished, too little-loved to survive the rigour of the sea voyage. It was difficult for the Heidelberg

169   GODFREY MILLER, *Unity in Blue*, canvas, 26 x 33, completed 1952,
Sydney

expatriates and their numerous followers to appreciate that the standards
of the Academy and the Paris Salons were not as firmly based and as
international as they appeared. The second phase of Australian art which
began about 1939, however, brought forth qualities of the Australian mind
and imagination tough enough to survive in other soil. Though nourished
upon European art, the work of Drysdale, Nolan and Tucker was embedded
firmly enough in Australian interests and attitudes to maintain distinctive-
ness from European art in general. By maintaining their Australianness, and
at times asserting it, they provided their art with room to breathe and
develop in its own fashion.

The story begins in 1949. In December of that year John Reed, with
the assistance of Peter Bellew, who had joined the art section of the
U.N.E.S.C.O. executive, arranged an exhibition of Nolan's Ned Kelly paintings at the U.N.E.S.C.O. headquarters in Paris. The introduction to the
catalogue was written by Jean Cassou, who had previously declined Reed's
request to exhibit the paintings at the *Musée National d'Art Moderne*. The
exhibition, however, was not reviewed, and received little attention. In the

170   JOHN PASSMORE, *Night in Harbour*, gouache on newspaper, 23½ x 32¾,
1956, Colonel Aubrey Gibson

following year the paintings were displayed by Gino Nibbi, who had returned to Italy, in his bookshop and gallery in Rome. Meanwhile, Sir Kenneth Clark, who had been acting as an adviser on major purchases for the National Gallery of Victoria, was invited to visit Australia by the Felton Bequest Committee. Joseph Burke, who had been appointed as the first Herald Professor of Fine Arts in the University of Melbourne in 1947, assisted Clark in the preparation of his itinerary, advising him, among other things, not to miss seeing something of Nolan's work, 'the most imaginative and original painter whose work I have seen in Australia'.[2] Clark arrived in January 1949, met Nolan and Drysdale in Sydney and was impressed by the work of both artists. 'I would not have accepted those upside down birds and flying harvesters,' he has since written of Nolan's work, 'if my eye had not been held by vivid communication of every touch, and by the truth of tone which is the surest sign of a natural painter.'[3] Clark also advised Drysdale to hold an exhibition in London, and became a good friend of Australian art following his return to England.

In November 1950 Drysdale held an exhibition at the Leicester Galleries in London. It met with fair success, the image of Australian outback life which he had fashioned during the war years making its first impact upon English art criticism. A painting entitled *War Memorial* was purchased by the Tate Gallery from the exhibition. At the Redfern Gallery, a couple of months later, Nolan held an exhibition of Central Australian landscapes painted from experience gained flying over the continent during 1949-50. Although it did not receive a great deal of attention the Tate bought a painting and the exhibition did something to complement and reinforce the new image of the outback beginning to crystallize in British art criticism.

Nolan had arrived the previous year. He settled for a time in Cambridge and then travelled during the winter of 1950-1 through France, Spain, Portugal and Italy. Upon his return to Australia he held an exhibition of small paintings at the Macquarie Galleries, Sydney, based upon his Mediterranean experiences, in which his visual wit, his fantasy, and his technical ingenuity were delightfully combined. Bird-like in the darting immediacy of his images, Nolan was less committed to an Australian iconography than Drysdale, making art out of his experience regardless of place.

Back in Australia, Nolan continued to work with immense energy. Commissioned by the Brisbane *Courier-Mail* in 1952 to make drawings in the drought areas of Central Australia, he visited the interior at a time when the Northern Territory, due to the failure of the monsoonal rains of 1952, was experiencing one of the most severe droughts in its history. In that summer an estimated 1,000,000 head of cattle valued at £25,000,000 died. Nolan painted with brutal realism and a sharp-edged economy of statement the cadavers of animals he had seen contorted in death by starvation and shrivelled by the sun. They were exhibited at the Stanley Coe Gallery, Melbourne, in March, and David Jones's Gallery, Sydney, in July 1952. Some of these drought paintings were shown in a second exhibition held at the Redfern Gallery in London in October 1952.

Australian contemporary work then began to appear more frequently in overseas exhibitions. In 1952 Australia was represented at the Carnegie International Exhibition of Contemporary Art by work from Dobell, Drysdale, Nolan and Friend. In June 1953 the Arts Council of Great Britain arranged a small exhibition of contemporary Australian painting at the New Burlington Galleries, London, on the occasion of the Coronation. It included paintings by Dobell, Drysdale, Nolan, Rees, Friend, O'Brien, Bellette, Constance Stokes, Arthur Boyd, Miller, Hinder and Balson. 'Australian painters', wrote *The Times* art critic reviewing the show, 'were anxious to produce a genuine national style, but also made every effort to keep up with the latest international art movements.'[4] The exotic element in the work attracted the critic most strongly. Nolan was 'the strongest and most curious'[5] of the artists showing; his works were 'suffused with a kind of pictorial folk-lore that has vanished from serious painting in Europe'[6] and 'painted in a sham-naïve manner derived from European and other Sunday painters'.[7] Drysdale's darker vision was not so much admired. He was, said the *Sunday Times* critic, turning 'Australian landscape into a transcript from Ezekiel and Australian womanhood into a set of low-spirited frumps'.[8] The Australian Immigration Department held similar objections. Quality not obviously Australian was less noticed in the exhibition. Nothing more was found in Dobell's art than 'an engaging broad humour', and the two 'brave' abstractionists were treated rather patronizingly.[9] *The Times* review was representative of London critical opinion of Australian art at that time. Exotica, raw-boned and vigorous, appealed; Australia was thought of as a land culturally primitive, whose most talented artists, appropriately enough, worked in a primitivistic manner, painting deserts, banditti and tough bushmen. Nolan's paintings from the exhibition were sent on later to the 1954 Biennale.

Albert Tucker's work attracted some attention on the Continent before it became known in London and New York. After leaving Melbourne he lived in London from October 1947 until March 1948. But at that time his expressionistic urban imagery fell into no readily recognizable Australian form. From 1948 until 1950 he lived in Paris (where the work of Dubuffet exercised an influence), and during 1951 in Germany, holding his first one-man show abroad in the Kunstzaal van Lier, Amsterdam, in that year. During the winter of 1951 and the spring of 1952 he was back in Paris, where he held a show at the Galerie Huit. Then in 1952 he lived most of the time at Noli in the Italian Riviera. Until this time he had continued to develop the expressive urban imagery he had begun in Melbourne in 1943, but under the impact of French and German contemporary art, his forms became more abstracted and dissociated, and his colours more dense and complex. At Noli, however, he turned to a series of religious paintings: among them are some of his finest works, such as his stark and monumental *Judas* (171). Many of these paintings were exhibited in his first exhibition in Rome, which was held in 1953 at the Galleria di Quattro Venti. In Rome, where he lived from 1954 until 1956, Tucker's work first began to attract more than passing critical attention, and in 1956 he received a personal invitation to submit work to the Venice Biennale. About 1954 he had begun to turn to Australian frontier images of explorers, bushrangers and the desert. Tucker's frontier, however, possessed neither the folksy charm of Nolan's, the pathetic heroism of Drysdale's, nor the monstrous tumult of Arthur Boyd's. It was tough, scarred, residual and humourless, and had absorbed into its leathery textures a good deal of *art brut* and the abstract art of Italian painters like Alberto Burri working with polyvinyl acetate in low tones and heavy textures. His 'machines link outpost and capital

R

with more certainty than other Commonwealth artists,' wrote Lawrence Alloway.[10] In Rome, and later in New York, the recognition of Australian art as a distinctive style based on frontier imagery has been due in large measure to Tucker's art. Late in 1956 he returned to London. During the following three years his art became known to critics in London and New York, where the Museum of Modern Art and the Guggenheim Museum purchased examples of his work.

Meanwhile Sidney Nolan had, in 1954, returned to Europe as a delegate for Australian documentary films at the Venice Film Festival, where *Back of Beyond*, produced by John Heyer (with whom Nolan had worked in Central Australia the year previously) won the *Grand Prix*. Then, after showing a group of his paintings at Venice and acting as Australian Commissioner at the Venice Biennale, he travelled in southern Italy, painting landscapes and compositions featuring the iron folk-art crucifixes which fascinated him at the time. In June he held a joint exhibition with Albert Tucker at the International Press Club in Rome, both artists exhibiting Australian desert and frontier paintings which attracted critical attention. Back in London in 1955, Nolan painted a new series of Ned Kelly paintings, exhibiting them with Italian crucifix themes at the Redfern in May 1955. Kelly had now become a familiar figure to London critics. John Russell, of *The Times*, spoke with great warmth about '. . . tender, brutal, universal Ned . . . the eyeslits of his steel helmet, sometimes alight with the joy of life, at times crimson with the threat of death'.[11] Nolan, however, now began to turn his attention from frontier to classical myth. Towards the end of the year, with Robert Graves's book on the Greek myths in his mind, he went

171   ALBERT TUCKER, *Judas*, hardboard, 38 x 51½,
1955, the artist

172   SIDNEY NOLAN, *Leda and the Swan*, polyvinyl acetate
on hardboard, 48 x 60, 1958, Sydney

off to paint landscapes in the island of Hydra where he lived from 1955 to 1956. From 1954 to 1956 he maintained contact with Australia by a series of exhibitions based mainly on Mediterranean themes held at the Macquarie Galleries, Sydney, in September 1954; at the Johnstone Gallery, Brisbane, in December 1954; and at the Macquarie Galleries, Sydney, in March 1955 and October 1956. During 1956-7 he moved about a good deal; from Greece to Italy on an Italian Government Scholarship, thence back to London for some months. Then, during a brief return visit to Australia, he was able to visit Greece, Turkey, India, Cambodia, Mexico and America, before returning to London for a large retrospective exhibition of his work held in the Whitechapel Gallery, London, during June and July 1957. This, the most important exhibition of his work yet held, covering the ten years from 1947 to 1957, was received with great enthusiasm by London critics. Nolan's work at the Whitechapel came to be accepted in its own right as painting rather than as exotica.

During the past four years (1957-61), Nolan has become one of the best-known painters at work in England. In June 1960 he held an exhibition of paintings in the Matthiesen Gallery based on the Leda and swan myth which had been inspired by his reading of Graves, an unpublished poem by Alwyn Lee, and his experiences in Greece (172). This movement into classical myth was a natural and normal development in Nolan's art, for his art has never been limited by a national mythology. Writing on this point,

Sir Kenneth Clark has suggested that the element of myth in Nolan's art need not be over-emphasized: 'though he has drawn his strength from a locality he is able to transcend it, the local becoming universal'.[12]

In June 1961 a large exhibition of contemporary Australian art was shown at the Whitechapel Gallery and was most favourably received. Many critics recognized a distinctive quality in the work at large. The detailed consideration of this exhibition and its historical importance lies beyond the scope of this book, but it may prove to be something of a landmark. In any case, Australian artists are now aware that they are confronted by a new situation. For the first time in the country's history a receptive audience for their work is appearing overseas, at the moment, mainly in England. The next ten years will reveal how they will respond. It is reasonable to conclude from the evidence that the energy and distinctivenes that still characterizes Australian art sprang initially from the stimulus of the war situation. Can the energy and vitality be sustained? Will the melancholy story of genesis, exodus and leviticus be told all over again? Fortunately that is most unlikely, for history is not cyclic like the seasons. But it would be most foolish to assume that the vitality of Australian art can be sustained unless it is nourished by a kindred vitality in Australian society.

The Growth of Abstract and Non-Figurative Painting

In 1950 abstract painting was still primarily geometric and constructivist in character in Sydney and pursued a path distinctive from the more fashionable neo-romantic painters around Paul Haefliger. New thought and experiment was, to begin with, more apparent among the sculptors than the painters. In February 1951, a Society of Sculptors and Associates was formed, with Lyndon Dadswell, the best-known sculptor and teacher of sculpture in the city, as its President. Dadswell advocated research, experiment and thought. For him the conventional divisions between architecture, sculpture and painting were becoming increasingly meaningless, and the new Society included architects and painters among its associates. It arranged Australia's first open-air exhibition of sculpture in the Botanic Gardens, Sydney, in November 1951 and helped to stimulate abstract experiment in the kindred arts. One of the younger members of the Society, Robert Klippel (b. 1920), who had returned to Sydney in 1950 after studying at the Slade, helped to arouse interest in open-form work and influenced some younger painters.

Of considerably more importance, however, was the work and example of Godfrey Miller (b. 1893), a New Zealander who had studied at the Slade and is now living in Sydney. His has been a lifetime of research into problems introduced by Cézanne, Seurat, Matisse and others, but for him never fully explored. Miller has set himself to capture a feeling for the essence of things in the flux of changing appearances: to find a pictorial

173 IAN FAIRWEATHER, *Monastery*, polyvinyl acetate on cardboard, 56¼ x 72½, 1960/1, Mr Wallace Thornton

technique capable of celebrating both permanence and change at the same time. Few Australian painters have possessed either the technical facility or the philosophical temperament to approach such problems, let alone pursue them single-mindedly through the course of a lifetime. His mature paintings are completed gradually, often over a period of many years. Natural appearances are never entirely eradicated, being held as it were in flight between intricate, interpenetrating grids. The tiny faceted mosaics of colour bear some reference to Seurat's *pointillisme*, but the visual and emotional effect are quite different. Miller's paintings are not attempts to impose order upon appearance, but allegories of a universe in which form and colour are continuously created and destroyed by energy and light (169). That Miller approaches painting in the manner of a mystic is not altogether unusual: what is exciting is the fact that his mysticism works as painting, that he finds truly pictorial equivalents for his vision of cosmic unity. Although he is probably the finest abstract painter at work in Australia today, his intricate technique is not readily transmitted and he has had few direct followers, but the inspiration of his art and his teaching has been widespread and profound.

The greatest single influence upon painting in Sydney during the first half of the 1950's was, however, John Passmore (*b*. 1904), a contemporary of Dobell at Julian Ashton's School, who left for study in Europe in 1933 and did not return until 1950. Passmore also developed a masterly style derived from a lifelong interest in Cézanne. In his work abstract construction, a mastery of tone, an unusually subtle feeling for colour, and feeling, too, for the hidden poetry of nature are combined with a firm grasp upon life (170). Although, like Miller, something of a recluse, Passmore became for the 1950's in Australia, through his work and his teaching, the painter's painter. Rich ambiguities of space, form and atmosphere lie hidden in the firm, painterly thrust of his work; and it is not surprising that it was of first importance for the post-war generation of art students.

The art of Ian Fairweather (*b*. 1890), though based, like that of Passmore, upon the figure, has also moved increasingly towards abstraction during the post-war years. But it looks back more to Modigliani than to Cézanne, being grounded upon the interrelation of flowing arabesques, and has been enriched by contact with Chinese, Indonesian and Australian aboriginal art (173). Fairweather served in the British Army during the First World War, after studying forestry in London and Edinburgh, and art at the Slade. He first came to Australia in the early 1930's, after painting in China and Indonesia. He has lived for several years in Melbourne, and also in tropical Australia. Peripatetic, eccentric and picturesque in his habits, Fairweather has left colourful tales behind him in his wanderings which have endowed his paintings with an associational charm. But the best of them can stand on their own. A master of fluent design full of springing energy and fine colour, Fairweather is one of the most inventive, personal and original of the semi-abstract painters at work in Australia today. It is only upon occasion that his fluency produces designs that are flaccid and repetitive.

The influence of Dadswell, Miller, Passmore and Fairweather lay in the direction of abstraction. So, all things considered, did the exhibition, 'French Painting Today', arranged by the French and Australian Governments, which toured the capital cities between January and September 1953. This was the most important exhibition held in the country since the Murdoch exhibition of 'French and British Modern Art' of 1939. Apart from the work of well-known artists like Braque, Chagall, Derain, Dufy, Ernst, Matisse, Picasso, Rouault, Utrillo and Vlaminck, original work of painters who had become known since the war became available to artists in the country for the first time. André Marchand's Picassoesque *Le Printemps*, with its lustrous colour, sonorous blacks and lively, spiky line was the most discussed painting; but the work of artists like Manessier, de Staël, Soulages, Vieira da Silva and Hans Hartung exercised a more lasting effect upon the work of younger artists.

174   CHARLES DOUTNEY, *Night Club*, canvas, 19½ x 27,
1952, Mr Hal Missingham

The exhibition was of special importance to the group of ex-servicemen who studied art under the Commonwealth Post-War Reconstruction Training Scheme. These artists, who came to exercise a great influence upon Australian art during the later 1950's, were divided between the claims of figurative and non-figurative art. In Sydney Charles Doutney, Bob Dickerson and Jon Molvig continued to work in figurative modes while such painters as Roy Fluke, John Coburn, Anthony Tuckson and Stan de Teliga sought to explore the newer post-war forms of abstraction. In Melbourne John Brack, Clifton Pugh and David Boyd developed their own styles of figurative painting.

Among the figurative painters of Sydney, Charles Doutney (1908-57) was somewhat older than most of the C.R.T.S. art students and had seen a good deal of life before the war. In a sense his work belongs spiritually to the realistic and expressive comment of the war years. But Doutney was not only, like Dobell, whose work he much admired, a keen and creative observer of life; he was also an artist of the finest perception. His best paintings possess a quiet authority of statement and an unusual beauty of colour and mood (174). He succeeded in carrying out an admirable series of paintings of Sydney life, especially the life of King's Cross which he knew so well, before an illness contracted in New Guinea claimed him. With his death, Australia lost one of its most talented post-war artists.[13]

Bob Dickerson (*b.* 1924) was a professional boxer before joining the R.A.A.F., and only settled to painting when he was stationed in Indonesia after the war. Today he is probably the best-known figurative painter at work in Sydney, and the only important artist of his generation in the city who remained immune to the mass-conversion to non-figurative painting which took place in Sydney during 1956 and 1957. He has developed his art out of a flat, posterish and naïve manner of painting. Like Sidney Nolan, however, Dickerson has a natural feeling for weight of tone and disposition of shape and mass, so that his paintings are usually constructed with distinction. From a limited technical vocabulary he has constructed a repertoire of cubic and expressive forms which he handles with great skill. It is a personal language with which he comments upon the human situation (175). 'I feel', he has written, 'we should try to paint the life we see around us—people and the way they feel about living today.'[14] It is a melancholy and pathetic vision of lonely and isolated people made tolerable by a certain amount of sentiment. Yet behind his image of tired men on park benches, furtive little clerks and touts and wide-eyed children lies the menacing allegory of universal isolation. His people are like A. D. Hope's wandering islands: no communication between them is possible.

> You cannot build bridges between the wandering islands;
> The Mind has no neighbours, and the unteachable heart
> Announces its armistice time after time, but spends
> Its love to draw them closer and closer apart.[15]

Dickerson's emphasis upon the isolation of the individual is a feature of the figurative painting of the post-war years. The element of wit, sardonic humour and the comments upon manners, so evident during the early 1940's in the work of such artists as Purves Smith, Dobell, Drysdale, Herman, Friend, Haxton and Flower, gave way during the post-war years to a new seriousness. People in their social roles, the comedy of manners, ceased to be interesting: attention turned once again to the individual isolated and yet encircled by an alien environment. The change in emphasis was already well in evidence during the later years of the war. In the paintings of Jean Bellette, Russell Drysdale and Albert Tucker, to name only three, the individual is figured standing out against society or nature; but the conception is still heroic. Dickerson and his contemporaries, notably John Brack and Charles Blackman, possess no such generous faith in the resources of the individual. People, in the mass or as individuals, are pathetic creatures at the mercy of forces beyond their control. This point of view is present both in the acidulous classicism of John Brack and the poignant romanticism of Charles Blackman.

John Brack (b. 1920), studied as a part-time student for two years (1938-40) before the war, and after service in the Army, for two years after the war as a full-time student at the National Gallery School (1948-9). Intellectual in attitude, well read, dry in manner, and no respecter of persons, Brack is something of a phenomenon among Australian artists. T. E. Hulme and Wyndham Lewis would have appreciated his art and

175 ROBERT DICKERSON, *Tired Man*, synthetic enamel
on hardboard, 54 x 60, 1957, Melbourne

176 JOHN BRACK, *Five o'clock Collins Street*, canvas, 45 x 64,
1956, Melbourne

disposition better than his own countrymen, for in a country whose artists have always tended towards romanticisms of some kind or other, Brack has become the leading anti-romantic, rejecting both the national romanticism of the frontier and the international romanticism of abstract expressionism. He is strongly opposed to the idea of creating a national style, regarding it as an anachronism, but also believes that the widespread desire to 'purify' painting by the abolition of subject-matter and image can only lead to ultimate sterility. Meanwhile, he maintains, the image remains 'impure and fecund'. In his own work he has sought for inspiration in the people he sees around him (176). 'I prefer to paint people simply because I find them more interesting than anything else.'[16] There is, however, nothing cosy about what he paints. His line is sharp, like a surgeon's scalpel, and just as cutting; and his colour can be as merciless as a sodium flare. There is nothing kindly in the way he depicts people with their masks off, but his art is a brave and timely reassertion of Matthew Arnold's belief in art as the criticism of society.

By contrast with Brack the art of Charles Blackman (b. 1928) is more personal. Blackman is a painter of women but not of flesh; a kind of belated reply to Norman Lindsay's pseudo-classical eroticism, an artist seeking to penetrate a feminine world of private sensations, hopes and fears (177). Blackman studied drawing at East Sydney and painting under Hayward Veal, a pupil of Max Meldrum. In 1950 he settled in Melbourne where he held his first exhibition in 1952 and helped to re-establish the Melbourne Contemporary Art Society the following year. Blackman is a skilled illusionist who owes not a little of his dramatic power to his Meldrum training. By combining tonal illusionism with forceful rudimentary images and rich, resonant colour, Blackman has created a personal art form of great beauty and poignant expressive power.

In the work of such artists as Doutney, Dickerson, Brack and Blackman the figurative tradition in Australian art survived with vigour into the 1950's. But in Sydney, especially, the desire to experiment with the new post-war form of abstract art current in Europe and America developed rapidly after the French exhibition of 1953. Significantly enough, the 1954 exhibition of the Sydney Group, the citadel of neo-romanticism for almost ten years, revealed the growing strength of abstract art in the work displayed by Passmore, Miller, Eric Smith, Michael Kmit and Ralph Balson. Furthermore, the hard-edged, geometric forms of abstract art gave way before forms freely fragmented and reconstructed into expressionistic rather than formal constructions.

During the early 1950's, art critics in Sydney gave only qualified support to abstract art. James Gleeson, for example, reviewing a joint exhibition of work by Ralph Balson and Robert Klippel, said: 'Generally speaking, ab-

177   CHARLES BLACKMAN, *Girl with Flowers*, hardboard, 47 x 41, 1959, Mrs Edith Kirwan

stract art offers an experience that is confined within very narrow frontiers. It has no content. We cannot relate it to ordinary life. The experience exists as a thing in itself, isolated in the art gallery by the moment of sensation.'[17] Even three years later Paul Haefliger, the critic of the *Sydney Morning Herald*, was still critical of abstract art as a mature form of expression. In March 1955, reviewing an exhibition of the Contemporary Art Society, he wrote:

The problem of abstract art as a means of expression for the younger generation seems formidable. Indeed, the fact that abstract art has conquered the world appears the best argument for not continuing it, since the cubist masters have exhausted most of its possibilities. If there are any aspects left in which to specialize Paris is exploring them—and not too happily. For our own young painters abstract art offers a splendid means to master composition. Apart from this it can only be a restatement, and as such, lacking in vitality.

At that time Haefliger, still oblivious of the American contribution, was thinking of Paris as the centre of abstract art. Yet taste was changing. Gleeson, despite his reservations, reacted sympathetically to the Balson, Klippel exhibition; and Haefliger was about to become a full-blooded champion of abstract expressionism.

By 1955 a new spirit of inquiry and discussion, a new curiosity about events abroad, stimulated by a younger generation of post-war artists and art students, began to reanimate the Contemporary Art Society in Sydney. It was given leadership and definition by Elwyn Lynn (b. 1917), a school-master and philosophy graduate with an interest in aesthetics, who had begun to paint in the later 1940's. Elected to the executive of the Society in 1955 and appointed editor of its *Broadsheet*, Lynn revived an interest in events overseas, promoted discussion, printed useful news and began a continuous questioning of the assumptions (especially the neo-romantic assumptions) of local Sydney critics. In the *Broadsheet* of March 1955 he was discussing the emotional element in American abstract expressionism; in April, how French and American action painters were reacting against commercialized abstraction. During 1956 and 1957 the C.A.S. *Broadsheet* discussed continuously abstract expressionism, tachism and action painting. This interest in the new developments in abstract art was assisted by several exhibitions from abroad, held between 1956 and 1959, such as the 'Exhibition of Modern German Graphic Art' (1956), 'Italian Art of the Twentieth Century' (1956), 'Contemporary Canadian Painting' (1957), 'British Abstract Painting' (1958-9), 'Contemporary Japanese Art' (1958-9) and 'Recent Painting: Seven British Artists'. Some visitors from the United States, Dr Grace McCann Morley (1956), Professor Dorothy Cogswell (1957) and the Australian, Mary Cecil Allen (1960), for example, helped to make the American contribution to post-war painting better known.

Meanwhile, in Melbourne, the interest in abstract art, both geometric and informal, was increasing. Roger Kemp (b. 1908), who had been trained at the Royal Melbourne Technical College and at the Gallery School, had already been working in a semi-abstract style for many years. He developed a personal style owing something to Italian futurism and sought, like Godfrey Miller, pictorial forms expressive of the relation between human-kind and the cosmic order.

Kemp's art exercised a considerable influence upon the work of Leonard French (b. 1928), who turned to a more abstract manner following a year or so abroad during 1949-50. French is a painter of power and vigour whose massive constructions are held in control by a hard-edged geometry of

178 LEONARD FRENCH, *The Burial*, synthetic enamel and gold
leaf on hessian-covered cardboard, 60 x 72, 1960, Mr R. Komon

form owing not a little to Léger, Delaunay and Manessier. He has produced
some fine murals. In recent years the personal language of symbolic forms
with which he invests his constructions has been simplified and clarified,
his compositions are more controlled, and his colour has become richer,
denser and more flexible (178). Avoiding the accidentalism of abstract
expressionism, French has evolved a sonorous and monumental art, richly
decorative in the best sense, and capable of expressing a wide range of
feeling. At the root of his art lies a craftsman's interest in materials and
techniques. His themes of recent years have revealed an increasingly
religious cast of thought. Given the opportunity, he could become, perhaps,
an ecclesiastical decorator of great distinction.

Somewhat apart in manner from French (around 1955) were a small
number of young artists and art students who, independently of events in
Sydney, had begun to experiment with the accidental, informal and romantic
aspects of abstract painting. The most important of these were Donald
Laycock, John Howley and Ian Sime. Both Laycock (*b.* 1931) and Howley
(*b.* 1932) had studied at the Gallery School, the latter also for short periods
at the Royal Melbourne Technical College and with George Bell. Both
artists became interested in the work of Roberto, Matta, Jackson Pollock

and Max Ernst. Laycock developed a rhythmical, linear and part-acci-
dentalist style, building his pictures into richly textured masses of colour,
in a desire to create pictorial analogies for the dispersion of energy and the
creation of matter (180). He was, if not the first, certainly one of the first
among local artists to develop a coherent personal style from the abstract
expressionist mode of invention. Howley developed a freer, more informal
and plastic style.

Ian Sime (*b*. 1924), like Laycock and Howley, has sought to develop an
art which avoids the conscious control of thought. As Miss Erica McGilchrist
wrote:

He regards the act of painting as an extension of the creative forces of nature
operating through man; and just as nature, within the framework of certain
fundamental laws produces a mountain or a toadstool or a sparrow, so the artist,
out of the principles of design, produces a painting. In both cases, the questions,
'What is it? What does it mean?' come close to destroying the capacity of the
observer to be emotionally affected by the object. The painting like the sparrow,
should be accepted for its own sake simply as another created thing.[18]

Sime's distrust and contempt for the operation of the intellect in painting
and his supreme faith in subconscious processes is shared widely by many
of his generation. His style, which has emerged, in part, from an organic
surrealist heritage reminiscent of Masson, possesses an explosive and disjunctive vitality (179). In his *Animist Paintings*, exhibited in 1956, he
sought to produce works independently of volition and premeditated meaning—'acts' of nature.

It was in Sydney, however, that the movement towards informal abstraction gathered the greatest momentum. It centred upon members of the
Contemporary Art Society, John Passmore and his pupils. In February 1955
one of them, John Olsen (*b*. 1928), held his first show at the Macquarie
Galleries. The paintings were semi-abstract, with masses and planes of
colour chunky and Cézannesque, revealing his teacher's influence. Robert
Klippel, the sculptor and a friend of Olsen, stressed the importance of
becoming more involved with the act of painting. 'Painting of the blood-
stream'[19] they called it. Later, in August 1955, Olsen moved down to
Melbourne and mingled with a group of artists that included John Howley,
Donald Laycock, Lawrence Daws and Leonard French. His work began
to move firmly in the direction of abstract expressionism. Soulages was
clearly an influence at that time; but some paintings by John Howley were
also germinal to his later development. In April 1956 he returned to Sydney
and in December organized with Klippel an exhibition at the Macquarie
Galleries called 'Direction 1', which included work by Passmore, Olsen,
Klippel, Eric Smith and William Rose. It launched abstract expressionism in
Sydney and the new mode was quickly accepted by the critics.

179 IAN SIME, *Painting*, hardboard, 36 x 48, 1955,
Museum of Modern Art of Australia, Melbourne

Events moved rapidly. In October 1956 the Orient Line, with the assistance of the National Gallery Society of New South Wales, organized an
exhibition of Contemporary Australian Paintings for display on the s.s.
Orcades in the ports of Auckland, Honolulu, Vancouver and San Francisco.
It gave special prominence to the new trends. Work by the better-known
figurative painters: Drysdale, Nolan, Arthur Boyd, Herman, Brack, Orban,
O'Brien and Friend was included; but the emphasis lay upon abstract and
semi-abstract work. It contained the work both of the older generation of
geometric abstractionists and constructivists, such as Miller, Passmore,
Kemp and Balson, and the younger generation, such as Lawrence Daws,
William Rose and Leonard French. It also included work by the abstract
expressionists Olsen, Howley and Laycock.

The Sydney critics praised the exhibition lavishly. Haefliger, whose praise
of abstraction had hitherto been guarded and qualified, found the exhibition
extremely exciting. 'Once again', he wrote, 'Australian art has sprung to life
in this most important of all exhibitions.'[20] Its importance, he asserted, could
not be overestimated. 'Painters with diverging interests have suddenly cast
aside their former manner of expression and, so to speak, jumped into the
maelstrom of abstract expressionism.' Gleeson, who travelled with the
exhibition to lecture, was equally enthusiastic. It was, he exclaimed in his
newspaper review of the exhibition, 'a honey of a show';[21] and in his foreword to the catalogue asserted that: 'European . . . art is an organic thing,

180   DONALD LAYCOCK, *As it was in the Beginning*, hardboard, 48 x 36,
1955-6, Colonel Aubrey Gibson

subject to immutable laws that cannot be artificially checked. . . . It must follow the current of History. It is not unlike a Calder mobile that takes its form from the pressures and tensions of History.' On his return he emphasized that the artists who aroused the greatest interest on the West Coast were 'those committed to the extreme forms of abstraction or abstract expressionism'.[22]

With Sydney critics thus enjoining artists to jump into the maelstrom, or on to the band-wagon of abstract expressionism in order to follow the current of History with a capital H (the metaphors varied), it is not surprising that the victory of the new mode and its variants was swift and surprisingly complete. John Olsen, personable, sensitive and poetic, was hailed as a master over night. Early in 1957, supported by a generous patron, he left for Europe. During his visit abroad he exhibited at the Salon de Mai, in the exhibition 'L'Oeil Neuf', Paris, and the Atelier 17 exhibition held at Basle. In August 1958 he sent an exhibition back to the Macquarie Galleries. 'He is the complete artist,' wrote Mr Laurie Thomas, the acting critic of the *Sun*, 'sensitive, intelligent, strong and courageous . . . but still the artist who responds to his intuitions. . . . He is probing into the depths of human nature, seeking the basic images which have satisfied mankind, for some reason or other from the beginning.'[23] The enthusiasm, though somewhat generous, was genuine enough. Olsen returned to Sydney, in February 1960, after travelling in Spain and living for a time in Majorca.

Like most abstract expressionists, John Olsen seeks to discover form and image in the actual process of painting (181). The poetry of Dylan Thomas and the sea-port paintings of John Passmore have deeply influenced his art. Pictorial animism, the possibility of automatic painting, has appealed to him, as it has to Ian Sime. 'The thing which I always endeavour to express is an animistic quality—a certain mystical throbbing throughout nature.'[24] He has abandoned painting landscapes from a fixed position which seems, he has said, to be quite out of keeping with present modes of travel and our changing conceptions of the universe.

The recognition of other painters experimenting in the new abstract mode followed upon Olsen's dramatic acceptance. In February 1957 Elwyn Lynn (182) won the Blake Prize with his *Betrayal* (Melbourne), an expressive abstract painting in which an affection for André Marchand still lingered. Later in the year he won prizes at Mosman and Bathurst. In August 1958 he exhibited a series of paintings at the Museum of Modern Art in Melbourne based upon *The Rime of the Ancient Mariner*, in the belief that abstract expressionism could communicate, symbolically, emotional states that were otherwise incommunicable.

The rise of Thomas Gleghorn (*b.* 1925) was more mercurial (185). He had studied art at Newcastle with advice and encouragement from Dobell,

181   JOHN OLSEN, *Digger Landscape*, charcoal and
gouache on paper, 27 x 20, Mr Daniel Thomas

but in 1957 was still virtually unknown. Then he won the Rockdale Art
Prize, and in 1958 the Blake *Christus* prize, and prizes at Bathurst, Tumut,
Mosman and Muswellbrook. In June 1958 he painted several abstracts of the
Nullarbor desert, and has concerned himself a good deal in recent years
with applying abstract expressionist methods to his experience of landscape.

John Coburn (*b*. 1925) has developed a firm, flat-surface style built upon
simple organic forms about which sonorous colours glow and play. His work
owes something to Manessier and Pre-Colombian art; and he is one of the
very few painters in Sydney who has succeeded in endowing non-figurative
work with genuine religious feeling (183).

Eric Smith (*b*. 1919), who worked with some success for several years
in a neo-Byzantine expressionistic manner and produced some notable
religious paintings in that mode, has endeavoured to convey religious feeling
in abstract work with less success. The art of Carl Plate (*b*. 1909) has
developed more slowly and is more urbane. It possesses a genuine feeling
for nature, at times a note of wit, and always a sense of good taste (184).

182   ELWYN LYNN, 1960, canvas, 72 x 72, 1960, Museum of Modern
Art of Australia, Melbourne

Among women in Sydney, Margo Lewers (*b.* 1908) is one of the most accomplished artists working with abstract form (186). Her interest in abstraction dates from a visit to England in 1933 with her husband, the sculptor, Gerald Lewers, when she became acquainted with the work of the artists associated with the Unit One group (1934, Mayor Gallery), such as Nicholson, Hepworth and Moore. During the past ten years her work has moved from a geometric to a more informal mode of abstraction and she has produced works of distinction in mosaic and tile, such as her large abstract composition for the Rex Capital Hotel, Canberra. In Melbourne, both Erica McGilchrist and Dawn Sime have produced competent work in abstract mural design.

By 1960 non-figurative painting had spread pretty generally throughout Australia from Perth to Sydney, from Brisbane to Hobart, and from the

183   JOHN COBURN, *Litany*, hardboard,
36 x 24, 1958, Sydney

Museum of Modern Art to the Secondary Schools. In Australia, as in most
other countries, it has brought with it an increasing preoccupation with the
processes and materials of art. In a very real sense art has become more
materialistic, less concerned with image and idea, and more concerned with
the creation, deliberately or adventitiously, of novel surfaces, edges and
textures. This obsession with surface has been accompanied by an equal
and opposite obsession with the nature of space, and both obsessions by a
growing intolerance of figurative painting. Abstract expressionism became,
furthermore, an exclusivist doctrine. It was, its champions maintained, the
only international art. It was the mainstream into which all contemporary
expression was to be channelled. Its advocates became the dupes of the
historicist fallacy. Abstract expressionism, they said, was the Instrument of
History and there was nothing anyone could do about it. Its champions

184   CARL PLATE, *Paradox of Sequence*, hardboard,
48 x 36, 1958-61, the artist

developed, like communists, a smug satisfaction in the inevitable triumph of their cause.

Innovation, however, is one thing, and quality another. Oddly enough, during the time when the swing to abstract art was gathering such momentum, William Dobell was preparing the sketches and studies for his portrait of Mary Gilmore, one of the finest and most representative of his paintings. After the Archibald Prize controversy and court case of 1943-4 Dobell's art, despite many fine portraits such as his *Mrs Frank Clune*, entered upon a period of uncertainty. He was not the kind of artist to take easily to the painting of commissioned portraits, except when the subjects interested him personally. Much of his work after 1945 was unequal and uneven, reflecting perhaps, something of the general uncertainty which many artists felt during

185　THOMAS GLEGHORN, *The Passion*, hardboard,
53½ x 24, 1958, Mrs Bernard Smith

186 MARGO LEWERS, *Irregular Shapes*, hardboard, 48 x 84, 1961, the artist

the years following the war. His New Guinea paintings, based on visits made in 1949 and 1950, are often of great beauty but are not to be numbered among his best works. He was not able to bring to his paintings of the native peoples of New Guinea the kind of insights which give such authority to his portrayal of the members of his own race. Indeed, they rarely reach beyond the picturesque.

Dobell found Dame Mary Gilmore a congenial subject to paint. The portrait (frontispiece) returns in some ways to his mannerist phase of the early 1940's, of which *The Cypriot* is the most notable example. The subject, seated in an alert and slightly tensed position, as though about to rise from her chair, is presented with great distinction, being composed in a pyramidal form of strength and dignity. The cool luminous blues and greens, of costume and background, serve as delicate foils to the fine, warm leathery texture of the head, and the painting of lace and hair has been accomplished with Dobell's mature technical mastery. The work as a whole endows his subject with an air of spiritual grandeur, a startling vitality of presence and, most justly, a queenly magnificence: the tribute of an artist to a poet.

The Survival of Figurative Painting in Melbourne, 1956–9

In Sydney the strength of figurative painting was sapped by a decade of neo-romanticism, Byzantinesque exoticism and genteel taste. Abstract expressionism brought new vigour, new life and a new cause to be fought for, to a rather stuffy art world. But in the process a good deal of Sydney's art began to look like a provincial expression of American painting: aesthetically, the city was ambitious to become, it seemed, a kind of south-western suburb of San Francisco. By 1957 Bob Dickerson was the only painter of

S

real quality among the post-war generation who was working entirely within the figurative mode. In Melbourne, however, figurative painting survived with vigour; maintained a critical edge upon life, and drew strength from a local tradition, still held in respect, that reached back to the Heidelberg School. In November 1956, a month after the s.s. *Orcades* had sailed for San Francisco with its exhibition, John Brack exhibited his *Racecourse Series* of paintings at the Peter Bray Gallery, Melbourne: the direct comments of an acidulous eye upon an everyday facet of local life. Such ordered and forthright statements about contemporary life would have found little favour in Sydney; in Melbourne it aroused the interest of critics and public alike.

In the same month, John Perceval held his first exhibition of paintings after having worked for several years in ceramics. It was an unusual return. The new paintings were quite different from the work of his Angry Penguin years. The subjects chosen were drawn from Williamstown, Melbourne's oldest port, and Gaffney's Creek, an old mining town (where Perceval painted with Boyd); and the artist, like Hans Heysen working at Ambleside, revealed an affection for the scenes he painted. This first exhibition following his return to painting was not, however, entirely successful. The speed with which he worked resulted in the production of many paintings that fell midway between mere paint and visual illusion. But as he developed his new manner, Perceval began to invent a truly novel interpretation of Australian bushland landscape. Radiant with high colour, it broke completely with the landscape of dry, open spaces, strange creatures, and tough heroes which Drysdale, Nolan, Arthur Boyd and Tucker have made so well known during the past twenty years. Just as their work may be viewed as a reinterpretation of ideas and feelings about Australian nature first quickened in colonial days, so Perceval's landscapes may be viewed as the products of an emotional attitude akin to that which produced the landscapes of the Heidelberg School. For Perceval's paintings are also visual and optimistic interpretations of the Australian countryside, full of the joy of life; but unlike the Heidelberg landscapes the imagery emerges vicariously from a tumult of pure colour and deeply corrugated, heavily impasted paint. It is a kind of action painting controlled by visual intuition rather than by non-visual and subconscious processes of the mind. In the act of painting before nature, *alla prima*, at high speed and pressure, drawing visual sensations not from one point of view but from all sides, a total impression drawn from new visual coherences, half-accidental, half-willed was found to emerge from the thickening and spreading paint (187). The approach has something in common with the later work of Van Gogh: but Van Gogh's method, even at its most expressionistic and exultant, was controlled by a repetitive act of emotive brushing derived from *pointillisme*. It created a deliberate, and

187 JOHN PERCEVAL, *River Foam*, hardboard, 30 x 36,
1960, Miss D. Dyason and Mesdames M. Campbell,
C. McComas, J. Davies and E. Falloon

more or less regular, textured weft over the canvas. Perceval's painting is far less controlled by systematic and repetitive brushwork or palette-knife work. It is a more random affair from which visual equivalences emerge, instead of being consciously asserted, from the painting process. In switching his attention from conceptual images to the pictorial problems of visual perception, Perceval has returned to one of the central problems of painting. His new approach could be of great significance for the future of Australian painting.

The work of Clifton Pugh (*b.* 1924) also testifies to the survival of figurative painting in Melbourne during the later 1950's. A C.R.T.S. trainee who had seen service against the Japanese in New Guinea, Pugh's personal style did not begin to emerge until about 1954. In 1955 and 1956 he exhibited with the 'Group of 4', which included Lawrence Daws, John Howley and Donald Laycock. Pugh has developed an imaginative and expressive portrait style, and is one of the better portrait painters at work in the country today. He is, however, better known for his landscapes which reveal his early interest in expressionism, his firm sense of design and his sustained interest in the appearance and structure of the visible world. But it is the savage and ruthless dichotomy beneath the surface of life, the hunter and the hunted, upon which his art is centred. Pugh sees nature as Thyestes devouring his own children: life battening upon life in an eternal

188 CLIFTON PUGH, *The World of Shane and Dailan*, synthetic enamel on hardboard, 36 x 54, 1957, Adelaide

cycle. Occasionally the more tender emotions appear, as in his *World of Shane and Dailan* (188), an admirable contemporary interpretation of a theme which has appealed to Australian writers and artists since colonial days.

In Melbourne the figurative tradition also found two able champions in the poetic humanism of Charles Blackman and the tragic vision of Arthur Boyd: Blackman with his *Alice in Wonderland* and *The Sleeping Beauty* series, and Boyd with his memorable *Love, Marriage and Death of a Half-Caste* series of allegorical paintings first exhibited at the Australian Galleries, Melbourne, in April 1958. These last were probably the most important series of subject pictures painted in Australia during the 1950's (189). They grew from observations made during a trip from Alice Springs to Arltunga in 1951, when Boyd became acutely aware of the dereliction and poverty of half-castes in Central Australia, and the great human problem involved. The paintings, however, do not refer to an actual event and recall few remembered observations: they are conceived as in a dream, a dream that owes something to Chagall, Rembrandt, surrealism and Boyd's circle of painter friends. Like John Brack's annotations on urban life, Boyd's paintings are a brilliant vindication of the role of the artist as a critic of society. Not that Boyd has a programme or a solution to expound. As Dr Hoff, who has discussed the paintings in detail, concludes:

There is no real end to the series; its importance lies in the individual situations in which Boyd appeals above all to our sense of sympathy. He leaves no message, offers no solution; but he presents problems inherent in the aborigine situation in a manner in which contemporary formal trends, and Boyd's own tradition of

189   ARTHUR BOYD, *Groom Waiting for his Bride to Grow Up*, hardboard, 54 x 72, 1958, Mr W. A. K. a'Beckett

poetic representation, combine to a successful climax of nearly twenty years of artistic endeavour.[25]

In these paintings Boyd succeeded better, perhaps, than any other member of the original Angry Penguin circle in elevating an Australian theme to a universal level, endowing it with a breadth of reference and feeling beyond the limits of nation or region.

In Melbourne the figurative image also survived in the work of David Boyd, who grew up under the influence of his elder brother, but developed a talent and imagination of his own. There is, as might be expected, a certain kinship in the response of both brothers to art and life. David first studied music at the Melbourne Conservatorium, and was trained in pottery and clay modelling in the family circle. After the war he also studied painting as a C.R.T.S. student at the National Gallery School and proceeded abroad where he worked and studied for five years (1950-5), mainly in the south of France and England. Upon his return he and his wife, Hermia, became well known throughout Australia for their pottery. Like his brother Arthur and brother-in-law John Perceval, David Boyd has also worked a good deal in ceramic sculpture. He held a one-man show of this branch of his work in Melbourne in 1957. In the same year he turned seriously for the first time to painting, beginning a series on the theme of Australian exploration. In 1959 he began a series based on the pathetic history of the Tasmanian aborigines. These early explorer and Tasmanian paintings are romantically conceived; the figures crowd upon the canvas grotesquely, and often possess

190   DAVID BOYD, *Truganini
and the Sealer*, hardboard, 48 x 36,
1959, the artist

a touch of the comic. All this was indubitably Boydian. But David Boyd's work is no mere imitation of his brother's. Arthur Boyd's *Love, Marriage and Death of a Half-Caste* paintings evoke a profound pathos. His morality, as Pater said of Botticelli, is all sympathy. His apprehension of tragedy is indirect. It is muffled by allegory and enters into the spirit of suffering without bitterness. David Boyd's work is more direct. He seeks his symbolism in historical events. In his later works his paintings are more highly modelled, more cubic and sculpturesque, less painterly and fluent than his brother's. Even in the early paintings of his explorer series, however, he revealed a clamorous vitality which was not the mark of a copyist. He was searching for a repertoire of images capable of expressing, within the nature and limitations of painting, moral issues of some complexity. In the later paintings produced during 1959 and 1960, the anecdotal element of the early work has been suppressed: the forms are cubic, simple and massive, an element of classicism entering into the expression. In the process of creating the series, the Tasmanian tragedy has grown into a universal expression of the conflict between white and coloured. The paintings belong to the world of Notting Hill riots, Little Rock, Sharpeville and the trial of Albert Namatjira. They are concerned with human conflict, guilt, love, compassion and forgiveness; and what they express they express as paintings, not as literature or propaganda. The image of Truganini (190), raped and dead, clinging to her sealer-lover in a timeless agony of hate and love, is an inverted image containing a dark truth which Dante (who placed purgatory down here in the southern hemisphere) would have understood. In such ways it is still possible for an artist to express the moral conscience of his time and assert his own freedom and the dignity of painting as one of the liberal arts (191).

The Melbourne Reaction against Abstraction

The conversion of artists and critics in Sydney to abstract expressionism was accomplished, as we have seen, with the enthusiasm, speed and efficiency of a modern evangelical crusade. Conversion brought with it a

191   DAVID BOYD, *Conflict*, hardboard, 48 x 36, 1959,
Monash University

fanatical devotion to the principles of abstract art and a rising intolerance
of figurative painting. The rivalry, always present between Sydney and
Melbourne, where figurative painting persisted with vigour, grew sharper
and more bitter. When, in October 1958, Arthur Boyd exhibited his *Love,
Marriage and Death of a Half-Caste* series of paintings in Sydney, it was
subjected to the most trenchant attacks. They were, it was said, bad paint-

ings: the artist had mistaken an idea for a painting.[26] Ideas in art had become the unforgivable sin. When, a month later, David Boyd exhibited some of his explorer series, he was accused outright in the Press of plagiarizing his brother.[27] To imitate Dubuffet, or Pollock, or Tapies from the glossy magazines was to be universal and progressive; to follow and add to a family tradition, like the Brueghels and the Le Nains, was to plagiarize! When, in February 1959, John Reed's pioneering collection of contemporary Australian painting, which included early works by Atyeo, Lawlor, Fairweather, Nolan, Tucker, Boyd, Perceval, Gleeson, Bergner, Counihan and Vassilieff, was exhibited in Sydney, the *Sydney Morning Herald* critic asserted that most of the collection possessed 'a decadent, inbred "hill-billy flavour" of tenth-rate German expressionism mixed with a dash of Picasso and at times reverting to the Australian primitive school'.[28] Under the pressure of the issues involved local criticism had degenerated into a slanging match. A reaction was bound to follow. Not surprisingly, it came from Melbourne. It had been foreshadowed by a statement made by Eric Westbrook, the Director of the National Gallery of Victoria, at a Council of Adult Education Summer School held at Albury in January 1958, in which he sweepingly condemned the more extreme forms of *avant-garde* painting:

Most of the pictures painted today were unintelligible nonsense. . . . If an artist were to kick a hole in his canvas and then exhibit this as a new work there would be some people who would say this was advancing the frontiers of art. Some of the public today think that any change or novelty necessarily means progress in painting.[29]

These comments were followed independently, a year later, by the formation of a group called the Antipodeans which contained seven artist members: Charles Blackman, Arthur Boyd, David Boyd, John Brack, Bob Dickerson (the only Sydney painter in the group), John Perceval and Clifton Pugh. The formation of the group was a reaction not so much against abstract art as one of the long-proven forms of contemporary expression as against the clamorous pretensions of the multitude of new converts to abstract expressionism and its varieties then rising upon all sides. The manifesto which the Antipodeans published in the catalogue of their exhibition, held at the Victorian Artists' Society rooms in August 1959, is best understood as a formal protest against the mass conversion to abstract expressionism of artists and critics.[30] Certainly, none of the members of the group was incapable of appreciating the aesthetic merits of abstract art. All of them had numbered abstract painters among their friends and associates. Pugh, for example, had been associated with Laycock and Howley in the 'Group of 4' exhibition. But with non-figurative art suddenly emerging as a mass movement arrogant and intolerant of all other forms, and one to which Press critics were becoming increasingly committed without much discrimination, it was felt that a trenchant defence of figurative painting was needed.

The manifesto began by identifying the group with the contemporary movement: 'Let it be said in the first place that we have all played a part in that movement which has sought for a better understanding of the work of contemporary artists both here and abroad.' But it proceeded to criticize the tendency of abstract painting to reduce all art to pattern and private gesture:

Modern art has liberated the artist from his bondage to the world of natural appearances; it has not imposed upon him the need to withdraw from life. The widespread desire, as it is claimed, to 'purify' painting has led many artists to claim that they have invented a new language. We see no evidence at all of the emergence of such a new language nor any likelihood of its appearance. Painting for us is more than paint.

The manifesto took its central stand upon the cardinal importance of the image in painting, which was defined without equivocation.

Art is for the artist, his speech, his way of communication. And the image, the recognizable shape, the meaningful symbol, is the basic unit of his language. Lines, shapes and colours, though they may be beautiful and expressive, are by no means images. For us the image is a figured shape or symbol fashioned by the artist from his perceptions and imaginative experience. It is born of past experience and refers back to past experience—and it communicates. It communicates because it has the capacity to refer to experiences that the artist shares with his audience.

Art is willed. No matter how much the artist may draw upon the instinctive and unconscious levels of his experience, a work of art remains a purposive act, a humanization of nature. The artist's purpose achieves vitality and power in his images. Take the great black bull of Lascaux, for example, an old beast and a powerful one, who has watched over the birth of many arts and many mythologies. He is endowed with a vitality which is an emblem of life itself. Destroy the living power of the image and you have humbled and humiliated the artist, have made him a blind and powerless Samson fit only to grind the corn of Philistines.

As Antipodeans we accept the image as representing some form of acceptance of and involvement in life. For the image has always been concerned with life, whether of the flesh or of the spirit. Art cannot live much longer feeding upon the disillusions of the generation of 1914. Today dada is as dead as the dodo and it is time we buried this antique hobby-horse of our fathers.

The Antipodeans asserted their right to draw upon the life and forms of nature about them for their art whilst explicitly denying any attempt to create a national style. Their attitude to myth has been much misunderstood. The Antipodean manifesto asserted the right of the artist not to invent myths of his own but rather to make use of myth in a creative way.

In the growth and transformation of its myths a society achieves its own sense of identity. In this process the artist may play a creative and liberating role.

The ways in which a society images its own feelings and attitudes in myth provides him with one of the deepest sources of art.

The manifesto was critical of the restraints placed upon artists by the advocates of social realism, and concluded with a specific denial of any delimiting patriotic or regional preoccupations. 'Our final obligation is neither to place nor nation. So far as we are concerned the society of man is indivisible and we are in it.'

The Antipodean exhibition and manifesto aroused a good deal of discussion and controversy in Melbourne and throughout Australia. Critics were either cautious or antagonistic. Willing enough to accept the work of the artists as individuals, they interpreted any collective criticism of non-figurative painting as a sign of conservatism and reaction. Many sought, despite the assertions of the manifesto to the contrary, to interpret it as a nationalistic *pronunciamento* preoccupied with what was quite mistakenly called regional painting or, more contemptuously, 'Australiana'. The Antipodean Exhibition itself asserted a position, like the 9 $\times$ 5 Exhibition of 1889, the synchromies exhibition of 1919 and Direction 1 of 1956.

Although the Antipodeans were not overtly nationalistic in outlook their exhibition did represent, among other things, an attempt to defend an indigenous tradition against the uncritical acceptance of currently fashionable overseas modes. In one sense the formation of the group may be seen as a part of a growing uneasiness among many Australians at the prospect of being swamped culturally by what Arthur Koestler has called 'coca-colonization'. Similar uneasiness was also expressed in the lectures and writings of Robin Boyd, the architect son of Penleigh Boyd and cousin of the artists, especially in his book *The Australian Ugliness* (1960), which proffered a trenchant criticism of modern vulgarities in contemporary Australian design that were also being justified in the name of progress. At a philosophical level, the essays entitled *The End of Modernity* (1959), by the poet, James McAuley, were also a reaction against the slothful acceptance of the *avant-garde* at any price. McAuley recalled the protests made by Plato and St Augustine against 'the degradation of *rhetoric*, the art of verbal communication, into *sophistic*, the art of verbal gratification and display'.[31] Arguing that greater use be made of contemporary art for ecclesiastical purposes he advised the clergy: 'Do not believe that artists are not interested in prescribed subjects, set themes, art for use's sake: consciously or not, they know very well that their art is dying of boredom and sterility for lack of use and meaning. No artist really wants to spend his days spinning irrelevant artifacts out of his navel.'[32]

'Irrelevant artifacts', however, *were* sought eagerly by a number of local Sydney artists a few months after McAuley's book appeared. The Antipodean Manifesto had been somewhat precipitate in declaring dada as dead as the dodo. In October 1959, as neo-dada it fluttered, albeit a little wearily, into Potts Point. (Barry Humphries, the actor and mimic, had already held three one-man neo-dada shows, one at Melbourne University in 1952, another at the Victorian Artists' Society (1958) and a third at the Museum of Modern Art.) The Sydney exhibition, which was called *Muffled Drums*, was arranged by Elwyn Lynn, Henry Salkauskas, John Coburn, John Ogburn and Oscar Edwards at Terry Clune's Gallery. It sought to be funny and ridicule the local art establishment of art gallery officials and critics. The show included Victorian paintings with rockets glued on; the *Vaucluse Venus*, an early art love unearthed; the Antipodean invasion, drawn upside down on a military map; and an old photograph of a lady (who had been given a Nolan-Kelly helmet) and a child, which was entitled *Someone had to be Picasso's Mother*. It was good, clean fun and the place was packed to the doors. But it was all a trifle *retardataire*.[33]

Significantly enough, the Muffled Drummers had their fun and made their points by means of visual images. The image which the abstract expressionists had so confidently swept out of the door instantly flew back in again through the window as neo-dada, and has been hovering about metamorphosed like a spritely god ever since, his shy theophany glimpsed at times as through a veil in the curious wiggles of John Olsen's recent paintings; or more boisterously as bulls *à la Lascaux*, with or without Europas; or as ravens and screeching cockatoos; and upon one occasion recently (1961) as an enormous white swan looking slightly lost and a little distrait.

The visual image was not to be put down easily. Nevertheless, it is to be stressed that as the 1950's drew to a close in Australia, most of the younger painters of the post-war generation were experimenting with some form of abstract painting which they felt suited their temperament. It is clear that the non-figurative modes of painting will continue to play a prominent part in Australian art in the foreseeable future. But the claim of abstract painters to be the sole Guardians of contemporary art is heard less in the land. It is unlikely that figurative painting will be replaced entirely by an art without images. But the course of Australian art after 1959 is beyond the scope of this book.

In a history of this kind it is not possible to make an extensive survey of the art of the present generation. It may be noted, however, by way of concluding this book, that many young artists (and others not so young) are actively at work today seeking to forge a personal style for themselves relevant to time and place. Others keep abreast of fashion. But just who among the artists of the present generation will produce work of enduring value is a question that only the future will decide. It may be noted, nevertheless, that work of interest and promise is being produced, at the moment of writing, by the following artists. In Sydney, where non-figurative and quasi-figurative modes largely prevail, by Earle Backen, Nancy Borlase, Judy Cassab, Oscar Edwards, Joy Ewart, Maximilian Feuerring, Roy Fluke, Hector Gilliland, Weaver Hawkins, Frank Hodgkinson, Leonard Hessing, Robert Hughes, Ross Morrow, William Peascod, Henry Salkauskas, Peter Upward and Douglas Watson. In Melbourne the range of style is more varied: from the realist work of David Armfield, Bernhard Rust and James Wigley to the abstract modes of such artists as Asher Bilou, Janet Dawson, James Meldrum and Gareth Jones-Roberts. Charles Bush, Ronald Greenaway, Michael Shannon, Gil Jamieson, Edwin Tanner, Ellen Rubbo and Fred Williams have all produced noteworthy work. In South Australia work of quality has been produced in recent years by Lawrence Daws, Wladyslaw Dutkiewicz, Jacqueline Hick, Anton Holzner, Louis James, Stanislaw Ostoiakotkowski and Francis Roy Thompson; in Western Australia by Robert Juniper, Guy Grey Smith and John Lunghi; and in Queensland by Jon Molvig and Andrew Sibley.

Australian art, as a living tradition, has come into existence during the past eighty years. It has been created by artists of independent mind and imagination who have gained inspiration and knowledge of their craft from the European tradition and applied them to their personal situation as artists in Australia. Some were revolutionaries; some were reactionaries; and some, at different times of their lives, succeeded in being both. But most of them found themselves, at the most creative moments in their lives, involved in challenging the values of Australian society. But they had to come to terms with it, or else spend their lives abroad until old age or death. This was no easy matter, for Australian society rarely takes its artists seriously until they begin to exhibit the conventional ambitions. This is partly due to the fact that the uneducated Australian is indifferent to art; and the educated Australian, upon whom the role of patronage normally falls, is, as often as not, a second-rate European with such a strong feeling of inferiority that he is embarrassed by the voices of his own countrymen. Lacking a folk-tradition of long standing from one section of society, or a well-informed aristocratic patronage of the arts from the other, Australian artists have constructed what is national and distinctive in their art in the face of the anti-art values of their society. That is why good Australian art is so often tough-minded and sardonic: not because of the desert but because of the people.

Australian art is today, however, a going concern which is gaining respect and some distinction abroad. But if Australia is to continue to produce an art of international standing it will be an art that emerges from Australian experience and gives a critical edge to it; an art that both celebrates and scarifies; diverse in its interests; encompassing everything from social realism to action painting within its ambience, while allowing the adherents of no doctrine to posture as an elect called by History to create the only true art of the time; an art combining tolerance with a lively clash of conflicting interests; an art contemptuous neither of ideas nor of intuition in the creative process; and an art which, at its best, can rise above the interests and limitations of the nation and the self.

FOOTNOTES

1 *See* A. A. PHILLIPS, 'The Cultural Cringe' in *The Australian Tradition*, Melbourne, 1958, pp. 89-95

2 J. T. A. Burke to Sir Kenneth Clark, *in litt.* 24 September 1948

3 The *Observer* (London), 12 June 1960, p. 17

4 Reported in the *Sydney Morning Herald*, 20 June 1953

5 *The Times* (London), 24 July 1953

6 The *Sunday Times* (London), 2 August 1953

7 *The Times* (London), 24 July 1953

8 The *Sunday Times* (London), 2 August 1953

9 ibid.

10 *Art News*, New York, Summer 1957, 62, 83. On Tucker *see also* 1960 Acquisitions, Art Gallery of N.S.W., pp. 30-1

11 *The Times* (London), May 1955

12 The *Observer* (London), 12 June 1960, p. 17

13 On Doutney *see also* B. SMITH, 'Notes on the Life and Art of Charles Doutney', *Meanjin*, xvi (1957), 420-4

14 *Modern Australian Painting and Sculpture* (Bonython), Adelaide, 1960, p. 15

15 A. D. HOPE, *The Wandering Islands*, 1955, p. 15

16 *Modern Australian Painting and Sculpture*, p. 43

17 The *Sun* (Sydney), 21 May 1952

18 *Modern Australian Art* (Museum of Modern Art, Melbourne), 1958, p. 52

19 *in litt.* 26 March 1961

20 The *Sydney Morning Herald*, 3 October 1956

21 The *Sun* (Sydney), 1 December 1956

22 ibid.

23 L. THOMAS, The *Sun* (Sydney), 6 August 1958

24 Statement in the catalogue of the s.s. *Orcades*, Pacific Loan Exhibition, 1956

25 U. HOFF, 'The Paintings of Arthur Boyd', *Meanjin*, xvii (1958), 143-7

26 L. THOMAS, The *Sun* (Sydney), 1 October 1958

27 L. THOMAS, The *Sun* (Sydney), 20 November 1958

28 The *Sydney Morning Herald*, 18 February 1959

29 The *Albury Mail*, 6 January 1958

30 The final draft of the manifesto was written by the present author, the only non-artist member of the group, in close collaboration with the artists and from discussions held between February and May 1959.

31 op. cit., p. 73

32 op. cit., pp. 106-7

33 *See also Modern Art News* (Melbourne), no. 2 (1959), 10

LIST OF ILLUSTRATIONS

335

A NOTE ON BOOKS AND PERIODICALS

References to individual artists and special aspects of Australian art are listed in the footnotes. This note is confined to publications of a more general nature.

Books   All students of Australian art are indebted to William Moore's *Story of Australian Art* (2 vols, Sydney, 1934), the pioneering study in the field. The present author's *Place, Taste and Tradition* (Sydney, 1945) owes much to Moore but seeks to relate Australian art to a background of European art and ideas. H. E. Badham's *Study of Australian Art* (Sydney, 1949) is derived largely from Moore but contains useful biographical information, not always available elsewhere, on artists flourishing between 1934 and 1949. Clive Turnbull's *Art Here* (Melbourne, 1947) is a brief and personal critical essay. *Masterpieces of the National Gallery of Victoria* (edited by Ursula Hoff, Melbourne, 1949) includes a section on Australian art. Short surveys of Australian art, part-historical, part-critical, have often featured as introductions to catalogues of exhibitions of Australian art held overseas and locally, for example, *The Exhibition of Australian Art in London* (1923); *Art in Australia* (Sydney, 1923); the excellent *Art of Australia 1788-1941*, edited by S. Ure Smith and published by the Carnegie Corporation of New York for the Museum of Modern Art, New York, for the exhibition assembled by Professor T. Sizer in 1940 to tour the United States; the *Arts Festival of the Olympic Games* (Melbourne, 1956); the *Jubilee Exhibition of Australian Art* (1951); and the exhibition of *Recent Australian Painting* (Whitechapel Gallery, London, 1961).

Biographical Information   No comprehensive biographical dictionary of Australian artists has been compiled. The dictionary in Moore (ii, 155-234) is invaluable for artists before 1934. This may be supplemented by the *Catalogue of Australian Oil Paintings in the National Art Gallery of New South Wales, 1875-1952* (Sydney, 1953) and the excellent catalogues of acquisitions published annually by that gallery; *The Catalogue of the National Gallery of Victoria* (Melbourne, 1948) and its appendices, 1950 and 1954; *The Catalogue of the National Gallery of South Australia* (1946) and its catalogue of drawings, 1948; the *Catalogue of the Australian Paintings and Drawings, Tasmanian Art Gallery* (Hobart, 1956) contains information on early Tasmanian painters; and the well-documented *Acquisitions 1960-1* of the Queensland Art Gallery. Kym Bonython's *Modern Australian Painting and Sculpture* (Adelaide, 1960) includes biographical notes on selected painters and sculptors of the last decade. Material on prominent artists will also be found in Percival Serle's *Dictionary of Australian Biography* (2 vols, Sydney, 1949) and the *Australian Encyclopaedia* (10 vols, Sydney, 1958), though entries in the latter are often abbreviated paraphrases of entries in the *Dictionary*.

Periodicals   Prior to 1900 there were no periodicals devoted exclusively to the visual arts. *The Bulletin* (1880-   ) *Table Talk* (1885-1937), *The Australasian Builders' and Contractors' News* (1887-95), *The Australasian Art Review* (1899-1900) are useful sources of information. *Art and Architecture* (1904-   ) and *The Salon* (1812-1916), published by the New South Wales chapter of the

Australian Institute of Architects are important for the Edwardian period and *art nouveau*. *Art in Australia* (1916-42) founded and edited by Sydney Ure Smith until 1938 remains the outstanding periodical. Well illustrated, it featured appreciative rather than independently critical articles. *Manuscripts* (1931-5), edited by H. Tatlock Miller, was an early *avant-garde* miscellany which included articles on art and design. *Angry Penguins* (Adelaide, 1941-2) (Melbourne, 1943-6), *avant garde* and highly controversial, is a basic source for the emergence of contemporary art in Australia. The literary quarterly, *Meanjin* (1940-), edited by Clem Christesen, has become, however, the chief vehicle for the publication of critical comment of quality in the visual arts. Special issues of *Studio* (London) have occasionally featured Australian art; for example, 'Art of the British Empire Overseas' (Winter 1916-17) and 'Australia in Art' (October 1942).

Periodicals published under the auspices of art societies have appeared sporadically and contain much useful information. The most notable include *The Society of Artists' Year Book* (five annual issues, 1942-6), edited by S. Ure Smith; *The Australian Artist* (six issues, 1947-9), edited by R. Haughton James for the Victorian Artists' Society (this Society also published its own Journal for a number of years); and the *Broadsheet* of the Contemporary Art Society of New South Wales, edited by Elwyn Lynn since 1955, an important source of information and comment on contemporary art. Recently (1960) a *Broadsheet* of the Victorian Contemporary Art Society has begun to appear. *Modern Art News* (two issues, 1959) was closely associated with the Victorian Contemporary Art Society.

INDEX

341